First Time Ever

PEGGY SEEGER

FIRST TIME EVER

A Memoir

FABER & FABER

First published in 2017
by Faber & Faber Ltd
Bloomsbury House
74–77 Great Russell Street
London WC1B 3DA

Typeset by Faber & Faber Ltd
Printed in the UK by CPI Group (UK) Ltd, Croydon, CRO 4YY

A CIP record for this book
is available from the British Library

ISBN 978–0–571–33679–1

FSC
www.fsc.org
MIX
Paper from
responsible sources
FSC® C020471

2 4 6 8 10 9 7 5 3 1

For my beloveds, Here and AfterHere.
You know who you are.

Contents

CONTENTS

Illustrations

Dio, Mike, Charlie, Peggy, *c.*1937. (*Photographer unknown*)
Mike, Penny, Dio, Peggy, Barbara, *c.*1947. (© *Williams*)
Elizabeth Cotten, early 1960s. (© *John Cohen*)
Pete Seeger, late 1930s. (*Photographer unknown*)
Peggy, high-school yearbook, 1953. (*Photographer unknown*)
Peggy, Ralph Rinzler and Lambretta, 1957. (© *Toshi Ohta Seeger*)
Peggy's German urchins in Belgium, early 1956. (© *Jos Vloebergh*)
The Ramblers, 1956. (*Photographer unknown*)
Peggy busking in Moscow, 1957. (*Photographer unknown*)
Peggy and Guy Carawan, Bolshoi Theatre, 1957. (*Photographer unknown*)
Peggy with Chinese and American comrades, 1957. (*Photographer unknown*)
Alf Edwards, early 1960s. (© *Peggy Seeger*)
Peggy and Betsy, mid-1960s. (© *Ewan MacColl*)
Peggy and baby Neill, 1960. (© *Ewan MacColl*)
Peggy and Ewan at Newport Folk Festival, 1960. (*Photographer unknown*)
Peggy and Ewan at work, late 1960s. (*Photographer unknown*)
Charles Parker, 1960s. (*Photographer unknown*)
Fitzroy Coleman, *c.*1961. (© *Eddis Thomas*)
The Stewarts of Blairgowrie with Hamish Henderson, *c.*1958. (© *Timothy Neat*)

Peggy and Ewan in Cuba, 1967. (*Photographer unknown*)

Peggy and Kitty, *c.* 1975. (© *Ewan MacColl*)

Alice Dawson, *c.* 1975. (© *Peggy Seeger*)

Calum, Ewan and Neill at the Singers' Club, *c.* 1978.
  (*Photographer unknown*)

Ewan, Calum, Kirsty and Neill at Kirsty's wedding, 1984.
  (*Photographer unknown*)

Kitty wearing Peggy's specs, early 1990s. (© *Peggy Seeger*)

Peggy recording, 1988. (© *Jim Maginn*)

Irene, *c.* 1990. (© *Gary Italiaander*)

Kerry Harvey-Piper, 2015. (© *Peggy Seeger*)

Justine Picardie and baby Jamie, 1990. (© *Peggy Seeger*)

Kate St John, 2015. (© *Neill MacColl*)

Kate Jones, *c.* 1990. (© *Peggy Seeger*)

Neill, Kitty and Calum recording, early 2000s. (© *Peggy
  Seeger*)

Mike, Peggy and Pete, 1995. (© *Dave Gahr*)

The Woodlawn Witches, early 2000s. (*Photographer unknown*)

Peggy and Maggie-the-Van, *c.* 2000. (© *Irene Pyper-Scott*)

Peggy and Irene's civil union, 15 December 2006. (© *Clare
  Chapman*)

Irene and the Fiery Cello, 2008. (© *Peggy Seeger*)

Peggy performing in Charlotte, NC, 1999. (© *Jen Fariello*)

Neill, Peggy, Calum and twelve guitars, 2017. (© *Vicky Sharp*)

Peggy about to turn eighty-two, 2017. (© *Vicky Sharp*)

Forethoughts

Please read this.

In his 1854 autobiography, American President Martin Van Buren forgot to mention his wife (née Hannah Hoes), mother of his five sons, to whom he had been married for twelve years. In *Journeyman*, the autobiography of my first life partner, Ewan MacColl missed mentioning the births of several of his children.

You may have been important in my life, yet you don't appear herein. I didn't forget you. Your scene was most likely cut because *someone overran* (see Chapter 32, 'The Occupants of Hell'). So you whom I idolise or whom I dearly love, like, dislike, or who might even qualify for inclusion in that chapter – you were most likely present in the long, unedited version of this book. I was the one who overran. I've also had to leave out various awards, Grammy nominations, an honorary doctorate, a flea circus and a sword swallower and friend, Justin Schwartz, who taught his cat to eat vegetables (including Brussels sprouts).

I began jotting down memories for this book in the early 1990s. There got to be so many notes – rather like the Post-its on the fridge door – that my friend Brian Reese offered to make a long rough draft of them, working towards a proper memoir. I owe him big time for this. I am grateful too for Jean Freedman's biography, *Peggy Seeger: A Life of Music, Love and Politics*. I used her book as a reference whenever my memory slipped up. Our two books are very different. The biography gives dates, times, facts, etc. It is strictly chronological and uses a plethora of authorised sources, taking us up to 2016. It presents me as I was, as I am. You'd do well to read it alongside this memoir, which presents me as I *think* I was, as I *believe* I am. My book roams freely around time, emotions, opinions, prejudices and a lot of whatever.

Memoir – memory. I have hardly used old letters and diaries at all – they were in the present of the past. This book has been written in the future of that past. It's how I feel *now* about *back then*, right up to this morning, when I woke up stiff from yesterday's training at the gym and slightly hungover from two large glasses of red at the Prince of Wales. You do get a rough narrative. I bring in subject-driven chapters when a necessary detour beckons, not for killing Time but for when Time tells me it's time to set up my easel and call on my vivid pictorial memory, that enormous gallery of snapshots that lives in my head. The narrative will always resume, so be patient.

Excerpts from some of my songs appear regularly throughout. Unless otherwise stated, all lyrics are mine. I've put together a CD of some of them, available from my website, www.peggyseeger.com. I am British, so spelling and much of the terminology is British – full stop, period. If it's easy to find an odd reference (like *Board of Inland Revenue* v. *Haddock*), then I generally don't explain it.

I'm Peggy. I wrote this book.

Oxford, 2017

I

1935–1955

I

Twice upon a Time

Summer, 1955. A barbecue at Butterfly Beach. I didn't fit in. I took off, headed west towards Santa Barbara's year-round Christmas lights. I was running. Ray, my six-foot Californian boyfriend, ran beside me. I would never stop. I would never be tired, hungry or thirsty. We came to a wide, shallow stream. Ray didn't want to wet his shoes. I piggy-backed him over and dumped him on the other side, literally and figuratively. I would never be weak or unable to carry a man. I ran, fusion of inner and outer space, force of nature hurtling forward, my hair streaming behind me, absorbed in the glory of being. I reached Santa Barbara having given birth to reckless optimism and a refusal to regard death as anything but another version of that five-mile flight from one reality to another. I was twenty and immortal.

*

February 1959, England. Ewan, my lover, has gone to see Hamish, his eight-year-old son. I am pregnant with our first child, due in early March. Betsy, Ewan's mother, has just arrived to live with us in our tiny upstairs apartment in Purley, Surrey. We are having a companionable cup of tea. In her lovely Scots brogue she comments, haiku-style:

You'll ne'er get him to leave Jean.
She's wi' bairn, due in October.
She's a loyal lass.

Her blue eyes have white circles in the middle, milky marbles looking right at me. She knows exactly where her dagger plunged, dangerously close to the baby's head. She doesn't know that I'm a loyal lass myself.

In the ballads and folk tales, the characters are clear-cut stereotypes, goodies and baddies, facilitated by natural and supernatural in-betweens. Women don't get very good press. Men and girls fare better. I loved the fairy tales. I was the brave mute sister of the seven brothers who had been changed into swans. Knitting the cloaks that would turn them back into men would also revive my ability to speak. Later, I would save my Latin and English teachers, Miss Loar and Miss Fielding, many times from car accidents. A prince was definitely going to kiss me – but he wouldn't be forty-four years old, married, with a son and a pregnant wife. So here was Betsy, straight out of a fairy tale, frustrated and vindictive, the size of tuppence, all tongue and temper, short on tenderness. She lived with us for sixteen years, during which time I was steeped in a Ewan–Betsy world via the traditional method: reminiscence and gossip. I only learned in later life about my own parents, from their very old friends, from my elder brothers, from various publications and from biographies, including my own.* But from my mother and father, who gave me a wonderful childhood – almost nothing.

* *Peggy Seeger: A Life of Music, Love and Politics* by Jean R. Freedman (University of Illinois Press, 2017).

Charles Louis Seeger was born in 1886 in Mexico and spent much of his early life there. Simple of speech, not given to tautological perorations, very slow to anger, he was incapable of punishing his children. We called him Charlie. We called our mother Dio – the closest my brother Mike could get to our father's affectionate *Ruthie dear.* Our parents were different in temperament and class. Even when drawn to anger, Charlie's most extreme expletive was *Ye gods and little fishes!* When Dio became irritated or angry at the chaotic dinner table, he would pat her shoulder, patronisingly, *Now, Ruthie dear, don't get peppy.* Velvet fist in velvet glove. She would smile and calm from boil to simmer.

Charlie went off to work every day in The Car. Back then, the grilles on automobiles made faces and expressed emotions. Our grey 1938 Chevy had a vertical fish-mouth and a fat lady's rump. If we were still playing in the unfenced yard when Charlie returned in the evening, he would stop at the bottom of the short drive and we would pile onto the running board, a feature now found only as a style accent or as a necessity on high vehicles. Slowly, he would pilot us up the drive and *bump the boxes, Charlie!* at the end of the garage. If we were in the nightly bath when he arrived, he would lift us out, one by one, and dry us slowly and tenderly on his lap between two towels.

Charlie was skin and bone. The veins on the backs of his hands stood out like blue tubes, as mine do now. We loved to slide those slippery pipelines back and forth under the mottled skin. He was very hard of hearing and would take the little receiver-box from his shirt pocket and hold it near the speaker for clarity. At the dinner table, he would turn his hearing aid off as the family decibels climbed ever upward. Dio would have to handle the battlefield on her own and could get peppy unhindered. Charlie's movements were unhurried. I never saw him run. He was incredibly limber and could stand on his head even in his nineties. He exuded inner peace, a quiet that ran through everything he did. He loved my mother with a constancy and depth that shone. She was his *twenty-three years of heaven* till the day he died. Like waves against a rock, she beat against him, moved around him, tide in, tide out. He was always there, never worn down. Later, he would never criticise the odd boys and men I brought home, never ever pass judgement on them. He would engage them in conversation and draw them out, interested in any male who was interested in his daughter.

I was my father's first girl after four boys – Charles, John and Pete from Constance Edson, his first wife, and Mike by our mother. Charlie had been waiting for me. He told me that. We communicated easily. I could talk to him about almost anything. Later, Ewan and I would take him on tour with us. He'd enter the club premises and stand stock still, a tall beanpole of a man, a pointer sniffing the air for grouse. Then he'd go and sit by his quarry, the most attractive female – under twenty-five – in the room. He'd charm her. If she had a friend or boyfriend with her, he'd charm them both. He just loved the sight, sound, smell and presence of young women. He wasn't always tactful. I was thirty-nine when out of the blue he confided, *Peggy, women look their best when they're under twenty-five.*

My parents would often stand with arms linked or in a halfhug. Flowers and jewellery were not their style. Charlie went to Paris on business and brought back a bottle of Arpège perfume, a whiff of which brings Dio back to me as I like to remember her. He also brought back a programme from the Folies-Bergère. He was an unreconstructed hedonist. When I was ten, the family went to Martha's Vineyard on a rare holiday. Dio and we children lay on the beach rug naked. When Charlie got up to swim I would go with him to the sea. He'd give me his trunks to hold while he swam. *Swimming with trunks on is like putting caps on your teeth before brushing them.* He wore feather-soft clothes. On one of his 1970s visits to us in England, he wanted to go to Simpsons in Jermyn Street for silk underwear. Breathe that empyrean air, emanating ancient privilege, as you watch Charlie, cane in hand, stride up to a posh young mannikin of a salesman. He describes what he wants. *We don't stock those, sir.* Charlie: *Oh, but you must. I bought mine here.* The manager is summoned, a David Niven lookalike, oozing Simpson deference. He listens, then widens the goal posts: *When would that be, sir?* Charlie, without hesitation: *1949.* I didn't carry a camera back then.

Charlie described helping his mother with her corsets. A teenager, he would put his knee into her back and she would take a big breath. *Now, Charles!* and he would pull the corset strings tight. After several such repetitions, my father's index fingers and thumbs would meet around her waist. She carried smelling salts in her reticule – a dainty drawstrung handbag. They were strangely close, mother and son. She confided to him that on her wedding night her mother told her that it was lady-like to pretend to faint when her husband's advances reached critical mass. Grandmother Seeger didn't mince words. When Charlie separated from Constance, she commiserated: *Well, Charles, you'll just have to live celibate now.* When Dio came along, her son had *married below himself.* Thank goodness. My mother came from 1800s 'poor white trash', the lowest rung of the white ladder that rests on black and brown ground. She was Midwestern plain, no-nonsense, an intensively creative woman. I have a photo of her with Carl Sandburg, the Chicago poet

– she's wearing knickerbockers and has an axe in her hand. Did she marry above herself? Her mother-in-law was a vertical Victorian would-be Lady, born in 1863, who wore long skirts and high button boots until her death in 1947. Grandfather Seeger had drawn up an intricate genealogy which, like thousands of others, traced the family back to the *Mayflower* with never a thought as to the possibility that Grandma Sarah Parsons might have slept with the milkman. When I was ten, I was sent to visit Grandmother Seeger in New York City. I took my books, *The Reds of the Midi* and *Little Women*. Grandmother removed them and brought me her reading matter: romance novelettes that she'd cut out from women's pulp magazines and pasted into a large scrapbook. She and I had nothing in common, but we circled each other with interest.

We children knew nothing of Charlie's Communist Party past. In 1952, when his son Pete was summonsed to Senator McCarthy's House Un-American Activities Committee (HUAC) hearings, Charlie resigned his job at the Pan-American Union, leaving *before I'm fired*. When pushed, we referred to our family's political stance as *progressive*. *Left-wing* was not a safe term in the States. Even now, *socialism* is a dirty word. I suspect that most Americans don't know what it actually is. They don't like *revolution* either. The American *Revolution* has morphed into the War of *Independence*. In 1961, when I asked Charlie why he'd hidden his 1930s political affiliations from us, he said it was *better that you children didn't know*. Ewan and Charlie got on very well. They were opposites, like me and Ewan. One active, one passive; one loud, one soft-spoken; one working-class, one middle-class; English, American; younger, older; schooled entirely differently, a yin–yang paradigm. Ewan's gut politics were created by life experience. Charlie

talked theories – everything was *interesting*. Ewan had mis-
treated his body in his Theatre Workshop days. Charlie had
attended the yoga school and gotten his body under control.
Ewan flew off the handle easily. Charlie's temper was shoved
down so far that it seemed not to exist. Conversationally, I was
no match for either of them. They baited each other, often saying outrageous things and watching each other hop on a hobby
horse and gallop away.

My mother, née Ruth Porter Crawford, was born in 1901.*
She was the first woman to win the Guggenheim Fellowship
for composition. It took her to Europe in 1930, where she would
turn up on the doorsteps of well-known composers, eager to
talk about *their work*, not her own. She had always wanted children and took eagerly to *composing babies*, as she put it. She was
always complaining that she *never got to her work*, as if children
were not work. Full of innocent energy, she would sing, jump,
make caves under the piano and magic herself into our world.
Like me, she never grew up. She waited to give me piano lessons till I asked, age six. She made up stories when we were
at the keyboard, illustrating them with leaps and arpeggios for
the rabbits, squeaks for the mice, thunder for the wicked step-
mothers and lions. The theory lessons were superb. The circle of fifths, resolutions, metre, signatures, cadences. When I
was about ten, she made me learn 'The Irish Washerwoman'
in every key on the piano and in every mode, including two
'Turkish' ones. I was very slow at sight-reading but thanks to
her I really know my way around the piano keyboard. When
it came to the Bach, Beethoven and Brahms that we both loved

* Judith Tick, *Ruth Crawford Seeger – A Composer's Search for American Music*
(Oxford University Press, 1997).

so much, I couldn't practise or play within earshot of her. We both knew she was listening critically. That was the beginning of my nerves problem. I never got through a recital in one piece and never got through one piece in a recital. One note wrong and I was finished. Hoping to conquer this, Dio sent me to a nervous little teacher, Miss Henbest. She and her piano were easily intimidated, but they did their hen-best. Our grand piano and my mother were hard acts to follow. I was transferred to Alexander Lipsky, a fiery man with huge hands – I Googled him today and was impressed. He terrified me. I improved but still couldn't practise at home. Arthur Lambert, the son of one of Dio's pupils, was a dreamboat. I suggested that I practise at Mrs Lambert's house. That was worse. Arthur was listening. At least I hoped he was.

As a young woman my mother had been stylish, hair bobbed, wearing the fashionable clothes of her time. Her letters tell me she was a 1920s feminist. She allowed motherhood and Charlie to turn her into a stocky peasant woman in plain dresses, men's shoes and braids over the top of her head. She wasn't a cuddler once you were out of childhood. She wore a stiff girdle which creaked if you hugged her. She never wore makeup – she didn't need to. When I wanted to do so, she said, *Fine, as long as it doesn't show.* I kept the lipstick in my school locker. When I was in my early teens, she came into my bedroom, a little shy, and gave me typed copies of some short stories she had written. She wanted my opinion. I was embarrassed, as the stories were romantic and adolescent, something I might have written myself. I know now that she was trying to close the gap between us. I know now that she wrote prose and poems aplenty in her school and college days and I feel yet again the regret of opportunities lost, hurts unmendable.

In 1952, Dio won the National Association for American Composers and Conductors' prize for the best piece of contemporary chamber music. She was in a panic as to what to wear at the acceptance ceremony. I ran up a long, full black taffeta skirt on the sewing machine – my sister Barbara and I drilled her on staircase routine. We took her shopping and bought a glowing red blouse. Charlie didn't like shiny clothes. As she went up the steps to the stage I saw that we hadn't bought proper shoes. I see her plainly now, dear, dear stranger-mother, in her definitely *un*fashionable everyday unpolished men's lace-ups, no jewellery at all, just her lovely colouring of black hair, very red cheeks and lively face – moving across the stage like a self-conscious child to accept her prize. It has been acknowledged that had she been a man, her work would have brought her greater recognition, and much sooner. She is in a class of her own now in the formal music world.

She read Perry Mason detective stories. She drank oceans of black coffee. Questions to which she didn't know the answer? She'd swing into the reply with which her mother had fobbed her off: *Not knowing with that degree of certainty which is so necessary in exigencies like the present, I shall not state, lest in so doing I should err therein.* She only needed to start with *Not knowing* and we'd wander off to find the answer elsewhere. When her biographers wanted to know about Ruth Crawford Seeger the Composer, I tried to remember her in that capacity. The picture is incomplete for I only knew her folk music persona, her classical piano playing, her attempts to cook. When I listen to her innovative compositions, many of which I do not understand and some of which make me feel physically uncomfortable, I am outraged that I never heard any of them except *Rissolty Rossolty* until I was in my mid-thirties. Dio the Composer virtually did not exist in my growing up. I love books. Dio is a book that was never fully opened.

Now, when I am older than my mother ever had the good fortune to be, I would give anything to sit down and talk with this woman who had all her children after the age of thirty-three; who considered her family more important than the music she composed; and part of whose creativity languished on the daily battlefield of household minutiae and music lessons for children with *fingers like cooked macaroni*. We are comrades-in-arms, Dio and I. We have so much in common: both united for decades to a man very many years our senior, always impatient to get to *our work*, endlessly trying to get across to our children as a person and being rejected not by direct lack of interest but by any child's unwavering belief that no life existed before its own birth.

2

Childhood

2441 P Street, Washington DC, a tiny terrace house, scene of my first memory, standing at the top of a steep staircase looking down into the well of darkness below. In 1938, we moved to Silver Spring, Maryland, just across the DC border, to a detached house surrounded by crabgrass lawn. When you play a guitar regularly it greets you even before you pluck it. Neglect it and it will sulk. Its strings will not resound, the wood will not respond. Similarly, when you enter a house you can feel its contentment or conflict as if the happiness or misery of its previous occupants has filled every cavity in walls, floor and ceiling. The vibrations of wood and plaster speak to those who know how to listen. 10,001 Dallas Avenue said *family*. The central rectangular room reached to the roof. A huge fireplace sat central on one long side and windows and French doors opened out to a large wooden porch on the opposite side. You couldn't fall on that porch without shards of wood entering some tender part of your body. One of my splinters was an inch long. I saved it for years in a little matchbox after Charlie removed it. We roamed in cowboy and Indian costumes on our wooden prairie, sailed boats on our porcupine sea. It had no railings, so we'd lie down and peer over the edge into the dark jungle of old lumber and rocks, searching for the black widow spiders that live under every such southern porch. Dio sat vigilant with her crochet and sewing needles, humming the songs she was transcribing. You could hear the trains from our house. They said *Lonesome-waaaaaaaah*. One night Charlie woke us all up at midnight and took us to the site of a train wreck. I am sitting on his shoulders. The big black steam engine is on its side, still puffing, the overturned train carriages snaking away into the dark embankment.

Dallas Avenue was one block long, about twenty houses facing each other across rough asphalt. At one end was a T-junction with a main road. The other end went wandering off, an earthen lane leading between corn fields to the unpaved farm road where we caught the school bus. A boy in my kindergarten class took a fancy to me, coming every day to stand by the kitchen door and walk me to the bus stop. I instructed Mike to stand by the closed door while I went to the far wall of the big living room. I'd dash for the kitchen door, Mike would open it and I'd sprint past Hopeful Harry. Bus rides were special and I wanted to experience them either with Mike or alone. A poultry farmer lived on one side of us, feathers and the smell of chicken blood everywhere. You could see the big chopping block from our yard. Charlie refused to let us have a pet chick. He said it would hear and understand the terrified squawking on what we called Chopping Day. On the other side of our house was an invisible line never to be crossed. Buddy and Kenneth, the Dallas Avenue bullies, lived beyond it. They both died in Korea. There was minimal social visiting. Dio wasn't the neighbourly, small-talk kind. She went from mother to music, music to mother day and night. She treasured what solitude she could find. Like my bus rides.

Boredom wasn't in our vocabulary. We were put out to play whenever the weather was fine. Cold or hot, we were on our scooters, then trikes, then bikes in the street. There was no

rat-running on Dallas Avenue. It led nowhere. In the winter there were snowsuits, sleds, snowmen and snow angels.
Galoshes went on over our shoes, mittens with a string between
them ran from sleeve to sleeve. In the summer, Charlie put up
a badminton net and constructed a dangerous merry-go-round
out of a stump, a bolt and a huge plank. Beyond our play space
was a field of four-leaf clovers, where, having relented, I sat
with Harry in the high grass. He had a seizure in an adjacent
classroom. He just put his head down on his desk and Fell
Asleep Forever, the same year as Mike's striped kitten, Tig.
Mike grieved properly, with tears, silence and the resolve never
to have a pet again. Harry was going to wake up and marry me.

Our childhood toys were simple and few. Marbles, jacks,
jump-rope, balls of all kinds, a suction-cup bow and arrow
set, cap-guns, sparkler wheels, lariats with long streamers of
crinkle-paper (crepe). If we got sick, we could play with the
Sick Toys, available only to those confined to bed. Many of
them were from Charlie's Mexican childhood: a village of
wooden houses, church, post office, none of them larger than
an inch in size; miniature pottery cups and saucers an eighth of
an inch high. My daughter Kitty has them now. The strangest
Sick Toy was a little book of several dozen Liberty cloth samples measuring about four inches by six. William Morris, for
upholstery and curtains. Feverish, sore throat, coughing, you'd
turn and turn the little pieces of figured fabric – then start
again at the beginning. Scrap-booking occupied us for hours,
cutting photos out of magazines and newspapers and pasting
them into a very large book of rough beige paper – the Dionne
Quintuplets and the young Princesses Elizabeth and Margaret,
Shirley Temple, Margaret O'Brien . . .

In the middle of the big living room was a couch facing the

fire, Dio's work desk behind it. Each corner of the room had a purpose. (1) The Puppet Show Corner, where wooden surrogates would tell our stories on a Charlie-made stage with Dio-made curtains. The puppets were large, about a foot high. I only remember Rastus, a stereotypical Negro – as the terminology went then. (2) The Sewing Machine Corner, where Dio sat mending and working the foot-treadle to make things out of cloth. (3) The Piano Corner, under which lurked the Electric Plug in the dark wall. The fourth corner should have been called Day and Night as one wall had the door that led outside, and the other opened onto the staircase to the two bedrooms above. Two downstairs bedrooms and a bathroom led off that short end of the living-room rectangle. At the other end was the ground-floor dining room and the little kitchen, where the sink looked into a windowless wall and the washing-machine tub ran endlessly. A chair would be drawn up to the sink and I would wash dishes with seven-year-old importance, or stand winding the handle of the mangle (*You're too young, Barbara, let go!*) and take the clothes that Dio fed through and lay them damp in the basket for hanging out on the clothesline with clothespins. The Cellar Door opened off the kitchen, the entrance into a land that you only dared visit with an adult. The rickety stairs wobble. Don't touch the walls on the way down for fear of thousand-leggers, huge centipedes that flowed when they were in a hurry. When the bare light bulb is switched on, small creatures *down there* rustle and scuttle on the earth floor. Then . . . quiet gloom. The only safe place was right below the light bulb, like on stage. When the coal arrived we'd go down and watch the clattering black waterfall fill the bunker. Charlie braved The Furnace, heroically opening the heavy door and shovelling the coal into the glowing fire.

16

Michael, Peggy and Barbara, each two years apart, that was us, a tangle of children. Barbara and I would bond later but now she was the baby. Mike and I were always close, hunkering down together to inspect ants and wormies, cutting the grass blade by blade with Dio's little sewing scissors. Next summer I intend to do that again to find out if it is still exciting after seventy-seven years. Fearful beings lived below the chinks in the floorboards. We dropped small items down those knotholes to appease them. When Dio wasn't looking, we'd open the bottle of carbon tetrachloride with which she cleaned the shiny records. Soak a wad of cotton in the colourless liquid, inhale and get woozy. At school we learned little dialogues and rattled them off as fast as we could:

Life's tough.
What's life?
A magazine.
Where d'you get it?
News stand.
How much?
Costs a dime.
Only got a nickel.
That's tough.
What's tough?
Life's tough . . .

We learned the dialogue ads on Mike's little radio and embroidered them with vocal and bodily histrionics.

JOHN: *Mary, please go out with me.*

MARY (hesitant): *No, John . . . I don't . . .*

JOHN: *Aw, Mary, please. We'll go get a soda and go to the movies and . . .*

MARY: *I'm going with Bill . . .*

17

JOHN (disappointed): *Aw, Mary, please . . .*
OFFICIOUS VOICE: *Too bad, John. You should have worn a hat.*
Then the address of where you could buy a hat.
Aw, Peggy, please . . .
Too bad, Mike, you should have worn galoshes.
Cackle-chortle, yuk yuk and start again.

*

During the Great Depression, Charlie had been one of President Franklin Roosevelt's cultural ambassadors to the Country of the American Populace. He was involved with setting up the Library of Congress Archive of American Folk Song. John and Alan Lomax, George Korson, Ben Botkin, Sidney Cowell and others deposited their recordings in this extraordinary archive. I'd go to the The Archive with Dio to help listen and choose the songs for her books, sneaking off to the little shop where I'd buy forbidden squares of fudge, gobbling as I sat on the toilet while the archivists transferred our choices onto bright sixteen-inch aluminium discs that you played with a thorn needle. When the needle got blunt it was the job of children to snap it into the little contraption, like a sparkler, that would whiz it around against a disc of fine sandpaper. Presto! a sharp needle, the only sharp item we were allowed to handle. You carried scissors with finger-holes upward. When I was five or so I got hold of a stylus and carved my brother's name M-I-K-E in big capital letters across the lid of the new baby grand piano that my parents had sweated blood and tears to buy. Dio was too angry to cry. Half crazy with fury, she dragged me methodically from one room to the next using first her hand and then her flat-backed hairbrush to whack my bottom. She took me in her lap and we cried together – then she continued transcribing the song that the Lomaxes had recorded in 1936 from Ozella Jones in the Raiford State Penitentiary in Florida. Jones had gotten life for murdering her lover and the trial and incarceration had traumatised her. It was a difficult song to transcribe and to get it right Dio had to play the first line over and over and over: *I been a bad, bad girl. I been a bad, bad girl.* Bottom sore, I sponged that song up: *Judge, please don't kill me, I won't be bad no more.* Later, when I was eleven Dio would teach me to transcribe simple tunes at a nickel a song, for Botkin's *Treasury of Western Folklore.* Make a rough transcription, get it approved. Then a fair copy – dip the pen in the ink bottle, tap it on the side and hope that the flow is even so the whole thing won't have to be done again.

We rarely played with neighbouring children, although we sometimes played with the children of our parents' friends. One such couple owned a 1930s Ford Roadster. We called it Rooster Roadster. Racing along at 30 mph with the wind in our hair, bouncing up and down in the rumble seat. Youngsters: these years are your *good old days.* I hope they are as good as mine were in the 1940s and 1950s. Our family needed no one but ourselves. We were a living reason for having multiple children. When Barbara was ready, Dio became the Music Mother at a nursery school in Silver Spring. This was the beginning of her crusade to bring folk songs to children. She made copies of the songs and bound them into books for the school. Method: Fill a letter-size tray with half an inch of clear jelly and let it harden till it's slightly sticky to the touch, like Jell-O cubes (before they decided to have Jell-O powder, which can't be sucked gradually into nothingness: tragic 'improvement'). Make an ink copy of the song. Let it dry – then lay it down on the jelly, where it will leave a reverse copy in purple. Press sheets of blank paper down on this image and you can make ten, twenty, thirty copies, all purple. Three children on the assembly line: Mike punches the holes and Peggy wets the reinforcements on Barbara's stuck-out tongue. Dio sings a together-song as she arranges the pages in order and puts latched rings in the holes to make 'notebooks'. Then she gets back to her records while we play and drink in more adult music, acting it out in the Puppet Corner – 'Another Man Done Gone', 'Go Down Old Hannah', the rich voices of the American southern blacks, the strained Puritan voices of poor southern whites. In the evenings, Charlie might do desk work or lie on the couch while Dio gave us all Mozart, Liszt, Chopin, the greats. If they talked, we could always hear my mother's voice, raised because of Charlie's semi-deafness. He always went to bed early. She would stay up playing the piano or just having blessed time to herself. Another day done gone.

*

All children love music till it's beaten or mocked out of them, or they're told to just mouth the words in choir because they don't sing in tune. Dio had singing bones and a child's delight in music. 'Cindy' played on the piano was a signal that the time had come to go to bed. If you didn't head quickly towards the stairs, she would sing 'Such a Getting Upstairs I Never Did See' or put a command to music. There were songs for choosing what to wear – 'Mary Wore Her Red Dress' – with your own name and garment slotted in. She sang continually during the lengthy summer process of checking our hair for ticks, mending clothes, cleaning house. She sang the songs she was transcribing. She made songs out of things we said. We could be cajoled into wearing anything via 'Tell Me What to Wear, Mommy, Mommy'. She even made songs for those boiling hot days when we had to bring every bit of woollen clothing or bedding out onto the lawn to bake in the sun. Hours of searching seams, hems, borders for moths and moth eggs. No songs, though, for the yearly spraying of every bedroom for bedbugs – handheld spraygun squiffing bug-poison onto mattresses, floors, empty bureau drawers – then shut the door tight, block up the gap at the bottom and sleep somewhere else for two or three days.

Dio loved the traditional rituals. She made Halloween costumes for us and we trick-or-treated the neighbourhood unchaperoned. We dyed Easter eggs and she hid them around the yard. Each of us had a little collecting basket with coins and small presents hidden in the shredded tissue paper. We went out carolling at Christmas with homemade carol books supplied by Dio. Her father had been a Methodist minister. She loathed organised religion but loved the songs. Dio celebrated Christmas in her own way. There would be exaggerated whisperings and significant looks beginning in early December. We made chains out of strips of coloured paper. Tantalising parcels would be placed on high shelves. On Christmas Eve, the tree was brought into the dining room. Charlie fastened the lights and we put the sparse decorations on. Then we would hole up with Dio in a dark bedroom and all the house lights would be turned off. She leads her little crocodile of children, eyes tight shut, through the darkened house. At the dining-room door she stops and signals to Charlie. Open your eyes and there's the tree, lit up and sparkling. I cannot bear over-decorated or fake trees – I need the smell and sight of Christmas, which for me is twofold: the smell of pine-tree needles and the zest-smell of tangerines, which you could only get at Christmastime. My parents' Christmas had nothing to do with God. Jesus was just a little baby. Angels were a little figure on the Christmas tree or the impression you left on the snow by lying down and swishing your arms and legs to make wings and gown. Christmas was a turkey, buying, making and wrapping presents, keeping secrets and creeping around a darkened house to dance at an enchanted tree.

Our parents' birthdays weren't celebrated, not even with cake and ice cream. Our own were observed simply but you always got something you wanted. The cake was invariably homemade, with your name written on the icing. When our friends had birthdays, Dio made cookies and iced their names on them, one letter per cookie. The longer your name, the more cookies you got. These would be carefully arranged on a tray lined with tissue paper. We were horribly embarrassed to give them. We wanted to give proper *bought* presents with bright paper and ribbon. Our friends were delighted with the cookies and ate their names for days.

We ate healthy food in those early days – Charlie's yoga diets. Dates, figs, cottage cheese on celery sticks with raisins and honey on top. Cheap meat – chicken and chicken and chicken and brains, liver, kidneys, whole beef hearts. Within my first couple of days in England, I was hooked on steamed treacle puddings with custard sauce, shepherd's pie, bacon sandwiches, brisket baked slowly so as to release an inch-deep layer of beef fat in which you roast potatoes, carrots, parsnips, onions and celery. Ewan–Betsy food, which warmed and endangered the heart while stacking the weight on.

I was nearly named Euphrosine, my father's preference. Dio objected but acceded to Margaret, the name of Charlie's first love, Margaret Taylor, who gave me a diamond ring when I was sixteen. When Ewan and I were in dire straits I sold it for enough to keep our little household for three weeks. I never liked diamonds. Opals . . . yes yes yes. Barbara is the only one of Charlie's seven children who got a nickname: Bopso. Barbara is the only one of us four who has a middle name: Mona, the name of Charlie's woman-friend between Wife One and Wife Two. On Christmas Eve 1944, after our Christmas tree ceremony, Dio lay down on the couch. Our baby was coming on Jesus' birthday! They went to the hospital and Charlie came home to sit with us by the fire. I took the phone call myself. A girl, just what I'd wanted. They brought her home, a tiny, mewling creature that I loved from the word GO. I was eight and she was mine. I nursed her, cradled her as Dio rolled about on the worn brown gym mat trying to lose post-partum belly fat. I sang my baby silly songs and trundled her about on my hip. She mustn't be allowed on the back porch, or near the cellar door, and only on someone's lap on the merry-go-round. Dio insisted on the name Penelope, Penny for short. Probably for the long-suffering wife of Ulysses.

The elder brothers Charles and John appeared sporadically, but big brother Pete was our main love. Whenever he came, Dio let us stay home from school, reckoning that Pete was as good an education for us as the teachers. Born in 1919, he would have been in his early twenties at that time. Skyscraper tall, the banjo neck as long as his arm, he'd sit by the fire, his long long legs and big big feet going like pistons, allowing us to damp, twang and retune the strings while he sang. He had left Harvard to hitch-hike around the South. He came back talking of George Pegram, Uncle Dave Macon, Aunt Molly Jackson, the Carter Family. He brought Woody Guthrie to Dallas Avenue. He hardly seemed much bigger than we were. Woody would *take the dog for a walk,* barking while he pulled his guitar around the floor by its strap. Pete brought his Japanese bride – Toshi Aline Ohta, exotic with her slanted eyes, lovely long black hair and caramel skin. I peeked in on her when she was bathing. Our little bathroom sang the Song of Solomon.

Alan Lomax and his father John came regularly, burly and loud-spoken. They were working with Dio on their new anthology, *Our Singing Country*. One time they brought with them a thickset, blue-black man, Lead Belly. New word-play for me and Mike, *LEADbelly, bellyLEAD* . . . Released from prison through the influence of the Lomaxes, he travelled with them. Mike and I put 'Goodnight, Irene' and 'Midnight Special' into our daily song-box. Lead Belly was soft-spoken, respectful. We went one night to see him and Pete singing – in a boxing ring.

In 1979, Mike, Penny and I went back to Dallas Avenue. The house now belonged to the Jessup family, who had records by Lead Belly, Woody, Pete, Mike, and Ewan and me. Linda Jessup, pregnant with her fourth child, said she had liked the house from the moment she walked into it. It exuded family. The house later became the Seeger House and concerts are held in it. I gave one there myself in October 2002, the stage being right in front of our big old fireplace. The rest of the house . . . its personality had vanished. Its sale value is now above $600,000. All the fields of my childhood are gone, covered by a pot-pourri patchwork collection of new houses. I've seen what consecutive residents have done to my childhood homes and immediately wiped the new images off my mind like chalk off a blackboard. 10,001 Dallas Avenue is intact in my memory. I may forget a word in a line, a line in a ballad – but I'll never forget the song of childhood.

3

Growing Up

When I was nine years old, we moved to Chevy Chase, Maryland, on the northwestern border of Washington. The move was a social leap towards city centre, buses, schools and Charlie's administrative job as Head of the Music Division of the Pan-American Union. Dio still needed to teach piano but now she could do so at home – from 9 a.m. to 6 p.m. six days a week. The music room was under my bedroom. I could hear every lesson. Her teaching methods were very unusual. Hugh Latimer, for instance: he loved jazz and his mother wanted him to learn classical. As regards the latter, Hugh planted his mule-feet on the ground but agreed to instruction in technique. Dio asked him to teach her to play jazz. She tried but wasn't good at it. After a few months, she gave Hugh one of the themes from Bach's Inventions and asked him to jazz it up. Bach would have loved the result. Then a theme from Mozart. Hugh began to love the melodies. When she played him a five-part fugue in which, as she put it, Bach was creating closely-structured eighteenth-century jazz, Hugh caved in, captivated. I could hear him improvising on the melody and countermelodies to make transient harmonies, a bar of unison, then back to chase-the-theme, catch-the-motifs and combine them. Then he played the fugue properly, note for note. *Play it more slowly than you need to, Hugh. Then play it faster than it should go. Then playing it at its proper pace will be easy.* I heard it all through the floor, envious that I wasn't able to learn from my mother any more. I could have learned anything from Dio after I was twenty. We never got the chance.

Many formal musicians are mystified by folk music. They have trouble engaging with its oral nature. So-called *serious* musicians often look down on folk music as embryonic, something that needs improving or that can be used in their new compositions. My mother had none of these hang-ups. She never looked on folk music as simple. Her folk song accompaniments are calculated but superb. She would agonise over this quarter-note or that chord and discuss the arrangements at length with Charlie when he came home at night. Sometimes while playing a classical piece she would dart into an improvisation on it, laugh, and then go back to where she and Bartók, Beethoven or Mozart had left off. If she played a piece that I wanted to play, I would thump the bedroom floor. She'd write down the name of it for me and I'd learn it. Dio had fire; Charlie had breezes. Dio was anxious; Charlie was patient. He and I played four-handed piano arrangements of Beethoven symphonies, either two of us at one piano or one at each of the grands we now owned. If I stumbled, we'd stop. Charlie would sit with his hands folded, gazing into space and letting me work till I got it right. He and I sang Spanish songs, me on the guitar and he singing a quarter-tone flat.

*

Chevy Chase was prestigious – and still is. It was founded as an upper-class community whose charter set out to protect it from Negroes and Time. 7 West Kirke Street is set in perfect *feng shui* position at a wide entrance from bustling Connecticut Avenue. It still looks exactly as it did in the 1950s, the only difference being that our large, wooden-slatted house has had its original wrap-around porch restored according to plans in the possession of the Chevy Chase Historical Society. Inside it has been totally stripped down and modernised. We had bare parquet floors and throw rugs. We weren't harum-scarum children. Romping was for the cellar or outdoors. The antique desks, chairs and tables sent down from Grandfather Seeger's house required care that they didn't get. The long, heavy mahogany table seemed to tremble with the weight of the letters that were laid in her lap each day. It was a family Rule never to lean on this old lady or touch her spindly legs. The grand roll-top desk shed daily its bright dandruff – tiny fragments of inlay. When you found a piece on the floor, you picked it up, opened the top of the desk and put the piece into a little box with previous escapees. Someone would come along sometime and somehow glue them back. The box is probably somewhere.

We were a close family, held together by music and by our parents' love for each other. We drifted together naturally on Friday nights and sang in the room where Dio and Charlie's desks stood back to back. An uneasy chair, a Puritan sofa and an austere ladder-back chair with flat seat and flat arms and no cushion, so uncomfortable that you sat up straight in an effort to have as little contact with it as possible. The fireplace took huge logs and there was no fire-guard. One afternoon Penny fell into the fire with both hands in front of her. My baby girl with huge blistered monster-hands in bandages for months. June, July, August – treasure-days. Dio and Charlie sat out on the lawn while we played Red Light–Green Light, Mother-May-I? and hide-and-seek everywhere within calling distance. These are the images that fill my head when I sing 'Everything Changes'.

The house I lived in when I was a child
Had woods . . . . we all ran wild,
You could hide . . . then come home – after a while.
The town I lived in when I was young,
Everybody knew my name,
The world was my own,
Safe in the dark, playing games
Till Mama called me home.

We caught the poor fireflies and put them in a jar with holes in the lid. When you caught enough, you could read under the covers by the light of their desperate mating signals. Probably one of the reasons why I was wearing glasses by the time I was ten. Open the window screen, let the little sparkles fly away, then fly away yourself to sleep. *Mama, it's late – time to call me home.*

Any little bit of green that wasn't lawn was a delight to me. There was a huge forsythia bush by the post office, a flower tent – perfect for Chevy Chase Indians. Lovers could lie down under it, as I would discover. Blackberrying in summer, returning scratched, blotched and sated. In the winter, ice skating on a lake, unsupervised. Dragging your sled to the golf course, three blocks away. Runners well-soaped, making your own new path down the immense white sheet of snow, you aimed at top speed for that little opening in the fence at the bottom of the hill. Fence? It was a series of posts, slatted between. The gap allowed about an inch on each side. Head down, bring your hands and every bit of body onto the sled and whiz through at a thousand miles per hour. You'd bash your brains out if you miscalculated.

Never bored as a child, never bored in pre-teens. There were always things to do. You could make clover necklaces. You could sneak into a neighbour's backyard, cut their zinnias, ribbon them into a bunch and sell them back at their front door. Bake endless cakes. Prepare Charlie's five o'clock orange juice or help Jesse, the handyman, hold the ladder while Charlie painted a house that was big enough to hide in. The cellar was big and uncluttered. We rollerskated round and around the central pillar, avoiding the coal bunker, swinging like monkeys on ropes that dangled from the ceiling, raising clouds of dust from the cement floor. The milkman left our quart glass bottles of milk on the back porch every morning, the cream risen to the top. Put lemon juice in to sour it and shake it, trying to make butter, which was still rationed. Oleomargarine came encased in very thick plastic, congealed white manufactured glop with a tiny capsule of yellow colouring somewhere in there. Squeeze till you find the capsule then squeeze and squeeze it till it bursts. We loved the word *squeeze*, saying it over and over as we squoze. Squeeeeeze and squeeeeeze until the colouring was all through the oleo, then cut off the corner and squeeze the contents out like toothpaste. Toothpaste tasted better.

The attic, a.k.a. third floor, was full of light. The rooms had sloping ceilings. Had we stayed there longer, I would have commandeered the chimney room, so called because there was a huge pillar smack in its middle, servicing the fireplaces on the two floors below. This room had a closet full of hand-me-down clothes from our cousin Mary, lovely outfits that fitted me until Mary went hourglass and I went straight up and down. A pull-down ladder led to the very roof of the house, a small, flat space. No railings – you could just walk right off it. Charlie took us up there once only, one at a time, stating in un-Charlie loud, clear language that this space was totally out of bounds. Mike dwelt on the third floor. He opted for seclusion from females and parents and for his own en suite bathroom. His room had paintings by brother Pete and Thomas Hart Benton and a rope ladder for escape if there were a fire. Mike sang a lot but so far hadn't shown interest in playing an instrument. He had taken the Kuder aptitude test (*Which would you rather do: empty the garbage or listen to the Moonlight Sonata?*), which is still used to match people to professions. He had scored lowest in music. Pete had just written his banjo manual and Mike, stricken by shingles in his eyes and condemned to six weeks on his back in a darkened room, scoffed, *You can't learn banjo from a book! Prove it*, said Dio and bought a five-string banjo from a nun in a local religious establishment. The old SS Stewart was a visual delight. It had inlay right up the neck and carving on the heel where it joined the head. Mike lay on his back and I read Pete's manual to him with a small flashlight. *Bump-diddy, bump-diddy*, placing his fingers where Pete said they should go. Then I'd grab the banjo and try it myself. Mike wasn't pleased. *You have the guitar. Go and play that.* But he was my Mike – he said it with a grin. When he began to play guitar as well, the SS became *ours*. Last heard of, it was in the vicinity of Chicago. Now, my name is burnt into the peg-end of every one of my instruments, simultaneously decreasing and increasing their value.

No family photos on the walls and very few pictures. A large portrait of Dio's father – Clark Crawford – was promi-nently hung in the dining room. He was undistinguished, bald and bland. Dio and Clara Alletta Graves had been unusually close for daughter and mother. Clara's portrait presided over the little dark hallway opposite Mike's third-storey bathroom door. I used to wonder about that. She looked like Barbara. She had long hair gathered up into a chignon. Her dress was high-necked and long-sleeved. She had posed for the painter in a scoop-necked, short-sleeved dress. When Grandfather

Crawford saw the finished work, he made the artist paint clothing more appropriate for the wife of God's earthly representative. The moment her husband died, Grandmother Crawford
blossomed. She widened her circle of friends, took painting
lessons, opened a boarding house and probably lowered her
neckline. She began taking music lessons from her daughter.
Fourteen years later, Clara was dead from cancer. Dio wrote it
all up as she tended her mother: the flowering, the peace, the
illness and the death. Until I read her diaries in 1979, I never
realised that Dio's cancer path followed that of her mother.
Penny, aged forty-nine, died of cancer in 1994. Her daughter
Sonya died of cancer, aged fifty, in 2015.

*

I began to realise that the behaviour of male visitors could be
altered by using my blue eyes and stance in a certain way. I
practised on Alan Lomax, flirting outrageously with him. He
said he was going to marry me when I grew up. At that time, I
would have promised myself to any man who could sing 'Abdul
the Bulbul Ameer' like Alan – but I *was* worried. I'd already
promised myself to Harry. When I was sixteen, Ramblin' Jack
Elliott and Guy Carawan rolled in together. Jack was flaky – a
wannabe Woody Guthrie and doing a pretty good job of it – but
Guy sewed his own clothes and could *make bread!* Hmmm . . .
he was a possibility, but he didn't ask me. They were untidy,
made good music and helped with the dishes. International visitors came and left. Many of them were Latin American, having to do with Charlie's job. One of them brought his gorgeous
son, who cornered me in the fireplace room and said he'd come
back for me in eight years and would I please wait. Yes – he

and Harry could fight for my hand. Not one of these suitors was true to his word, but then neither was I. The composer Hanns Eisler turned up at Kirke Street before his deportation in 1948. He was old – fifty – and balding. When it was time for him to leave, Charlie and I walked him to the front gate. I'd been practising what Grandmother Seeger called *the come-hither look*. Flowering forsythia made an arch over the entrance and I positioned myself strategically, peering out from behind the branch, like Meg in *Little Women*. Hanns came up to me. *You're doing that on purpose, aren't you? Don't.*

One visitor spread a square of canvas on the big front porch and laid out pots of paint. Barefoot, the Seeger siblings hunkered down to watch as he poured great pools of colour onto the beige expanse. He invited us to walk in the paint, which we did with leaps and skips and slides that took us onto our hands and bottoms. He most likely discarded the painting, even though it was no doubt better than his well-known style, which Ewan once described as Pollock's bollocks. *I have no fear of making changes, destroying the image . . . because the painting has a life of its own.* (Jackson himself.) We tracked the colours through the house. Dio in a fury was a force to be reckoned with – torrents of anger, pictorial threats. *I could thrash you within an inch of your life*, probably subconsciously aimed that day at Mr Pollock. The *life of its own* certainly lived on as our mother scrubbed paint off floors, throw rugs and children. Dio never swore. We children weren't allowed to swear. If we did, she would wash our mouths out with soap.*

* Swearing has gotten boring. I couldn't watch the TV series *The Wire* because every third or fourth word was *fuck* or one of its permutations. We swear by what is sacred – mother, sex, God. *Motherfucker* must be lethal. For creative cursing, investigate the *Carmina Gadelica*, a collection of folklore

After-supper dishwashing was communal. When we began to play portable instruments, one of us was deployed to sit in the corner and play and choose the songs while the others washed, wiped and put away. On weekend nights, we'd occasionally find other neighbourhood kids and have a square dance in the dining room. The throw rugs would get thrown, chairs and tables pushed to the side. Arthur Lambert and big, red-haired Timmy, Nina Powell, myself . . . we were fifteen and sixteen in the world of Frank Sinatra, Hedy Lamarr, Veronica Lake (the stars and starlets for whose large, autographed photos I would send off as instructed on the back of the cereal box) – and here we were square-dancing in very upscale Chevy Chase. In the living room, the rickety mail table would shiver and shake. The old folks would drink coffee while we girls did our best to avoid dancing with Timmy.

Mike was my chief companion and Barbara was my companion sister. We did each other's hair, played endless games of Saturday-morning canasta with four packs of cards, talking about boys. In a family of left-wingers, Barbara turned right. She was the real rebel in a family of *progressives*. She branded herself the *white sheep of the family*. Aware that I was Charlie's favourite girl child, Barbara embarked on activities of which Charlie disapproved, things that I never dared to do. Dio may have clapped from the wings as Barbara stepped out in makeup and high heels, as she decamped to watch a neighbour's television (we didn't have one). She attended ballroom dance classes at Miss Murray's Dancing School over at the post office. I played piano

and poetry from the Doric and Gaelic-speaking regions of Scotland (1860 to 1909), gathered together by Alexander Campbell. My first husband had that name.

33

for these evenings for a dollar a night. 'Smoke Gets in Your Eyes', 'Tennessee Waltz', 'Now Is the Hour'. I would sneak 'Barbara Allen' in to annoy Barbara as she smooched closer to a boy in a dark corner. Miss Murray would go round from couple to couple prising them apart as they danced. She was everything our mother wasn't: overly made-up, over-dressed, over-perfumed, a social climber who thought the middle rung of the ladder was the top. Built like a battleship, she wore little girly dresses and championed pink Cadillacs, platonic love and dancing at least six inches apart. The other denizens of the building were the garbage men, down in the stinky, dark, dirty basement, camouflaged by their varying shades of black. In between shifts they would congregate next to the furnace. I took them maple-sugar candy, which I dearly loved, because I felt sorry about the job they had. They were very kind to the little white child coming in with offerings of maple-sugar leaves ...

A very tall pine tree stood just outside our fence, in full view of Dio's teaching room. Its branches were perfect for climbing, its top so supple that you could hang on and sway back and forth. Poor Dio, watching me climb fifty feet up, holding on with one hand and waving a sandwich in the other. Good teacher. She kept running her pupils through their paces. Good mother. Never once did she call me down or command me not to climb up. The swing was also outside her window. It was a real swing like those in the paintings, the lady with her long skirts and the gentleman pushing her. We were hoydens in shorts and several of us would get on this two-foot plank suspended by twenty feet of rope from a long-suffering limb. We would go halfway to heaven, with baby Penny clutched tight between us. We could see Dio, so she could obviously see us. Dear mother. Brave mother.

34

Life was ordered but strangely free – few dos and fewer don'ts. Every morning for years I had an early paper round, a huge basket on my handlebars. By the time I was twelve, I was cooking occasional family meals. I'd get home from school to a note from Dio: *Meatloaf, page 354, get hamburger and parsley. Don't pay more than 41¢ per pound and don't overcook it. Mashed potatoes and spinach. Take Penny.* A quick check of *The Joy of Cooking* and off I went on my bike, pulling my four-year-old sister in the big shallow wooden wagon. Down Connecticut Avenue, swooping around Chevy Chase Circle to the Safeway, Penny squealing with pleasure as we dodged the cars, the wagon tipping onto two wheels around corners. Every Friday for years we went to the movies – the cartoon, the news, then the cowboy feature, the ice-cream lady patrolling the aisles with her little tray. When I was older there were romantic films. After seeing *The Bells of St Mary's* I wanted to be a nun – for a week. I went with brother Mike and my first lover, Jeremy Foster, to see *the breast film*, a Swedish movie in which a young girl's breast was actually – intake of breath! – *totally uncovered*.

Charlie features heavily in the photo album in my head. Charlie recording me singing children's songs in 1945, at the Pan-American Union. He put a big smooth black disc onto a turntable and the needle cut the grooves as I sang, Charlie gathering the thread-like waste up in handfuls. Charlie on a Sunday teaching us to balance the three-legged cups in which his mother had served tea to those out of favour in her circle. Those *in favour* got solid-bottomed cups. Charlie coaching me in Esperanto, which neither of us liked. Charlie neither agnostic nor atheistic. Leland Junior High School wants to know my religious affiliation. *Put Zoroastrian, Peggy.* He was called in to talk to the principal. He came home with a new regime for

Sunday mornings, when we all piled into their double bed for hugs and reading. He would give us a chapter from the Bible followed by a chapter from *The Decameron*, in which *the nightingale outside the girl's window, children, is not really a nightingale.*

Mike and I played music together in our teens. Neither of us had fitted into the high-school social scene. Dio and Charlie encouraged both of us to take proper classical guitar lessons with Sophocles Papas. Massively overweight, he had thick, sausage fingers like his teacher Segovia and he insisted on our learning to sight-read, to follow the notes exactly. Mike quit and got lucky: he put himself under the tutelage of Charlie Byrd, the great jazz guitarist. I stayed but refused to sight-read. I would listen to Papas and then give him back, by ear, what he had just played. I was dismissed. Mike and I wound the Victrola up and listened to the Carter Family instead. We were a good mix – he was quiet, exact and somewhat of a recluse, and I was a lolloping, spontaneous loner who studied, made no friends, who sewed most of her own clothing, the high and low examples of which were a billowing tulle/satin/net ball gown and a bathing suit. I wore the former once only, discovering that I loathed the fol-de-rol of the high-school prom. I wore the latter once only because it came apart when we were playing netball on a beach.

Could a girl grow up in a middle-class suburb in the Western world like that now, not caring for peer pressure or fashion, still roller-skating to school on brick sidewalks at age sixteen, adventurous and ready for anything? Innocent freedom. We dressed like children, even into early teenage. Our parents set the thermals and we each rode our own breeze until we fell back to earth – on 18 November 1953.

4

The Songs and the Singers

Whenever I had a bout of croup, Dio would hold me over a steaming open-top kettle to help me breathe, just as I would do thirty years later with my Kitty. This night Charlie put the lidless kettle right beside the bed. I stepped out straight into near-boiling water and was rushed to hospital, where I contracted septic scarlet fever and was put into quarantine – no visitors. My bed is a shelf and my parents are smiling at me from behind a large window. They could hear me singing down the maze of corridors, *Sweet Will Yum on his deaf bed lay, For love of Baaaaarbra Allen.* 1937 – two years old – and the songs had entered my bloodstream.

My mother was a folklorist's delight. She transcribed a song onto staff paper so accurately that anyone wishing to sing it would have difficulty in reading the intricate transcription. Until teenage, I learned by listening and I kept the songs more or less as I'd heard them – from field recordings, from brother Pete and from singers passing through. They were transient, so I had no consistent feedback in terms of listeners. Once I began to learn songs from print I became less adept at learning them from an oral source. I also began to mess with them. I began to collate texts, to look for more satisfying tunes – even to make up new ones if I didn't like the ones in the books. Don't tell anyone. I was so steeped in the northeastern American tradition that I felt equipped to do this – but then I was not testing my versions

37

out on a stable home community. There was one Scots ballad that I wanted to sing but I don't sing in Scots on stage – my vowels make the Scots irritable. I couldn't find an American version. Solution: translate as closely as possible into Yankee-speak and sing it in until it is comfortable in the mouth. Instant folk process and folklorist's nightmare. That ballad is already being sung by other singers as traditional. So far, no folklorist has picked me up on it. They may have asked me *where did you get that version from?* to which I'd reply that I couldn't remember. True, for I constructed it in a now out-of-reach section of my brain. My excuse? The story was too wonderful to be lost, the directly translatable sections too precious.

The songs: I am theirs and they are mine while I'm here. I call them *mine* since I have nurtured them like children and brought them forth with me in time. Like my physical children, they form my core. I revel in them, tasting the words as I sing, entering earlier eras and other people's lives. Unlike my physical children, they have grown towards me rather than away. I have studied and internalised their textual and melodic disciplines. Their texts and tunes fit so well together that I can easily spot a decayed version, a rogue word or an ill-fitting melody in print or performance. This makes me a closet purist, although Ewan and I didn't closet our vociferous and hypocritical purisms. Even though we doctored, pruned, edited and experimented with the songs and singing styles of traditions that were in noticeable decline, we believed that we were sticking as faithfully as possible to the style and intent of the original makers and carriers of the songs.

In the 1970s, Belle Stewart, a Scots Traveller woman, took us to meet The Memory, an old, old, really old man. By his bedside sat a boy in his late teens. No notes or notebook. The old man was reciting the Stewart genealogy and the boy repeated each sentence after him, committing the family lineage to memory. Every now and then the old man would backtrack and ask the boy about some long-deceased, long-ago-mentioned ancestor. The boy had to place the departed one on a branch or twig of the family tree, with names of spouse and children, siblings and parents. He came week after week and the old man talked week after week. The boy would become The Memory when the old man died. We stayed for about an hour. The old and the young never stopped their discourse. Books can be burned, archives can be pillaged, cities and nations laid to waste, but you cannot destroy what is passed via memory from mouth to ear to mouth.

Up until fifty years ago, I wanted a *beautiful* voice, that voice that sometimes seems to find itself more interesting than what it's singing. In my teens, I imitated my greats whenever they visited me on my little radio – Mary Ford, Rosemary Clooney, Patti Page, Margaret Whiting. No use. Ewan called mine a *character* voice, more suitable for singing folk songs. So the singers on my mother's records didn't have *beautiful* voices? They had extraordinary voices – rough, limited, the unique character of each voice as important to the story as the words. Text, tune, voice: I tried to reproduce them as an unbreakable unit. 'Goodnight, Irene': listen to the Weavers' version, then listen to Lead Belly singing it. One is an overdressed copy and the other is the real thing. I'm not the real 100 per cent thing – but I do know that a mellifluous voice might have trouble singing 'Poor Ellen Smith',* which needs the high lonesome style of Texas Gladden and the fast rippling banjo of her brother Hobart

* Ellen Smith was shot by her lover in North Carolina in 1894.

39

Smith. I don't try to copy. I just sing for the story, the maker, the actual words. But I would love to sing like Jean Ritchie, birdlike and pure. Or like Hally Wood, way down there far below middle C.

How you sing doesn't only matter to me. In 1995, my friend Irene and I were touristing in Charleston, South Carolina. We took a guided tour – its title included *Slaves and Slavery*, probably called *Heritage* these days. In our little bus were two pink Brits and half a dozen brown and black female friends who kept up a hilarious running commentary for the whole ninety minutes. Living in Asheville at the time, I told them I had often passed by the African American churches on a Sunday. I first heard that whole body-and-soul singing while Dio transcribed it. As an adult I longed to join in whenever I heard it. I asked our tour companions, *How do you feel when white folks walk into your church on a Sunday? Just fine, honeybunch, just don't try to sing!* We all got a belly laugh from that. You have to live in a community or culture to be a true part of it.

The word *community* runs through this book like a heartbeat because it is basic human nutrition. A community energises individuals to take on co-operative roles which maintain the cohesion of the whole. I have a community of four or five hundred songs rattling around in my head, in various stages of retention, supporting each other. They are all huddled together in the same place in my brain, each telling me how to sing it so as to best communicate the circumstances that created it. On stage, I become as the narrow neck of an hourglass, bringing stories and singers from the past to the present; a relay runner hoping that someone will take the song from me and carry it into the future.

5

The Helpers

At Dallas Avenue, whenever Dio went out to teach piano, we were put under the care of a succession of young women, most of them from further south. Brown, black, tan, whitish, on their way north, they'd knock on the door. *Does Missus need help today?* That was how lovely Dorothy came to us, sleeping in our little bedroom. She must have been about eighteen, coffee-coloured with long, naturally straight hair. Mike would stand and watch her dress, until she realised the true nature of his interest. Privacy was downstairs in the only bathroom, so she donned her day garments whilst still under the sheets. I watched too, for I wanted to see how you could dress while you were still in bed. Dorothy would writhe and twist under her blanket, reaching an arm out here and a foot out there to pick up and drop garments. Then she would emerge, a butterfly out of its cocoon, ready for her day. Dorothy left. Another knock on the door. Dio gave a cake recipe to the only really white one who turned up. When the recipe asked for starch, our minder (who had never baked or been near an oven) put in washing starch instead of corn starch and entertained us *in absentia* as my father tried to cut the solid brick of cake. Another knock on the door. Back then you could entrust your three children under ten years old to a passing stranger.

When we moved to Kirke Street, Dio taught at home so we had a rota of permanent helpers. Mamie Harrison had occasionally come to us at Dallas Avenue and she now came to Kirke Street, on Sundays after church. Charlie called her *a first-century Christian*. She lived the Bible. She had turned the other cheek so often that her face was flat, all bone. She lived on onions, bread, sassafras tea and God. She lived His Word and He was her only life partner. I loved Mamie. She was good-tempered, lean and worn, active as a whippet. She was dark brown and ill-educated but with a keen desire to *speak proper*. Determined to unlearn *ain't* and cure the habit of dropping her *gs* she would give us a penny to correct her speech. Her response to *thank you* was the old form of *be welcome*. For pennies she learned our *you're welcome*. She wanted straight hair. She'd lay her tight black curls down on the ironing board and get me, a child, to iron them straight. We didn't charge her for that. She plaited our hair with coloured ribbons and held us passionately to her flat chest. She'd leave after dark, her working shoes wrapped in her apron in a bag, a late-evening version of Betsy in Ewan's poignant song 'Nobody Knew She Was There'.

> *Working shoes are wrapped in working apron*
> *Rolled in an oilcloth bag across her knees.*
> *The swaying tram assaults the morning,*
> *Steely, blue grey day is dawning,*
> *Draining the last few dregs of sleep away.*

Mary Ann James came from Monday to Friday. Lighter brown than Mamie, large, comfortable Mary Ann had taught at Tuskegee Institute.* I think she was better educated than Dio.

---

* Tuskegee, Alabama. The school was founded on 4 July 1881 as the Tuskegee Normal School for Colored Teachers.

She had come north to live with an ill sister and never went back. She corrected our grammar, my algebra, and told us a great deal about the history of the South. I loved Mary Ann. She was up for cuddling and wore no creaking girdles. You confessed the day at school to her and listened to her talking about her life while she ironed and made supper. She was a splendid cook. She didn't make meals – she made banquets. Scrumptious baking powder biscuits, chocolate cakes, southern fried chicken, chicken-and-dumplings, collard greens with pork. Fresh rolls with butter tucked into a fold that resembled a baby's bottom. An entire shad, fourteen inches long with roe inside, served on one of Grandmother's fragile oval china platters. Cakes like towers. Cheese soufflés and spoon bread. I asked her how to make the biscuits – a kind of scone – that we so loved. *Take two fistfuls of flour, honey, a serving spoon of butter, put this amount of salt in your palm, the jelly glass with the little girl on it full of milk* . . . At dinner-time, Charlie would press the button under the table – I felt shame when he did that. Mary Ann – dignity personified – would sail in like a galleon to bring in or clear away, never speaking. The family usually did the final clearing and washed the dishes, but when Mary Ann worked late she'd stay overnight in the basement bedroom. That was shameful too and I said so at the time. There were two empty, light, dry bedrooms on Mike's third floor, but no – women without whom the house would have come to a full stop slept in the cellar, where every surface was covered with a thin layer of cement dust. The smell of mildew and the sight of tiny paw prints in the dust kept me out of that room. I'm sure Dio would have offered the upstairs rooms to our dear Helpers. But would they have . . .? Sometimes, unfortunately, the person who keeps the *status* in the *quo* position is the person who least benefits from it.

I was always wandering off somewhere, a tendency that can lead to a variety of interesting results. When I was about four, I vanished from the little paddler's puddle that had been provided for children at a busy New York City swimming pool complex. I was found edging my way around the deep end of the grown-up pool. In 1948, I wandered off in Lansburgh's department store in Washington and a tall, calm, very black woman found me and stayed with me till Dio came – Elizabeth Cotten. Penny nicknamed her Libba and the name stuck. She and Dio struck up a friendship immediately. I loved Libba. For five years she came to us on Saturdays. Libba got on with Mamie but she and Mary Ann chose their corners and came out slugging with pin-pricks, deft asides, songs and cake recipes. Libba had been schooled till she got her periods and was married off. She was resentful of Mary Ann's single life and education. She discovered that we liked frosting and filling thicker than the cake itself and became Queen of the Chocolate Cake. When I was away at boarding school, she would whip up one of these delectable mini-skyscrapers, about a foot high. Dio would box it, write THIS SIDE UP on all four sides and take it down to the post office, Vermont-bound. It would arrive five hundred miles away in one right-side-up piece. From 1792 onwards, the United States Postal Service was legendary – it would send anything anywhere. It sent a whole bank building from the east coast to the west coast and lost not one brick. I was the flavour of the month at Putney School when those cakes arrived.

The family guitar was hung on a wall in the kitchen. I came in after school one day and found Libba playing it left-handed, index finger swinging away doing the job of the thumb, her thumb relegated to fingerdom. We heard 'Freight Train' for the first time. Mike and I learned to play it left-handed. Libba

44

became a major centre of attention. Mary Ann simmered as she ironed on a Saturday morning, occasionally dropping comments about lack of education. She began making *very* tall chocolate cakes. That surely would be better than *any* song that Libba could sing. This sounds humorous, and in a way it was – but in another way it was tragic, as each of our substitute black mothers had something special to offer. They were both in the same boat but were pulling in different directions – as people have always done, dividing themselves before the rulers get a chance. Mary Ann's encroachment on Cake Territory wasn't lost on Libba. She dragged songs out of her childhood, polished them up and sang them on Saturdays. Her church in North Carolina had deemed guitar playing unsuitable for a married woman so, a girl bride, Libba had laid the instrument *down by the riverside*. The Lord is fond of second comings. Libba picked up the guitar once more in a Chevy Chase kitchen and she damn well wasn't going to lay it down again. After Kirke Street, it was Mike who bought Libba a guitar of her own, recorded her and got her on stage. It was Mike who toured with her, opened for her and handled her professionally, for in her later days once she got on stage she couldn't be gotten off. Mike became her guardian angel and stayed so till she died in 1987.

All three black women bonded with my mother but it was always *Mamie* and *Mrs Seeger*, *Libba* and *Mrs Seeger*, *Mary Ann* and *Mrs Seeger*. My mother tried in vain to get them to call her Ruth, but the built-in black–white, southern–northern, worker–employer dynamics prevailed. Since Charlie had been brought up with servants in the house, the real, live distance between him and the three black women was to be expected. It wouldn't have occurred to any of us to invite them to sit down with us at the dinner they'd cooked. Even had we asked, they would not have done so, not even Mary Ann, well educated as she was. Mamie would have sat bolt upright and worried about manners, worried about grammar, polite and horribly embarrassed. Libba . . . maybe. Mamie and Libba sat down with a whole passel of us at a reunion supper in the 1970s with no qualms at all.

*

As we moved into teenage we had lots of jobs. We cleaned the bathrooms, Barbara and I – by candlelight. We ironed our own clothes, mopped the kitchen floor. We shopped and cooked and mowed the lawn. Our rooms had to be neat, beds made. Dio called me back from junior high school once because my bed wasn't made. She worked hard, her income vital to the family economy – but she was always in the piano room with a pupil. Mamie, Libba and Mary Ann: I wanted to know what their lives were like. That's probably why I tried to make friends with Glover, the janitor at Leland Junior High. I was taken aside by the principal of the school and told that this kind of contact wasn't to be allowed. Glover seemed more real than many of the other Leland adults. He did work that seemed like work. So many people who had physical work were brown that I associated brown people with that kind of labour. The dark Latin American and African diplomats and associates of my father were different, and they knew they were different by dint of their history, country, class and demeanour. Occasionally they came to dinner. Charlie would press the button under the table and brown Mary Ann – daughter of a child of a child of a child of slaves – would sweep in with food for the white family and the brown visitors. Charlie had been a communist in the thirties. Dio was the daughter of a boarding-house keeper. Mary Ann had a master's degree from a southern college. Perhaps an ancestor of one of the diners had sold the ancestor of the cook into slavery. The button still got pressed.

6

School

Old Glory stands in the corner of every classroom. Stand up, hand on heart, face the red, white and blue piece of cloth and group-chant: *I pledge allegiance to the flag of the United States of America and to the republic for which it stands, one nation (under God) with liberty and justice for all.* Officially, the USA is a republic, not a democracy. We bow our heads and recite the Lord's Prayer. Officially, church and state are separated. At assembly, we sing 'The Star-Spangled Banner', 'America the Beautiful' and, if we are unlucky, our state song, 'Maryland, My Maryland'. By the time President Eisenhower added *under God* to the Pledge of Allegiance in 1954 I was at college, pledging allegiance to freedom from pledging allegiance to anything but studying and having a good time.

*

It was sunny and warm on the first day I went to school, aged five. I walked between Mike and Dio in a pinafore dress of tiny orange and white checks, swinging my little lunchbox. I tore my dress that first day and refused to wear it once it was mended. When I was twelve, I was skilled enough to play piano for the school assemblies. When I was fourteen, I entered myself for the talent show. Clad in a top hat and a black, ill-fitting formal suit, I sang 'My Mother-in-Law', pretending to be drunk:

My life is all trouble, no pleasure I see,
Wherever I go that old lady watches me.
I'd rather be drug off to jail or to Congress
Than live all my life with my mother-in-law.

Talk about seeing into the future. My legs were shaking so hard that I thought I was going to collapse. My classmates thought I portrayed inebriation and fear of the old lady very well. I was a voracious reader but my only requirement was a good story. I devoured the entire *Nancy Drew* series, *Little Women*, my mother's Perry Mason series, *Anna Karenina*, *War and Peace*, *The Reds of the Midi* . . .

From the beginning, I loved school and wanted to do well. Wanting to do well gets in the way of real learning. I became competitive and got straight As. I was adept at memorising and at pleasing the teachers. The exam system encourages students to learn what they will need for the exam and no more. This was (and still is) my downfall. I tend to do many things half-way. High-school chemistry was gripping, a peek into what the world is made of. The chemistry teacher, Mr Rowe, with whom I was infatuated for several weeks, gave us a valuable lesson in memory: *If you tell yourself to forget something, you will remember it.* He gave us a three-digit number to forget. It was a bonus question on his final exam. We all remembered it. I still do.

School music was compulsory and stifling. Had I not had a musical home, school would have stripped me of any interest in music. I never had a music teacher at school who seemed to really *love* music. At the piano, their arms rose and fell as if they were expecting their hands to play even when they were in mid-air. They oozed those stereotyped emotions that dictate what kind of music best accompanies a situation in a film or a radio show. Slow has got to be soupy; fast has got to be like little mice gone mad on a wedge of cheese; sad has to be in minor. At Leland Junior High, our pudding of a music teacher was ill for a week and a visitor from the Milky Way was drafted in – a retired opera singer. He had waxed mustachios and a little pointy beard. He spent the whole of each lesson talking about where and what he had sung. He sang his opera parts for us when we were supposed to be learning 'Tora Ora'. He wasn't *teaching* music – he *was* music, wonderfully overblown and passionate. He filled our classroom with his presence. He took us to Vienna, London, Milan, backstage, on stage and into the presence of royalty. You could hear him singing from the far edges of the playground. Pudding returned, a doughy dessert after we'd been stuffed with nutritious meat and veg.

Boys. They always went after the pretty girls, the ones who'd already achieved a waistline with complementary Above and Below. We competed with our female classmates for the attention of the poor fellows. I fell for the class president, Eddie Haskins. My best friend immediately hijacked him. We girls hid our real selves, parading what the boys wanted – if we had it. Karen sat in class self-harming, scraping the back of her hand with a bobby pin until it was bloody. She looks miserable. *Why do you do that, Karen? You have big breasts.* The boys called her The Dairy and tried to feel her up during change of classes. The principal of the school had haemophilia. He avoided the halls, standing flat against the wall while student hordes passed, some of us whistling or humming a tune, the words of which we knew he knew:

> *We never stumble, we never fall,*
> *We sober up on wood alcohol.*

Send old Mason out for gin,
Don't let a sober teacher in.

I believe in school uniforms. Janice's mother made her a new skirt for *everyday*. I tried to keep up but Dio refused to buy that volume of cloth. When I learned to sew, I stitched vertical strips of baleen into the skirt waistbands so they wouldn't be sucked into the crevices of my puppy fat. Advertisements (*which twin has the Toni?*) talked my classmates into perms, shampoos and rinses that Dio refused to buy. We Kirke Street women washed our hair with bars of Ivory soap and put vinegar or beaten-up egg white into the penultimate rinse.

Dio acquiesced when I asked for a teenage party at our house, both boys and girls. It got out of hand. We played Spin the Bottle and one by one we girls were dragged under the grand piano and our mouths deflowered at length while the others looked on. Not pleasant. We played Post Office and I insisted on drier delivery. We were under parental supervision but not interrupted. Charlie always came to each of us at bed-time, sitting for five or ten minutes talking about this and that. Tonight, post-party, he wanted to talk about this and this, obvi-ously deputed by Dio. He put it in plain terms: a kiss leads to petting to *At some time, Peggy, you will want a good, strong penis to go into you* . . . Bet my classmates aren't getting this. The phrase, delivered dry and gentle, was burned into my memory. I wasn't embarrassed, probably because I couldn't see his face clearly and because I was more comfortable with him than with Dio. They'd both walked around naked on summer Sundays at Dallas Avenue so I knew what the item was – but I found it difficult to imagine that Mike's little one and Charlie's floppy one could go anywhere.

My mother could never have said those words. She had trouble with saying anything as far as sex or the female body was concerned. Before I went off to boarding school at fifteen she said, *It's possible your womanly manifestations will be starting soon, so you should get used to what Kotex feels like.* I was mortified when she brought out a pad and one of those elastic contraptions they used to have. She made me walk around with it for an afternoon. Courageous mother, doing your best. So between them, Dio and Charlie gave me a kind of sex education that was far and away better than the silly sex films they subjected us to at Leland, those coy productions that show you everything except the process by which the sperm gets delivered. The girls sat downstairs in the auditorium and the boys hung over the banisters of the upstairs halls, dropping paper airplanes and wads of masticated chewing gum on us.

I was becoming a problem at home, sassing my mother and being sulky. Teenage children were not my mother's forte. Are they anybody's? I don't think I was very good with my teenagers either. What is a good mother, anyway? You've put yourself in thrall to charming little people who change to big people who all of a sudden begin to treat you like an intruder in their lives. One companion mother suggested to me that we put all the teenagers in a gladiatorial arena and let them fight it out among themselves. And yet, and yet – *Mother* awakens in most of us a subliminal allegiance. At a festival in Tasmania, Ewan and I would witness a flyting between a Uruguayan and a Paraguayan. Flyting is a stylised contest in which participants exchange improvised insults, sung or spoken in rhyme or free verse. Hammer and tongs, the South Americans went at it with guitar and voice, louder and faster, competing for loudest and fastest till the Uruguayan broke his guitar over the Paraguayan's head. Blood, curses, fists, mayhem. I asked a Spanish speaker what the Paraguayan had said. *He insulted the Uruguayan's mother.*

Most animals know when to kick the kids out. Kangaroos don't seem to bother. We're in Australia and a huge joey, its front end in the pouch, is trying to get its back end in while Mama peacefully munches on something and gazes into space. A good mother. Gannets – avian seaplanes – feed their solo chick in a nest high on a cliff until it's as fat as a pin-feathered basketball. One day, just before it can grow proper wings, the Good Gannet Parents ease it out of the nest with their beaks. It bounces hundreds of feet down the cliff, hitting rocks, other nests, often dislodging kindergarten fledglings before their time. If it is one of the fittest, it survives, landing with a WHACK on or among its stunned contemporaries, knowing bugger all about flying or feeding itself. Its layers of fat keep it afloat and alive until its feathers and wings grow, taking it into the air so that it can dive for fish. Good parents are parents who give you what you need to survive – body, brain, courage, trust and the possibility of wings. The best parents open a bank account in your name. Perhaps for the therapist you may need later?

My buddy Mike, also a problem teenager, had been sent off earlier to Woodstock Country School in Vermont. Now the same had to be done to me. I had talked vaguely of becoming a farmer's wife, so in the autumn of 1950 Dio and Charlie drove me up to Putney School, also in Vermont. I was happy to go. Carmelita Hinton, headmistress and owner of Putney, was thickset and eccentric, white hair and ice-blue eyes. She had started the school with a gaggle of children and a flock of goats and treated both similarly. She wanted a place where youngsters could learn to farm, raise vegetables and get plenty of fresh air. She came down hard on secret smoking, budding sexuality, truancy, roaming the fields at night. They billeted me in Kelly House, which lay at the end of a lane that turned into a path that turned into a squirrel run and turned right into the front door. It was a log cabin that had been brought by Carmelita from the southern mountains. The big room upstairs housed Sandy Spencer, Joan Brooks, Lin Frothingham, Liz Arakie and me. Peggy Miller, our house mother, was too young, unprepared for governing five girls with a communal leaning towards soft sadism. One tiny bathroom served all six of us. It was never free of laundry hanging on racks in the tub, on lines hung from the ceiling, on every hook and in every nook. There was no central heating, just a wood fire downstairs and a little single-filament electric heater for our room upstairs, an area about thirty by thirty feet with no insulation. We froze. Many's the night we five pushed two beds together and negotiated for the centre position, flanked on either side by warm bodies, hoping we wouldn't get pushed to the edge where unprotected body parts were exposed to the Arctic. Think male emperor penguins, with their eggs between their feet, hunched, shuffling and sharing in turn the warm centre of the huddle. We would put on all our vests, socks, sweaters and coats, pile on every bit of blanketing and still feel the frost developing at the outer edge of our mound. In those post-Hiroshima days, we called it the *Atomic Pile*. Carmelita called it character-building.

Putney School was a school for oddballs, so it was the first time I had female friends. You could easily visit other dormitories, sit for hours in other girls' rooms. Carmelita trusted us to ramble over the lovely countryside wherever and with whomever we wished, provided we were on time for lessons, meals, kitchen/field duty or curfew. The Good Ship Putney sailed on a sea of hormones. Every week or two the Kitchen Dining Unit would be cleared of tables. A band would arrive and the mock-courtship ritual known as dancing would begin. We danced in twos, arms around waists, hands holding hands, bodies close as possible. Carmelita prowled among the couples with a little piece of wood in her hands, exactly six inches long. She'd graduated from the same school as Miss Murray. The couples froze then sprang apart as Carmelita's headlights bore down on them. *Six inches, please*, she would say in her officious New England-with-an-underlay-of-North-Carolina voice, shoving the wooden bar between each couple. Some of us were canny and steered ourselves around the hall either away from her path or following directly behind her. Carmelita sailed, creating a wash in which the couples latched together again once she'd passed. If you weren't dancing at the time, it was hilarious to watch. Mind you, if you were dancing with someone you didn't fancy, Carmelita's *six inches, please* would definitely please a lady.

The farm work began immediately. The rain was teeming down. Our boots were taking on twice, three times their own weight in thick mud but you had to dig those potatoes, lift those carrots, pull up those tomato plants, straw those strawberries, *tote that barge, lift that bale, get a little drunk and . . .* fat chance of that. Not a drop of alcohol anywhere on the official premises. Official. One lad made hooch in the chemistry classroom. It was several weeks before he was discovered and sent home – but not before handing the recipe on. Our long-suffering Kelly House Mother did make us mulled wine one night under promise of silence.

Everyone had to work. I chose brushing the cows in the early morning. For six months, I rose in the dark and struggled into my barn clothes: two or three layers of shirts and vests, my heavy overalls, as many socks as I could find, high rubber work boots, top coat, hat, scarf and heavy mittens. I stank of barn, a pleasant manure and hay smell when the odour was new, offensive when it wasn't. My gear was so permeated with caked mud, cow-dirt and my-dirt that it stood up by itself. The malodorous items only got washed every couple of weeks because I needed them daily and there was no place to dry them.

The trudge to the barn took maybe ten minutes. In the fall and spring it wasn't bad. In the winter it was a struggle but beautiful. There are so many clear skies in Vermont. The stars might still be out. Moonlight caught in the xylophone of icicles on the cabin's overhang. If there had been a fresh snowfall overnight, you waded through clouds, an untrodden, knee-high sea of white flakes fine as dust. It's still snowing and the silence is holy. An occasional electric *crack!* of a branch breaking. When you saw the lights of the barn and heard the mooing and the machinery, anticipation of the warmth moved your legs faster. The boss of the barn was a rough Vermont countryman. He loved the cows. He talked to them, knew all their names. They would stand still as he fixed the milking machine to the tired udders. He could shoot from the cow's hip and hit me with a spritz of milk when I came within range. He overheard my proud announcement to Sandy and Lin that my periods had started at last. Thereafter he greeted me with bawdy comments every four weeks, the first man who ever paid complimentary attention to my monthlies. There were about sixty or seventy cows harnessed in two long rows, munching away, *moo-moo-mooing* and waiting for my ministrations. Put the circular metal scraper on over my work gloves and start scraping dried shit. Cows' bums are as distinctive as their faces. At first, the sight of those vertical, dirty openings is repulsive. I'd never had a look

at myself *down there*. I have since and it bears an unmistak-
able resemblance. I was responsible for cleaning about a foot on
either side of the place where the tail joins the body and down
the inside back of each leg. I cared gently for their no-longer-
private parts. Poor things. They couldn't walk while they shat,
so how could they keep clean? They would look around and
say *lovely lovely* with their eyes when you did something they
liked. They have clitorises too. Maybe I was more than just the
cleaning lady.

Everything about Putney School was exciting. Some students didn't go home over a half-term holiday. A group of these
boys disliked one of the vacationing teachers so, in cohort with
lads from the town garage, they took his car apart and put it
back together in his room. We went swimming at the little lake,
always with a buddy. A boy jumped in from the diving board
and didn't come up. His buddy went down, found him stuck in
the mud and pulled him back up. They took away the diving
board. Playing piano in the practice rooms in the cellar of the
main house with Mike Vidor on the banjo, Pete Seeger's sister
and King Vidor's son making music of several sorts together.
The freedom was exhilarating. Slap peanut butter and jelly into
sandwiches on a Saturday morning and careen downhill on the
bike to the little town of Putney. Thrilling – paid for by having
to walk your gearless bike back up the long hill in time for dinner or duties. Weekdays, and a bell tolled the change of classes
over the whole hilltop. Up till then I had thrived on competition. My astrological sign is Gemini – twins. I even managed
to make *them* compete with each other. At Putney, competitive
attitude or behaviour was discouraged. I was only there thanks
to Pete, who had agreed to do two free concerts in exchange for
my tuition. I kept breaking rules. Had I been a model student

I think my continual overstepping of freedom limits, playing hooky at night and – yes – putting snowballs in Carmelita's bed on a regular basis might have been overlooked. Having spent the year misbehaving, it was goodbye to my Kelly House cabal, to the hills and farm work, to John Peasley, who let me in on his science experiments in his little hut in return for dancing with him on six-inch Saturdays. I was returned home unceremoniously after a year.

*

I was back in a learning factory, a homing pigeon returning from its first release. Bethesda-Chevy Chase High School (BCC) was huge – two thousand pupils. I felt out of place, a loner again, but I didn't mind. What I did mind was the Gender Game. It had entered the curriculum. The gym teacher was in charge of it. *Stand up straight with your shoulders back. Those bumps were put there for a purpose!* I wonder what she would have made of Madonna. The male arts teacher taught us girls how to put makeup on, how to dress. Was he gay? Advice comes from everywhere. Tips on dating. *Don't giggle or fiddle with your hair. Sit attentively with your legs crossed and don't make any sudden, unfeminine movements. Listen to Him and don't talk a lot about yourself. Don't talk to or about other boys when you are with Him.* How to respond when *His first telephone call* came, how to tell *Him* what kind of orchid you wanted on your ball gown, how to keep *Him* from going too far – nothing about how to keep yourself from going too far. No problem for me. I was the class swot and no one asked me out.

I had always been surprised that anyone recognised me. I would look in the mirror, trying to remember my face.

Actually, I was vivacious, full of life. I played several musical instruments, sang, sewed, danced and was physically active. I had long, wavy egg-white-rinsed hair. I wore glasses. Men and *girls*. Dorothy Parker coined the phrase *Men seldom make passes at girls who wear glasses* – but when they did (at college) their starting gun was primed and ready before mine had even been loaded. My Jeremy was a beautiful boy, my brother Mike's best friend, nineteen years old to my seventeen. He was in a hurry. He coaxed me under the forsythia bush on Connecticut Avenue and laid me down on a carpet of stones and twigs. Pedestrians and traffic were only yards away and it felt as if our feet were sticking out in plain sight. I was not prepared, although he was – canny boy. The whole thing was hurried and distressing. I was a virgin, then all of a painful sudden, I wasn't. The loss of virginity didn't bother me. It was the disappointment. The old story, *Well, is that what all the fuss is about?* Children: the first total physical encounter with a lover is crucial. Consider mutual orchestration, care, thought and just the right mixture of affection and passion. True to form, however, I went home and wrote a romantic poem about my deflowering. Even my diary was not to be party to how thrust upon I felt. I began to look on boys as predators. Even through the most attentive foreplay I felt as if my body – not me – was being prepared like a succulent dish at a banquet. Check out *nyotaimori*, the samurai tradition of serving sushi on the body of a woman.

I've described the actual loss of my virginity in two objective sentences, one sentence for each of the minutes that it took for the deed to be done. That sensitive boy, inexperienced himself, later broke my inexperienced heart. My inexperienced reaction broke his. One strike and we were both out. He couldn't help himself – his body was in turmoil. His brain and heart were

59

quite romantic. He looked soulfully at me. We bathed naked in moonlit southern creeks. We lay under the harvest moon in a southern pasture. He carved me a little wooden heart inlaid in ebony with *JF* on one side and *PS* on the other. I still have it.

*

All over the world, millions of humans behind steering wheels are co-operating together like shoals of fish. BCC offered a year-long driver training course. We were taken to the bedsides of traffic victims. One was a man who had lost his wife and two daughters when a windblown newspaper flew across his windscreen. He steered head-on into another car and was now paralysed totally for the rest of his life. Some people with terminal illnesses devote the remainder of their short lives to raising funds for medical research, to calling the attention of the public to early warning symptoms. This ruined man dedicated himself to talking to learner drivers. He had one message for us: observe and memorise the whole scene in front of you in case it is suddenly blanked out. This lesson served me well on a cold winter night early in 1963. We had a second-hand Citroën DS whose downward-sloping bonnet opened upwards from the front in one large section. Our load was five and a half passengers and a double bass. I was the driver, heavily pregnant with my second child. We stopped at a garage on the M1 to check the oil. We started out again. The new-fangled latching of the bonnet hadn't caught and at 70 mph it flew up and over the car, blocking off all vision except a small sliver across the bottom of the windscreen. Hunching down to peer through the crack, plus my habitual memorisation of the traffic ahead, around and behind, probably saved our lives. Thank you, kind quadriplegic man.

Mike was also back home. When he and I drove out together he made it plain that the 1938 Chevy was *his*. The night before my driving test, Charlie took me out at rush hour in the Pontiac station wagon. We drove north up the divided highway of Connecticut Avenue. Turn left and make a U-turn at East-West Highway *and let's go home, Peggy.* A moment later he doubled over, paper-white. *Get ... me ... home ... to ... Dio ...* I leaned on the horn, put the accelerator down, signalled my left and right intentions, wove in and out down Connecticut Avenue, through a red light at Bradley Boulevard. In my passenger seat, *Get-Me-Home-to-Dio* was choking. Turn right at the post office and into the drive. Charlie straightened up, his colour returned. He smiled and said, *Very good, Peggy.* After that, my driving test was a doddle. Years of advanced yoga pay off in odd ways.

I had one real friend at BCC – Annette Dapp. Wiry, dark-haired, smart. We went through primary, junior and high schools together. We'd often walk home together, occasionally do homework together. She still holds onto me now, occasionally emailing me, interested in my life. I'm interested in hers but – as is my sad pattern – once I leave a location I leave its occupants. Annette is my only connection to my teenage years and I treasure her. But on the whole I made myself invisible at BCC, although my biography tells me I entered into quite a bit of high-school life. I isolated myself in a corner of the dining hall with a book and my lunch of chicken drumstick, honey sandwich and apple. I had one superb teacher who began at the back of the history book, not the front. Honour-bound not to look at the previous chapter, we had to guess what cause had led to this effect. Our teacher was fired. A boy in our class murders his parents and his co-adopted sister. The homeroom teacher unfolds the story and its warning: if Daddy refuses to lend you the car keys, don't run for the family gun. Fact = warning: class-mate Romaine Sanders goes for an aerial joy-ride with some older men and the plane crashes. I was Class President for one of those years. Sounds prestigious. It actually meant that when Miss Divers – blond and very pretty and whose forthcoming marriage fascinated us – was called out of the room, it was my job to pick up where she'd left off in the text book. No problem. If Mrs Brown has a bushel of apples and gives twenty to Johnny, seven to Susie, nine to the postman, eats one herself and Miss Divers is absent, no one cares how many peaches are left. Tom Fleming has double-booked our after-school appointment with Janine for a kiss in the teacherless classroom. I sit doing home-work for twenty minutes while they become a live, clothed standing version of *The Kiss*, wandering hands and movement forbidden. My turn. Tom wants movement and I abort the flight. We head off to his front yard to kick a ball around.

One football game. One prom. One graduation, with hon-ours, to the tune of 'Pomp and Circumstance'. On the last occa-sion, I was wearing high heels for the first time but I hadn't practised on stairs. I managed getting up onto the stage but fell flat on my face coming down. A fitting farewell to public school.

7

1953

Pete and Toshi had bought land high on a hill near Beacon, New York. We four were often shuttled off to live with them in the summer. It was my first brush with a marriage dynamic different from that of my parents. Brother Pete was a peaceful, flowing river. Toshi was Mount Vesuvius. When she began to explode – with plenty of reason – Pete would just meander away without a word. The equivalent of storming out of the room slowly, having the last word silently, slamming the door without closing it. You'd find him outdoors under a tree reading a book, leaving Toshi to fume alone. Then lava-talk, then hot springs, then 98°F dialogue and soon they'd be sitting close together on the seat that looked fifty miles over to the far-off Catskill Mountains. There was an unending torrent of Pete's fans coming to help build the little homestead and everyone had to work. Pete made a wooden yoke for my shoulders and I became the Water Girl. A five-minute downhill path-walk to the stream, always barefoot, pails swinging, dozens of times a day. *Bring me a little water, Sylvie* – living Pete's dream and loving it.

*

In July 1953, Jeremy came to fetch me home from Beacon, via New York City, where he behaved very badly. Poor me – very young and with no understanding of that fearful hormonal urgency that grips teenage males, be they eighteen or forty-one. Poor Jeremy – no father like those reputed to take their lusty sons to an experienced woman who can teach them that the Fellow Downstairs needs instruction in delicacy, control and patience. Poor nouveaux lovers – neither of us (in the words of 'Aunt Sal's Song') *knew how to court*. Meanwhile, my dark-eyed boy had figuratively stabbed me in the heart as surely as the murderer Tom Dula had actually done to Laura Foster in May 1866. I pulled the knife out and metamorphosed into Atalanta, vowing to run from any man at the first whiff of trouble, carrying my own golden apples.

I went AWOL in the Third Dark of night, taking my broken heart to the Brooklyn doorstep of Earl Robinson, left-wing composer and family friend. He welcomed me in, then took me along to a political meeting at the apartment of Earl Browder, ex-leader of the Communist Party USA, where I sat trying to understand the fearful whispered conversations. My Earl took me to several houses of terrified writers and actors whose passports had been cancelled and who were trying to work out how to get to Canada, Mexico, Europe, anywhere. I took a Greyhound bus home to find that Dio had been in hospital – an operation for cancer, a disease that hadn't yet become an epidemic. She was in a private room, looking unusually tired but with her usual colour. No one mentioned how grim the situation was or that she'd offered herself as a guinea pig for a new treatment – radiation. They burned her up inside. She came home and spent the long, hot, humid days sitting up in bed working on her next children's songbook while I prepared myself and my clothes for college. Charlie took me shopping and bought a set of sky-blue suitcases and a typewriter. I don't remember a special goodbye hug from Dio. A long drive, up to Cambridge, Massachusetts, a lovely trip. The leaves were just beginning to change. Charlie talked more than usual – about his student days, about Dio. It was strange that she hadn't come along – they'd both taken me up to Putney. It was also odd that she hadn't been teaching for several months. Charlie deposited me at Peach House and drove back home.

Radcliffe College for the females, Harvard for the males. We shared Harvard staff, lecture facilities, campus and world-famous library. My social life was patchy but the banjo and guitar proved to be my ticket to almost anywhere. The International House hosted students from many countries and had Friday-night singalongs. Anne Yeomans and I led the singing from the big rough-typed book of songs in many languages. I knew a lot of Pete's songs and I imitated his song-leading and banjo styles. I became *Pete Seeger's sister*. I never minded that.* In 1953, the United States was in the grip of the Cold War. HUAC was running every show in town. McCarthy was everywhere, robbing my generation of political freedom and hope. The blacklist stripped my country of its best cultural dreamers and creators. Obedient captains and docile crews were put in charge of education, entertainment, government, social organisation. Waves of fear swept over *the land of the brave and the home of the free*. Any country can be home port for SS *Fear and Loathing* if we give it a chance. Pete's appearance before HUAC was looming. I read now about things that happened then, names that pop up like cut-out characters, and I am appalled, for in our house

---

* But I did mind when in 1998 I was lumping all my gear into a hall for my solo gig and there's the poster: *PETE SEEGER'S SISTER IS SINGING TONIGHT!*

there was no anger, no indignation, no sound and no fury. At Radcliffe, the same. No politics, no progressive dialogue. I was a good girl. I studied, I memorised, I got As. My college days memories are haphazard.

I took one course I will never forget: Theories of the Origins of the Universe. The lecture hall was raked upward away from the stage, on which sat a baronial table. On one end was a bunch of grapes in a white birdbath bowl, a small table microphone beside it. Five minutes went by, then ten. Several hundred students begin the crowd babble that radio producers achieve by getting the cast to repeat (un-together) *rhubarb-rhubarb-rhubarb*. Finally, the professor arrived in a white chiton. Sweeping on stage, he didn't even look at us. He lay down on the table facing us – elbow and hand supporting his head – and began placing grapes one by one into his mouth. He chewed as he gazed into a distant past. Pencils poised. Eyes glued. Someone began to titter. Our prof's gaze stopped that with a swift, direct eye-bullet. He leaned close to the little microphone and spoke very slowly. *Well? What do you want to know?* He'd learned that trick from *Alice in Wonderland*. Some of us wrote it down anyway. *There's nothing left to know. Zeus is all-powerful. The gods and goddesses are sporting and that's that.* Another grape. His mouth dripping with juice, he told us about his world. Athens was a jolly town, the Romans were looming on the horizon. The sun went round the earth by day, the stars ditto by night. The moon was a shiny flat discus thrown by the gods. The earth was flat. You'd fall off its edge if you walked or sailed too far. That's what had happened to boats that never returned home. More grapes. Lecture over, we walked carefully out of the room. Perhaps the cliff-edge was there at the end of the corridor or at the bottom of Concord Street? It was a fragile week. Many of us who had sailed out of sight of land probably thought we hadn't sailed far enough to fall off. Our man appeared the following week, professor-dressed. *How many of you think the earth is flat?* Hands went up. As the semester progressed he took us through the years of barbarism, into the Dark Ages. Mankind was served up like a Sunday dinner on a table top, the heavens upside down over us like a bowl, keeping the food warm. A now kindly, now vengeful God sat waiting out of sight with a fork and knife. We began to feel at home on a flat world.

Dissenters began to appear and Senator McCarthy and his henchmen marched into our lecture hall. In this corner, the Inquisition, moral lightweights with institutional clout. In that corner Giordano Bruno and Galileo, heavy on mental capacity but light on allies. The bell sounds and we cheer as the battle begins. For whom we cheered depended on how far down the road of disbelief we had travelled. *Hands up*, the master roared one morning, *those of you who are heretics and think the world is round!* Fear rippled through the lecture hall. We who knew what had happened to Bruno and who knew about HUAC had to take stock of our own bravery in order to hold up a hand. The Galileos (you know who you are, octogenarians, even now after all these years) sat on the fence rehearsing recantation speeches. The diehard group was surprisingly large in number. A formal debate followed, a champion for each cause. Many of us were burned at the stake, in honoured company. Unlike HUAC days, none of us informed on each other. The debates continued until we all agreed that the earth was indeed round.

*

Dio . . . I must have known subconsciously. One autumn evening I sat down at my little typewriter and wrote a letter to my mother and father, thanking them for giving me such a good life. Any parent would have loved to get such a letter from their child. In the second week of November, I got a phone call from Charlie telling me to come home. Dio was ill. My first flight, Boston to Washington. Charlie, with Dio's brother Carl, at the airport. My mother, with whom I had yet to get properly acquainted, had a week to live. Since I had left for college she had metamorphosed from a rosy-cheeked, plump, lively woman into a half-skeleton with yellowed skin, lank hair and dull eyes. Home hospice without any professionals. Charlie administered morphine whenever it was needed. Feverish and drugged, Dio lay in the ice-cold bedroom. I was glad to sit with her, Eskimo-large in sweater, coats and scarf. She would sleep then wake, calling or wanting water. She knew who I was and was glad to see me. I am still angry that I wasn't called home before she slipped so far away. Perhaps we could have had some mending time between us. I had so much to tell her – but would I have known how?

I'd never seen anyone die. Now, having been requested a dozen or so times to come and sing to a dying friend or lover, I am more capable at a deathbed. But back then, I sat through those November days with Dio, sang to her, held her hand and watched and waited, numbed with cold. On 17 November, in the evening, she sat upright, half delirious and wanting to work on her book. I sat on the bed behind her, combed her hair and plaited it, put it on the top of her head and dressed her in her shiny red blouse. Her eyes were not so dull and she leaned against me. I was hopeful. I now know that this is the remission that comes just before death. Around noon the next day, a gush of black liquid came from her mouth and she went limp in my arms. I laid her back down and called Charlie. He came up, went downstairs again and made a phone call. When he returned, he pulled the sheets back, cleaned her body, combed her hair and put her in a peaceful position. Men in black suits brought her down and out the front door. I walked with Charlie to the front gate. As the hearse moved off slowly, he started down the road after it. He walked right down the centre of the road with that leisurely, long-legged gait of his. He never asked me to come. He just walked off after her. Shock silenced us. Charlie set post-mortem protocol in motion. I go to my room. The heart waits until it is totally alone before it breaks.

We went to the crematorium a day or two later and waited in the little chapel. There was a niche in the wall about seven feet wide. The open coffin slid into view, and my mother appeared, her face waxen, yellow and shrunken, unrecognisable, not my mother. There were flowers on her body. Mike stood rigid, staring straight ahead. My father bent and kissed her cheek. I followed suit, unprepared for the deathly cold of her skin, the rock solidity which was not like flesh at all. The next time I would experience that granite, glacial cold would be when I kissed Pete goodbye at the viewing in the Beacon funeral home. Dio's coffin slid out of sight into the right-hand wall. We went into the mortuary gardens, waited an hour and came away with a small brown box of ashes. Dio.

I want to know where Dio is. I try to see and hear things for her, to lure her spirit back from the lost body. I muttered to her as I did odd jobs that week. I apologised out loud for all the times I had dismissed her, been rude, for all the symphonies I stubbornly hadn't attended with her, for the Kotex I'd forgotten to take to her at the hospital. Letters, cards and flowers flowed in. We sent thank-you notes, answered the phone, met friends and pupils who came to the door. We sat at our usual places at dinner, Dio's place set but her chair empty. Mary Ann brought dinner in, her face wet with tears. The parental bedroom was cleared of death paraphernalia, its Stygian atmosphere swept, dusted, washed, scoured, swilled and willed away. Mike went back to conscientious objector duty in a Baltimore TB hospital. My sisters went to school. Charlie took over Dio's piano pupils and put me on the train back to Radcliffe, as Dio had requested. He and Barbara and Penny would improvise the fragmented, single-themed coda that brought the bustling symphony of family life to its end. *Dio is dead.* Barbara wrote to say that Charlie slept with Dio's nightdress in his arms. She found him crying at Dio's desk.

I came home for Christmas. The house echoed: *Dio is dead. Dio is dead.* Make it a Dio Christmas for Penny's sake. Stockings were filled. Presents were wrapped. *Dio is dead.* Like Karen and her bobby pin, I repeated the phrase out loud to myself to increase the hurt as the mechanical holiday prolonged the funeral march. *Dio is dead.* Kafka's needle could not have done a better job as 24 December approached, Penny's tenth birthday. Dio was not there to help Penny blow her cake candles out, to douse the lights and dance into the tree-lit room with us. Mother lost is home lost. I wept in private. Charlie wept in private. Our playful Penny-child went silent. Mike played the banjo in his room. Barbara stayed out with her friends. Mary Ann came less often, Libba more often. Mamie was at church praying for my mother's soul.

Back at college, I searched myself, sure that she was in me somewhere. There was only me or the sky. In time the sky became smaller, friendlier. Then my mother was everywhere around me. I sang her favourite songs. The singing might reach her where talking had not. I felt closer to her dead than alive – that was what hurt the most. In my seventies I wrote a poem for Dio. I update it yearly as I age. Read poetry and delirium out loud. If you read silently, you may read the former too fast and the latter too slowly.

My mother is younger than me.
She died at fifty-two
With plump red cheeks and black black braids.

My hair is grey now, my cheeks are lined.
She sits at my knee, her head inclined
To accept my care.
I comb and braid her hair
As she once did mine.
And as I sing
She tells me things
About her new school.

As I grew my wings
She opened the window
And out she flew.

I am eighty-two
She is fifty-two.
Strange – my mother is younger than me.

8

North, West and East

We greeted 1954 *à l'ordinaire.* Charlie whipped up eggnog in the big Chinese bowl and our decimated family stood on the little back porch listening for the church bells. Dio came back to Radcliffe with me. My heroine, Jean Ritchie, came to Cambridge to sing, as did John Jacob Niles, a lover embracing his eight-string dulcimer on stage. Bill Broonzy and Josh White sang to rooms full of white kids. I got drunk on straight gin, two whole tumblers full, given to me by laughing young men. I'm slumped over the toilet crying for Dio and spewing up more than I thought possible. The following day, grey-green and white with the dry heaves, I began work on my first record, *Songs of Courting and Complaint.* It sounds more sober than I actually was. Three MIT buddies broached the project, Jay Ball and Jean-Pierre Radley bankrolling it and Clark Weissman playing guitar. They formed the Signet Record Company in order to bring it out.* My own, very own record. I played it

---

* Later, it was issued by Folkways, but I never received any royalties for it. Ewan and I didn't receive anything from Folkways either. We mentioned this to Moe Asch (a.k.a. Mr Folkways) at our Carnegie Hall concert in December 1959. Folkways had a huge catalogue. Moe brought out records by obscure poets and singers and was pleased if they sold a dozen copies. Ewan was curious. *How do you finance these records, Moe?* Moe replied, *I don't. You do.* We hinted that a little royalty cheque now and then wouldn't go amiss. There and then he wrote out a cheque for $243.52 or some such and we walked the

proudly to the family at Beacon, everyone happy but Mike, who kept looking at me quizzically, probably because I'd changed some chord or verse from the original. Then a great big smile and a hug.

Radcliffe was bang in the middle of Cambridge life. Music was everywhere. It's the only time in my life when I was part of a wandering group of singers and musicians. We went far afield looking for hootenannies. If we couldn't find one, we'd find an empty room and start one. I'd take the banjo along to square dances and sit in with the band when they'd allow it. Occasionally I thumped away on the piano to provide some rhythm and harmonic density. One night Tom Lehrer entertained us in an MIT common room. Black humour, political and funny. Singing like *that* when McCarthy was listening all the way from Washington DC? In December 1953, eight of us rented a hearse and drove down overnight via Yale to Princeton, New Jersey. I had kept diaries for years – detailed, articulate, a pictorial style in clear, readable handwriting. That trip gets a full page, complete with one tyre that explodes, another that catches fire, eight quarts of oil into the worn-out crank-case, and a policeman stopping us. We sit in the back of the police car singing while he reports to his superiors on the two-way radio that he's inspecting *a 1937 death-trap packed with college-age juveniles.*

The following spring, Mike and I attended the folk festival at Swarthmore College, near Philadelphia. A tall, red-haired, blue-eyed boy was standing next to us in the registration queue

---

New York streets listening to him tell us what the city had been like when he was young. I could do the same now with almost any aspect of life, for the world into which I was born has changed beyond recognition.

– Ralph Rinzler. I was shivering and he ran off to his dorm to get me a sweater. The three of us rattled around the campus for three days looking for jam sessions and eating hoagies loaded with salami, lettuce, tomatoes and cupfuls of mayonnaise. Ralph is – he died, but he is still in my present tense – the only man with whom I have had a deep platonic relationship. He never made a pass. He just didn't fancy me is more like it – or was gay. He said it was because I was Mike's sister. We slept in the same room many a time; in the trailer at Pete and Toshi's, where I was so cold one night that my feet went dead with Reynaud's Syndrome, an immune-system problem that affects circulation. The capillaries constrict and your fingers go yellow-white. If you injure them before the blood returns, you can get gangrene. Ralph brought me into his bed, with my bare feet under his armpits. In 1958, at Lucienne Idoine's apartment in Paris, he made himself a pallet on the floor in his tiny room and gave me his little truckle bed. A week later we took a fortnight driving Diane Hamilton's Bentley from Paris to Rome for her. For once in my life, I had a man *friend* on whom I could depend at any time, with whom I didn't feel vulnerable or victimised. In 1995, I wrote a good song for him – 'Old Friend'. We chatted, laughed, played music, kept in touch. Until Ewan.

College days – I had boundless energy. I walked or bicycled everywhere. I wore knee-length, peasant-style skirts, sweaters, saddle shoes with white socks, jeans, roomy shirts, big scarves in the winter. I wore my hair free, or in braids or ponytail. I never dieted or worried about my weight, but I did wish I was as slender as that black-eyed, short-haired nymph in the Theories class. Her sweaters were very short and when she bent forward you could see several inches of bare lower back with a subtle hint of the beginning of the buttock cleavage. No sign of

vest or underpants. I wished I had the nerve. I came back home
at Easter 1954. The Christmas tree was still up, bare, decorated
branches with a deep pile of dusty needles under it. Skeleton
tree for a skeletal family, father and three girls of eighteen, sixteen and ten. Charlie is lost and I have to grow up. He and I are
now a unit, discussing and planning as he and Dio had done.
The house would have to be sold and the family would move
to Cambridge so I could continue with college. I vetted the pro-
spective buyers and turned down the ones I didn't like. I settled
on the Hollanders, who told me years later that I interviewed
them as if they were applying for a job. In August 1954, Charlie
gave me an impossible budget which barely covered rental of a
tiny third-floor apartment – 1039 Massachusetts Avenue, near
Harvard Square. Next door to a nunnery and across from a
bustling supermarket, it was a sobering comedown for Charlie
and much too small for the four of us. The living room and two
minuscule bedrooms, hall, kitchen, linen closet and bathroom
would have fitted as neatly as puzzle pieces into half of our
Kirke Street bottom floor. Charlie has sent a grand piano up
from Kirke Street. It won't fit in the elevator. The nuns gather
at their window across the alley to watch it being winched up
and through our living-room window.

I studied in the linen closet – it had floor room for one narrow
kitchen chair, a shelf for my typewriter. The living-room talk,
dishwashing and radio necessitated closing the door, which I'd
open intermittently for a shot of oxygen. At Penny's bedtime,
I took the guitar and banjo into the bedroom and Barbara and
I would sing all the songs we knew and the new ones I was
learning. Charlie sang along, quarter-tone flat as usual. My
motherless little sister lay there, her big eyes open, her stringy
limbs keeping time until she fell off to sleep. Sometimes friends

crowded in for the singsong. Three sisters, we washed our clothes together and dried them on the rack that stood up in the bathtub. The apartment smelled of cooking and laundry all the time. It was probably as close to a stereotypical working-class lifestyle as I will ever get in my life. The three sisters thrived.

Poor Charlie, heartbroken, sixty-nine-year-old widower, living in a manner and emotional mindset to which he had no desire to become accustomed. Over the winter he began flying off regularly to California, and in the spring of 1955 he came back a changed man. His piano playing had always lacked energy, been somewhat wishy-washy. Now he began to sit up late into the night composing florid, complicated songs which he crooned in his strangled singing voice – the voice of a man who had done little or no heavy labour and who sang with too much effort. The melodies were hard to discern, but his passion was not. Charlie was in love. One evening he sat us down formally on the sofa to talk. Dio was the love of his life and could never be replaced. Then he announced that he had asked his first sweetheart to marry him. Margaret Adams Taylor, the woman after whom I had been named, had said *yes*. He was going west to live with Mar in her house in Santa Barbara, a beautiful home with garden all around. Penny was assured that there would be no more children. It all happened very fast. They married in California with little fuss. Charlie suggested that I take a year off from college to go to Holland and visit brother Charles. I jumped at it. Meanwhile we had to drive west – Charlie, Mar, Peggy and Barbara in the Pontiac station wagon, a baggage trailer hitched on, loaded dangerously full. Penny was left behind in Killooleet, brother John's summer camp in Vermont.

What a feeling, to be on the east coast of the continent,

heading for the west coast on the legendary Route 66, right across the whole country. Ohio . . . Indiana . . . Illinois . . . then the mud flats that flank the Mississippi River. Missouri . . . Oklahoma . . . Texas . . . into New Mexico. We stopped at diners and junk-food eateries. We ate food that Charlie and Dio had avoided all those years: tamales, hamburgers, real chili con carne – and those grilled cheese sandwiches that, when made with flatpack Velveeta and blotting paper bread, presented as flat, greasy square tiles about a half-inch thick. We gorged ourselves on Howard Johnson's ice-cream sundaes.

Charlie and Mar made an odd pair. He was string-bean tall, pale, nearly bald, a would-be European minor aristocrat. Mar was brisk, no-nonsense, under five foot, dark-haired, compact, well dressed and so, *so* American. They were really in love. In fairy tales there are tests for true lovers. Here comes one. Today it was Arizona hell-hot. We were on the edge of the Mojave Desert. We had just had the car fitted with an air-conditioner which you rented on one side of the desert and turned in on the other side at a specified garage. At a pit stop, Mar bought an ice-cold beer. We'd only had wine in our Seeger house – beer was *common*. Seegers didn't drink it. Mar offered me a swig. It was freezing cold Schlitz in a bottle and it remains one of my dearest gastronomical memories. As it trickled down my throat, I recognised my oesophagus for the treasure it was, the beer triggering every jingle bell in my palate on its descent from mouth to belly. Charlie's face was rigid. Mar bought me a beer of my own and I surreptitiously offered underage Barbara a swig. Mar bought a whole case of beer and a cooler. The Pontiac began to smell like a bar. I cracked a second bottle. The desert became even more glorious. The atmosphere in the front seat was arctic.

Mar's house was in Montecito, an exclusive suburb of Santa
Barbara. It was luxurious, a little six-bedroom palace, land-
scaped with lawns and big trees. Most of the rooms were wall-
to-wall carpeted, something we Seegers never had anything to
do with. Barbara and I slept in the little guest house and occasionally some of Mar's five children – lovely Edith and Rufus –
came home to *their* rooms in the big house. Apparently this was
Charlie's arrangement, not Mar's. I placed an advertisement in
the local paper for someone to teach me Dutch. Mr Pollman
answered it. He had been a Resistance fighter and at one point
his womenfolk had hidden him, nailed under the floorboards
of their house in Amsterdam. He went into a trance while he
described the thumping of his heart as Nazi soldiers trod over
his head with only an inch of planking between them. If the
women had been arrested and taken away . . . He retold and
retold the story as he taught me basic Dutch. His life as a grocer
in Santa Barbara was heaven on earth.

In 1930, Charlie had driven Dio up to Quebec and seen her
off on the steamship to take up her Guggenheim Fellowship
in Europe. On the way, in Vermont on a covered bridge, they
had realised that they were in love, and just days later she sailed
away. Now he was driving me up to Quebec, whence my ship,
the SS *Maasdam*, was sailing. He tried to tell me what the city
meant to him but I was too young, too young. Part of me was
already on board. He needed me to hug him close and give him
some support. Too young, too young. From alone with Charlie
to the hubbub of the ship. Jack Elliott was on board, with his
new wife, June. We gathered a bunch of kindred souls around
us and made a nuisance of ourselves over the whole ship, singing all the way across the Atlantic. We only slept when unable
to stay awake. Best of all was just to stand at the back of the

boat and bond with the wash of the waves and the swooping gulls. Brother Charles, wife Inez and their three boys, Jemmo, Matthew and Nicky, were at the quay. They hadn't expected me to bring so much luggage: two suitcases, a banjo, a guitar, a knapsack, a typewriter, a bicycle – would you believe it, I shipped my *bicycle* over to Holland! – and a steamer trunk you could open up sideways to reveal drawers and hangers. September 1955 – how wonderful, coming to live with family and children again. Wrong. I came into a home writhing in the coils of a dying marriage.

II

1955–1960s

9

Europe

In the inner sections of our outer space there are millions of pieces of mechanical junk in orbit around the earth. In the outer section of our inner space there are billions of metallic needles that were shot upwards by the United States military in the 1960s. Pre facto, my brother Charles, a high-ranking astronomer in the NASA search for extra-terrestrial intelligence by the time he died, had gone to Washington with a battalion of scientists to beg the US government not to meddle anywhere in space. The military are notably hard of hearing. They assumed that the little shards would stay together and (according to Charles) be part of global surveillance transmission. Nope. They dispersed and are thought to have pierced the Van Allen radiation belts, thus contributing to climate change. In 1955, Charles worked at the Leiden Observatory and a spacious house came with the job. He and Inez gave me a lovely ground-floor bedroom overlooking a lawn that swept down to the canal. That household wasn't ready for a twenty-year-old American teenager. I was a bull in a china shop and every corner or conversation in that house had something breakable waiting for me.

The baker's boy came every morning on a bicycle equipped with a little trailer filled with hot bread. For weeks I would rush out to get the bread, cut the heel, slather it with butter and go to heaven. I learned *weeks* later that until my arrival the high spot of Inez's day was the early morning after her troops had left. That was her time to sit at the kitchen table with the buttered heel of the bread, a cup of coffee and solitude. I was also eating all of the family's daily supply of butter for breakfast. The young are so . . . young. I tried to help with housework and bed-making but I'm only a 50 per cent perfectionist. Inez was 100 per cent and nothing I did was ever done right. She and Charles loved the old songs and the boys worshipped Pete. We sat one evening in the kitchen talking and singing. Did I know 'The Jam on Gerry's Rocks'? Yes, indeed I did, and off I went like a greyhound from the slips. Inez rushed out of the room crying, *You've changed it, you've changed it!* I probably had. I didn't pay the microscopic attention to words, music and style of singing that Mike did. Inez gradually turned into the Ice Queen and began to talk to me only when necessary. Such a heavy-hearted house. Her children came to me for hugs. They're still very huggable.

*

At Radcliffe I'd been heading for my junior year. Leiden University, the oldest in the Netherlands, tested me and put me in as a freshman. Freshman orientation is peculiar to many institutions of higher learning. Its purpose is to introduce new students to each other and to certain college rituals. At Radcliffe, the occasion had been humiliating, chiefly due to the presence of packs of feral Harvard boys whose job was to choose Miss Freshman Radcliffe 1953. Another Butterfly Beach – but I had stayed to watch. In Leiden, the new female students could gather to meet each other unhindered by fresh men snapping at our heels. Each of us had to stand on a table and answer questions posed by a panel of female seniors. When I took my turn up on the table, they gave me the option to answer in English or Dutch. I chose Dutch. *What's your name?* Easy, that one. *Your birthday?* *17 June 1935.* *Where were you born?* I asked back, *Waar of waarom?* which means, *Where or why?* Ice broken. For several hours we all drifted around, among, away, towards each other, searching for a would-be sisterhood, a *vereniging*, a togetherness. Each *vereniging* was to have thirteen members. Mine was a warm, close group of young women, the only pride of lionesses I have ever had. We named ourself De Woezle, after the Woozles in *Winnie the Pooh.* My special comrade was Anneke Rueb – dead now from cancer. We thirteen met once a week to sing, talk, joke and dip pieces of dry Dutch honey-cake in weak, milky coffee. I would practise my Dutch and they would practise their English. They had the words of the Woozle in Dutch and asked me to make it into a song:

Zoek je de Woezle (Seek ye the Woozle),
Find je jezelf (You find yourself).
Zoek je jezelf (Seek ye yourself),
Dan find je de Woezle (Then you find the Woozle).
Zoek je de Woezle (Seek ye the Woozle),
Find je elkaar (You find each other).
Zoek je elkaar (Seek ye each other),
Dan find je de Woezle (Then you find the Woozle).

I composed a catchy round and we kept it ready for any gathering at which our image would need to be projected. The next ritual was a rite of passage for all freshmen and you weren't allowed to talk about it once you had undergone it. As the ceremony approached, a frisson went through the freshman community. Just in case, sixty years later, there are freshwomen in

Leiden who are still initiated in this way, I shan't tell you about it – only that it involved a lot of candles, darkness, interrogation and threats in deep faux-male voices. Anneke invited me to her home in Arnhem. They talked a lot about the war. A German soldier had been billeted on them. Many such soldiers didn't survive this. *He broke his neck coming down the narrow stairs in our humble house. A tragedy, Herr Kommandant.* I went to Hermine van Veen's house and sang her little siblings to sleep. My lovely *vereniging*. I lost track of them after I left Leiden. I'd love to meet any of them again . . .

I hung out with Jewish-American students who hadn't made it into the United States Medical Association's *Jewish quota*. Another chapter of that old let's-shoot-ourselves-in-the-foot saga. I'd registered at the university to study Russian. It was taught in the language of Dutch. It was also a farce so I got on my bike and rode around the town and its countryside. Concerts, Woezle parties, hitch-hiking up to Amsterdam and Utrecht. In need of money, I contacted the several nearby US air bases and went along to entertain the boys. Boys they were. They neither chatted me up, listened nor really cared whether I was there. Many of them sat reading comic books through my stint. I wasn't bothered as long as I was paid. All in all, it was a grand un-academic autumn.

The Dutch Christmas separates commerce and religion. On St Nicholas's Day, 6 December, you creep up to a friend's door, leave a gift on the step, and run away and hide. The recipient comes to the door, makes a show of looking around for the giver, opens the gift and shows appreciation. 25 December takes us to church. Gather hot water bottles, heavy socks, coat and every sweater you own, bring a blanket and sit in Leiden cathedral for the midnight mass. Steam rising from the breathing of the crowd – singing, organ music, instrumental ensembles, it lasted about four hours. Stupendous. The ice thickened on the canal outside my room and the skaters came out, muffled up in long coat-skirts. Johannes Vermeer and Frans Hals took up residence on our lawn. Businessmen went to work on skates; women on skates pushed prams on runners; little ones in padded coats on inch-long blades wobbled, fell and got up again; lovers skated in pairs; boy racers, our three among them, zipped from right to left and back, ignoring the frame of the painting. Charles sat by me as I played the piano we'd rented, watching my hands. Inez had stopped talking to me altogether.

My childhood friend Nina Powell turned up and suggested that we go travelling. Of course. Why stay in a marital fridge? Off we went, hitch-hiking in December. It's what greenhorns do during the white months. The first large town we hit was Alkmaar, where they rolled the huge cheeses down the main street right through horse manure and tourist droppings. Ancient churches pull me in – the stained-glass windows, stonework, engraved tombs, wood carvings. Alkmaar's cathedral was colder inside than it was outside. The organ music rose up to the roof. We sat for several hours listening until the organist came out. Her face was familiar and her accent American. She was the sister of my friend Abigail – Marian Sibley, who'd been one of my mother's prize pupils.

Nina and I had no itinerary – we were just going up country. We were crossing the Afsluitdijk, that magnificent barrier between the North Sea and the IJsselmeer, the latter being a huge series of waterworks that keep the deep heart of lowland Holland from flooding. On the top of the dyke was a nineteen-mile-long narrow two-lane road connecting North Holland to Fryslân (Friesland). A Jehovah's Witness picked us up on the western end, driving a beat-up truck. His small son sat by him in the front seat, Nina and I in the back. When Jehovah's man discovered that I spoke Dutch he took both hands off the wheel, swivelled his whole body around, put his elbows on the back of the front seat and set about converting us. Shove over to make room for the Creator of All Things. The truck was being operated not by divine power but by the father's foot on the accelerator and the left hand of the little boy holding the steering wheel. The windscreen was totally frosted over. The unfenced edge of the dyke dropped away down a chasm to our right and opposing traffic scraped by on the left. Yes, yes, yes, I'm a believer! Just turn around and take the goddamn steering wheel.

Fryslân. The language is a guttural variant of Dutch. The first town we hit had been struck by a power cut and the inhabitants were walking around in the winter dark. Heavy wool capes, huge flambeaux and large pikestaffs, Brueghel over there setting up his easel. Those old artists do get around. We pushed on. Nearing Christmas, it came upon a midnight clear when we found a youth hostel in our YHA book, then found it in actuality. It was shut December-tight. There was no visible town nearby, no lights, no shops. We followed yon Yule star, a window with a candle in it. We knocked. It opened and amber warmth and the smell of cooking poured out. Do you know what the lady of the house did to two frozen, starving young female strangers on that December night? She unlocked the hostel and ushered us into a Siberian chamber in Dante's Hell. No heat, no light, no water, no cooking facilities. With a torch, she showed us where the damp, cold blankets were. Then she went home to her dinner and warm fire – taking the flashlight with her. She'd have turned Joseph and Mary away.

Groningen, in a light Christmas-card snowstorm. In a small

grocery shop, we fell into conversation with a grandmotherly woman. She took us home, fed us royally and showed us – with pride – her enormous collection of tiny coffee spoons with cathedrals on them. Soft towels for a bath, then she put us to bed. The next day she did our laundry. I have stored up a plethora of such kindnesses in my heart and hope that I have in turn offered enough succour and hospitality to others in need whose paths I've crossed. The bright side of the human condition.

A few days later we were about fifteen miles from Luxembourg. I remember the distance because we had walked much of it – plenty of time to read the road signs. Car after truck after bus passed us by even though night and heavy snow were falling. Our bones were rattling with cold. A big, bluff Catholic priest stopped for us. He looked at the guitar and banjo. Did we play and sing? I've often been asked by people who see me with instruments, *Do you play that thing?* Duuhhh. *No, I just carry it around.* Father J. E. Vloebergh was interested in singers and musicians because . . . Nina and I were asleep. The haven to which he took us had the same atmosphere as the YHA warden's home, but these strangers welcomed us. They ran hot baths for us, warmed our change of clothes by the fire, fed us mountains of hot food. Precious strangers from the past: I hope that someone gave you as precious a gift as you gave us that night. Nina and I sang for them. Jos had a religious theatre company. They were taking a Christmas show to West Berlin. Would we come as musicians? Of course, why not? We met the troupe in Antwerp and began rehearsing. The Flemish Christmas carols were charming, set in a modern nativity play. The guitar went perfectly with them. We'd all bonded by the time we headed east.

At Dallas Avenue, the air-raid sirens had sounded occasionally during World War II. We'd turn out all the lights and Charlie would pull the blackout curtains down. German airplanes are going to fly three thousand miles across the Atlantic to bomb Washington? Well – Pearl Harbor . . . Charlie had read out the war news every Sunday at the breakfast table. There was a steady barrage of propaganda against the Germans and Japanese – posters everywhere announcing that *enemy ears are about*. Toshi's Japanese family were interned. I had learned early: Germany was a place to stay away from. But here I am now in an impromptu *vereniging* of Belgian thespians barrelling across bleak West Germany into bleak East Germany, destination the political island of West Berlin. The troupe were cheerful, but in heavy Flemish, a language that even many Belgians don't understand. Maurice van de Putte was my special friend – elf-like face, pointy ears, thin mouth and a huge Mephistophelian smile. A friendly devil. I christened him *Teufel*. Strange – he never questioned the German nickname. He loved my songs, spoke English as much as possible to me and never got fresh. Mind you, with Father Jos aboard, nobody would even *think* fresh, much less *get* fresh.

Spool forward: in September 1958 Ewan asked me to go to East Berlin to pick up a Leica camera for him. His play *The Travellers* was a hit there but the royalties had to be spent in East Germany. This was only a little more than a decade after the end of World War II. There was no Berlin Wall back then – you could go from forgetting to remembering by just getting on a train. West Berlin: a German Times Square. East Berlin: still war-torn but honest – huge photos of the concentration camps postered on and in public buildings. They carried one message: WE DID THIS. NEVER AGAIN. In 1957, I would turn down the opportunity of visiting the Kraków-Płaszów camp when I was in Poland, repulsed by the idea of viewing the loot from the millions who had been murdered there. Barrels of gold tooth fillings and jewellery; shoes of every shape and size; mountains of spectacles and clothing; rooms of children's toys. I didn't need to see it – it had already filled my mind in the 1940s, photos in *Life* magazine, mountains of skeletons, then the aftermath of Hiroshima. It never occurred to me that Seeger is an Austro-German name.

Our little Belgian troupe performed two or three times. Now Jos's main objective was made manifest. He had come to bring back seventeen displaced Catholic children whose parents had fled East Germany. The little ones were aged from six to thirteen, and the trip back to Belgium was a trial for all. He took us to Montigny-le-Tilleul, a small mining village where he was parish priest. He placed six of the children with volunteer families and took eleven to his tiny house. A nurse was brought in to check on the children's health and the community provided clothing and shoes. Jos asked me to stay. I was going to anyway. Who would desert those waifs? I became washerwoman, cook, scullion, drudge, nanny and Kleine Mutti. German for my little ones.

How did little Protestant Adolph ever get included in this bunch? He was about eight years old, a sorry little mite, a lamb who was assigned a pack of wolves as travel-mates. The older children taunted him, stole his food when they could, poked him in the ribs, pulled his hair and insulted his religion. The younger ones didn't dare defend him. Most of this happened while the adults weren't looking. I tried to catch them at it, but they were canny. Adolph fastened himself to me in the daytime and Jos protected him at night in the boys' bed. I slept with the girls, six of us in a huge double bed. At least one of them would wet the bed every night. The oldest girl (Gerda? Gaby?), blond and blue-eyed, was my bossy ally. She took it on herself to organise the girls and did a good job of it. She got them helping me with laundry, mending and peeling the endless potatoes. Big Kurt organised the boys into mock-Nazi storm troopers. They marched the Montigny streets, goose-stepping with their fists clenched, thumbs east–west under their noses – Hitler's youth. Kleine Mutti took the job seriously. All the children were hugged, fed and kept in clean, warm clothing. Things soothed down. One day, I had trouble detaching Kurt from a hug. He was sobbing like the baby he was. Children – the bottom-line victims of war.

Every afternoon we would go for a walk over the snow-covered fields, alternately slushy or frozen with little shards that could pierce the stoutest boot. My crocodile of girls and Jos's alligator of boys. On this day, we visited a local monastery where we got huge bowls of hot soup. When we were coming back across the wastelands, Jos pointed to a large ancient building in the near distance. *That's where the nuns are. If you stay, I could head the monastery, and you could head the nunnery.* Local children came to the house to recite their catechism every morning. Our eleven would join them, Adolph included. He was trying. There were prayers on rising, prayers on going to bed. Be it noon or midnight, when Jos went out to give extreme unction he would have those little ones up and kneeling on chairs until he came back, praying for the soul of the dear about-to-depart. I stayed in bed and refused to get up. My girls liked that, because the bed was still warm when they got back. At the end of each day Jos and I would stay up late talking, he trying to convert me, me worn out with children and housework. He gave me a rosary and taught me to tell it. He illustrated the heavenly circles on which cherubim and seraphim coasted around Our Lord like electrons. The Holy Ghost was a hyphen between God and Jesus. The Virgin Mary was . . . a period probably. We sang a lot, the kids and I – 'Skip to My Lou', 'Rissolty Rossolty'. Jos joined in with priestly dignity. He was the Father Figure and it was his job to draw God's line and make sure everyone toed it. My little flock: if any of you read this book, please contact me. I would love to see you again and find out how you have fared since those bitter months of early 1956.

I sent letters describing my life to my *Maasdam* friends Sally and Hu Lindsay, who were living in Amsterdam. They turned up unannounced one Sunday in early March, at dinner-time. So many tableaux here in these war-torn flat lands, *the low, lowlands of Holland* that were used as battlefields for European wars from the Middle Ages onward. It's that painting thing again – the sparse dining room, darkness around the edges; candles and one bare light bulb illuminating the long dinner table, me at one end and Jos in priest-wear at the other; Sally, Hu and the children waiting to eat till prayers had been said and all our rosaries told, mine included. After dinner Sally took my rosary away. *Pack your bags, we're going.* I was too tired to resist. They took me back to Leiden and my battling relatives. I should have saved the rosary. Charles and Inez needed my prayers.

Jump-cut: Jos turned up at the Singers' Club several years later, in civvies. With two beautiful young women in tow, he had forsaken what he called his *clown suit*. He listened to half of the programme and departed with *You are lost, my child*. Takes one to recognise one. Fifty years later I reconnected with him via Teufel. He'd married and sired children. He died a few years ago. Maurice and I – Teufel and Mutti – are communicating

93

again. He has all the letters I sent him. He is hard of hearing and refuses to wear a hearing aid, so we communicate via his son, my friend Peter, who visits me yearly. I have been handed on to the younger generation.

*

What am I doing in this unhappy house? Alan Lomax phones from England. A TV company in London is producing *Dark of the Moon* and they absolutely *have* to have an American female who can sing and play the five-string banjo. We don't have much of a budget so let's get a folk singer. Both of Gemini-me for one fee.* Perhaps Alan also mentioned something about forming a group? Alan – England . . .? Sally and Hu are concerned. They are going to drive to Denmark. Would I like to come with them while I decide? After Jos's house, I am in need of parenting, so of course. Of course. I have a bird at hand. I'll catch the bird in the bush later, Alan. Suitcases, bike, steamer trunk into storage, downsize into knapsack, guitar and banjo. I am stuffed into the back seat of a tiny Fiat and off we go, northeast. It is curative, the three of us setting out together. But I wonder how my urchins are doing tonight without me . . . Whenever we stop for a meal, a snack, a pee or a look around, I'm winkled out of the back seat so stiff that my legs have to be straightened manually, gently. The baggage caves into the space I've left and we have to dig out a hole for me to crawl back into. On the outskirts of Odense we stop for dinner. A cosy fug of a room and mashed potatoes rolled into balls, deep-fried in batter and served with a caramel sauce, side by side

* It turned out to be a bit part, only two days on site. Alan used it as bait.

with meat and cabbage and washed down with flagons of cold beer. There are many heavens.

Copenhagen – and our money begins to give out. We move into a youth hostel. Amnon, a genial Israeli boy, is on the prowl. He loves my songs, tells me my eyes are *the colour of time*, a phrase I stole and put into the mouth of Prince Charming in my Cinderella song 'Gotta Get Home by Midnight'. He asks me to go with him to a logging camp in Finland where the work's hard and the money's easy. Of course, I'd be earning too – as a cook. In the Australian song, she is invited to accompany him to the outback and *wash his dirty moleskins on the banks of the Condamine*. Irresistible. In the USA, women headed west in overfilled Conestoga wagons with children and the parapher-nalia of a foregone, comfortable life. The film industry permed their hair, ironed their aprons and set them on the front seat beside their men. Occasionally they held the reins. Full orches-tras hid behind the tumbleweed. Follow the tragic track of jettisoned bedding, household furniture, mirrors, crockery, skeletons of human and beast across the plains and western mountains of North America – the white man's self-imposed Trail of Tears. Finland? The Yes Girl says OK. Hu and Sally rescue me a second time. *The money will be better in England, Peggy, and you can sing and play. Finnish is a very strange language and it's even colder up there.* London sounds more why-nottish. Wash your own dirty moleskins. I'm off to England.

10

England

Waterloo Station in the early morning of 27 March 1956 – a big, bluff Alan-hug and news that the television job might not materialise, but *there are some folks I want you to meet*. His girlfriend, Susan Mills, greeted me in their Chelsea basement apartment. Striking and confident, she took one look, sniffed one sniff and indicated the shower. After throwing my jeans into the waste basket, she scrubbed me down, checked nooks and crannies, complimented me on my hair, which at that time reached halfway down my back. What remains of my vanity regrets that there are few people around now who remember me when I was young. Susan inspected my knapsack. Probably too big to go into the waste basket. She opened her wardrobe and began pulling out dresses, shoes, frillies of all sorts. I understand that the Queen has someone who dresses her. Susan dressed me, complete with nylon stockings and a pair of high-heeled shoes. She back-combed my hair and swept it up into a high bouffant beehive. She fastened it with clips, hairpins and Kirby grips – bobby pins – before nailing it into place with lacquer. Makeup and lipstick, then a necklace that Dio would have removed immediately and earrings that could have graced a Christmas tree. I rather liked the look – but who was that in the mirror?

At 10.30 a.m., banjo in hand, I tottered in on high heels to meet my next thirty-three years. One woman and a tribe of older men and so much smoke in the room that I didn't notice him at first. The penny dropped. This was an audition and this was Alan's proposed project, *England's answer to the Weavers*. He hadn't asked me. He just assumed that what he wanted was what I could be persuaded to want. He perched me on a high stool and commanded me to *sing, honey*. He had a way with women, adding *honey* in that seductive Texas drawl and giving you a command with a twinkle in his eye. It nudged you towards doing almost anything he asked. Almost. I never play on stools – the floor is too far away. And high heels . . . how did Ginger Rogers do it? Duty called and I called again upon my old friend 'The House Carpenter', high lonesome voice and hedgehog banjo. There was applause, but not from the man in the corner diagonal to me. He was sitting very still, a cigarette burning down to his fingers, just looking, staring. He came over and introduced himself – Ewan MacColl. His ears stuck out. He had thick, straight, black hair and a very red beard. He was singing in a stage show, *The Threepenny Opera*, and would I like a complimentary ticket for tomorrow's show? Complimentary *anything*, that was me. I had no money and I loved the theatre.

Of course, I had already *met* Ewan but didn't make the connection. The first time ever I heard him sing was in 1954, when my friend Rob Loud played me a few verses of 'The Four-loom Weaver' on the Columbia World Series set of recordings. Mrs Gaskell writes about the song in *Mary Barton*: 'The air to which this is sung is a kind of droning recitative, depending much on expression and feeling. To read it, it may, perhaps, seem humorous; but it is that humour which is near akin to pathos, and to those who have seen the distress it describes it is a powerfully pathetic song.' I thought the singing on the record was appalling – whining and with garbled words. I didn't connect that odd singer with this odd man until I heard him sing that odd song in person – and was intrigued by all.

Learn to use the London Underground and look to the right when you step off the sidewalk. *The pavement.* Plush theatre seat in the balcony, goodies for sale during the intervals, well-dressed people. Up goes the curtain and a beery, leery old man enters singing. What a lovely voice! I was entranced.

> *O, the shark has pretty teeth, dear,*
> *And he shows them pearly white;*
> *Just a jack-knife has MacHeath, dear,*
> *And he keeps it out of sight.*

It's Ewan, his hairy, fat, naked belly poking out, clad in ill-fitting trousers, suspenders, no shirt, a ragged jacket and a filthy lid of stovepipe hat aslant like a garbage can. He looked ancient. After the show I went to see him backstage. I saw the show and went backstage many times. Once he made me up as an old, old woman. Another time he asked fellow actor George Cooper to fart. Down come George's pants and Ewan lights a match. A blowtorch of fire spurts out between the two cheeks. Backstage banter becomes courtship stuff. But this first time ever, he was spruced up, neat and clean, looking a little younger. He'd said he was thirty-eight. He was actually forty-one. Thirty-eight, forty-one . . . both were *old.* I must have looked raggle-taggle young, hair down my back, wrinkled man's shirt and jeans res-cued from Susan's waste basket. *Let's have a drink and I'll drive you back to Alan's.* While we drove back, he did most of the talk-ing, as he did for the next three decades. We parked out front. He thought I was beautiful and he wanted to make love to me. I'd been dallying with boys who never talked beauty. They either wanted to learn the banjo or get as far down my body as possible. This man didn't touch me. He just sat there holding the steering wheel, looking straight ahead. He'd fallen in love with me yesterday. Well, I tell you, it was thrilling. There I was, just shy of twenty-one, with this married English singer who said he wanted to *make love* to me! Children, that's the right way to go about it, even if *make love* was a new term to me. He didn't ask or fumble. He just turned and proceeded with a kiss that curled my toes.

I kept a sporadic diary in those days. There's nothing about my meeting with Ewan, nothing till 1 April. *When Ewan talks I listen. My mind is at his command. He is a true poet . . . Funny person, wholly sure of himself . . .* 11 April. *Ewan MacColl is in love with me. And I with him. He is married, with a boy of five years . . . I would lose my personality were I to marry him. He is too pronounced a personality, too complete a person to really need me.* Feminism was far off in my future back then. I had entered a maelstrom of *want*. Ewan wanted me. The BBC wanted to put my songs in their archives. Alan, now with Shirley Collins, wanted the Manchester Ramblers for a new series on Granada TV. Bill Leader of Topic Records wanted me to record. I had no CV for the record, but Alan could create folklore as well as collect it. He wrote glowing bogus critics' reviews of my mythical performances to go on the album cover. *Ropes of honey-brown hair, etc*. I had bad acne. Alan strong-arms the television producers into paying for complete dermatological abrasion. They bathe my face in a drying agent. My skin begins to crack all over, as if dozens of little puzzle pieces have moved away from one another, revealing red-raw ridges underneath. Soak them continually in Dettol – agony, for the cracks are open wounds. *The first time ever I saw your face?* I look like a big walnut with eyes and mouth. Ewan is still passionate. After six weeks, they cover my face with a mask of starch. While it hardens, you have to think nice thoughts so that your expression doesn't change. I had very few un-nice thoughts back then. When they lift the mask off there is skin as smooth as a baby's bottom underneath.

I saw *The Threepenny Opera* umpteen times and umpteen times he took me back to the little cheaply furnished flat that Alan had rented for me. Umpteen kisses. We were digging ourselves into a hole. For the most part, Ewan's six-days-a-week schedule was Croydon to the Strand, the Strand to Croydon. Mine was Chelsea to the Strand, the Strand back to Chelsea. One night he didn't come. The ocean tides had stopped. I had never been stood up. I sat till morning on the step of the little terrace house, aching for the smell of nicotine on his fingers, the man-smell of his jacket and the bulk of his shoulders. Day-dreaming at night, desolate. No mobile phones back then, no phone in my little room. Ewan's wife, Jean, had come to see the show. He'd had to go home *with* his wife instead of *to* his wife. Alan knew, Shirley knew, the Ramblers knew – everyone knew but the wife. It was especially hard to hide our goings-on when we had recording sessions at the MacColl flat in Croydon, Betsy and Jean making meals for us all. I'd never been involved with a married man and I swore I wouldn't carry on with it. I loved him but I wasn't blinded by love. He was. I was alarmed by the intensity of his passion. I needed to get away. I went back to Belgium in May for a month to see my abandoned children.

One night, Ewan brought me home after a rehearsal. Little ones: if you are really in love, go for romance, music, subtle lighting, wine and dinner beforehand if possible. Book a nice room, not a worn-out, grey cubicle in which all the life has been sucked out of wood, wool, windows and the very air by a relay of temporary tenants. Two cracked mugs, spoons that you can bend and a kettle with which to make tea on the little gas ring in the corner. Warming yourself at the tiny gas fire, shish kebab style. A single cot bed with rough sheets on which to lie down with your first real love. No, no. This is not right. Even Jeremy's forsythia bush was better than this. I was too young and Ewan should have known better. He said later that he was alarmed at how quickly I took my clothes off. I was undressed and in bed before he was. He couldn't play his part. He was mortified. He told me later that he was breathless with passion and beside himself with love. We said goodnight and he crept home. The second time was the first time referred to in the third verse of our song, semantics be damned. *A rose by any other name, et cetera.* And besides: *second time ever I lay with you* doesn't really cut it, metrically or otherwise. *A standing prick has no conscience*. It was Ewan's favourite sport. His sudden amorous urges could occur anywhere, any time. He'd commandeer the dressing room at the Strand Theatre for fifteen minutes . . . the disreputable relaxation room at Topic Records, where egg-boxes on the walls guaranteed sound-proofing. Just time for a quickie – what an insulting term. I was discomfited but compliant. I loved him and granting what one of the folk songs calls *a small relief* seemed kind. Cardinal Cap Alley up against the wall of No. 49 Bankside, the oldest house in London.* My busy lover stops mid-flight and I open my eyes. A policeman's truncheon is tapping on his shoulder.

Moving on. The Manchester Ramblers were rambling along

---

* It boasts a plaque declaring that here *in 1502, Catherine, Infanta of Castille* [*sic*] *& Aragon, afterwards first Queen of Henry VIII, took shelter on her first landing in London.* She was discomfited too, big-time.

nicely, working up programmes for a weekly show in Manchester. At one time, I believe George Martin produced and directed us, but his good sense would have made it a one-off. We were a haphazard assemblage of excellent musicians: West Indian guitarist and singer Fitzroy Coleman; Nat Atkins, Nigerian drummer; bassist Jim Bray; clarinet and sax player Bruce Turner; Brian Daly, session guitarist; Johnny Cole, harmonica player; Bert Lloyd, Ewan MacColl and Shirley Collins, unaccompanied English folk singers; Alan Lomax and myself. We made a passable sound but the directors sat me on bales of straw, from which I get hay fever. Shirley languished at fence gates, with spotlights on her bright yellow hair. Ewan and Bert clung to mock-ups of ships' rigging like spiders in a web. 1950s tacky. Eleven weeks of long train trips up and back every weekend, with two days in Manchester in between. Eleven weeks – long enough for the Ramblers to know we wouldn't make it. Long enough for Ewan and me to lay down a solid foundation which would crack and mend and crack and mend.

When the Granada contract was over, I bought a Lambretta scooter and took off for Scotland, leaving my boxes and belongings in Ewan's workroom in Croydon. The trip through northern England and Scotland was my first major adventure totally alone. I got soaked right through so many times that often I had not a single stitch of dry clothing with me. Caught by nightfall, I would knock on farm doors and ask to sleep in a barn or outbuilding. No one ever said no. Angels are guiding me to other angels. I stop overnight at a pub near Kendal and the landlady, seeing how drenched I am, strips me in a little room next to the kitchen, puts me into pyjamas, dressing gown and slippers, gives me a meal and puts me to bed. Overnight she dries my clothes and sets me on my way again. One Highland Scots woman saw the guitar and said if I would sing to her guests I could sleep in her daughter's room. The daughter was a wide-eyed one-year-old, cooing at me through the bars of the crib the next morning. She'll be sixty now.

Ewan had given me letters of introduction to poets Norman MacCaig, Hugh MacDiarmid, Thurso Berwick; to folklorist Hamish Henderson; to political activists Norman and Janey Buchan and their students. Jimmie MacGregor, beautiful boy at twenty-six. Beautiful man at eighty-seven – sunrise smile and bedroom eyes. Stick to the subject, Peggy. My mother's people, the Crawfords, came from Lowland Scotland, so I went to the Edinburgh shop that sells clan tartans. I didn't like the Crawford colours. There was a German ordering a Schwartz plaid, six weeks for delivery. Unlike me, he could order any colours he wanted. *Och, the puir laddie*, said the proprietor, impaling the German's order unnecessarily hard on the spike. In the sixties, Ewan and I would meet a stately German in Freiburg, in full tartan kit, who confessed that he was *studying to be a Scot*.

I got as far as Aberdeen before turning back south. Jean had opened my boxes and read my diaries, in which I had been keeping a blow-by-blow account of her husband's love affair. It didn't stop us. I flushed from foot to head whenever I was in her company. I felt furtive but not soiled, wrong but not sinful. LOVE should have been the eleventh commandment. We fitted perfectly together musically and I gloried in the experience and knowledge of an older man.

The Ballads and Blues folk club met weekly. Alan and Shirley had moved to Highgate, where there was room for me – along with his daughter, his first wife and her lover, respectively Anna, Elizabeth and Herbert, who'd been living in Spain and who'd written a book about Franco's fascist government right under Franco's nose – and smuggled it out. Ewan came over regularly and we closeted ourselves. We quarrel and make up and my diaries avow that *he is my entire existence, jealousy and all.* He is depressed, too. *A look that comes on his face, the living embodiment of doubt and . . . fear of his inadequacy . . . It seems a marvel that we convince ourselves that we are hiding any-thing . . .* [tonight] *there is no . . . valid reason for why he should be on his way back home when his home is here.* The diary of a child who just wanted to go swimming, dancing and running on Hampstead Heath with her lover. Ewan didn't swim, dance or run – he just wanted to go to bed.

We went to see *Edward II*, directed by Joan Littlewood, Ewan's first wife, with whom he'd started the pioneering Theatre Workshop. There we are in a row, Man with Women 1, 2 & 3 side by side, watching the action: Joan, Jean, Ewan and Peggy, energy frizzling along the four seats as we all pretend that *the play's the thing.* I swanned around London, singing at coffee-houses and hootenannies, relishing the freedom that comes with being *the other woman*, not the wife. It was at the Bread Basket in Cleveland Street that, at their behest, I taught Libba's song 'Freight Train' to two skifflers, Nancy Whiskey and Charles McDevitt. Folk musicians share. We teach and learn from each other, paying no attention to ownership or copyright. Libba had patiently taught 'Freight Train' to Mike and me. Nancy and Charles sit at my feet and I teach them the song and accompaniment. Glimpse into the future: When I came back from China I found that 'Freight Train', sung and copyrighted by Whiskey and McDevitt, had whizzed to the top of the Hit Parade. I found that my Topic recording of 'Freight Train' had also been issued with their names on it as authors. Nancy and I chanced to meet one day on Charing Cross Road.

She greeted me like an old friend. She must have been thinking of the royalties. Libba was in poverty. A lawsuit began. Royalties were frozen and put into the hands of a neutral party, who neutrally ran off with them.

I began to get fits of depression. I went to a Harley Street psychiatrist, Eustace Chesser, who had written a sex manual entitled *Love without Fear.* I spent the first two sessions clamming up while he talked about himself and his daughter. At our third session of expensive silence, the dam broke. I couldn't stop crying. He put me into his adjoining office, where I wept for several hours. My grief at Dio's death had been too deep for tears – but I was crying for her now, crying for the loss of so many things I had taken for granted, of which not being in love with a married man was one. *I have to go home, Ewan. I have to go.* We walked around London not knowing what to say to each other. We sat in our cafes. We paced our favourite squares, Golden and Soho. I couldn't stop eating. I devoured tureens of oxtail soup, brigades of steak and ale pies, ecstasies of steamed treacle pudding topped with custard and golden syrup. Ewan made me promise to come back next summer for the Moscow Youth Festival. Two nights before I left, we went to Manchester together. He told Jean it was a goodbye weekend. We took a room in a nice hotel, what we should have had for our *first time ever.* Soft sheets, warm lighting and a tiny, luxurious bathroom. Renoir paints while Ewan washes my back, slowly soaping me all over as he sits by the side of the bathtub. *Love, O love, O careless love.* We've been careless, love.

We came back to London yesterday and today I took the train for Liverpool. The look in his eyes as the train pulled out from the station . . . his face was blank and bloodless, his mouth half open as if his life force was being drawn out through it. He seemed not to blink, as if to miss not a single moment of my departure. I leaned out of the window and he walked with the moving train to the end of the platform, never changing that expression. *I looked down the track, far as I could see. A little bitty hand waving after me.* I cried all the way to Liverpool Docks. I would know exactly how Ewan felt thirty-two years later when it was my turn to drown in Love.

Santa Barbara and Chicago

Steamships. No little trays on your lap, no squirming in minuscule leg-room, no entering a loo that two hundred people have
already used. You are transported in luxury in a dignified manner – if it doesn't hit an iceberg. You are stewarded, attended,
cared for. My favourite occupation was – and still is on any
motorised water vehicle – to stand at the stern and watch the
wash that wags like the tails of two furry white dogs. We were
two days out when it struck, storm force 10. The big liner
became a nutshell in a washing machine. The public spaces of
the boat emptied. Put all movables in your rooms into the closet.
Remain movable yourself only when necessary. Horizontal is
the only thing possible. Every violent illness seems to be the
worst you could possibly have, but seasickness is a special
state. It is not a locatable pain. It disorientates all of the senses
and closes down hunger and balance, the only sign of hope
being the swaying, vertical stewards bearing bottles of drinking water. Crawl on hands and knees to the loo, brought onto
your back suddenly as the ship rolls. Symphony of misery: tuba
squawks of wood scraping wood, drum-drone of the engine,
cello pizzicatos as dropped water bottles hit walls, violins play
joist, joint and hinge in motion flat and sharp. Then the omi-
nous nanosecond of silence as our ship tops a wave, then it all
starts again. Every sound told us exactly what our craft was
made of, outlining the dimensions of our prison, reminding us

of the fragility of life and the uselessness of human endeavour.

On the fourth day, I got to the bathroom on two legs. The public rooms were the only part of the ship that didn't smell of vomit. I made it to the dining room, where breakfast was set out. The Demonic Composer of the last four days was now writing mellifluous chamber music, performed by Hearing, Taste, Touch, Sight and Smell. In the early evening, I went out on deck into the cold, December salt-spray wind. The sun was setting and the gulls were still with us, snatching up the ship's edible leavings. The crew tossed all unwanted items overboard. They're probably swirling around right now in the Great Pacific Garbage Patch. Neptune had not abandoned his pitchfork-and-toss, but his associates had put up signs warning everyone not to stir without a hand on one of the ropes which were strung warp and weft from rigging to rail. The boat was bucking like a horse, nose up, nose down, up the sky, down the sea, what goes down must come up, so I'm horizontal even while standing, holding onto the ropes and shouting *Hi Ho Silver, Awaaaaay!* The Lone Ranger rides the waves. The dinner hooter hoots. Born again in my dripping clothes, I sit down in a nearly empty dining room and eat several dinners.

Our ship's destination had been New York but the storm diverted us to Canada. We docked in St John's on Christmas Eve. Grey and freezing, adapting slowly to walking on ground that didn't move. Canadian Customs decided that I would miss the coach to Boston while they opened up every suitcase and instrument, took the bodywork off the scooter, searched my purse, my boots, my coat and me. Several hours later, my picture-puzzle-packed belongings were all over the custom-house floor. Customs officials are outside any law. They have extraterrestrial powers. They can turn your life, house and bank accounts upside down. They don't repack your luggage. There was a midnight southbound coach waiting for the Unfortunate Chosen. I had to leave the scooter behind as it would not fit on, in or above our bus. The shipping company would send it. There are good kernels in every bushel of bad corn – a nice boy was sitting next to me. We held hands for the whole trip and fell asleep with our heads together. Where are you now, my 1956 one-night sit? The warm, inviting New England be-Yuled settlements passed by. Christmas . . . *Dio is dead.*

On to Baltimore. Mike's front door was unlocked. Following the sound of the music, I found him squatting on the eight-inch-deep radiator, playing the fiddle. Like Charlie, Mike could fold himself up like a cricket. Fly west after New Year. *Home* was wherever Charlie and my sisters were. Now it was Mar's house in Santa Barbara. This time Charlie rented the house next door for me – a comfy little two-bedroom flat, a parlour full of interesting books, a piano and a tiny kitchen where I experienced my first earthquake, trembling floor and cups swinging on their hooks. Penny moved in with me, twelve years old now, quiet and with a great sense of humour. Barbara was living in town and we recorded our album *The Three Sisters*, with Charlie playing the guitar in the very far background and singing, yes, as usual, a quarter of a tone flat. One morning after breakfast, I stood up, got vertigo and fell down, hitting my back on the corner of a low table. I couldn't move. The pain kept me flat on the floor for several hours until Penny came home. Quick-quick to a chiropractor who crack-cracked my spine, my little vertebrae leaping home in sequence. I saw the chiro once a week for a month. I should have been X-rayed, properly and completely dealt with. Subsequent X-rays would reveal that I'd compressed a vertebra. Unfinished business, halfway journeys.

With Nature, people and machines, I learn only what information I need immediately. A repeating pattern – life-threatening with my body, heart-breaking with people.

Ewan wrote, made a phone call whenever he could afford it. One day, I told him a Los Angeles radio show had asked me for a very short, modern love song. *How about this one?* and he sang 'The First Time Ever I Saw Your Face'. Yes, that'll do nicely. Ewan never sang it again. Unspoken: it was mine to sing. To him. I sang it folk style, gave it a wandering guitar accompaniment. When we first heard the Roberta Flack version we were shocked. Ewan said he wrote it as an hors d'oeuvre and it had been turned into the main course. Charlie was still supporting me, so when an offer came through in March to play at the Gate of Horn in Chicago, both of us leapt at it – my first professional, long-lasting engagement. Good Ralph Rinzler had collected my scooter from the shipping company. He drove it to Philadelphia to meet me.

Nine hundred miles to go, I set out for Chicago on a rainy spring evening with the banjo and guitar on the scooter-flanks, an enormous knapsack perched on the little luggage rack over the back wheel. Where angels fear to tread. I started out at dusk and headed towards the remains of a sunset. I'd memorised the map – kind of. It was the first time I had ridden the scooter in the USA. The cars were bigger, the trucks were monolithic, the roads were wider and traffic was faster than in the Old Country. I merged onto the highway behind an enormous moving van and was immediately swept into its slipstream, unable to break free. My undertow swimming technique didn't work. It was one of the old-style highways, pitted with potholes, littered with debris. I couldn't see any booby traps until I was upon them, right behind the truck tail-lights. I strove not to panic. Fortunately, those old-style highways had traffic lights. The truck slowed down and stopped. I lectured myself: travel only in daylight; ride on the shoulder on highways; small roads now; buy mirrors for the handlebars.

In 1957, scooters were very rare in the USA. Motorcycles are the American style – man stuff. In Harrisburg, I was hauled over by two overweight policemen. My licence didn't cover scooter driving. They escorted me to an obstacle course for motorcyclists. I had scootered to the top of Scotland and back. I had negotiated London traffic in rush hour, once with oversize Alan Lomax riding pillion yelling *whoopi ti yi yo* around the roundabouts. No part of the Lambretta or its burden touched a single cone or spike in Pennsylvania. I got the licence and bought a helmet. My long hair flowed out from under it like a banner. A nightmare of a beginning but a dream of a trip. I learned to ride the slipstreams of the better highways like a fish or a surfer. Truckers smiled and waved and leaned out of windows. Cars gave me a wide berth. When I described this twenty-five years later to Charlie, he just sat silent, staring at me and uttered one word: *Peggy* . . . In Cincinnati, I had to get the Lambretta serviced. It was late in the afternoon. I found a mechanic who would do this immediately. A man was lounging in the office. He asked if I wanted to see Cincinnati. Why not? I jumped into his car. OMG. Dusk, a stranger, nobody knows where I am or who I'm with and I don't know where I'm staying tonight. For two hours, my man showed me Cincinnati, talking and sightseeing. No groping, no suggestions, nothing – just a nice man. Thank you, fellow traveller, from sixty years in the future of our past.

Roads straight enough to impress the Romans, fields on one side and more fields on the other, boring to the point of idiocy. The road dwindled into a pinpoint in the distance. Moving pinpoints in the distance came nearer and passed, continuous Doppler rise-and-fall. I sang and talked to myself. It was wonderful to be going to a job that would earn money, to Carl Sandburg's Chicago, the town in which my mother had lived and worked. I took a detour to where she was born, East Liverpool, Ohio. I hoped it was more interesting in her day. I arrived after six days, a week before I was to start the job. I went straight to the house of the agent who had hired me, Albert Grossman. An unappetising man, fish mouth, little pebble glasses, little pebble eyes. Like looking at a fish in a fishbowl. He said I was welcome to stay in his house with him and be his girlfriend while I was in town. Offer made with entitled self-confidence and turned down with the same.

He took me to the digs provided by the Gate, the top floor of an old warehouse. The only entrance to the huge building was in the back alley. Four floors up, no elevator, just trash-littered stairs. My new home was a huge room about twenty by fifteen by twenty by fifteen giant steps. In the middle was a spacious, unswept floor space. In that far corner was a big double bed with a chair and table. In this near corner was a very basic kitchen set-up, its window looking out four storeys down into the alleyway. In the corner to my right was a tiny bathroom and in the diagonal far corner a stinking pile of historic filth. These days I would quit the job if that was where I was to live for three months – or one day. In March 1957, I just set to. Boxes and bags of trash, old clothes, grocery packaging and rotting personal items went down to the dumpster. I swept and scrubbed and scraped and polished, went through gallons of ammonia and bleach until the place was shining. Studs Terkel – quirky, fascinating writer, broadcaster and author – had interviewed me for his radio show and given me names of local musicians, singers and wonderful, interesting strangers. By the time the room was clean, I had enough friends to have a big party. A band in one corner, singers in another, dancing in the middle and, American style, they helped clean up before they left.

The Gate of Horn was a basement dive with a performance space and a kitchen/bar/dining unit adjoining, clean enough to be safe, dirty enough to be friendly. When I went back in 1961 it had achieved hygienic anonymity. In 1957, it boasted the best hamburger I had ever tasted, sharing its laurels with the Great American Music Hall in San Francisco. The singers were allowed free meals, so I arrived hungry at ten at night and left burgered-out at three thirty in the morning. That left only a mountainous brunch at noon on my dime. My contract stipulated singing thirty-minute sets six nights a week. The two acts were equal; no one opened for anyone else. Fifteen-minute break for everyone every so often. Singers came and went but one of them was more than special: Big Bill Broonzy. He spent most of his time off stage in the little bar with bottles of brandy which he drank neat. During the breaks we'd sit together. Neither of us were small-talkers, just quiet eating and drinking. Bill was not a performer. No stage chat. He just played and soared and pretended he was somewhere else. My songs felt innocuous compared to his. He had stayed with Ewan back in the 1950s. He said that Ewan sang *like a white nigger.* Ewan was thrilled when I told him. Sometimes my friends would linger till the Gate closed and then we would racket around Chicago and carouse by the lake till it was time for me to scooter home and sleep. Chicago was the biggest, roughest town I had ever lived in and my housing was not in a residential area – but in those days a solo woman could ride home safely to a warehouse at five in the morning, park in a back alley and let herself in through a little dark doorway. The only thing that ever went missing was my rear-view mirror. My body rhythms went haywire. I slept from dawn till mid-afternoon. I had breakfast at lunchtime, no lunch – then burgers all night, with dill pickles serving as vegetables. In the late afternoon, I might visit Dawn and Nate Greening, my Chicago family, who ran a sanctuary for folk singers of any ilk. I gloried in the attention I got at the Gate. I loved flying solo. 'The First Time Ever' was now a staple of my repertoire, but Ewan was far away. We wrote occasionally, telephoned rarely. It felt . . . over. I didn't know how to carry on a long-distance love affair any more than I knew how to carry on a near one.

Peter Schlein sat in the front row nearly every night – a nuclear physicist, a completely nice man. True to the fairy tales of my girlhood reading, I gave him a task: jump into icy Lake Michigan with me and you can ride back to New York City with me at the end of June. Peter did it, brave soul, both of us gasping as our friends hauled us out in high spirits, dragging us to the nearest bar for a major breakfast and higher spirits from a bottle. The trip back east was slow. There was Peter (not a small man), his luggage, my knapsack, guitar, banjo and me on those two little wheels across Chicago, out onto the plains and those boring Midwestern arteries towards New York at no more than 50 mph. One day it rained so hard that a trucker took pity on us. He stopped, put us in the passenger seats and hauled the overloaded scooter onto the back of his pickup. St Someone Upstairs better be chalking up all these thank yous. I hope you are Believers as it's probably Collect Upon Entry. Even though Peter is gone now, I like remembering his birthday – 18 November. The birth of a friend on the date my mother died. Balance.

I'd promised Ewan that I'd return to go to the Moscow Youth Festival. Ralph saw me off at one of those gigantic docks on New York's west side where the big liners were set like race horses at the starting line. He was jumping up and down, waving a white handkerchief as the boat moved away. So innocent, so childlike, so joyful. That was Ralph. I left the scooter with him. Funny to think of him on the little Lambretta with his long frog legs sticking out. I had written to Ewan to tell him that I was coming. He would be in Liverpool to greet me. He didn't come. The person who thought she didn't care enough *did* care and wept like the child she was. Ewan wasn't there.

12

Break a Leg

I disappeared from my first appearance on stage. Head down, costumed from hooved shoes to blanketed shoulder, hands around the waist of a classmate, I was the back end of a horse in a primary-school production of Dr Seuss's *And to Think That I Saw It on Mulberry Street*. I forgot my dance steps and, distraught at not being perfect, I let go. Head sticking out of my 'saddle' but not abandoning my role, I cantered off, bent over, through the wings. I ran home, hid under the covers and refused to go to school the next day.

Don't say *good luck* to someone who's about to go on stage. That's bad luck. Say *break a leg*. That's good luck. The Greeks stamped their feet for applause, so the admonition may be meant for the audience: stamp your legs enthusiastically enough to break one of them. Or perhaps it refers to the audience jumping to a standing ovation so quickly that they break bones. The audiences at the Gate of Horn were small but appreciative. I had no smart chat, no jokes, no *routine* as such. I knew who I was: a suburban middle-class female who'd had a superb exposure to folk song and classical music. I sang songs that I treasured. I was a link in the chain of oral tradition. But now after decades of professional singing – *Who am I?* A performer? An entertainer? A social therapist, trying to mould a gathering of individuals into a temporary community? An opportunist chasing that elusive fifteen minutes? A seeker of a lifetime of royalties? A peddler of

my own ego? Or am I just a singer and instrumentalist, an interpreter of a past tradition and writer of songs of socio/political
significance that may never make it to a wider audience?

You reveal yourself the minute you go on stage. You present
who you are, who you have been and how you want to be thought
of. Your behaviour on and off stage tells all to the practised eye
– if you have one persona on stage and another off, that can be
tricky, for if these two entities do not work well together they
will trudge on like a tired marriage or one will begin to dominate
or both will make you wonder who you really are. The audience
is cannier than you think. They will only be fooled if they want
to be fooled. But sometimes they may not know they've been led
down this or that path until it opens into a clearing where we
can all sit down and have the picnic. A good concert is made up
of co-operation between performer and the assembled company.
End of concert is one of many telling moments.

Possible Scenario No. 1: The last song has been shocking –
Ewan's 'Disc of Sun' in stark unison. Marx's theory of aliena-
tion. Bring the Vietnam war on stage, here, now, and you're
going to watch and be part of human savagery. Four economi-
cal verses, ending with:

> *Programmed war, efficiency team,*
> *Punch cards fed to thinking machines,*
> *Computered death and the murder plan,*
> *Total destruction of Vietnam.*
> *O brother, have you got no shame?*
> *O Jesus! They're killing in my name.*

Total quiet for several seconds. No one – including us – wants
applause, but knee-jerk tradition takes over and a tide of almost

resentful hand-clapping rolls towards us. They've been shown a horror film. Now they need a mug of Horlick's and tucking up in bed. *Thank you for coming, for singing so well. Let's sing one last one together* – an encore that will enable them to stand up and head for home. Possible Scenario No. 2: The last song was nutritious, word-full, contemplative – 'Everything Changes' or 'Bring Me Home'. Emotions that we all share. Several seconds of quiet before generous applause. We're all still digesting, so maybe no need for dessert. Possible Scenario No. 3: The last song has been humorous, a rousing chorus. Laughter and enthusiastic applause. Send them home happy.

There are degrees of standing ovation in my own history, their quality visible from the stage. There is the all-together-now dignified mass rising. There is the little snowball rolling down the hill, set in motion by the short, beardy man in the front row. If it increases in size quickly, it becomes a Standing Ovation. If the rise is slow, there may be many reasons: they have dicky knees; they are lukewarm about the evening but admire my stamina at my age; they don't want to stand out as dissenters; they stand up neutrally, glad of a reason to gather coats, bags et cetera. A friend once confessed to me after a concert: *Peggy, I was almost too tired to stand up for you. Your songs have so many WORDS.*

The Big Scenario: Audience immediately vertical, applause that begins at the shoulders, calls for encores. Singer grabs the mic, *I LOVE YOU ALL!* Blown kisses, extravagant bowing, smiles that show the tonsils, exit-and-re-enter times three, finger-flick kisses that floor those in the back row, encores that everyone knew were coming anyway. Of course we love the audience. We want them to love us back and beg us for more. Sometimes, at the humungous pop concerts, they applaud so loudly that they cannot even hear the music they've paid good money to enjoy. It's cathartic, understandable. We need to get out of our own skins and participate in someone else's world for a while even if it does resemble a controlled riot. But *I love you all* feels false to me, an easy get-out. It's a bit like left-wingers who declare, *I love people.* Hitler? Donald Trump? Jihadi John? Irma Grese, who flayed Belsen inmates and had their skins made into lampshades? The audience seeks love too and the applause increases with each *I LOVE YOU ALL!* I have *never* said this, by the way, nor has any performer I respect. What we really love is the adulation. What we really want is for someone to tell us that we've done well even if deep down we know that we haven't.

When Ewan died, I didn't know who I was on stage, by myself, solo. Don't believe the press or your fans – they don't know who you are either. They only know who you are on stage. *Fan* – the diminutive of *fanatic*. John Lennon was murdered by one of his. One of Ewan's tried to beat him up in a folk club. *Who I am* is written in invisible ink all over me and I'm holding myself over a flame in this memoir hoping to discover a definitive identity. I need to know before I reach the Goal Post (hopefully with little or no warning). Comical, isn't it? A human photon quarking around an electron stage erratically circumnavigating a huge gaseous proton lost in a finite galaxy in an infinite universe wants to know who she is and what part she's played before she enters the black hole. She hopes it will make dying easier. Talking about it in the third person singular does that already.

13

Moscow

We were strangers. Ewan tried to reconnect, but I was lost. He hadn't come to meet me at the ship because I hadn't mailed the letter. Years later, I found it in an old suitcase. We made love in a friend's house. Strange, making love from a distance. We walked along the Thames, forlorn and quiet. We sat in Golden Square, feeding the pigeons from a joint bag of peanuts. We went to Torino's on Old Compton Street, a cafe frequented by artists, writers, media bods, politicians. Eavesdropping was de rigueur so you tried to make interesting conversation. Ewan and I sit uncommunicative over lamentable food. Minestrone, transparent right to the bottom of the bowl. Roast beef floating in watery cabbage gravy soaked up by lumpy mashed potatoes. Steamed pudding, heavy and greasy, floating in Bird's egg-free imitation custard. There is a fashionable joint there now, great pasta and insistent Muzak.

I longed to be off for Moscow and out of Ewan's company. He and Jean were flying in with Joan Littlewood and Theatre Workshop. Ewan's Woman No. 3 took the terra trip, first aqua and then firma. The boat to Calais was overloaded with young people from everywhere. Every seat, aisle and inch of floor space on the train was taken. Mr and Mrs Health and Safety hadn't been born yet. Every time the train stopped at a station, we flew off like locusts and emptied any food stalls we could find. Long queues for the toilet, where there was usually no water or paper left. For three days, we travelled through Belgium, Germany, Poland and into Russia – three days of nonstop music and talk. You could walk the length of the train and never be out of hearing of live music. The McPeakes of Belfast never stopped playing, but then you never wanted them to stop. Guy Carawan and I gathered our own crowd with banjos and guitars. We slept on the floors, in the luggage racks, between cars, on our feet, sitting up, across a stranger's lap. The lucky few got to lie down stretched out.

In Moscow, each nationality was billeted separately to ease language and organisational difficulties. I was put with the American *delegation*, but delegation we were not. We each came of our own accord, many of us determined not to be tarred with anyone else's brush. We were given schedules, maps, banners, badges, interpreters, guides, vouchers for restaurants and forms to fill out stating what we wanted to see and do, which museums, what mausolea, what other nationalities we wanted to exchange pleasantries, politics or ourselves with. The communist and socialist countries *really* knew how to do this. Cuba and China were the same. Every need seen to, every want met, every cultural idiosyncrasy catered for. Ewan came often from the British quarters to see me. He was out of place among all the young people in our digs and we both knew it. He had that same beseeching look in his eyes that he'd had on the train platform last year. He was in love with a brick wall, unable to stop beating his head against it. It would have been kinder just to tell him it was over, but I couldn't. Jean came with him once. She linked her arm into his possessively, calling him *lovey*. He didn't seem to notice. She loved him the way he wanted to be loved. She looked at him the way he looked at me. She saved his life and her life. She assured the lives of our children. She hated flying and insisted that they return to Britain by train. They gave their air tickets to a young Danish newlywed couple. The plane crashed, killing all aboard.

The Cold War played out at lower levels when the Russians challenged the men in our group to a drinking contest. Our poor lads didn't have a chance against those whose urban prairies are graced by statues reputed to be not of stone but of ice – important citizens (a ship-full of sheets to the wind), frozen stiff as they tried to cross Red Square in January. Our lads didn't know that the trick is to scoff down a quarter of a pound of butter beforehand. It lines the stomach so that glass after glass of straight vodka goes straight through and out. The Russians were kind about it – they soothed our puppies and settled them in chairs to sleep it off. Later, when we were at a diplomatic charade at the Chinese embassy in London, Her Upstairs gave the Russians payback. The Chinese served dainty porcelain sippy-cups of a whitish liquid. Ewan warned me not to drink it. The Russians haw-hawed and slugged it down like vodka. One minute they were standing and the next minute they were flat on the floor. Most of them were large. Most of the Chinese were small. The latter trotted in bearing stretchers, carting unconscious Russians away to a room set aside in anticipation of this outcome.

We were transported to the opening ceremony in open trucks, each labelled with the nationality of its occupants. About forty of us standing on the fenced platform of each, we were up above the oceans of people stretching as far as the eye could see. It seemed that all of Moscow had turned out to see the young people from all over the world. That a group of young Americans was present at all in the city was worthy of attention. Мир и дружба – *Mir i Druzhba! Peace and friendship! We don't like your government, but YOU are welcome!* We

leaned over the side of the truck shaking hands until our finger bones felt liquid. My diary: *We began shouting back, leaning over the trucks to kiss people, shake their hands, touch them,
exchange whatever little we had. For miles ahead – two or three
at least, this stretched, sometimes 100,000 people* [nearer millions,
I would guess now] *in a large square . . . my heart almost burst
and our tears certainly did. I am hoarse from my own enthusiasm
and shrieking, but for miles . . . how many faces and eyes did I look
into, how many hands did I touch, how many times hear 'мир'
and 'дружба' I will never forget, for my heart has counted them:
there is no numerical system for them . . . God help me to describe
it to people who have not seen or cannot imagine it. It will be an
incentive to everything that I do or think.* The Muscovites surged
around the trucks, holding up autograph books, tokens, trin-
kets, badges that read мир и дружба. Some of the latter were
small, very well made, enamelled or moulded, like union/fra-
ternity/attainment badges. During the following ten days, I
amassed a little hoard of them.

The crowds were beached as the trucks swept through
guarded entrances into the stadium. The ceremony was mirac-
ulous. The entire field was filled over and over again with suc-
ceeding waves of athletes, dancers, scarf-wavers, musicians and
acrobats all in synchronised movement, young girls whose skirts
ballooned out like the dancing mushrooms in Walt Disney's
Fantasia, regiments of women hurling batons and balls with
faultless co-ordination, several thousand boys and men marching in step, a moving mat of humanity in the grass oval. It lasted
four hours, then back to our dormitories via the empty squares
and wide thoroughfares.

The festival began in earnest. The Russians pressed the
American delegation to present something cultural. Guy and

I cobbled a programme together, gathering a 1957 Coalition of the Willing into an informal presentation of musical Anglo-Americana. It consisted of several dozen of us trooping barefoot on stage and treating the hallowed boards like a playground. The only songs we all knew together were religious, patriotic or children's ditties. Big, raggle-taggle, playful children in skirts and jeans, we performed a rough square dance then sat down to sing. Thanks to a year of intensive Russian at Radcliffe, I could speak about the songs. The Russians clapped and clapped. We bowed and bowed. As an encore, we sang 'We Shall Overcome' – probably not the most diplomatic choice – and trooped off unceremoniously. It was appalling artistically, but the Russians loved its innocence. The USA is, after all, a teenage country. All the old countries know that. They used to make allowances for us. Now they just can't believe the things we do. We can't believe it either.

Ewan had been attending meetings with cultural-politicos of his acquaintance. He told them of this wonderful young singer who knew American union and workers' songs. I agreed to come and sing. Ewan gathered famous writers, dignitaries, poets and artists to listen. I was due there at noon. I turned up at twelve thirty with Guy. Ewan didn't like Guy's singing. Furious, he nevertheless spoke well about the American political songs and waxed lyrical about me. Guy and I proceeded to sing religious songs, then more religious songs, the type which so far had brought the Russian theatre audiences to their feet. We followed these with some light children's pieces, trying to get the audience to sing the silly choruses. Not a union or worker's song passed our lips. The interpreters translated the words. The audience settled into a stony, polite silence. Ewan asked me to sing 'Which Side Are You On?' I said no, Guy wants to sing

'Come and Go with Me to That Land'. People began to wander out. Even as I write I blush with shame. Here was a gathering of gigantic figures in Russian literature and politics. We had sung nursery rhymes. Ewan was too angry to speak. He told me later that he swore he would end his pursuit of me, that I was fickle, childish and shallow. His humiliation in front of his peers must have embarrassed him terribly, especially as it was undoubtedly obvious to them that he was infatuated with this egotistical singer whose only good points appeared to be youth, honey-coloured hair and a longneck five-string banjo. I didn't see him for the rest of the festival.

On the final day of the festivities, there was a closing ceremony at the Bolshoi Theatre. Each nationality was sending one act, seven to eight minutes in duration. Guy and I were invited. Founded in 1776, the Bolshoi represents Russia culturally. I hadn't realised the theatre's size until I saw the act preceding ours, a Chinese dragon dance with twenty or thirty running dancers holding sticks that support segments of the huge, undulating, cloth-paper-wire puppet. Standing in the wings, we watched it race past us long before it got to the centre of the stage. Red-blue-green-white-gold, it turned and twisted to the twanging birdsong orchestra, upstage to downstage, right to left, the dancers' bare feet making no sound, coming near then far, the dragon alive on its thousand-legger feet. It whooshed past us back into the wings to a storm of applause. After the Lord Mayor's show comes the dust-cart: Guy and I were announced.

We mistimed our entrance. It took about fifty steps to get to the centre. *Kumbaya! Michael row the boat ashore! Join in on the chorus!* We sing, they stand, they cheer, we bow. The lights went on and I nearly passed out with fright. Balcony after balcony rose up and up and up until you have to crane your neck to see the peanut gallery. Chandeliers, blood-red drapes storeys tall and every seat filled, though at the moment most of the audience were standing, clapping, shouting. There are photographs of us – me in my red polka-dot dress and Guy in his casuals – smiling and acknowledging our unearned ovation. Ewan was out there, still volcanic with love and rage.

14

China

All hell broke loose when Mao's government invited all of the American attendees to China. The US media went into a feeding frenzy. We were tools in the hands of communists; we were willing to go anywhere, do anything for a free ride; we were unaware of the harm we were inflicting on the American people, et-boring-cetera. We went because we came from liberal, progressive families reared on union songs and the Henry Wallace presidential campaign; we went because we were exercising our right to travel; we went for adventure for its own sake. In 1957, our American passports were *not valid for travel to the following areas under control of authorities with which the United States does not have diplomatic relations: Albania, Bulgaria and those portions of China, Korea and Viet-nam under Communist control.* Christian Herter, Undersecretary of State to John Foster Dulles, phoned each of us separately threatening revocation of our passports, thousands of dollars in fines and political ostracism for us, for our families and friends, forever, Amen. Charlie said, *Go, Peggy. You'll never get a chance like this again. We'll sort it out when you get back.* Jake Rosen, one of our number and later our chosen spokesman, did an expert job of negotiations. Forty-one of us would travel right across Russia, all expenses paid by the Chinese government. In August we boarded a very long train, each carriage containing a different nationality and rows of four-bed compartments. The journey would take a little more than a week – nine memorable days of watching the countryside change, watching the Slavic facial features transform slowly into East Asian ones. The Chinese had sent interpreters to accompany us. They tried to teach us some basic Mandarin, a tonal language with four distinctive contours. We entertained them with our attempts before giving up and settling for *hello, goodbye, please, thank you* and *comrade* – each pronounced like porcupines making love: very carefully. Producing the wrong tone or contour could completely alter the meaning.

Invitations were issued to and from the length of the train. Such formalities were necessary because you could wander the whole length, get lost and arrive back home too late for dinner. The train didn't stop at every station. Many's the village we swept through at high speed, sometimes in the middle of the night, the faces on the platform blurring, hands waving, voices shouting *MIR I DRUZHBA!* Some ceremonial stops were planned, mostly at farming communities where there were only mud roads and one-storey huts, where the people were a stereotype of what the average American thinks an average Russian looks like: stolid, kerchief round the head, weather-worn faces. A few heavy trucks and many carts with huge wooden wheels drawn by bullocks. Toothless ancients and shy children. Peasant women offering plates of cakes and selling small artefacts. A member of one of the delegations would make a brief speech, translated right there on the platform. When such halts occurred in the middle of the night, we'd wake bleary-eyed to participate, even the most recalcitrant of our group aware that we had a responsibility here. Discord was already developing – are we an entity or an assortment of individuals? Example: One day a large American flag is stretched along three of our carriage windows. Who had brought such an item with them? We'd passed through several towns with this outrageous token of authority on the outside of our carriage before the Chinese aboard got wind of it. Apparently, we'd terrified village people who thought the US invasion had begun. The budding dissension among our ranks solidified at that point and never ceased till we left China.

At the border we were each given a loose visa – no record of our entry or exit would appear on our passports. We got showers, medical inspection and emergency enemas to empty bowels that had been solidified by a nine-day diet of meat, potatoes, black bread and the carbonated drink that we dubbed People's Pop. We stood out in a country where all the eyes were slanted and dark, all skin was tan, all hair was black, all clothes were denim blues and no one was overweight. Most of the Chinese were shorter than me. I have a photo of us striding along a street in a factory town – we tower above our hosts and we all seem to have huge feet.*

Dalian. This day, early in the morning, the weather was fine but chilly. The footpaths up the surrounding hills were covered in people exercising, saluting the morning sun with yoga, deep breathing and meditation. We joined them. Everyone stared or smiled but no one sought conversation. This was a time that was set aside by Mao for Chinese citizens to contemplate and prepare for the coming day. It was in Dalian that we first realised that the bodies and breath of Chinese people had a certain odour, a little sour but not unpleasant. At one point, Louis

---

* Read *The Crippled Tree*, the first volume of Han Suyin's autobiography, beginning with the life of her European mother, who married into an outback aristocratic Chinese family, all of whose women had bound feet.

– older than the rest of us and, shall we say, unsubtle in all his dealings – informed our interpreter, *You all have bad breath and you smell strange.* She cast a look at her associate, who gave a little nod of assent that probably meant *Yes, we should tell them.* Her attention came back to us and, nice as ninepence: *That must explain why all of you smell so strange to us. You smell like corpses.* If someone else's breath smells strange to you, then yours may smell strange to them.

The trip lasted forty days. We went from Manchuria, far north, right down to Guangzhou, far south. I became aware of living conditions such as I'd only ever read about and optimism the like of which dreamers would deem impossible. Whenever we reached a destination, we were given a choice of things to do: visit a local family; go to any number of small arts co-operatives or businesses; walk around a palace, park, factory, educational establishment; or just explore without interpreters or guides. A nursery, run by cheerful ancient toothless women. A housing complex with communal kitchens – optional attendance, freeing women of constant kitchen duty. A bridge is being built across a very wide river. The scaffolding is entirely bamboo, many storeys high, reminding me of our childhood Tinkertoy towers. A swarm of workers trundle up the slatted footways carrying stone, wood, cement, huge steel girders; running back down to refill empty hods, wheelbarrows and shoulders. A neighbourhood committee in one of the large towns: an adolescent thief is being questioned by his peers and neighbours. *Why did you do this, comrade? If you needed that pair of shoes, why did you not ask?* The boy gets a sentence of four community work-hours. The Great Wall, before it became a tourist attraction . . . workers all over it in the punishing wind and sandstorm. We climb to the top. The stone snake slithers across the distant hills in both directions. It can be seen from outer space and has kept invaders out for millennia. It will not be able to repel the new marauders from inside and outside, the personal and corporate greed, the opportunists, the market economy which by the new century will destroy old China and imprison its people in a new form of serfdom. We pull our scarves across our faces.

We visit a hospital in Kiangsu province. My first sight of acupuncture, little children lying still with hair-thin needles stuck in them. Excerpts from my China Diary: *Tradition of Chinese medicine was looked down upon by foreigners . . . Doctors are sent out from here to difficult cases elsewhere. To develop medical heritage and mix it with western method . . . The Chinese medicine is 3,000 yrs old – it has supplied the Chinese people with the only care they had . . . Limitations were put (legally) by the Kuomintang on development of trad. med. Open prohibition of Chinese doctors to practise or teach their art! No schools or hospitals allowed to use it. Very good for meningitis. Some diseases are referred to Chinese methods, and some to western ones. Acupuncture: . . . better for chronic diseases . . . most fit for internal medicine . . . lungs, brain system (the nerves) and digestive tract. Good for malaria and whooping cough, heart disease and TB. Use of baked herbs against influenza in summer, sunburn, malaria. He emphasizes summer diseases. Preventative med. taken in accordance with changes in the weather! And if the gov't finds any quacks, it educates them into the medicine they are pretending to know . . . Midwives trained by gov't. Education for natural childbirth begins 2 or 3 months before delivery (lectures, pamphlets, etc.). Mother mortality rate: extremely few. Acupuncture also takes care of some of the mental illnesses. Psychiatrists? Yes – this is a part of trad. med.'s coordination with west. med. Not much mental illness in China.*

In Tianjin an enormous machine on a wheeled platform is

being pulled by fifty or sixty men with long ropes. One of them called out to us cheerfully as they passed. A passer-by translated: *Remember that it will not always be like this*. Everyone must work, including visitors. We were taken to an orchard where we picked apples all day. On another day, we visited a village where we had to push the huge millstone wheel around, grinding the grain to flour. We attended the anniversary celebration in Beijing, an all-day spectacle in Tiananmen Square. China flowed past us. Acrobats and little girls dancing with ribbons on sticks; representatives of all the ethnic minorities; hundreds of musicians, thousands of dancers; processions of monks and nuns. Soldiers and their materiel, the men marching in goose-step, that universal silly walk in which each man seems to be kicking the backside of the man ahead of him. Would women march thus? There were potters, weavers, wood-turners, cooks, waving the tools of their trade. Divisions of grannies with babies and toddlers; an infantry of teenagers waving books; platoons of women in aprons. Each section had its own music, and those who accompanied them swayed, marched and danced in time. A vibrant mix of colours and styles – pink/orange/red, blue/green/purple scarves, flags, banners, streamers. Everyone saluted our section of the bleachers for above and behind us was the government: Lin Biao, Mao Zedong, Zhu De, Zhou Enlai, comrade veterans of the struggle for China in their blue denims and caps, waving and saluting. The whole day proclaimed *We are China*.

In the big cities, much of the fine upper-class architecture of old China still remained, beautifully decorated in green, red and gold. In Beijing's Summer Palace and Gardens, I was walking through the scenes painted on Grandmother's porcelain plates. Round a bend and there's a musician sitting on a bench playing the *erhu*, a two-string fiddle. Little wooden bridges crossed streamlets bordered by crooked dwarf trees. Serenity as far as the eye could see and, like many of our public parks, originally meant exclusively for royalty and their relatives and friends – and visiting enemies needing reminders as to whom they were dealing with. The Russian revolutionaries killed off their aristocracy and most of their wealthy, upper-class, privileged government and business citizens. The Chinese communist government absorbed and utilised those who'd not been summarily slaughtered by the peasants' rage. A former rural landlord who had been cruel to his tenants: his life was granted on the condition that he and his family live and work among his erstwhile serfs. He was not a happy man. He described his life before the revolution and referred to his present life as unsupportable misery. The interpreter was sympathetic. *His despair is natural but necessary.* She also told us that the man lived marginally better than his peasants – two rooms instead of one – because he would have died otherwise. The man whined as he talked and tears welled up in his eyes. His wife was stone-faced. *At least we are still alive.*

A group of us visited the home of an ex-factory owner in Beijing. Prior to the revolution, he had been a good employer, so he was kept on as the manager. He was a happy man. He compared his present to his previous position and preferred the present. No fear of worker uprisings, of having to look for markets, of being responsible for everything from before A to beyond Z. The new government needed him and his knowledge of the business and acknowledged that he would not work efficiently if he were reduced to living as a peasant. So he lived very modestly but had kept a few relics of his old way of life, one very memorable: a chair, its tall straight back made of a rectangle of highly polished marble, with smooth wooden framing to protect its edges. This slab was about one inch thick, twenty inches wide and three feet high. A brown cat sat clearly delineated against a white background, its paw on a perfectly round brown ball. The chances of such a formation occurring in nature . . . but the chances of *finding* it in a chunk of marble . . .? Our host gave us a truly royal meal, lamenting the loss of a particular gastronomic delight from his old days to which (fortunately) he could not treat us. After a big meal you would swallow whole a couple of newborn mice, dipped in honey. For the short time they lived in your stomach they would wriggle about, trampling your meal down and helping the digestive juices before those juices digested them.

In Beijing bicycles were everywhere. We asked for bikes. *We'll see, comrades.* We asked again. Politely: *No, comrades.* The Yankee children are insistent: *Why, Mommy?* Our girl-woman interpreter: *Comrades, you are guests of the Chinese government. You are unofficial diplomatic visitors. Can you imagine the concern in your country if one of you should fall off your bicycle and injure yourself? Can you understand the problems it would create in our two countries if one of you should injure a child? No, comrades, putting you on bicycles could possibly create an international crisis.*

We could walk wherever and whenever we wished. We did just that in each city we visited. No maps, guides or interpreters unless we requested one, although I'm sure we were followed discreetly. Once you got away from the centre the streets were of hard-trodden earth, twisting and narrow. We carried a note in Chinese to use if we got lost. Our finders always laughed upon reading it. It probably said something like *Help us. We are poor silly Americans and we are lost. Please take us to such-and-such hotel.* We got seriously lost on one of our Beijing peregrinations.

Every child in sight was following us, touching our clothes, smiling and clapping as we sang. We showed them our note. They giggled and took us in tow. On the way home, Guy and I started singing 'Skip to My Lou':

> *Lou, lou, skip to my lou,*
> *Lou, lou, skip to my lou,*
> *Lou, lou, skip to my lou,*
> *Skip to my lou, my darling.*

The children began chanting it. They couldn't get the fourth line so they just sang the first two lines over and over all the way to our hotel, still singing as they ran off.

A three-day trip down the Yangtze River from Wuhan to Nanjing in a large riverboat that was made in Shanghai by an English company, its engine Scottish. We had the upper-class cabins above, a beehive of little rooms and narrow corridors. Four of us to a room, each with facilities which would have been luxurious to the Chinese passengers in steerage below, who sat huddled close day and night on wooden benches. Several had brought geese and baskets of produce. One had a huge pig on a rope. The first morning on the boat we were awakened by singing, a work song as like as could be to 'Pick a Bale of Cotton', recorded by the Lomaxes in the American South.

One evening at dusk we stopped at a small river port where all the old people were blind or near-blind. Chattering as we trooped down the gangplank, we were greeted by a crowd of old men and women, their eyes milky-white with cataracts caused, we were told, by the pre-revolution untreated water supply. Each ancient had a child guide. A tall, toothless, bone-thin old woman turned her face towards us. She had heard the foreign accents and was drawn instinctively to beg. Her little Girl Guide tugged at her skirts, lilting over and over in a soothing voice: *No, Granny, no, Granny! We don't do that any more! We don't need to do that any more!* I want to cry.

In Nanjing we visited a weaving commune. There was dust everywhere. Women and children sat in the shadows along one wall, sorting silk thread and winding it onto spools. The weaver sat on a bamboo platform about eight feet above the floor, a sort of assembly line below him. Two rolls of colour, one bearing the warp thread and the other the finished cloth. The five-foot-wide loom is caught between them, laced into the parallel rainbow threads. The weaver has ranks of foot-pedals and hand-hooks which move the warp up or down. His hands and feet take a second or two to set each combination for the pattern. The lines of bright warp silk shift subtly. The weaver pulls a lever to fix the combination on the loom below and gives a sharp call. A worker on the far side shoots the shuttle through. The shuttle person on the near side either shoots the shuttle back or engages shuttles with different weft colours and awaits a new call from the weaver on high. Every few shots, another two workers lift, lower and press the warp-wide comb against the woven material to tighten it. Children turn the huge rolls to keep the warp tension right. Pedal-pedal-pedal-hook-hook-hook, fixing-lever, call, shuttle-lever, weft-comb, pedal-pedal-pedal . . . thousands of combinations making up the pattern, which repeats every six or seven feet, an intricate bright silk tableau of flowers, birds and little people on little bridges, in little houses. The women are singing, the rhythm of the contraption is hypnotic, the vision is dreamlike. The shed is dark, its only light coming from high up, where one skylight allows the sun to spotlight the weaver, who, like the shuttlers, knows the woven story by heart. The drifting snowstorm of lint and dust sparkles in the sunbeam, beautiful and deadly.

An ivory and jade carving commune. A traditional fable was being released from the deep recesses of an enormous elephant tusk. The carver was ancient, shrunken and toothless, with tree-bark skin, his hand rock-steady. He pointed out how the hero, half an inch tall, fought a dragon here and stopped there in the deep forest for a drink of water. The story wended its way from right to left, from narrow to wide, down the tusk in intricate 3D. The old man was about three inches from the root end of the tusk. As he talked he picked out a fragment of ivory from the dress of a maiden at a gate. He had been working on this tusk all his life and hoped to finish it before he died. *What if you die before you finish it?* Matter-of-fact: *Then my son will finish it.* We wonder if the old man's father began it. There's a carved tusk such as this on display in the Snell Library at Northeastern University in Boston. The one his son finished after he died . . .?

Our Chinese interpreters lived mostly on rice and vegetables. The food we were given was too rich for them. The dishes bore little relation to the Chinese food served in Western restaurants. Try a jam omelette: drooling delicious. Sometimes the food was served in big pots – you just dipped in and took what you wanted. Shanghai – a regal meal today: dim sum. A huge platter arrives filled with delicate bite-size pieces, artfully arranged. We are told, *Two for each of you, comrades.* One of our company takes four pieces instead of his two. *Comrade, you've taken someone else's share.* He sulks and puts it back. Third, fourth, fifth courses come along, each of them so mouth-watering that you soon learn to eat your two little bites very slowly. We begin heralding each new platter by calling its number out loud, right up to forty. Shanghai – China's financial hub, the city divided up by ensuing legions of invaders, some of whose street signs had been left in place. BRITISH QUARTER. NO CHINESE OR DOGS ALLOWED. Shanghai – the sun is rising. The Yangtze is packed with junks, flotillas of floating homesteads. Soundscape of washing, singing, cooking, conversation, commerce, children, home and market. There was no trash riding the river currents. There was no trash on the streets. Every piece of manufactured or reusable material was recycled. Discarded items were rare but picked up, sorted and distributed – habitual in China for centuries. Even body waste was not wasted. The night-soil collectors came around in the early hours of the morning to take human excretions, unpolluted by chemicals and junk food, away to manure the fields. Even the little revolting plugs of hawked-up mucus and spit in the street were organic and swept up for fertiliser.

On to Guangzhou, the southernmost point of our trip. A monsoon hit and a sky-sized bucket of rain waterfalled us for several days. The inhabitants sloshed through it, briefcases, baskets, baby-slings and footwear held high. We Westerners were transported in rickshaws under a half-roof or holding an umbrella – kind of OK when the driver was on a bicycle but shaming when we were pulled by barefoot men, thin as reeds, soaking wet, their legs sunk to mid-calf in water and mud. Much has been written about China since the 1949 revolution. I only became aware later of the complicated implications of the Anti-Rightist Movements and the Cultural Revolution, all of which were happening or about to happen at the time of our visit. Zhou Enlai sat down with us for an hour or two.

... 15) Is it true that there are dissensions in the leadership regarding the 100 flowers policy and does it include a 'struggle for power?' Ans. (Chou is very amused at this . . .) This is a rumor. 16) Would

New China enter the UN even if nationalist China is represented there? Ans. NO! (very terse). We cannot agree to the creation of 2 Chinas. Thank you for raising this question. 17) What products could new China trade for U.S. goods in the event of free trade? Ans. Chou has little knowledge of the needs of the American market. Chou will not venture to add his ignorant supposition to that of the State Department. At first trade would be uneven.

My 1957 China Diary was written daily in tiny script in notebooks four inches by three. Typed up, it is ninety pages long. Every page describes unremitting physical labour and optimism and national commitment on a mind-boggling scale. *Made in China* on every possible sort of manufactured goods does not tell the story of an extraordinary country that grew up too quickly, which pulled itself up by bootstraps on bare feet. The scale of the journey from bestial feudalism to bestial capitalism in the space of some seventy years is awe-inspiring.* My little books recorded a once-in-a-lifetime journey made by a girl who took the trip because she believed in Of-Course-Why-Not. She was more politically aware than I have since given her credit for. Before I reread them, I thought that my political education began with Ewan. In fact, I already had an understanding of the complexity of China's transition and was invigorated by the vistas of Hope that our group ploughed so lightly through. Unlike many places I visited in my youth, I have no desire to see the new China. I prefer to remember it newly revolutionised and with breathable air. I saw the results of a thousand steps

* Acts of courage, horror, hope, ambition, greed, altruism, tragedy – it's all there to be soaked up frcm eyewitness accounts, biographies and documentaries to denigrating, slanted, destructive reportage. Start with Edgar Snow's *Red Star over China* and progress to William Hinton's *Fanshen* before reading Jung Chang's *Wild Swans*.

forward and don't wish to see the five hundred steps back into the free-market future.

Zhou Enlai signed my banjo. I shook Mao's hand at a reception. Their China was only eight years old when we came. What children we were! We skipped and twinkled through these encounters and the old heroes were *so* polite, *so* patient. Most of us knew little or nothing of the history of the revolution, the hardships of the Long March, the horrors of the Japanese occupation, the degradation and torture that many of these dignitaries had suffered as other countries came, saw, conquered, divided and exploited China. Would Mao and Zhou wish to visit China in the 2000s? Probably. The old revolutionaries had vision but they were pragmatic and understood human nature, the urge to destroy always nipping at the heels of the urge to create.

15

Russia and Poland

It was September when we flew back to Moscow. There were already signs of Winter, the Eminence that has defended Russia's western borders for centuries. Moscow Radio arranged for Guy and me to stay on as musical ambassadors. Would we pair up with a group of Chilean musicians and tour various cities through October and November? We boarded the train, crowned with ear-flapped astrakhan caps. The Chileans spoke no English. We spoke no Spanish. Our interpreters had only Russian in common. We performers laughed and gestured, and the interpreters went off for a drink. Some damn fool suggested that we all do several songs together in each concert. 'Skip to My Lou' with charango and banjo, 'Michael Row the Boat Ashore' with Chileans on the *Alleluia* refrain . . . Our support to their songs must have been equally bizarre, but I wasn't a purist back then and we all had fun. When we sang 'Kalinka', the Russians' singing drowned us out. More badges, more pictures of Lenin, little dolls and painted boxes and then it's back to Moscow. It was early October and I was ill – those familiar fevers and chills of my recurring childhood ailment, tonsillitis. Moscow medicos wanted me to guinea-pig a new cure for it, a slow burning-out of the tonsils. I'll think about it. In the meantime we were bil-leted in a massive hotel where I wasn't too ill to gorge on cheese blintzes, sour cream and caviar.

I wrote to Peter and Maurice, but Ewan . . .? None of my

letters to him are left. Sometime in the early 1980s we were cleaning out the Paper Room, our overflow filing system in the attic. Ewan proposed that we burn our love letters. No anger, no passion, just . . . tidying up of old business, I guess. He did burn mine, ceremonially in the living-room fire. They weren't very interesting anyway – not the kind of love letters one keeps. His letters were passionate, flowery, poetic, very bawdy and frequent. I carried his early ones around with me in my knapsack as I travelled. I still have them. I'm still 'travelling' but now it's to visit the strange country of Myself a few more times. One very long letter dealt with the Twentieth Congress of the Communist Party, in February 1956, at which Khrushchev denounced Stalin. Such a brave thing for a world leader to do, such real courage for a nation to look honestly at itself even if (a) someone else was going to do it soon anyway, (b) it was high time, or (c) it was a power game cover-up. I read that letter aloud to Lyev and Kostya and our boisterous Moscow friends. It caused an unprecedented deep political discussion. Shortly afterward we were given two days' notice to leave Russia. I was overwhelmed and felt too ill to hit the road again. Suddenly – too late – I wanted my tonsillitis cured. A rare postponement of Of-Course-Why-Not hadn't been a good idea. Guy, his wife Noel and I were escorted to the Polish border in early November.

*

The Nazis had deported Poland's Jews, homosexuals, disabled people, Gypsies and political opponents to the concentration camps and then systematically razed the Warsaw ghetto, slaughtering the remaining two hundred thousand residents. Hitler vowed that Poland would never rise again. *Oh, yes, it will.* Poles came back from all over the world. Some saw the devastation and committed suicide. Others just began rebuilding. By the time I arrived in 1957, the Market Place was the only part of Warsaw that had been reconstructed exactly as it had been, to the last brick and cobblestone. They even found – and brought back – the woman who had traditionally sold peanuts in the square. I bought peanuts from an old woman there . . . After the vengeful carpet bombing of Dresden by the Allies in February 1945, the Dresdeners also rebuilt their historic centre as it had been. Tragic and ironic – both sides rising like the phoenix from mutually imposed destruction.

The rest of Warsaw was emerging in Emergency Style. The Russians had helped to build the enormous Palace of Culture in a huge open space right in the middle of town. Some of the trams were running. Every one of the few automobiles was packed tightly with passengers. If a car had an empty seat, the law allowed you to flag it down and get in. If there were too many bicycles and pedestrians in the street, a car could travel on the sidewalk. The trams tailgated and were dangerously full. Passengers hung not only onto the poles at the back, but onto people who hung onto people who . . . Someone fell off this extruding chain of passengers and was cut in half by the following tram. I didn't know a human body could contain so much blood.

The Polish government put the three of us up in a hotel, accommodation only. We gravitated towards the university, where we found a noisy bistro-cum-nightclub. It was dark and smoky, roistering students, full and empty beer bottles everywhere. We sang and coins were dropped in the open guitar case. I was taken up by two of the students. One was Bogdan, a shy, dome-headed man whose chief ambition was to marry me and leave Poland. The other was Jan – blond, dapper, engaged to be married. He was a musician, fascinated by the banjo and guitar. He kissed the back of my hand whenever we met. I asked him about his fiancée. *She is a cow. She is for children. She will be my wife. You are my friend.* I was not a feminist back then.

The ghetto in Warsaw was fenced off with barbed wire. Billows of rubble, waves and crests of stone, glass, metal, wire and remains of shattered household furniture. I stood at the fence for hours, stupefied. The photos in *Life* magazine were childhood fare for me. The little boy among the Jews herded out of the ghetto who looked just like Mike; the skeletal inmates of the concentration camps; a starving child vomiting up milk offered by an American soldier, the sudden nutrition too rich for its swollen belly. My Woezle Anneke had seen it in real life, Nazi soldiers marching endless lines of men, women and children past her Arnhem home. She and her friends brought sandwiches to give to the children as they walked eastward to extinction.

Jan took me down a nondescript street of new brick buildings. He linked his arm in mine in front of one of these featureless edifices and grew several inches taller: *That wall, Peggy. See the windows at the end of the building on the right, on the second floor? Start at the top right-hand corner of the one on the right. Count three hundred bricks over to the left and then seven rows up. Back to the right now, to the wall. That makes a rectangle, yes? I laid those bricks.* His face lit up with pride. A bricklaying musician who believed in Warsaw. Jan had a flair for business and had hopes for Guy and me. Would we give a concert in Łódź, west of Warsaw? No reason why not. Much of the population were living under the ruins. We were put up in the remaining half of a small tavern in the middle of a wasteland.

Paths had been cleared through the remains of the city and little signs helped pedestrians to avoid danger spots. Half of an opera house was the only public building left standing, pockmarked with bullet holes, guarded by headless, handless statues. It must have been wondrous in its time. The stage is huge. The audience sit wrapped in blankets, metal army canteens filled with hot water on their laps. Guy and I start with our Protestant religious standards in a Catholic communist country. My turn solo. The theatre is in blackness, broken here and there with bare thirty-watt light bulbs hanging on wires. I am singing my own story in a devastated historic city, alone on stage in this frigid, half-demolished erstwhile scene of glittering performances enjoyed by the upper classes, many of whom were party to their own downfall. I'm singing 'Barbara Allen' for a handful of desolate survivors of the worst war in human history. So far. I close my eyes to watch Sweet William and Barbara move from right to left, deathbed to cemetery. The audience begins to murmur. I open my eyes slightly. Traversing the front of the stage, lit by the pathetic footlights, is a huge mother rat leading her young from stage right to stage left.

We returned to Warsaw. The Poles did not, could not, would not, should not have to keep us in the manner to which the Russians had accustomed us. They took away our accommodation. Commendable. This country was trying desperately to heal itself, not to play host to wandering American troubadours. Guy and Noel left. I still had some of the money that I had earned from the concerts in Moscow. I moved into a student dormitory, a cold, bleak, dark maze of rooms, each bed with a straw mattress, a brick-hard pillow and two blankets. The kitchen had two gas burners and no food anywhere. I wandered around in the bone-piercing cold until tonsillitis floored me, mutated and confined me to bed. The students, all women, came and went, but mostly went as far as I was concerned. Caring for layabout visitors was not in their curricula. No one worried about diplomatic incidents here. I didn't even know the Polish words for *Help me.* I became a shivering, sweating mass of self-pity when one of the girls came and sat on my bed. She spoke broken English. She called a doctor who didn't charge, who diagnosed pleurisy, gave me some pills and vanished. The girls piled blankets on me, placed beakers of water by the bed – and went. Each morning they brought me a sloppy grain breakfast, much like oatmeal – and went. They brought a hot drink at night, then everyone slept. I believe they saved my life. I was sick forever – and then I wasn't. A government official turned up and told me I had to leave. *We need your bed – and the Polish government cannot afford you.*

I blush now for my presumption. The Poles were lifting their country out of the grave. I had not done any bricklaying or cleared any rubble. I had not helped in any way. Polish politics were in turmoil. The aftershocks of Khrushchev's speech were watering the early seeds of Lech Wałęsa's Solidarity movement. And yet . . . Prime Minister Władysław Gomulka, who lived near our dormitory, could walk without bodyguards among his people. Jan came to the station with me. He cried and collected his tears in a thimble. *Tears are my precious soul pouring out.* He saluted me with the thimble and I boarded the westbound train. Three devastated communist countries had treated me royally without charging. The Free World gives free rides only to the rich.

16

Marking Time

My 1955 US passport is stained and battered and hotchpotched with entrance and departure stamps and signatures. I travelled back and forth with seemingly no purpose in '56 and '57 – Germany to France to Switzerland, the Netherlands. My childhood journals come to a complete stop after 23 November 1957. I fetched up in England again on New Year's Eve that year with a three-month visa. Alan Lomax had no room for me so he asked Maud Karpeles to put me up in her small Swiss Cottage flat. Alan and Maud (her last name pronounced *KAR-pull-eeze*) had been crossing swords for years – more likely fencing, a fitting sport for two academics who loved the nitty-gritty of important trivia. The following example of their jousting, told to me by Charlie, took place at one of the conventions of the American Folklore Society, where once again the folklorists were trying to hammer out a coherent definition of folk song. They may still be doing that. Maud, a bent-over, pint-sized English lady, demands that a song should not be labelled *traditional* unless it is at least three hundred years old. Alan, a large, combative Texan, jumps to his feet and throws himself verbally across the room. *Maud, do you mean to disqualify all of the indigenous folk songs of America?* Maud, smiling: *Yes, Alan.*

Maud had accompanied Cecil Sharp on his collecting trips in the southern Appalachian Mountains between 1916 and 1918. Sharp had definite opinions about 'Negroes', and Maud was reputed to have gone ahead of him into the mountain communities preparing the ground: *Mr Sharp doesn't want to hear nigger music*, which presumably meant music accompanied by guitars and banjos or sung by African Americans or maybe any dark person. Sharp did, indeed, collect a great deal of unaccompanied, white-European-based material. Maud had the stereotypical chin-and-nose profile of the wicked witch. She was a hospitable soul and a friend of Charlie and Dio's. I first met her when she came to our house in Chevy Chase in the early 1950s. It was during our Spike Jones period, when Mike and I had 'Laura' and 'Dance of the Hours' constantly on the phonograph, our laughter helping Spike along. Charlie would smile indulgently, but Dio loved the oddball music. So did Maud. At one point, she upped her long black skirts and pranced around the room, laughing with us.

Maud's flat was several storeys up in an apartment building and consisted of one bedroom, one large public room, a bathroom and a kitchen. I was to sleep on the sofa, at the head of which was a life-size bust of Cecil Sharp. She asked if I wanted a cup of tea. Yes – and would I please make it while she continued working? She came into the kitchen when I was just about to put the tea leaves into the teapot. Gulliver voice from a Lilliputian woman: *NO! YOU WARM THE TEAPOT FIRST. THEN PUT THE TEA LEAVES IN!* She showed me the elaborate ritual that has made the English cup of tea famous the world over. It takes time, but it's worth it. I'll elaborate when we're next in a kitchen together. The basic ingredients are quality loose tea, a teapot, thin china cups with saucers, creamy whole milk, white sugar and McVitie's digestive biscuits.

When bedtime came, Maud confided, *I have a night-time*

ritual that may alarm you, Peggy. I need to give a little scream once a day. The neighbours are all used to it. Understood. Maud went into her bedroom. The shriek that ensued . . . Jack the Ripper would have wet himself. It went on and on and on, after which she came into the kitchen smiling. *That's better.* There she was next morning at the breakfast table, cheeks glowing, black hair pulled straight back from her face, eating her toast and drinking the tea that I made properly. Maud had heard that Ewan MacColl and I were entangled. She called him *that dreadful man* and hoped I wasn't getting deeply involved with him. He was a known womaniser and he was – she had trouble saying the word out loud – *political*. But then, she was one of a group of trustees (Princess Margaret was another) of Cecil Sharp House, the English Folk Dance and Song Society – the establishment organisation supporting English folk traditions. A priceless institution.

Spool forward to 1987 for a moment. The EFDSS has decided to give a Gold Badge Award to Ewan and me – a real honour. The ceremony had the atmosphere of a Montague–Capulet wedding. The traditional sponsors and members of the society occupied the left side of the aisle – dressed for an occasion, sitting vertical and deep in *sotto voce* conversation. Our raucous, streetwise, comradely, casually dressed folk-club friends congregated on the right side, laughing, talking, lounging and socialising *forte voce*. Maud was long gone by that time but she'd have relished the sight of the warring factions trying to share the aisle. She would have sat with the Right, who, strangely, had chosen to sit on the left-hand side of the hall. Spooling back again, Maud and I were not on *sympathique* terms, but we got on well. To my surprise, she left me in charge of her flat when she went abroad for a couple of weeks. The *dreadful man* came over to record my album for Folkways, *Animal Folk Songs for Children*, lugging his elephantine Ferrograph tape machine up four flights of stairs.* Love is.

While I had been in Poland, work had begun on *The Ballad of John Axon*, a true English Casey Jones story set to music. It was our first Radio Ballad, a sixty-minute aural tapestry with a warp of music (both instrumental and vocal) and weft of actuality (recorded speech and sound effects). The Radio Ballads were woven together by a master dramatist and songwriter (Ewan MacColl); a seasoned BBC radio producer (Charles Parker); and a classically trained folk musician (Peggy Seeger), tripling as instrumentalist, amateur music arranger and director. In very simple terms: they were originally meant to narrate the impact of work on those who perform it. A temporary work permit was arranged for me. This was my first really big creative job and the programme was breaking new ground in radio. It tested me to the limit. I was so inexperienced – but I was the daughter of a woman who, in her late twenties, had travelled solo through Europe in the early 1930s seeking out experimental composers like herself. I was also Charlie's self-confident angel/fool. I danced fearlessly on pinheads. I was now working with a small group of mature male session musicians, all of whom had known one another for decades. A session musician is one you hire by the hour or by the job. They were mostly unionised back

---

* In my lifetime, recording apparatus has progressed from weighing too much to carry to being hard to find if you misplace it. Sound formats have moved from acoustic to electric to magnetic to digital, from earth to aether: stylus and record-cutting machine (Charlie recording me at age seven), the discs being metal, cardboard, vinyl; wire recorders; analogue tape, single- then multi-track; cassettes; Betamax/VHS cartridges for video sound; DATs; CDs; to digital audio files (MP3s) . . . all within my eight decades.

then and incredibly skilled. They were seasoned swimmers and I was out of my depth. I made so many mistakes and they were so patient with me. I didn't know that you had to transpose the clarinet key when scoring it. I wrote for the English concertina as if it was an accordion. One member of my little orchestra bought me a present: Henry Mancini's guide to orchestration, *Sounds and Scores*, commenting that it would put everyone out of their misery.

The Musicians' Union requires a fifteen-minute break in the middle of a three-hour session. That's when we'd stop to smoke, pee, chat or talk about whatever. I'll find a quiet corner and remember an old friend.

17

Alf Edwards

Alf Edwards was the only musician who played on all eight of the Radio Ballads. He was the son of circus performers – *augustes*, he called them, aerial circus entertainers who traversed Europe up until World War I. His mother could *play the fiddle standing on her head on a tightrope when she was pregnant*, said Alf with ruler-straight face. He was proud of having been born backstage and cradled in a props basket. His mother gave him a sixpence every time he learned a new instrument. He was passable on the trombone, clarinet, ocarina and any number of others but unsurpassed on the English concertina, an angelic instrument that's devilish to learn. Alf was a courtly man, old-fashioned and slow-moving. He was five foot eight, somewhat overweight, with a pasty-white complexion – probably due to the fact that he lived in a basement flat and spent most of his time in recording studios. He was old-style with women, would always open doors for me and rise to offer me his seat. He was proper to a T, which occasionally wound up the less restrained members of our musical sodality. When Alf turned up to a session with a broken toe and the excuse of turning over in bed, he got, *Oh yes, mate, just thrashing around in bed all on your tod!*

---

* Cockney rhyming slang, abbreviation for *all on your Tod Sloan* – all on your own.

The concertina was new to me until *The Ballad of John Axon*. Alf blanched when he saw his score but remained calm. He would point at one of the score-sheets: *You can't do that on the concertina, Peg-Tops, but I'll try if you write out the notes for me.* Never call me Peg. Peg was Ewan's speciality. If you've been calling me Peg for ages and I haven't corrected you, that means I like it. Peggy-O, Peg o' My Heart, Peggy Sue, anything but Peg. Back at rehearsal, Peg-Tops wrote out what she wanted Alf to play: a melody line with chords signified by the letters – G, G7, D7, etc. This is what you'd do for a folk guitarist who plays by ear and who can just barely sight-read anything. Alf couldn't play by ear, couldn't improvise. He had to have every damn crotchet, rest and bar-line written down. He could play Bach's Two-Part Inventions on the English concertina. He could sight-read anything, in any key, at any pace, and for as long as you wanted him to play. But a G7 chord . . .? Dear Alf – he moved his glasses further down his nose and rewrote my score into something doable. It wasn't until I learned to play the English concertina myself that I discovered that Alf had actually been playing the impossible. Years later, the Nigerian griot Tunde Jegede would do the same for me on the kora.

In 1962, dissatisfied with many of my guitar and banjo accompaniments for Ewan's songs, I bought a Lachenal English concertina and went up to London every fortnight for lessons with Alf. It's the hardest instrument I have ever tackled, the major difficulty being that the buttons on the right hand play the notes that are in spaces on the musical staff and the left hand plays the notes that are on staff lines. On most instruments, the left and right hands have different functions – one frets, the other strums; one plays chords, the other plays melody; one plays bass, the other plays treble, etc. The hands do equal duty on the English concertina. My right hand was stronger than my left and we spent many lessons trying to equalise them. Alf didn't allow me to pick the concertina up and search visually for the desired button. You picked it up and immediately found the key you wanted by feel alone. We spent a month on the easiest key, C major. Arpeggios, scales, octaves – like the hated Czerny exercises that Dio had given me on the piano. When I had the key of C under my belt, Alf added a sharp to the signature and we ran through the same routine in the key of G. Subtract a sharp and add a flat and run through the routine and random finds in F. Alf decided that I would become a good player and instructed me to order a fifty-six-button Wheatstone – I got one of the last concertinas that Wheatstone made, soft reeds for accompanying singing and buttons that needed next to no effort.

Alf and his wife Jean lived in Holland Park, in the basement of a Victorian terrace house. It was a subterranean nest of rooms that consisted of a kitchen for half a person, a bathroom the same, Alf's windowless music room, and the front room that doubled as a bedroom. A large sofa, which could be made up into a double bed, backed onto the huge front windows that looked out, sous-terrain, onto the legs and up the skirts of passers-by. My lessons were held in this room. Jean had terminal cancer. Their relationship was one of sorrow and bitterness. They had wanted children, but she needed an operation to unblock her fallopian tubes. The operation cost £20, a galactic amount at the time. By the time they had saved up £20, the price had gone up to £40. By the time they had £40 . . . and so on. When the folk revival came along and Alf was in demand, Jean was past childbearing age. Now, lying on the sofa, dying, she retold daily her devastating disappointment and the story of the £20 that haunted her. My weekly presence at that time was her last straw: by then, I was expecting my second child. When I ballooned out into full pregnancy, we moved from the living/bed/sick room to Alf's work-cave.

One day Jean wasn't there. She'd requested hospice care and died shortly after. Alf began to look old and sad but he wanted to talk about how I felt as my nine months progressed. I invited him to put his hand on my belly. The baby moved its whole body around and Alf's eyes filled with tears. We both chuckled as I tried to balance the concertina on my belly. In early March we had a last lesson before my confinement. On this occasion, he produced a superb steak and a bottle of St Emilion. He was as excellent and precise a cook as he was a musician. He served the dinner ceremonially, with tablecloth and napkins. He held his glass of wine up against the candle flame. Looking through it before sipping it with his little finger crooked ever so properly, he said softly, *You know, Peg-Tops, I really wanted children.*

Alf was born around the turn of the century. He and I worked well together despite our difference in age. He respected the folk aspects of my upbringing, admired that I could improvise, play by ear and play the banjo while directing the musicians. I admired his ability to sight-read anything on so many instruments. For years he was the one and only English concertina player we had. He taught me, knowing all the while that I would probably take his place accompanying Ewan and Bert Lloyd on sea shanties and country songs. Alf didn't have a malicious, jealous or harsh bone in his body. He was our old-world gentleman musician. After the Radio Ballads were discontinued, we only saw him infrequently. Parkinson's had ambushed him. He showed me how he could no longer hold his hand steady to copy his mammoth scores. He signed himself into an old people's home in Worthing. It is to Ewan's and my eternal shame that we never visited him there. I'd phone him up occasionally and his friend John Campbell would sometimes phone me to say that Alf would like to hear from us. I phoned the home in the autumn of 1985 and was told he'd died. I was six months too late. Years too late.

Concertina players remember him as the pivot point at which the instrument arrived and thrived on the folk scene, even though his accompaniments for folk song are a little mechanical, his real skills untapped. He was indeed a relic from times gone past. I wanted you to know him just a little, for you to help me keep him alive and coming forward with us. His collection of concertinas, tiny treble to huge bass, were sold one by one. Sometimes they appear on eBay. The family of concertina players in the English revival are the children he craved.

18

Conversation in France

After that fifteen-minute break we pick up the session again in spring 1958. Maud has returned from her travels. She is a model of diplomacy. Suddenly, Bert Lloyd, whose wavery-savoury style of singing had always charmed me, invites me to stay at his home in Greenwich, a historic terrace house facing the observatory and the park. Bert's wife, Charlotte, deaf since her teens, had just had a fenestration operation to restore her hearing. A four-string fretless banshee had taken up residence in her home: Peggy was learning the fiddle. Even those with lifelong hearing would have had trouble with that – Charlotte found it insupportable. With nowhere to practise, the fiddle gave me up. I'd never have made a good fiddle player anyway. In 1956, Ewan had taken me to visit his artist friend L. S. Lowry. A jumble of frames, paint, brushes, turps; scattered and hung squares of canvas, featuring formalised factories, peas-in-a-pod terraces of two-up-two-down houses, grey skies. His bone-thin figures walked all over the room and up the walls. I loved his work. He kept some of his brushes in an old Toby jug. Bert Lloyd was a Toby jug – wide smile and jolly face. At meal-times he had a huge napkin tucked up under his triple chin. Charlotte was a Lowry woman, spindly-thin and quick. She disliked Ewan intensely, warning me off him as Maud had done. *He's a weak man. You need someone more reliable.* She never mentioned the fact that he was married and had a son.

I'd displaced the four-string banjo player who'd plucked for the British folk revival so far. A member of his family pointed out to the Home Office that Peggy Seeger's work permit had expired several weeks ago. In May, before *John Axon* was finished, I received two days' notice to quit the country. I pointed out that I played the *five*-string banjo, the true subject of all those banjo jokes. Britain needed laughter. The Home Office didn't laugh. Mid-May I went down to Dover and over to Boulogne. Anyone with a microgram of common sense would have waited a month and returned via Portsmouth – in those pre-internet days it would take weeks for Portsmouth to communicate with Dover. But no, two weeks later I returned via Dover. I was taken from Customs directly to the headquarters of the marine police. Unsaid: *Private Britain was saluting General America.* Said: *I was to be sent back to Boulogne in the morning.* Their excuse: my lack of money, although money was awaiting me at American Express in London. My problem: I had to collect it personally. Not possible. I'm in jail. I phoned Ewan in a panic. He hired a London taxi – one of those iconic British jobbies that can do a U-turn on a ha'penny piece – and came down to Dover. £10 without tip – an enormous amount for someone who never had enough money. Love is, once again. I'm lying on a bunk in a cell, crying. *England is beginning to feel like home, Ewan.* Head down, he is holding my hand. *I'll see what I can do. I love you, Peg.* His cigarette glows in the dark.

The next morning, I was on the boat back to Boulogne, a heavy black ink X over yesterday's entrance stamp on my passport. Comrades from the China trip had told me to keep a good firm grip on my passport when in the presence of authority. Confiscation of documents at entry and exit points was one of the most common ways of making sure that we would have to return home. Over the next week the French authorities slipped me over the border into Belgium. The Belgians dumped me on the Dutch, who put me right back over the Belgian border. All the transfers were done at night, politely, with no stamping of the passport onto which I held tightly. Within one week I was in four countries, after which the French either slipped up or gave up.

Something was keeping me from just going back to the States. By early June I was in Paris looking up some of Charlie's contacts. In 1955, he had printed up visiting cards for me – *Introducing my daughter, Peggy*, etc. I was to knock on the door of said contact, leave the card on the silver tray brought by the butler, wait for the answer or make an arrangement to come back when convenient. I never met a butler. Maud had accepted her card with solemnity and without a silver tray. Now, worn out with being shoved across borders, I was at the door of Charlie's old friend Luiz Heitor Corrêa de Azevedo, the Brazilian journalist, musicologist and folklorist. He hugged me, my card in his hand. He adored Pont-l'Évêque cheese. He and his wife had sent one to Kirke Street for Christmas in the early 1950s. The parcel arrived in late November and sat unopened in the corner of the dining room for several weeks before we sussed out that the fart smells were cheese, not any of us children. The Azevedo flat reeked of it, but by the time you've tucked into a good ripe one at a candle-lit table with a South American aristocrat, a bottle of Nuits-Saint-Georges and a fresh baguette the aroma just adds to the joy. I slept on a feather bed, wore beautiful Cherie Azevedo nightgowns and probably drove Luiz Heitor mad with banjo playing. After a week, I moved into a very cheap hotel near the university. Many floors up under the eaves, the room was about ten feet long and seven or eight feet wide with a sloping roof. The little window looked out onto the other three sides of the square that formed the courtyard. The life across and below was like a movie. I sat on a high stool by the barred window, playing the banjo and singing to the young mother across the courtyard as she hung diapers out. I wrote letters to Charlie while lovers in the next room gave forth with a trio of sounds: bed-springs whanging, him grunting, and her sighing then shouting *Henri! Henri! HENRI!* I spent days walking around Paris, making my breakfast of half a dozen croissants dipped in café-au-lait last nearly till dinner-time. Money from *John Axon* paid for another Lambretta.

Late May 1958 – a perfect time not to be alone in Paris. Ewan and I were a mismatch and at odds, but all of a sudden I wanted very much to see him. He always came when I called, poor man. I scootered up to Boulogne, then east to Cap Gris Nez and found a little inn right near the water. I took the room because of the colour of the wallpaper – a lovely pale salmon-orange. Ewer and basin to wash in and a window that looked out over the dunes to the sea. On a fine day I thought I could see the pencil-thin line of the white cliffs of Dover. At that time, Boulogne was not a place where the English went to fill up on duty-free goods. It was just a northern French coastal town with a modest fishing port, ferries to England and a vibrant market place. Ewan came off the boat with his old knapsack on. He was fit and slender, in walking boots and shorts. He had good legs, good shoulders – appealing, almost boyish. His freckles had all joined up and he looked continental. He came up to me without smiling. *I've only come to say goodbye, Peg. It's time to finish with it.* Two years ago he'd declared his willingness to leave Jean. He'd waited for two years for me to decide and now he wanted out. The tension in Croydon was tearing him apart. We scootered to the inn, left his knapsack and walked over the dunes. There were little places to sit, sheltered from the wind, stone benches worn down by centuries of sitters. With lovemaking off his mind, we could talk. We sat holding hands and talked. Have you heard this one? One man confides to the other, *She had her way with me. We talked all night.* We talked along the beach, talked into sunset and went into town for supper. We'd known each other now for two and a half tumultuous years. The chase became a dance. Hunter and quarry shape-shift into a pas de deux. In that one day things came right between us. So right that when we came back to our little room with its apricot walls, we could talk in bed. *I'll do anything for you, Peg, even marry you.* Through the night we talked about working together, about his divorce. *Let's have a baby . . .* We were delighted with ourselves, even as we tumbled into a financial abyss. He stayed several days, during which we walked, bathed, ate, underslept and overslept. He was worried. Did I really mean what I said? Truly? *Yes.*

> *Two rivers turn and flow into one*
> *The ocean lies waiting, it gleams in the sun . . .*
> ('Autumn Wedding')

He went home to tell his family. I scootered back to Paris and my fleapit hotels. I couldn't get into England and we'd have no work in France. He tried to contact people in radio and television who could arrange work that would bring me to England. The Americans wanted me back and the British Home Office has long tentacles. We were stuck. In late June, I woke up nauseous every morning. *Let's have a baby . . .* July was a long month. Morning sickness can last well into the day, every day for weeks. I found a shop that sold Dutch salted herrings and boosted its income noticeably. I became acquainted with an American girl, Laura Pincus. She loved the scooter. *Let's go to Brittany*. Did I consider that I was now responsible for the life of another human being? Did I think about preparing for an event that would change my life forever? Did I study up on what to eat, what to expect during the next nine months, the next twenty years? *Brittany? Why not? Let's go.* I was going further away from Ewan, where his letters couldn't reach me, where he wouldn't know from day to day where or how we were. Already I am *we*.

Laura and I had very little money and no itinerary. We stopped at a farmhouse and asked if we could sleep in the barn. We curled up in our sleeping bags and slept like two babies. Three. In the morning, the daughter of the house came out with a tray – two huge plates of strawberries and cream and two bowls of strong café-au-lait. *Practise random kindness and senseless acts of beauty* may be cheesy, but random kindness can last a long time. In the middle of the next day there was a sudden downpour. We huddled in a barn with a group of country people on their way to market with produce and livestock. *Do your parents know you are doing this? Nice French girls don't do this.* Our huddle-mates gave us some fruit and we took off as soon as the storm was over. After seeing Mont St Michel Laura headed back to Paris. Ewan was due to come over in several weeks, so I began looking for a romantic retreat. Beyond St Malo, at the very end of one of those little appendices that poke out into the Channel, there's a modest family hotel. Isolated. Quiet. Perfect. I took a room in a family hotel and painted the scooter silver. Ewan flew into Cherbourg on the big pot-bellied plane that brought vehicles over to north-west France. He stayed for longer this time. He was worn out with the strife at home but he never brought the trouble to me – like the plumber in Edward Lewis Wallant's superb novel *Human Season* who, however dirty his job had been in the day, always came clean into the marital bed at night.

Ewan was delighted that I was pregnant. *I knew at the time that I put a baby in you, Peg.* He'd brought his little Gilwell camping set. We made tea and cooked meals on the beach. He was teaching me to rock-climb. There was one place where the path narrowed, skirted a cliff face and led to a three-sided stone room with a floor that sloped downward. The fourth side was a fifty-foot drop to the sea. We had to edge around the cliff using inch-wide foot- and hand-holds. We took this route regularly and he'd hold me and talk to me so that I could push my fear down to manageable levels. I didn't like the sport. Ewan loved it. Later, when he'd gone back to England, I dared myself to go alone to our little room – once and never again. The next time Ewan came, he brought with him the score of *The Death of Hector*, with music by Mátyás Seiber. It was a complicated piece, twenty minutes long. He was to record it with several musicians in a few weeks' time. He didn't read music, so I taught him the whole thing by rote as we sat on the cliffs and beaches. I sang the instrumental parts, counted out the rests and cue phrases and he would come in with that rich, self-confident, chocolate voice.

One morning, sitting at breakfast, I had absolutely nothing to say to him. He had been doing all the talking. I felt like a piece of blank paper. Our table was sunlit, a still-life of crois-sants, café-au-lait and my featureless person. For once, Ewan fell silent. We sat there awkwardly. Our landlord's fifth daugh-ter had been born in the night. Crestfallen, he came in to toast the little one's health with us. *La dernière. No more, no more, no son . . . no son.* Ewan took my hand. *We don't have to talk, you know, Peg. You don't have to talk. I've just gotten so used to talking. You have to stop me if I go on too long.* It was as if he had read my mind. The next time he said that was after a lengthy interview with a journalist, a year or two before he died. *You have to stop me if I go on too long, Peg . . .*

Early September. The American embassy hadn't found me and the French weren't bothering. I was plump, tanned and very fit. I spent long days on the beach, on the hills. One hot day, I just lay under the trees and watched the clouds change shape all afternoon. I played with the landlord's new baby. I polished up the scooter. The silver was wearing off – I'd used the wrong kind of paint. I headed back to Paris via the inland roads. Rainbow autumn leaves, the scattered treasure of northern realms everywhere. Ewan and I communicated via poste restante when I was en route. Ralph and I had no such hotline, but somehow I found him in Paris staying at the home of a friend. His room was tiny but we shared it. *Do you know anyone I can stay with, Ralph? I really need it.*

Lucienne Idoine. Ralph called her by her surname (pronounced *eed-WAN*) and thus so did I. She was a handsome woman, between thirty-five and forty years of age, about my height, with dark hair and piercing, sunken eyes. Her face was lined and she looked easily ten or fifteen years older than she was. She'd been in the French Resistance movement and had been captured and sent to Ravensbrück concentration camp, where she *existed*, as she put it, for several years. I tried not to imagine what that really meant. She couldn't bear to touch or be touched physically. Political to her core, she taught at the university and made her home a way station for anyone in need. She took me in without hesitation. No. 5 Rue Jacob was a large courtyard monitored by a female Cerberus guarding the gates of her very own Overworld. Every now and then the gift of a bottle of wine brought a snaggle-toothed smile. It was five storeys up to Idoine's minuscule flat. You entered directly into her parlour, a room about seven feet wide by thirteen feet long, just big enough for a bookcase, a sofa and a fold-up table, opened up at meal-times. The opposite door led into a wee kitchen where another door led out to a garret that held Idoine's bedspace, with a shower and toilet shared with the occupants of the adjoining flat. *Where is there room for me here?* On the living-room sofa-bed. My knapsack just fitted at the bottom of the bed and the instruments were stowed away behind the entrance door. Ralph partook of some couscous, gave me a hug and departed. I didn't see him again for a long, long time.

I wrote to Charlie and told him I was pregnant. As a joke, I wrote *Special Devilry* on the envelope. He wrote back, worried that his daughter – who had come fifth in the all-Washington DC spelling bee at age twelve – had misspelt *delivery.* The word the proper spelling of which would have kept me in the competition was *papacy.* Godless Charlie, sitting in the front row with ex-Methodist Dio, put his head in his hands. I knew about the Pope but not the papacy. Now Charlie telegraphed. *Shall I come over? Are you all right? Is Ewan going to take care of you? Keep in touch. I'll come if necessary.* I could more than manage the situation. I became a powerhouse. I was in and out of Idoine's flat several times a day, roaming around Paris either on scooter or off. I'd take the five storeys of steps two at a time both up and down, sometimes with both instruments, off to this or that club, this or that street corner. To play, not sing. My voice was unheard above the traffic. I lived at Idoine's for nearly three months. She never asked for rent – lucky, because I only had what I earned by busking or singing in little clubs. Instead, I took over the housework and shopping, for which she was grateful as she was rarely at home. I was a good girl. I kept the kitchen spotless. I swept, washed the floors and windows, did laundry, ironing and occasional mending. I was good at seeing what had to be done. I made my bed up afresh each night and turned it back into a sofa in the daytime. I began to dream in French.

I was waiting for Ewan to arrive in Boulogne. I'd taken a hotel room and was having supper in its little restaurant. For several days, I'd been watching the progress of the operations to rescue miners trapped underground at Springhill in Nova Scotia.* I wrote 'The Ballad of Springhill' over a bowl of grey tripe and onions. Ewan liked the song – but it needed a verse that sounded as if I'd been down a mine. He added it:

> *Down at the coalface miners working,*
> *Rattle of the belt and the cutter's blade,*
> *Rumble of rock and the walls close round*
> *The living and the dead men two miles down.*

We sang the song for the whole of his visit. I was very proud of it, my first good song. Many people think Ewan wrote it – I regard that as a compliment. It has now been adopted officially by the community of Springhill, even though the mine closed after the 1958 'bump' and never reopened.†

* The rescue operation after the earthquake at Springhill mine on 23 October 1958 was the first of its kind to be televised. Ninety-nine miners survived, some after enduring many days trapped below ground, but seventy-four died.
† In July 1997, on my way to the Canso Festival at the tip of Nova Scotia, I detoured to Springhill and met Caleb Rushton, celebrated in the song for keeping up the spirits of twelve entombed miners for eight days till rescue

Back and forth we went, he from Croydon to Boulogne
and back, me from Paris to Boulogne and back, right into
December. One day Idoine came in while I was on my hands
and knees washing the lovely old dark-red tiled floor of the little living space. She stood there observing me, ostensibly waiting for the floor to dry. *Tu est enceinte?* Unavoidable now. *Yes.*
She was adamant. *Off your knees – and no more washing of floors.*
I was healthy and only twenty-three. *As long as I can, I will
wash the floors.* She had never asked me about myself but now
she wanted to know about the baby's father. Wary of Home
Office investigation, of French morals regarding married men
and unmarried motherhood, I hadn't told her where I went
when I disappeared. Idoine said that I should invite Ewan to
the Rue Jacob instead of making the trip to Boulogne in below-
zero weather. They took to each other immediately. They were
the same age, their politics were identical, their histories were
sympathetic and my, but they were both talkers! They jabbered
on, for Idoine's English was heavily accented but excellent. She
cooked Algerian food for the three of us. The little flat was cosy
and warm. I came to the narrow sofa bed and Ewan's arms
slipped round me. We lay like two spoons in a drawer, a complete Being. Me, him, and the baby – us. We lit a candle and

---

arrived. The song was sung regularly at school and church functions. It was
Caleb's job, when he attended these occasions, to stand up at the appropriate
point and sing his line:

> Three days passed and the lamps gave out
> And Caleb Rushton he up and said,
> 'There's no more water nor light nor bread
> So we'll live on songs and hope instead,
> Live on songs and hope instead.'

watched the ebb and flow of the little head moving in my belly. We blew the candle out, laughed and talked and fell asleep.

> *When first we loved and when our life was new*
> *Time lay before us like the space around a star . . .*
> ('Thoughts of Time')

Christmas. I bought a small tree and decorated it. I put a few presents under it and held a little ceremony with candles and wine. Idoine was delighted. She asked where I was going to have the baby. Charlie, Idoine and Ewan are doing the worrying. I'm just coasting along. *When is it due?* I didn't know. *Shall we see a doctor and arrange to have the baby born in Paris?* I don't know. What kind of mother am I going to be with this kind of non-planning? The true reality had never hit me. I just had this precious invader who kept moving around inside me. That was entertainment all on its own. I would lie and watch the head come up into a great hump and then subside. Then a little heel or elbow would jut out on the side of my stomach and I'd have to shift my position or I'd get a cramp. I'd try to work out which part of it was poking out. I could be lying perfectly still, then, all of a sudden, there was an eggbeater in there, thrashing in all directions. The thought of our ever being separated was inconceivable. I had never been good at looking forward – but maybe we had better make plans. Tomorrow. Ewan came over for New Year's Eve. We bought ourselves a bottle of excellent port and some cheese and bread and took ourselves off to larger, more private quarters for the night. We had two objectives: (1) To talk about what we were going to do in the New Year regarding getting me and our baby-song over to England. (2) To finish the bottle of port.

19

A New Family

I love you so much, Ewan, that I'll marry someone else. We
decided that I should become a British wife – but whose? Alex
Campbell was the obvious choice. He thought a lot of Ewan
and knew that my bump was of Ewan's doing. Yes – he's kind
enough, single enough and daft enough to be just the right person. A tall, rangy Scot with wild red hair and beard, he was a
good-natured rake and a heavy drinker. Alex caroused for a
living. He sang in the streets, his woolly hat on the pavement,
his red-wine smile ever blooming. I hadn't the knack or voice
for street singing and my hands responded too quickly to cold
weather. I went regularly with Alex and worked the crowd with
a child's potty for donations. Pregnant with a brave, put-on,
poor-me face plus his thin, half-starved physique brought the
money rolling in. Every now and then we'd break for my frequent pee-stops or for a *croque-monsieur*, those ham and cheese
toasties that play a definite first fiddle to the American grilled
cheese sandwich. Alex was more than willing to do us a favour.
Idoine helped me figure out that I was due in a little under two
months, so we'd have to hurry. Speed was not the style of the
American embassy but I had to have their co-operation. They'd
been looking for me but they weren't pleased to see me. *She's
whaaat? Lost her passport, the most valuable of her worldly possessions?* Add pregnant and unmarried to that and I was their
perfect storm. The embassy wanted to deport me back home,

but there was that problem belly and my weepy face. *I can't go home. What would the baby do without its father? What would Alex do without me? He's going to do the right thing.* Doing the right thing is part of the American Dream, especially if it pays off. They didn't want to add a small international incident to their endless list of ginormous big ones. I could get married on my youth hostel card. Two birds with one stone – me off their hands and one less Red at home.

Four and three-quarters of us in a French church on 24 January 1959: an official representative of God and the USA in sneakers and dirty surplice; me and Mine with a size-20 coat over our front porch; scruffy Alex in his best torn jeans; and our one witness and very bestest, best man, Derroll Adams, the ever-so-laid back American Banjoman and singer, who happened to be in town – another treasure of a person. Alex and I vow to love each other till death do us part. I think I had to obey him as well. After the little ceremony, we signed the papers and Surplice-and-Sneakers beckoned Alex into the vestry. *A word with you, Sonny.* After twenty minutes, Alex came out trying to look chastened. We four – my bump legitimate now – trooped out at pregnant pace into crisp, cold Paris. Once in the street, Alex whooped and hollered, a memorable bout of hysterical laughter. We bundled him into the nearest bistro, where we killed a bottle of champagne, thanks to 'The Road and the Miles to Dundee' and 'Auld Lang Syne', which we'd busked pre-wedding at one of the main traffic intersections. When you have a story, tell it well – and Alex did. God's man had seared him on the coals of Christianity for getting me into this condition and for waiting so long to make an honest woman of me. He warned Alex of the trials and tribulations of marriage and gave him advice regarding the volatility, changeability and impossibility of women, especially the sexual unavailability of heavily pregnant ones. He offered congratulations on the impending birth and expostulated on the duties and pleasures of fatherhood. None of us wanted to calm down. We rollicked until Derroll saw us off on the night sleeper to London.

25 January – Robert Burns's two hundredth birthday and Ewan's forty-fourth. He was there on the platform when the train pulled into Waterloo Station. Alex took my hand and placed it in Ewan's. *Here's your woman.* Was I, so newly acquired, being given away already? I wasn't a feminist back then. *Thank you, thank you,* and a little kick of farewell from the little one to its legal daddy, who's off to rant and roar in Soho. Alex is long dead now and I am left with deep regret that I didn't thank him enough. I was Mrs Alex Campbell until 1961, when Alex asked for a divorce so as to marry his Pat. Thank you both, Pat and Alex. After two weeks, we found a first-floor flat – called a second-floor apartment in the USA – in a small semi-detached house. 55 Godstone Road, Purley, Surrey. Funky little place, set back around forty feet from a busy bus route that – west to east – connected two of the big north-to-south spoke-roads out of London. It was owned by Mr and Mrs Crabbe, who were so concerned for the wellbeing of their cast-off carpets that they put them into No. 55 upside down, filthy underside up. British itty-bitty standard basic gas fires, postage-stamp front and back grass patches which we were supposed to care for. No fridge. Keep the milk on the ledge of the single-glazed window. We took a one-year lease.

We had one night together before Betsy came. Jean: *If your son goes, you go too.* Poor old lady, of course she can live with us. She can sleep in the little single bed in the tiny front bed-room. In Jean's house, she's knitted a complicated traditional shawl for my baby. It's beautiful – about four foot square, in four-ply blue wool. A lovely gift. She is now knitting one for Jean's baby in my house – poetic justice of a sort. Betsy knits like the Parisian women at the guillotine. Betsy knits in parlour and kitchen, a spider in the midst of a massive expanding white web. She seems to know not to make it blue. She was less than five feet tall, a tough-heart to my tenderfoot. She had muddy moods, draining away the emotional energy of the house. She'd look at me as if I was responsible for every disappointing thing that had ever happened to her. It was our house when Betsy was in good spirits, hers when she wasn't. And yet . . . whenever Ewan and I came in late after a gig, the kettle was always on the hob, just about to boil. Our plates would be set, bread on the breadboard and butter and jam in little pots on the table. *There was a little girl who had a little curl* . . . Sometimes Betsy would still be up and she and Ewan would chat sociably.

Once I learned about her life, it became easier. Born in 1886 in Auchterarder, Scotland, one of fourteen children, she left school at fourteen. She wanted to be a nurse and would have been an excellent one, but her father sent her into service in the Reverend Goodall's house. Her face would contort when she talked about her sixteen-hour workday as a skivvy under the housekeeper, her older sister Belle. Her meagre but welcome wages were brought home to the huge family of siblings. Her husband, Will Miller – an iron-moulder with debilitating asthma – was continually blacklisted because of his political activities. Betsy went out charring and cleaning houses in Salford to keep the family afloat. Plagued with devastating, full-body psoriasis for six months of every year, she lived on a self-imposed diet of bread and butter, builder's tea and occasional protein. She had two late miscarriages, then a daughter who died shortly after birth, then her little Billy dead at the age of three. Ewan nearly died of gastroenteritis when he was eight. Ewan was her jewel, her one deep joy – and Ewan was in love with an upstart American twenty years his junior. The last straw in her disappointing life.

A son's a son till he takes a wife. A daughter's a daughter for all of her life. In jokes and funny songs, the mother-in-law is always the wife's mother. Poking fun at her, rendering her ridiculous to her daughter, helps to alienate the two women – a necessary part of wife-stealing. Not so the husband's mother. In the jokes and ballads she is terrifying, desperate to be the most important woman in her son's life. Ridicule places adversaries above and below. Anger puts adversaries on an equal level, his mother in this corner, his bride in that one. In 'Prince Robert' – No. 87 of the magnificent Francis Child ballad collection – mother kills son so wife cannot have him. In 'Willie's Lady' – No. 6 – husband's mother puts a spell on his pregnant wife, making it impossible for her to give birth. Spoiler: Willie's wife *does* outsmart the old lady. I had no desire to outsmart Betsy. I just wanted to live peaceably with her. Without her we could not have managed in those early years. She opened up a world I would never have seen otherwise, but she kept herself closed. An impenetrable shell protected her central core. The Salford Saga – the pre-Jean and pre-Peggy story – was straight out of Dickens or Smollett, a world of Betsies. It swamped my life story, in which neither mother-in-law nor son showed much interest. Memories of Betsy fill me more with compassion than anger. She represents millions of women who have lives like hers and must work for or alongside women who have lives like mine.

That night I said nothing to Ewan until we were in bed. *Betsy says Jean's having a baby. It's not true, is it?* Yes, it was. He cursed Betsy for telling me before my confinement, saying he should never have brought her near me. He cursed Jean, cursed her baby. *Oh, no, no, no. It's a baby, Ewan! It's your baby. It doesn't matter.* He told me all the circumstances under which it had happened – so understandable, a tragedy avoided. Betsy corroborated the story later, in passing. Ewan's arms were around me, mine around him, close as if trying to mend the vessel of love that now had a major hole in it. He was crying, not the first time I had seen him cry. I'm sure some of his tears were for what he suspected he had lost but hoped he hadn't. I trusted his love. *Making your wife pregnant . . . isn't infidelity . . . is it? But don't you have to feel desire to be able to . . .? And doesn't he love me more than . . .?* Shameful thought: *I hope he loves my baby more than hers.* He said over and over how wonderfully I was taking it, how wonderfully. Nothing mattered more at that moment than comforting his terrible sorrow, so yes, I was wonderful. Later, I wouldn't be. Much later, having fallen hopelessly in love with someone else, I would understand that you can love two people at once. I needed that understanding in 1959.

We found a kindly GP down in Purley Village. He plied me with iron pills, told me to wear a bra at night and arranged a midwife and a home delivery. *Midwife??? Where am I? Dio had gone to the hospital . . .* Mrs Crabbe wanted assurance that I wouldn't be having the baby on her property. There would be blood splashed all over her downside-up carpets. Even while arranging for a home birth, we assured her that the baby wouldn't be born at home. On 3 March we went to town on the scooter to have lunch with the head of Mills Music, who were bringing out *The Singing Island*, a small book of songs that we'd hastily drawn up together. A very happy Someone burst into the room. 'Side Saddle', a Mills property, had hit the top of the charts. It featured Russ Conway playing the piano, a catchy but most unlikely candidate for a No. 1 hit. One moment we were discussing an anthology of English folk songs and the next moment we were on a football pitch, our Mills Man a manic referee, the players competing for the position of finding the songwriter who would take over from Russ when 'Side Saddle' began to slip sideways. Desk-jockeys were going to *tell musicians what to do? Where am I? It should have a solo piano, yes, but maybe add another instrument; try changing the key. No, don't change the metre, keep it in major; we need the feel of 'Side Saddle' with . . . just that little something new.* Mills Man: *I want it by Monday!* The players left. MM turned back to us. *Now, where were we?* Music moves the savage purse, quickly.

I had to drive the scooter home because my bump was too big for riding pillion. By the time we turned into the uphill drive-way of No. 55, I was in labour. Call the Midwife. Betsy laid out towels and hot water and darted out to the little shops a block away to get more tea, milk and bread. Ewan had never attended a birth before but he stayed with me right through it. I hadn't expected that. Hoping that her grandchild would be born today, 3 March, her birthday, Betsy hovered outside the birthing bedroom. I should have asked her to come in. From age fourteen she had assisted her midwife mother at many a birth. Ewan was grey with fear and far too sensitive for all the blood and liquids. Two hours after midnight and it was over. Once the baby is put in our arms, we forget the excruciating pain of childbirth, described by Carol Burnett as *taking your lower lip and forcing it over your head*. Our neighbours down-stairs didn't even know until morning that a child had been born above their heads. Ewan congratulated me on not scream-ing. I think screaming would have helped.

They laid him on my chest and waited for the afterbirth. I love remembering all this. His little fingers wrapped around my thumb and I just dissolved. Part of me was still a child and this was the present I'd always wanted. They cleaned me up, revived Ewan and we all slept. We'd bought no cradle and had only one or two pieces of baby wear – Betsy had said it was bad luck to buy specially in advance in case the baby died. Neill was clad in a long flannel baby-dress and laid in the bottom drawer of the big wardrobe. Betsy softened. She loved babies. Whenever I was weary or working – usually both – she took Neill from me and sat crooning to him. She'd bring him in to be nursed, carry him out to change him. We both handwashed the nappies and Betsy wrung them out with her working wom-an's hands. Until our first decent fee bought a spin-dryer, we hung the white squares out on the line, brought them in fresh from the wind and draped them over the wall radiator in the bathroom. In damp old England you didn't bring clothes in and just fold them and put them away. You *aired* them at room temperature or exposed them to indoor heat to make sure the damp was completely out of the seams. The spiders loved those warm layers of towelling and scuttled out when I shook and folded them. Betsy made nourishing soups and stews, tripe and onions in milk – white, not grey like French tripe. Ewan and I were working on the albums *Songs of Robert Burns* and *Songs of Two Rebellions*. Neill lay beside me while I taught Ewan the tunes out of the *Scots Musical Museum* and worked at accompa-niments. We four coalesced into a family.

Betsy lived as frugally as if she were still in Salford, refusing to take money from us. She was full of warnings. Don't put green on the baby – wrap him in the colour of the fairies and they will come for him. Superstitions die hard. How many green automobiles do you see on the road? Don't let your child look in a mirror till he's a year old – he'll be seeing himself in the afterlife. As each of the children came along, she opened up a penny-a-week burial insurance policy for them. It was the 1960s and she still paid for Ewan's policy, opened at his birth in 1915. Just in case. Once every three months, the insurance man came to the door in our prosperous south London suburb. Betsy would give him two shillings and sixpence and he'd stamp her little books. *She's paying pennies to bury herself, her son or her grandchildren if they were to die? Where am I?* I had been brought up in cloud cuckoo land, a.k.a. the middle class.

Ewan and I laughed a lot. One night the phone rang. It was on the ground floor, shared with our downstairs neighbours, who would answer it, ringing our doorbell if the call was for us. I was feeding Neill in his high chair, so Ewan went down. A BBC producer wanted me for a programme – me, not us. As he took over the chocolate pudding spoon, Ewan gave some curt instructions: *Stay focused. Short sentences. No ums. Be businesslike. Don't sound too eager. Refer them to Felix* (our agent at the time). Down I go. I am doing my best when I hear a little whistle from the landing. Ewan is standing there, his stomach poked out, dressed only in my very skimpy bikini, into the bra of which he has stuffed huge wads of clean nappies. He's posing and making suggestive moves with his hips, a lecherous grin on his face. I finish the conversation and hang up. We sit on the stairs falling to pieces with laughter. *Good-oh, Peg. Don't allow yourself to be distracted when you're doing your job.*

My American passport had no expiry date but it was obviously not reliable as a travel document. Be safe. 22 April 1959 finds me in a seedy little solicitor's office in Lincoln's Inn Fields, in front of a flyblown photo of a Royal Woman whose progress I'd followed via my childhood scrapbook. I, Margaret Campbell, swore that I would be *faithful and bear true allegiance to Her Majesty Queen Elizabeth, her heirs and successors, according to law. So help me God.* From now on I would be sailing under British colours. We sang every week at the Ballads and Blues Club, in the upstairs room of the Princess Louise on High Holborn, London. I'd come back late at night, gorged with milk, bringing to 100 my 99 per cent identification with the cows in the barn at Putney. Betsy brings Neill in. *The dairy's arrived!* She knew dozens of Scots songs but diddled the tunes, *dow-die, dow-die, dow-die, dow*, to Neill as she dandled him on her knee. Neill began crowing *dowdie dowdie*, which gave rise to the name by which we all knew her till she died: Dodo. The five of us – Ewan, Peggy, Neill, Betsy and the Shawl – would have a companionable late-night snack and go to bed. In the morning, Betsy would bring us a cup of tea, take Neill and clean him up, and bring him back to bed shining and ready for the breast. She laboured without complaint, carried more than her own scant weight. We both became possible to live with. Maybe if warring dictators had to share care of a baby . . .?

Jean's white shawl grew daily. The wife was now *the other woman*. We had both been pregnant at the same time and each of us had been pregnant when the other wasn't, un-pregnant when the other *was*. For the last three weeks of February and through the long hot summer while I was nursing, Betsy knitted for a baby whose coming drove a thin but permanent wedge into the unity that Ewan and I had taken so long to build. Ewan

Dio, Mike, Charlie and me, c. 1937

Clockwise from top left, Mike, Penny, Charlie, Dio, me, Barbara, c. 1947.
The photo is probably by a 'Mrs Williams' who turned up every three
or four years to capture us, yet again

Elizabeth 'Libba' Cotten, early 1960s

Pete (*centre*) as we'd have known him in our childhood. Woody
Guthrie is on the left, late 1930s

The *face,* three years before Ewan saw it. High-school yearbook, 1953

Me, Ralph Rinzler and Lambretta, 1957

My German urchins in Belgium, early 1956

The Ramblers, 1956. *Clockwise from top left*, Alan Lomax, Bruce
Turner, Jim Bray, Brian Daly, Shirley Collins, Ewan, me

Busking in Moscow, 1957

With Guy Carawan at the Bolshoi Theatre, 1957

With Chinese and American comrades, 1957. I am on the far right

Alf Edwards, master of the English concertina, early 1960s

Mother-in-law with daughter-in-law, mid-1960s

With baby Neill, 1960

With Ewan at Newport Folk Festival, 1960

Ewan and me working on something or other. Judging from the hairstyle and the Ampex tape machine, late 1960s

Charles Parker, master editor and producer, 1960s

Fitzroy Coleman in full flight, *c.* 1961

The Stewarts of Blairgowrie, with folklorist Hamish Henderson, outside their cottage at Rattray, Perthshire, *c.*1958. *From left*, Alec, Hamish Henderson, Belle, Sheila, Cathy and Rena with Sheila and Cathy's children

Clockwise from top left, Karl Marx, Friedrich Engels, Vladimir Lenin, me and Ewan, the last two severely dehydrated in Cuba, 1967

never stopped her from knitting in my presence. Somewhere during those first two or three months, he went back to live in the upstairs flat of the Croydon house. Jean's baby was due in October and Hamish was in crisis. Ewan found leaving his son harder than leaving his wife. A few years later, we were walking on Bleaklow Moor in Derbyshire when all of a sudden Ewan began to cry. He sat down on a big boulder, overcome with convulsive sobbing. *Here, Peg, I hit him, Peg, I hit him, I hit him right here.* It came out in a rush. Back in 1958 he'd taken Hamish for a moorland walk to tell him he was leaving. *But you're my dad. You can't leave. You can't.* Little boy – he was only eight. In a fury at being torn in two directions, Ewan had lashed out, hitting him repeatedly, then held him till he stopped weeping. Ewan had a lot to live with in his head. He never spoke of it again. Perhaps during that year when he returned to Croydon he was trying to steady himself as well as Hamish. He was living in his old office, one floor up from Jean's flat. He came to Purley every day on the scooter.

Betsy put up a photo in her room: a quality studio shot of Hamish and a very pregnant Jean sitting back-to-back, both of them smiling broadly. There were times when I loathed Betsy with every bone in my body. How could she put up that, of all pictures, in *my* house, on the mantel right next to Neill's crib – especially when she spent so much of her time telling me how badly Jean had treated her? On other days I was so grateful for her presence and her knowledge that I would have hugged her, had she let me. I nursed Neill for several months and then weaned him – we had to tour for the money. Betsy bound my breasts in the old manner, tight against my body, forcing the milk back.

Neill was learning to turn over and push himself up on his

elbows. Many's the morning I awoke to see his toothless mouth clamped to the side of the little pram, his big eyes looking at me. Charlie had had four boys and yearned for a daughter. It had given me the impression that fathers wanted daughters more than anything else. Ewan must be the same, two sons and now ... I hadn't cared one way or the other if my child was daughter or son. But now I just didn't want *Jean's* baby to be Ewan's first girl. Ewan was non-committal. *A child is a child.* We rarely spoke of it. I couldn't – and he didn't want to. In early October, Betsy also went back to Croydon to help. Ewan was with me on that October day when Jean phoned. Her labour had begun. Would Ewan come and stay with Hamish? Of course. Betsy was with Hamish, so he probably went to the hospital. Lots of unspoken territory here but, well, he *was* the father. We'd bought a paraffin – kerosene – heater to supplement Mrs Crabbe's parsimonious heating arrangements. We kept tins of paraffin in the garden shed. It was dark. I was in the shed filling up the paraffin can when the scooter came whizzing up the gravel drive. He parked it and walked down the path to the shed, taking his helmet off. The can was full. My heart was full. *Peg, it's a girl.*

My skin emptied out and filled with tears. It hadn't been real until now. I put the top on the can and walked past him into the house without a word. I hated Jean, her baby, Ewan, Betsy, everything but Neill. I wanted to go home. Neill was grizzling in his cot. I picked him up and held him in my arms, rocking and crying and crying. I use that memory when I need to identify with grief in a song or ballad. The flat that had been lit by untroubled love for one day before Betsy arrived now appeared in its true lack of colours. Dirty carpets, tiny gas fires, a mean little place, Ewan mute and ashamed, making tea in the dingy little kitchen. When we had been talking in France about what to name our baby, Ewan had suggested Kirsty if it was a girl, no suggestion if it was a boy. Now Kirsty was the name of Jean's baby. I didn't know what to do with my mind, my anger, love and hatred boiling up and nowhere to go. We were both miserable but for different reasons. Neill saved us. We took such pleasure in him, the proof of our disgrace. His beautiful disposition held us together through trials that might have parted most couples under similar circumstances. The music saved us. It was exhilarating. I loved to hear Ewan sing. The joint struggle of living on a financial knife-edge saved us. Love saved us.

*

We sang together, fitted together. Our work saved us, the politics, the recording projects, the next Radio Ballad, the new songs we were learning and writing. On tour, we made a point of taking routes we'd never travelled before. This was before the time of the big motorways and we had cloth-backed Ordnance Survey maps. Spool forward to 1988: I undertake a sponsored swim for the Campaign for Nuclear Disarmament (CND), priced at £1 per lap. My friend Irene is there keeping tally and her husband Philip grins and waves at me. Swimming lengths in a large pool is boring. I keep myself focused by counting the laps via the numbers of British roads. The A5, that three-lane death-trap across the lower Midlands, England's answer to Cape Cod's Suicide Alley; the A25, around London's southern rim, where traffic can be slower than a horse and buggy; the A74, where Ewan would occasionally hit 110 mph coming back from Scotland. I finish on lap 127, swimming from London to Southend and shocking my sponsors. You couldn't always trust the maps, though. Once on holiday, a moorland lane on the

OS map became a stream-bed down which, unable to reverse uphill, we had to build a rough Roman road of rocks for the rented car to bump along – ours was in a garage recovering from travelling on the new M1 with Ewan at the wheel. Neill, in his little car seat, was crowing with excitement at every hump and bump; Betsy was white with fear.

Together always. We toured together, gloried together in the wild countryside. Often we would just stop, put our boots on and take off up a hill. Ewan knew so much about every part of the country – and what he didn't know he made up. It almost didn't matter whether it was true or not, he was so interesting with it. Driving through thick mist in the North Yorkshire Dales while Ewan tells me about the people who lived in Keld and Muker. In the winter they had to ferry their dead over the moors to gentler country because the frozen, rocky home ground made grave-digging impossible.

Betsy was now at Park Hill Rise with Jean, Hamish, Kirsty and Ewan. When we toured we left Neill with Fay Tracinsky, who lived on the other side of Godstone Road, where the little terrace houses announced, by their very size, design and proximity to the railway, a difference in social class. Two up and two down and a tiny backyard, it was filled with Fay, her husband, their five children and a lot of love. Coming off tour, I'd drop Ewan at Croydon and head for Fay's. That afternoon, Neill was in the high chair with a little spoon in his fist, his favourite pudding all over his cheeks. When he saw me, he stretched his chocolate-spattered hands and arms towards me and we both burst into tears. I lifted him out, shouldered his bag of clothes and dirty nappies, said goodnight to Fay and we both went out into the night clutching each other in a toothsome, brown embrace. I wrote my song 'The Lifeboat Mona' in December

1959 while feeding Neill chocolate pudding. When news of the loss came on the radio it was dark and cold outside – I was warm and happy in the little Purley kitchen. Negative and positive. Life and art feeding each other chocolate pudding.

I sit cross-legged in front of the little gas fire playing the banjo, Neill in the scarlet carry-cot beside me. I'm being watched by a painter – and by a big spider under the bed. Like crowds assembling when you're street-singing, one would come – then another and another until there was a little row of sparkling eyes reflecting the fire. I'm frightened of large spiders and these were big ones, three or so inches across, but they were company. Lonely mother, me. 1960, and summer rain day after day. Ewan's not here yet but we had excitement this morning, Neill and I. He's in the living room in his playpen and I'm in the kitchen making our breakfast. All of a sudden he gives a whoop of joy and rattles the bars. I rush in, wanting to share his happiness. The laundry rack has fallen over onto the paraffin heater and the clothes are on fire. My baby loves the leaping flames. Rotten mother. Dreadful mother. Neill had persistent croup – day after restless day of coughing and fretting. I was exhausted with walking him up and down. So tired. *Just drop him.* My ballad, 'The Cruel Mother' – she kills two children.

> *She took out her wee pen knife,*
> *All alone and aloney-o,*
> *There she took her two babes' life*
> *Down by the Greenwood sidey-o.*

One night the doorbell rang. Jean. As usual, I went cold all over. I'm on trial. She came upstairs and sat down at the kitchen table. *Come over for Christmas. Now that I've got my man back, I think we should* . . . yes, be civilised about the situation. *He loves our daughter.* That word – Ewan still called her *the baby.* Now she's *their daughter.* I plunge the knife in *Charlie's daughter.* It digs deeper. Let's turn it, shall we? Jean sat there with dejected bravado. All was as it should be in Park Hill Rise. Hamish had calmed down and we should start preparing for how we were going to continue. *What on earth has he told her about his return? Was he really sleeping upstairs?* So easy to distrust . . . I begin to realise how deeply wounded she is. I had been living in my own selfish bubble. She asked to see Neill. Poor Jean, forcing herself to look at my sleeping baby – Ewan's *son.* Poor me, contemplating Ewan's *daughter.* Poor Ewan, poor all of us. Blank-faced, appealing to me, Jean came out with the real point of her visit. We could have a *ménage à trois*, all of us living together. *Our babies could* . . . *No.* She went home.

Had I been older, wiser, less of a child, I would have seen the situation in a more objective light. It wasn't a competition – it was kind of fair: I had Ewan, she had Kirsty. Back then, I knew he'd chosen me and I just didn't want to share him or his love. I knew that when he was over there he held Kirsty, crooned to her, all of that, and it soured me. I shoved shovelfuls of resentment down, deep deep way way down inside. I let it cloud what should have been good days. Ewan's birthday-mate, Robert Burns, had scattered his seed far and wide, even bringing one or two of his offspring home to his wife, another Jean. I used to wonder about her. Up to now our story had been a one-episode love song like those peonies that burst from bud into full blossom in a day. Now it was becoming a narrative, a ballad with turns and twists in the plot where he is guilty, she is angry, but *they* love deeply.

I sank into depression. Ewan came over from Croydon every morning as soon as he could. It's a day of English gloom, grey and windy. It's gloomy inside our grey flat. I'm lying naked, crosswise along the bottom of our bed. Ewan is sitting on a chair, his back to the gas fire. Neill lies naked between us. Rokeby Venus in Purley – we are reflected in Ewan's glasses. Syzygy on Godstone Road – three generations caught in a moment of passage: the man, his seniority and maleness filling the room, the woman feeling as if her body still held the child lying naked between, gurgling and squirming as they stroke his edible bare bottom. We made him together. Now we're discussing parting. *You don't have to stay with me, Peg. You know that. You're free to go. We can part. We'll work out the finances somehow. We can still sing together. You don't have to stay.* He's not begging. He's accepting the situation, however it might turn out. I'm free to go. Therefore, I'll stay.

20

Folk Revival

From the floor, Germans sang Greek songs, Greeks sang Israeli songs, Israelis sang Spanish songs, Hackney kids sang American and Americans sang a lot of et cetera. Folk clubs were a free-for-all. From the stage Peggy sang French songs alongside childhood favourites; Ewan sang Scots songs, a smattering of English, occasional tear-jerkers and parodies and American songs he'd learned from Alan Lomax, who only sang the songs he and his father had collected. Ralph Rinzler stuck to North America's eastern states. Fitzroy Coleman wouldn't have stooped to singing anything that didn't come from Trinidad. Dean Gitter sang anything that was entertaining. The atmosphere was light-hearted and informal and the audiences flocked in. Resident singers would bring sandwiches and graze on stage. Guitar players were encouraged to perch in the front row like sparrows on a washing line. Some of them had only bought their guitar that day. We'd arrive early to tune all of these instruments, many of which would have made inferior firewood. We allowed forty-five minutes for this but a lifetime wouldn't have done the job. Like painting the Albert Bridge: by the time you got to the southern end it was time to start again across the Thames. When you sing with the sound-holes of twenty randomly tuned guitars aimed straight at you, you choose simple songs because their minders joined in on absolutely *everything*. Democracy gone wild. Before each song,

you'd teach the chord patterns while the un-instrumented customers drummed mental fingers.

I never played on Fitz's songs. He was just too good. He only
wanted to play with his equals – and he was the only player
present who was his equal. He wasn't a snob – he was a professional. He never told the sparrows not to play. He'd begin.
Two bars of F13. He knew that most of them couldn't finger
the *barré* chord up from E position, much less work out what a
13th was. Some knew that if they put a capo on, they'd have to
convert in their minds from F to E, B-flat to A, C7 to B7 – but
you'd only do that if the whole song was in F. Fitz never told
us what key the song was in. That F13 chord convinced half
of the birdies to put their heads under their wings. *Four and
a half bars of A-flat 9.* His left hand takes and leaves the position quickly. Speed is all. The singer Ed McCurdy, cruising a
buffet table, suddenly brought his penis out and laid it on the
table between two halves of a hot-dog bun. Lightning quick,
the woman next to him plastered it with mustard and pickles
and closed the bun with force. Speed is definitely all. The traps
are up and Fitz is a greyhound, chanting. *Two and a half bars
of C7, one bar of B-flat 9, two bars of G7, one bar of C7,* and he
swings immediately into the song. Indeed, it *would* have two
bars of F13, four and a half bars of A-flat 9, et cetera, all correct.
By the time he'd done one verse, he'd lost all but one or two
diehards who, eyes swivelling frantically from Fitz's hands to
their own, laboriously formed each chord several bars too late.
If anyone hung in there for too long, Fitzroy – *be gentle with me,
dear* – would exaggerate the Caribbean placement of accents to
soften the blow: *Song too low for me to sing. We transpose up to
F-sharp!* Fitzroy could play capo-less in any key, anywhere. One
survivor left. Fitz sends his brown spider-hands up the neck

into inversions of the chords, leaving him in full command of the field. It sounds cruel and elitist – but what was anathema to other musical disciplines was supposed to be OK for folk music. Off stage, Fitz fumed. *You learn to play, then you play for other peoples. You don't play for other peoples while you learn.*

The British public house is a unique institution, first set in place by the Romans, who needed way stations for their troops. Pubs come in all shapes, sizes, decor styles, atmosphere. Anyone from any class can go into any pub unless snobbery (both up and down) or fear for your safety or your ego keeps you out. Unless you are underage you buy your drink in the bar and either consume it there or go into the public room, which is cheap to hire for social events. This night one of the up-and-coming floor singers was executing 'Rock Island Line' – verb chosen for accuracy. I'd heard Lead Belly's pulsing, steam-engine voice singing 'Rock Island Line' on steady tracks since the year dot. Now here it is with charming Cockney vowels – smart, clipped, aboard the Wabash Cannonball and in high tenor. My gut reaction was to laugh. It was rude, outrageous – but I couldn't stop. I had to be taken out of the room. After the show, the other resident singers insisted that we talk about it. Members of the audience were invited. The singer came, downcast. Maybe he hadn't sung the song well enough . . .? I apologised and accounted for my behaviour: *East London vowels don't really fit with Lead Belly and you sang it so fast* . . . at which point, one of the French audience members said he didn't like my singing of French songs. Stung, I passed the aggro on to Ewan: *Well, I don't really like it when you sing 'Sam Bass' with an exaggerated American accent.* Then Isla Cameron objected to Bert singing songs from Scotland. A trail of dominoes – we all lost but in the process found a policy for our club and our club only. Repeat:

The Policy was for our club only. Repeat, repeat, repeat because the Policy has been blown up out of all proportion. Repeat: It was only meant for onstage singing. On our stage you sing songs that come from your own culture or language-base. Sing whatever you want elsewhere but on this stage you only sing foreign-language songs if you can speak that language competently or if you come from that culture. When ironing, bubble-bathing, humming at home, it's your show. On stage here – rules. Kind of like if you're at a trad jazz club you don't do modern jazz from the floor. The meeting was so fruitful that we formed an official Audience Committee.

Our usable repertoire shrank. Then a new issue surfaced. It seemed that we had been singing the old faithful songs to death. Quality Control spawned Quantity Control. The committee ruled that a resident could sing that particular traditional song only once every three months. New songs were exempt, having shorter half-lives. So the overall choice shrinks further and the Book is born, listing the titles of the songs sung each week and by whom. Tonight it's my turn. I give the title. The Keeper of the Book thumbs through the previous three months. *No, you sang it seven weeks ago.* We found ways around it, of course. Ewan would give the song a different title from the one in the Book. Bert would flash his Toby jug smile and say that this version of 'Lady Isabel and the Elf Knight' was different from the one he sang in May. Peggy was hard to interrupt. Some of those banjo jokes are true. Spontaneity gave way to planning. The atmosphere sobered. Our full houses became half-houses then quarter-houses. Floor singers were cautious. Ewan and I internalised the Book when out on tour and became our own Audience Committee. For each concert we prepared five-by-eight-inch index cards on which the list of *possibles* had been culled from our master lists. On the other side of the card were columns of what we'd sung at that club before, so as not to risk repeating exactly what we'd sung on our previous visit. At home, we'd enter the night's titles into our Programme Book, with income from sales of records at the bottom of the page. These Books, documenting over two thousand gigs, were invaluable when I needed to date our original songs for the two songbooks. I'm on Book 13 now, but without merch prices. In the 1990s, I was part of a New York concert devoted to my mother's folk song transcriptions and her own compositions. The pianist and I were talking about such lists, for she kept them as well. *And do you put what you've worn at the bottom of each list? Yes, but only since Ewan died.* She high-fived me. *So do I. We're divas.*

The Policy made it harder for Brits to sing the blues – a North American format at that time – at our club. Also, Alan's name for the club, Ballads and Blues, was reassigned by our booking agent, Malcolm Nixon, to his own new Policy-less pholk club. We chose a new name for ourselves – the Singers' Club – and began having theme nights: love songs, trickster songs, crime and criminals, war and peace, the Big City. An evening of matching songs would have residents singing different versions of 'Barbara Allen' or 'Maids, When You're Young'. It became interesting and fun – full houses again. The *You Name It, We Sing It* evenings were the most entertaining. You needed a referee and three or more singers with large repertoires. The audience would write subjects on little slips of paper: a girl playing hard to get; a transvestite; a baulky mount. We'd take turns being first. The subject: one unarmed bloke and the other with two swords. If Singer No. 1 took more than ten seconds to produce a pertinent song, then Singer No. 2 had five seconds, after which Singer No. 3 had to sing one immediately. No one got a second chance. The writer of the slip would decode the subject if necessary: 'Little Musgrave', of course. We worked on a points system. The Cheshire Cat smiled and swore blind that the text he'd just made up wholesale was a traditional folk song – and collected his points.

News of the Policy spread to other clubs. Sometimes it was widely derided or misconstrued – but where it was adopted it spawned the phenomenon known as the *weekend collector*. Armed with little tape machines, folk song enthusiasts went out into their local pubs, working men's clubs and old people's homes to collect songs. Bob Thompson and Mike Herring were good singers and founders of the Royal Air Force folk club on the air base near Stamford, Lincolnshire. Little Uher cassette machine slung on shoulder, Bob entered his pub, where a phalanx of old boys were holding up the bar. *Does anyone here know a song called 'Lamkin'?* All heads turned. One oldster nodded and sang it there and then. The weekend collectors proudly brought their haul into the club and thence into the revival, bringing the Policy in through the back door. Some of them brought the old singers as well. Like many new movements, the concept of the Policy was occasionally taken to extremes. A Lancashire club didn't allow the singing of Yorkshire songs – a new War of the Roses. Like *Truth* and *Love*, *the Policy* meant many things to many people and was taken to new heights and depths. Some clubs interpreted the Policy as allowing only unaccompanied songs. One club declared me non-traditional because I sang American songs. Another wanted to hire Ewan on his own as Peggy played all those *untraditional instruments*. The Policy was valuable in that it made the song the baseline, not the singer. I figure that the Policy was largely responsible for the huge resurgence of interest in British material. This in turn gave rise to the staggering number of skilled singers and players of English, Scottish, Welsh and Irish folk music that we have today.

Our 'Rock Island Line' singer was a skiffler. When I arrived in 1956, the skiffle movement was at its height.* It depended largely on American folk, blues, jazz and roots repertoire, played on homemade or improvised instruments like the washboard and the washtub bass. Wonderful, but oh dear – here come American guitar styles and banjo players: all of a sudden 'Glasgow Peggy' accompanied by Chevy Chase Peggy is up-tempo and sounding like something out of the Appalachians. Accompanied, 'The Twa Magicians' has no pulse any more, just rhythm. Ill-considered accompaniments wreaked havoc. An instrumentalist would turn a 5/4 song into 4/4 to fit with the duple metres preferred by the five-string banjo. Songs would speed up, passengers on a runaway train rocketing along on metrically precise rails. I blush with shame when I hear some of my early backing for Ewan's songs and the speed at which I sang some of my own. I use recordings of them for cannon fodder when I teach accompaniment.

The Audience Committee announced the arrival of autumn, encouraging the front row of instrumentalists to fly south – permanently. Fifteen minutes were set aside at the beginning for floor singers instead, auditions to be held before the show started. I abolished onstage munching. Imagine: you're in the audience, you're hungry, and you're sitting there five feet from a singer scoffing a sausage buttie or a newspaper cone of fish and chips. Imagine: you're singing a passionate love song with

---

* For more on the skiffle movement, check out Billy Bragg's excellent *Roots, Radicals and Rockers* (Faber and Faber, 2017).

Alan Lomax sitting next to you chomping on a double-decker BLT with crisp lettuce. Alan's jaw cracked when he ate. The Audience Committee criticised diplomatically at meetings. Gail Petersen took the job on solo one night at New Merlin's Cave on Margery Street, King's Cross. Ewan and I had been recording all day and were too tired to sing – a bad workman blames his tools. To close the first half, we sang 'Lassie wi' the Yellow Coatie' as a duet, maple-syrup harmonies lying on green velvet single-string guitar arpeggios. Gail – stocky and with a mission – came up to the stage during the interval, a thundercloud looming across her face. *Hello, Gail! Good to see you. How are you?* Matter of fact: *Pregnant.* Then, furious, very loud: *Don't you EVER sing that song like that again!* The whole club went quiet. *It was soppy. Slushy – and the accompaniment is terrible.* She turned away and went to the bar for a drink. Ewan sang it by himself in the second half. He prefaced it with a description of his father singing it in front of the tiny fire at Coburg Street. Just right. The Audience Committee was a very good idea.

Ewan and I were evolving a stage routine that we were to keep for the rest of our professional life. I would open with a song like 'Sweet Willie', with fast, rippling banjo accompaniment, the chief purpose of which was to quieten and focus the audience. It's unfortunate, but people are impressed by fast playing – in fact, it's often harder to play slowly. Ewan would follow with something like 'Broomfield Hill', myself on the Appalachian dulcimer, or 'To the Begging I Will Go', me leisurely on the concertina. Then we'd relax into the two-for-me/two-for-you routine, with occasional songs together. Neither of us knew what the other was going to sing and would often change our choice for contrast. If you needed a third song, so be it. We never argued about who had the most time, the most songs, the most applause. Our early concerts were immensely long – too long by my present standards – and were far more traditional than the later ones. As time went on, we began to include more contemporary songs simply because we were writing so many, often producing new ones before the previous new ones were out of date.

The deep concentration that we were generating on stage was new to me. I had achieved this depth when performing ballads, but now we got two hours of quality attention from a motley group of people for a motley group of songs. I'd seen Pete's concerts, where he threw himself out into the audience with that warmth and involvement that were his speciality. I'd taken part in the anything-goes havoc that had characterised the Ballads and Blues evenings. This new *intensity* was gripping, almost theatrical. Ewan had always stood up when he sang lusty chorus songs or shanties with Bert. Now we just sat, which made for a non-performance atmosphere. We were riveted to our chairs for the whole evening for the next thirty years, surrounded by instruments. Ewan kept his chair around backwards, elbow on chair-back and hand to ear. Misinterpreted, like the Policy, that stance has been dubbed *finger-in-the-ear singing* by jokesters. It's often used to make fun of Ewan. You don't put your finger in your ear. Your cupped hand pushes the whole ear slightly forward to create an echo chamber. Many traditional singers do it – it helps in setting your pitch and sends your voice forward and around you. Try it.

The folk revival that began in the 1950s has been an extraordinary cultural movement. The grassroots part of it was never captured wholesale by the establishment. Singers were lured away from it but there were always new singers taking their place, making sure that the revival itself has remained a vital part of the UK's subterranean cultural life. It is fed and watered by the network of folk clubs whose breeding and stamping ground is the pub. Keep grassroots movements down in the grass. We are cultural wildlife in danger of extinction. Grow the grass higher so we won't be seen and gobbled up. Make the stage informal so that newcomers can cut their teeth in front of a sympathetic audience. In a folk club, you could hear pure genius or self-indulgent twaddle. You could join in on the chorus – or not. You didn't have a feeling of being *on stage* when you sang at a folk club. The audience was often near enough to touch. Keep folk music *in here, down here*. There's always someone wanting to change it from what it is into something more saleable. The pub is, for the most part, honest and humble – some pubs are brand new but most of them are so old that, like my guitar, the walls give and take the music. Sometimes it feels as if someone sang from this corner to a room full of friends centuries ago . . .

21

Wallpaper and the Meaning of Music

Hemingway sentences so's we don't freeze our tonsils. *Why are you standing out here? Music's too loud. Why don't you turn it down? The manager wants it that way. We'll go talk to him. He's not here.* The earth-shattering music from behind the closed door was rattling the plate-glass windows. It was one of those English winter days when the damp frozen air drills through high boots, woollen tights, scarf, coat, sweater, Damart thermal vest, hair, skin, flesh, bone, marrow and stiff upper lip to intimidate your very vitals. You don't lounge about outdoors – but here were three women clad only in their logoed uniforms, preferring the cold outside to the music inside.

Circa 2015, Queen Street, Oxford. The damp, frozen air was drilling through high boots (etc.). I'm caught by an enticing long grey cardigan in the shop window. I open the door and am shoved backward viscerally by the universal, pounding war-cry, always in duple time with the drums leading the cavalry. I shout to the assistant about the sweater in the window. She shouts back, *Window?* Lip reading and sign language should be required skills for shop assistants. I lead her outside the door to point at my prey. I shout my usual question: *How can you stand listening to this all day?* She shouts the usual answer: *You get used to it. Don't notice it after a while.* Surf the internet for *frogs in boiling water.*

Music creates meaning when used commercially. In 1922,

George Owen Squier formed a company, Wired Radio, which then became Muzak, known as *elevator music, easy listening, mood music* – music while you eat, while you shop, while you travel, 'The First Time Ever I Saw Your Face' while I sat on the loo in Selfridges last week. When they installed Muzak on the bus from Silver Spring to Washington, my mother marched up to the driver and commanded him to turn it off. *Sorry, I can't, ma'am. Company policy, ma'am.* She took her children, ages five, seven and nine, off the bus and walked us to our destination. The Muzak company went bankrupt, unmourned, in 2009, by which time Squier's idea, much like that of Henry Ford, had morphed into a monster. Music was originally meant to be listened to. Now it is created not to be heard as music, only as aural wallpaper.*

*

One of the things I love about folk music is that it generally chooses a style of *being* that allows the listener to settle in. It's like a cardiograph: the form being the graph paper and the content the heartbeat. If it's steady, we're comforted. At a certain time in music history, consistency gave way to change, even in classical music. I go to a symphony concert – *change* is central

---

* Pipedown – the Campaign for Freedom from Piped Music – will supply you with cards to leave with the manager of a musical inferno seconds after you walk in, telling her/him why you are now going to walk out. Pipedown's website says: 'Unwanted and inescapable piped music has an adverse effect on human health. Like all unwanted noise, it RAISES the blood pressure and DEPRESSES the immune system.' (The capitals are theirs.) The 100 per cent monotonous presence of music in our lives is largely responsible for the devaluing of music – but we *can* do something about it.

to the symphonic form but the form has become traditional. If I'm in the mood and if the contrasting movements are well put together, I appreciate its similarity to the Painted Lady houses in which prescribed muted colours are combined. But when Chopin takes me on a smooth, sunny trip across grass lawns then all of a sudden has me jolting over boulders and potholes and then I'm back on the green sward again, I just have to ask, *Why?** I'd chop the dissonant, restless bars out and join the opening and closing parts so that the same would stay the same old same. A classical music lover's nightmare. I just want the seasons kept separate, with change when *I am ready for change.* I'm marching with a banner: EQUAL RIGHTS FOR LISTENERS! MY WAY OR NO WAY!

*

Music creates meaning each time it is heard. You hear 'First Time Ever' with your lover when you have just fallen in love. Listen to it the day after he leaves you or beats you up and its meaning will have changed. My first exploratory kiss with a dear Someone was in the dark by garbage cans, too new and unfamiliar to taste of love. If I'm thinking of that during the Kiss Verse of 'First Time Ever', I just have to laugh – a different kind of joy. In *A Clockwork Orange*, a piece of music was one man's meat and another man's Chinese water torture. 'Salt River' played by Walt Koken can make me envious of his banjo playing, can make me wash the dishes faster, can remind me that I won't ever play banjo with Mike again. Some music

---

* The answer is in *The Necessity of Art*, a Marxist-orientated meditation on the importance of art by Ernst Fischer.

is made for a purpose – marching music, hymns for church, music for dances. But you can hum hymns while climbing a mountain, dance to the marching music, leading to the possibility that usage = meaning. Music certainly has uses – seven and a half billion of them, perhaps $7.5 \times 7.5^{\infty}$, depending upon the changing circumstances under which each listener listens.

*

The folk tales, songs and dances are the oldest music we have. If they have meaning, it is to keep us connected to one another, to the past from which we come – all of us, each culture in its own way with the one purpose: to perpetuate togetherness – survival. The big old ballads are of this web. Arundhati Roy describes the kathakali dancers meeting in the temple to apologise to their god for corrupting the Great Stories, *encashing their identities* by dancing for disinterested foreign tourists in the market, hawking 'the only thing [they own]. The stories that [their bodies] can tell.'* In the temple, they dance – ragged, drunk, stoned and in scarlet rage.

> It didn't matter that the story had begun, because kathakali discovered long ago that the secret of the Great Stories is that they have no secrets. The Great Stories are the ones you have heard and want to hear again. The ones you can enter anywhere and inhabit comfortably. They don't deceive you with thrills and trick endings. They don't surprise you with the unforeseen. They are as familiar as the house you live in. Or the smell of your lover's skin. You know how they end, yet

* *The God of Small Things*, chapter 12.

you listen as though you don't. In the way that although you
know that one day you will die, you live as though you won't
... That is their mystery and their magic.

In the early days of the present folk revival in Britain, there were only a few traditional singers left and most of those were in the late autumn or winter of their years. They knew how the songs should be sung but most of their vocal ability was gone. There was enough left of their singing style to indicate that they sang as they spoke, i.e. without melodramatic input; no increase in decibels or over-dramatisation of the story; no mid-song shift to a different key; no slowing down at the end of the song; no externally imposed vocal tricks. They just *sang straight*. Change the style of folk songs and their 'meaning' and purpose changes.

Music creates meaning when it is made for sale, patronage or personal aggrandisement; when it is stolen without credit to create new compositions; when its original meaning is prostituted, demeaned or wiped out completely; when it loses its original name (like women when we marry). Classical composers, believing folk melodies to be embryonic, appropriate those melodies because of their beauty – but they don't call their compositions 'folk music'. Classically trained singers with more than a passing interest in Victorian morals sang the songs with *beautiful* voices and cleaned them up for audiences of *good taste* – but didn't call their performances 'folk music'. In the 1950s, here come the ubiquitous guitar and classical harmony progressions. Here come performers more determined to entertain than to carry a tradition forward – they call it 'folk music'. The plots thin. The accompaniment thickens. The excitement escalates. Much to apologise for in the temple. Do a similar thing to Vivaldi and no one will call it 'classical music'. Vivaldi was written down. Even if you change Vivaldi drastically, there will still be those who know how it was meant to be played, who hope that the remake won't be the only Vivaldi that is remembered in the future. Dress up 'Midnight Special' often enough and no one will remember how Lead Belly sang it, for it is not hewn on durable materials. Why should this matter? Obviously, it matters to me, having sung the folk stories all my life. I only have a problem when it is *called* 'folk music', for the term *folk music* means something very special to me.

We constantly use music created for one purpose to enhance the meaning of something entirely different, so why look for meaning in the first place? Music just means music. Meaning has meaning too.

22

The End of the Beginning

Late autumn 1959, we trundle up to the ticket desk in the airport with three instruments, three large suitcases and a six-month-old baby. A tour of Canada had come through – our first experience of touring together. We were in high spirits. My created family was going to meet my birth family. In all US entry ports, records were being kept of the China miscreants. Our flight went via Boston. Logan airport at 2 a.m. was no place to land with a hungry, weaned baby and three hours to wait. Past the exit door was my home country and an all-night eatery. We could see it. We could smell it. *Give the baby to your 'friend' and come in here.* They took me into a pitch 6 cubicle, speaking in pitch 72. *How could you give up your American passport, the most valuable of your possessions?* I can hear Neill crying. *Can my friend get some milk from the cafe?* Neutral: *Transit passengers are not allowed out of the transit lounge.* Begging: *My baby is hungry.* Sardonic, almost pleased: *Not our problem, ma'am.* I sit for over an hour, interrogated by full-bellied, bellicose officials wanting to know what kind of American would allow their passport to expire. *Sit – here – and – remember – this.*

Neill was allergic to motorised travel. He vomited with every bump and swerve of anything on wheels. He vomited in cars. He vomited when the plane took off. He vomited when it landed. He wriggled violently when we held the vomit bag near his mouth. The odour and stains of barf were badges of parenthood as far as we were concerned. On that tour, many a member of the reception committee recoiled as we walked through the arrivals door. Arranging babysitters while we went to give concerts and interviews, coming home late, waking up with Neill once or twice a night. I used towelling nappies for all three of my children.* On tour, it was scrub, wring, hang and hope to dry them. I did it – Ewan didn't. I wasn't a feminist back then. What did nomadic people do about their babies' excretory needs? Bird-watchers go birding. I was fruit-batting in Australia and way high up Mama-bat holds her pup close under wing. Suddenly wing opens, baby is held out. *Poop poop*, and it's fold up wing and baby is body-close again. Why aren't humans like that? Hold him over the toilet, a drain in the gutter – a baby on disposables for a thousand days can use up a sequoia. Lecture over, we pack everything up, travel to the next town and start the whole rigmarole again.

We were worn out after a week. Charlie was waiting when we landed in Vancouver and I put Neill in his arms almost like a present. He admired dutifully, even though he already had eight similar gifts. Our host, Vancouver angel Jeannie Cox, opened her arms. *I'll take the baby.* I handed him over without a murmur and collapsed into bed. Mike was there with his new wife, our Marge, who saw Neill and decided to get one of her own. She got three in quick succession. Next destination: Port Arthur, with Charlie waving goodbye from the observation platform. The propeller of our turboprop was making a terrible clatter. Airborne, a banner of flame is streaking backward from the engine. The plane banks sharply. We're heading back to Vancouver with an engine on fire. Assured that there

---

* Mothers of sons: cloth diapers are better for his little jewels than disposables.

was no danger, we land, heads down in crash position, between rows of fire engines and ambulances. We transfer to another plane. A kind union official met us in Port Arthur, the familiar wrinkled-nose greeting. *We have a day or two to spare. How would you like to give a concert in Geraldton? It's a gold-mining town some four or five hours' drive north. It'll be bumpy and cold. Maybe leave the baby . . .?* We spoke in unison: *Of course.*

No time for *why not?* Kind Man's Kind Wife takes Neill and we're off. It began as a four-lane double carriageway, became a two-lane road with no shoulders, winding among small lakes and scrub, turning into a cardboard road of frozen mud. Little communities of native Canadians and European immigrants, broken-down barns, skeletal trees and forlorn houses. It was snowing by the time the road devolved into the gravel track that led into Geraldton. It was a frontier settlement, straight out of Jack London – a single main street with low wooden houses, low wooden shops and a two-storey wooden hotel. A church organ of icicles hung from the low eaves and the windows were shuttered tight. Through the storm door, then through swinging half-doors into one of my childhood Friday-night westerns. The bar had a long polished wooden counter. The drinkers watched us in the embossed mirror behind the bartender then turned around to survey us. Heavy country-wear and low-slung hats, booted feet up on the long brass rail, they were expecting John Wayne. They nodded. The bartender nodded. Geraldton-speak for *howdy.* Kind Man took us to the hotel section at the end of the bar. A little green desk lamp with a two-watt bulb sat on a small table next to a register. We were signed in and shown upstairs. A bare light bulb hung in the middle of the room. Ewan declares it colder than an Eskimo's balls. *How do you know?* We're too cold to laugh.

We crossed the empty street and went into the wooden community hall. *Where is everyone?* It's moose season. We should have known – of *course* a whole town empties to shoot moose. *They'll be back for the concert. They've been looking forward to it. Entertainers don't bother to come up here.* We thought we were folk singers. Set the stage up and test the 1876 microphones. Curtain time, with no curtains and no audience. Eight thirty. A few stragglers come in with blood-soaked bags of moose meat and moose heads with antlers attached to prove they haven't shot an adolescent. Nine thirty. The grisly pile in the corner is growing and the hall reeks of blood. All seats full – men, women, teenagers. Children playing on the floor, babies at the breast. The starting gun and I'm off with fast banjo and high, lonesome singing. A wave of applause. Ewan sings an unaccompanied Scots ballad. A wave of applause. A political song, a really funny one – not a snicker, not a titter, then . . . a wave of applause at the same level. The children were well-behaved and the whole assemblage was attentive. Nobody was leaving, the attention was not dutiful but . . . what's going on here? Whenever things got tough we sang for each other. Ours not to reason why – at least the show wasn't dying.

During the interval, we were plied with drinks, handshakes, invitations to inspect moose heads. We tried conversation but there was such a hubbub that we couldn't understand a word. Everyone eating enormous sandwiches and drinking hot tea and hooch out of Thermos bottles. The children were sitting in groups, the boys whittling antler prongs with pocket knives, the girls with dolls or younger siblings. We asked our union friend how he thought it was going. *They're loving it. Of course, they don't understand a word. They only speak Finnish.* We spent the second half of the concert with an interpreter and varied the style and pace – bitter-sweet love songs, songs with a very, very easy chorus. They liked 'Skip to My Lou' and 'John the Rabbit' as much as the Beijing children had. The final applause was raucous and appreciative. One of the gold miners invited us back to his home. Open the door and a blast of garlic rushes out. Vintage moose sausage.

The house was diminutive and crowded. *Feast* doesn't adequately describe their hospitality. They emptied the enormous fridge of its contents onto the family dining table. Their English was almost non-existent but Kind Man did his best. Within minutes several of the men were under the table demonstrating how to mine gold and we women were talking about our children. They had trouble understanding how I could have left Neill behind. So did I – until I remembered our glacial bedroom. Early morning was dawning. Our host asked if we would take some moose sausage to his relatives in Port Arthur. He brought out a huge glass bowl and we followed him to a back room. An old bathtub was filled with moose meat. Moose sausage has personality: one-third each of breadcrumbs, garlic and moose meat. The sausage went into the bowl, the bowl went into the car and the green grass grows all around and around. We drove back to our hotel, where a celestial being had put a hot-water bottle into our bed. Next morning the garlic was waiting for us in the car. We picked up a hitch-hiker, who flinched as the door opened. His expression was familiar. But wait . . . Neill's not with us . . . Ah yes, garlic. After a short while our green-complected passenger begged Kind Man to stop and let him out. Weakling. Port Arthur and we drop the sausage off and head for our precious baby. Mrs Kind Man reacted when we entered the house – as one does. Neill recoiled too. She put our clothes in the washing machine.

She probably scrubbed down the instruments and their cases while we were asleep.

This tour was not arranged geographically. Winnipeg, then Edmonton, whence our host would drive us to Saskatoon, about four or five hours away. At the last minute, the wife of our host decided to come along for the ride – with her baby. We piled our joint luggage in one of those station wagons that are close land-kin to yachts. The prairie stretched away in all directions. Five or ten miles away to the left, there's a grain elevator. To the right, in the very far distance, there's another. Three or four miles ahead, at the end of the spaghetti-thin, spaghetti-straight road, there's two or three more. Every half-hour a car or truck came the other way. The drivers saluted each other, occasionally stopping mid-highway to chat. Ships at sea. Our car broke down. We panicked – we'd be late for the concert. Our hosts were nonchalant. *No problem – we'll hitch a ride.* Two men, two women, two babies and a pile of luggage that we all could have hidden behind. *Of course* someone would pick us up. Of course, the first car that came along stopped. *Where are you bound?* Silly question – the road only went to one place. *Hop in.* We did – fast, before our saviour could change his mind. Garlic and vomit linger on – like love. He was a neat, middle-aged exec with his briefcase on the seat beside him. When we squeezed in, I sat right behind our man with Neill in my lap, not thinking, not remembering all those take-offs and landings. The car swerved to avoid a pothole. Neill ejected the contents of his stomach forward with its usual velocity, volume and scent. It dripped down the man's head, all over his suit, beneath his collar, down the front seat and over his briefcase. He laughed and said he had children himself. And *don't worry. It's a company car.* Talk about making a virtue of necessity – such a gracious response. Our rolling vomitorium cruised smoothly into Saskatoon and we were deposited at the very door of the concert organiser. One of humanity's finest drove away and we didn't even take his name.

*

In January 1960, I had my first abortion. Sharing experience demystifies the process and strengthens female bonds. We'd had Neill on purpose as a seal on our union. We were just scraping by – if we had another baby both families would be in real trouble. Abortion was illegal, moral opprobrium and secrecy firmly attached. We debated far too long. By the time my tipping point arrived, Ewan had to go north with Charles Parker, recording for our third Radio Ballad, *Singing the Fishing*. I would stay home with Neill, take a well-paid television job and see to the abortion myself. The woman lived in Hanley, a long way from Purley, southeast to northwest, right across London. With motoring gloves, long woollen scarf, helmet and winter coat, I scootered through the cold, badly-lit suburbs to rid myself of the fruits of love for the sake of love. The terrace house was in a dark narrow street. A fat little woman came to the door. She surveyed the street up and down and pulled me in. The house was dingy and dark and smelled sour. No *hello dearie*, no cup of tea, no reassurance, just a long, high table in a little back room. Legs up, Mother Brown. *I want my mother, I want . . .* Dio would not have understood my despatching a baby thus. I'd been told it would hurt and by God it did. Syringe of soapy water, no post-procedure advice, hand over £20, close the door and flee for home. Pick Neill up from Fay's and take him to bed with me, cuddling and crying.

208

An abortion is not simply a heavy period. I flowed as if a tap had been turned on, the blood clear and bright red with great clots in it. I bled through the night, lying down unless I had to feed or change Neill. In 1989, I wrote 'The Judge's Chair', setting forth some of my experience but with a different outcome:

> *Slowly, slowly up the stair*
> *Into her childhood room;*
> *Her bed filled up with red, red blood,*
> *Annie died alone.*

Wake up disorientated and dizzy. Drop Neill off, scooter up to London, bleeding heavily. When I wasn't needed, I lay on the studio floor, too weary to stand up. The TV programme was about race relations in London. One very black cast member – Big Tom, a lovely man – commented with concern that today I was a *really white person*. He was the one who pointed out the brown and black girls always chatting up men lighter than they were. *I haven't a chance there. They don't want dark babies.* I had despatched my white baby and I'm crying in a television studio.

The next morning it was as if a dam had broken. Blood poured out when I sat on the toilet. The phone is downstairs, Neill is crying and I can't even stand up. Ewan is on the herring boats, two days out at sea. *How could he? How do I contact shore-to-ship? Not his fault, not his fault. Who can I phone? We should have known. I want my mother. How could I know? I'm twenty-five and he's forty-five. I hate him. He should have known, damn him. How do I stop this? Dio . . . please . . .* I put two nappies on Neill, three nappies on myself, got into bed and prepared to die. I remembered the show. Which must go on. I got up, took

Neill to Fay's and scootered into London. Something in me did die. I never told Ewan how bad it had been.

Mrs Crabbe, our po-faced landlady, gave us notice. On her last visit, she'd seen that Neill was just about to walk. Once mobile, children deface walls, drop things down toilets, scratch woodwork with sharp implements, pee on upside-down carpets. We needed a bigger place anyway. Betsy would be coming back. We'd exchanged the scooter for a second-hand car on the never-never – instalment plan – a Citroën Light 15, royal, deep burgundy. It had a bosom – bulbous front fenders – and the gear-stick rose from the floor like a tropical flower bud. Whichever of us was passenger would put a lover's hand on the hand of the driver as the gear-change was made. That car was cherished. It got a wash and hoover-out every Sunday. We went out once a week to the country for a picnic or down to the sea. In those days Citroëns were rare, as were garages that would service them. Citroën owners dipped lights to each other on the road. When the M1 motorway was finished, it became a playground for would-be Jackie Stewarts and you had to keep up to the minimum speed. Our poor little 15 was too Light for the job. It wore her out and we had to put her out of her misery. Honeymoons were over.

23

Settling Down

By the time Ewan and I were invited to the 1960 Newport Festival, Fear and Loathing had produced Checkpoint Charlies at every entrance to the United States. Harold Leventhal (our US agent) and the American Civil Liberties Union filled out reams of forms to get us in. He and the ACLU lawyers were up on the balcony of the entrance hall when we arrived. You could actually stand and watch the person you were meeting being accepted or turned away. Wave hello or wave goodbye. Upon arrival, you were presented with a form containing yes/no choices, one of which was *Are you entering the United States for the purpose of overthrowing the democratically elected government?* or some such. I believe it was the journalist Gilbert Harding who – upon entering the USA from Canada – answered: *Sole purpose of visit.* He was interrogated for hours and nearly deported before they discovered who he was. Never joke with jokers.

Questions and forms are old-fashioned. You get a visa online now but you still have to shuffle around like sheep in a pen, hello Homeland Security USA, give your thumb print, have your photo taken. Iridology is probably already embedded. Many of the US officials are friendly and welcoming now, but back in 1960 each passport official had a little kingdom in which, mounted on a mini-lectern, was a tome large enough to be a telephone book for the world: the List of Undesirables. Our officer in 1960 was heavy-set and suspicious. He thumbed through the paper-thin pages of the directory and found us on page 8563 or so. He turned the leaves of Ewan's battered passport, a seasoned document filled with entry visas to every possible communist country. He looked up at Ewan in between each page. When he'd finished, he held the dear little book up in front of Ewan's face and drawled in a slow monotone: *What – is – this?* Theatre training runs deep. Ewan smiled. His face went childlike. *I travel a lot.* Less is more. They stared at each other in silence. The official slammed the passport down and thunked the entry stamp onto it so loud that the gallery greeters heard it and cheered.

We came home with money. Cash. We were terrified of debt but decided to buy a flat. It was – and may still be – difficult for musicians to get a mortgage. As everyone knows, we are short on reliability and long on drugs, alcohol and random sex. We bought in Beckenham – *Bec* for brook and *ham* for settlement – village by the brook. It was one of the many dozens of old villages that were swallowed up by insatiable London but there was still one little Tudor house and a forlorn filthy stream down at Shortlands. One of the women working at the only Beckenham hairdresser grew up on a farm which was where the Odeon Cinema stands now. She'd take milk across to the other farm, which is now the library and swimming pool. She was in her sixties, describing her good old days, not realising that her bad new days were my good old ones. We old ones must remember, when lamenting the state of the world, that our bad new days are the good old days against which our grandchildren will measure *their* bad new days in the future that I fear is coming. In 1960, onion sellers from France came down our suburban street, beautiful braided ropes of onions dangling from the handlebars of their bikes. The knife-and-scissors man came regularly, a grinding wheel affixed to his grown-up's tricycle. The rag-and-bone and metal collectors drove slowly past the big old Victorian houses. All these entrepreneurs had distinctive street calls. The winding High Street still retained many of the traditional village features. A few of its pavements were higher than street level, a one-storey stone ziggurat, with stairs to the shops above. A real hardware store that would sell you one screw. A draper's shop with school uniforms for children from five to thirteen years of age, where you were served by a courteous older man in full pinstriped suit, waistcoat and tie and impeccable manners. A workers' cafe, a small chemist, a quality clothes shop, a bakery, a fishmonger, half a dozen pubs, one of which – the George Inn – went back to the early 1700s. At the butcher shop, Paul would lean with a leer across the counter as he trimmed some fat off the belly of pork I'd ordered. *Would you like your belly scratched, madam?* A Sainsbury's where the staff wore long white aprons and high white caps. Dairy was on the left-hand side, preserved meat products on the right and packaged goods and tins at the back counter. You could have one slice of bacon and an ounce of butter, which was cut off from a 5 lb round. Nothing was vacuum-packed in plastic and you went to each counter separately, the money owed written on a slip of paper, payment to be made at the door. A connoisseur's delicatessen on a backstreet, run by Alan Watson, who'd co-ordinated the cameras at the Bikini atom bomb tests in the 1940s. A behind-the-scenes group of old Beckenhamites worked hard to keep their – and my – good old days from ending. Time, franchises, speculators and the drug trade wiped all of old Beckenham out by the 1990s.

We needed to be near Ewan's other family and we were desperate to get settled. We purchased 35 Stanley Avenue after one viewing. We didn't have it surveyed. We never questioned the crazy joint freehold we shared with old Mrs Cole downstairs, who wanted to charge Betsy sixpence whenever she gave her a lift to the Bromley Road shops. We never questioned whether we wanted to live in six and a half rooms on the upper two storeys of a large Victorian house. We just loved the flat. Light poured through the large windows into the spacious, high rooms. It fitted our budget at £4600. We put £300 down, borrowed £2500 from Charlie and put the rest on a mortgage at £15 a month. It was in bad repair. The tiny kitchen had hot water on demand, a pop-up Formica-covered table, ancient hob and oven and a fridge with space for a couple of pints of milk, a pound of butter and six eggs crowded in. There were four different types of electric plug, all lethal and all set at floor level. There were only two small gas fires in the whole place. As money came in we had the chimneys swept, opened up all of the six fireplaces and installed coal stoves. We conquered the iffy walls with paint brushes, filler, rawlplugs, plaster, wallpaper, hammers and the nesting instincts of early love. Ewan had a fetish about painting walls different pastel colours, a concept entirely foreign to me but which quite appealed to my sense of the absurd. We brought Neill's playpen to wherever we were working, put on one of our two jazz records and brought our home alive with our own special brand of imperfectionism.

We moved in at the end of August 1960 with a single and a double bed, three chairs, a table, clothes, instruments, books, Neill's cot, a gramophone player and optimism. We bought furniture from charity shops, bought the worn-out wall-to-wall carpeting for £50. A steal – for the previous owner, Dr McClintock. I ran up curtains on a treadle Singer sewing machine just like Dio's. Betsy – kicked out by Jean a second time – got the best and biggest room in the house from the very start. It would be her sitting-room-cum-bedroom. We'd all have some privacy that way. That arrangement remained until she was encouraged to move out in 1974. The overgrown garden was a beautiful, wild place – bullfinches, hedgehogs, foxes, a tortoise. McClintock had worked for the National Coal Board and he'd laced his raspberry, celery and tomato beds with conveyor belts that had once transported the coal from the face to the tubs. There were about a dozen of these monsters, each roughly twenty feet long and three feet wide, two-inch-thick rubber with metal cleats underneath. It took hours to roll one of them up the garden path around the garage and out to the street. We unearthed a complete motorcycle, dozens of rusted garden tools and enough ashes and clinker to pave hell. We laid down a lawn that brought moles – blind bundles with fur like dry water. We clipped hedges and planted flower beds. A sandpit and a swing for Neill. One of the ancient apple trees fell down, revealing a multi-generational village of stag beetles, now an endangered species. Ewan had never owned a single inch of land till now. This space was his kingdom. Baron MacColl of Beckenham went to inspect it every morning. Where did we get the money for this? All the above improvements were done over the space of two or three years. We never saved anything. Sing yesterday, buy some more paint today. Sing on Sunday, buy a sofa on Monday. Spend today. Tomorrow the IRS and NHS back payments will catch up with you, ensuring a hard couple of years. Good days – hopeful days.

Another tour was planned in the autumn of 1961 – three months, well laid out, Canadian and US dates, visas and work permit required. At that time, the US embassy was in one of those lovely Georgian terrace houses in Upper Grosvenor Street.

The consul himself interviewed everyone, dossier on his desk. That really opened my blue eyes wide. My dossier was about an inch and a half thick, with photographs of me in Russia, China and Poland. It had verbatim transcripts of conversations I'd had with other members of the 1957 trip. In no way was I dangerous politically other than being Charles Seeger's daughter, Pete Seeger's sister, Ewan MacColl's mistress, not yet my own woman – and having visited communist countries. My papers came through. Ewan was denied permission to enter the USA. We desperately needed this money. We could repay Charlie. We could fill up our savings account. We could get off the un-merry-go-round. The show had to go on. Need of money: the first commandment of many a questionable credo. I'd have to do the tour alone.

Our bedroom was the least enticing room in the house. Still in love, we lit it with our presence. This would be the first time we'd been parted since joining ourselves together. I cried, Ewan cried. We were awake the whole night, weeping, angry and full of passionate vows. Neill and Ewan waved me off at the airport in the old traditional style, standing high up on the top of the terminal and waving white handkerchiefs. Girl-mother, bawling like a baby as the plane took off. More than once I turned up at a concert venue to see a long line of people at the box office wanting refunds. I was just one of a growing number of long-haired female folk singers – dubbed *mushroom sitters* early on – whose songs they thought they already knew. The audiences wanted Ewan. When we'd been there in 1959, requests had piled up on the stage: 'Eppie Morrie', 'Johnnie o'Breadislie' – they wanted the unaccompanied voice singing texts they could barely understand. Years later, they wanted Ewan singing 'Freeborn Man', 'Shoals of Herring'. My persistent requests

– but much later – were for 'I'm Gonna Be an Engineer', 'The Ballad of Springhill' and 'The First Time Ever I Saw Your Face'. I came home after three months with $3000 in cash and we paid Charlie off. I was proud – I had earned it all myself. Ewan had a surprise for me – and he was proud. He had taught himself to play the guitar. He knew nearly every chord in the book. He began to sing, strumming awkwardly. It was heart-breaking and funny. He couldn't sing and play at the same time. *Just sing, Ewan. I'll play.* Relieved, he laid the guitar down. Relieved, he confessed that he'd been afraid that I might just stay in the States.

We weren't very good at family planning. I blame both of us, irresponsible and spontaneous. In 1961, the same financial conditions and my second abortion. Ewan drove me to Edmonton – another down-at-heel two-up-two-down with a not-so-clean, overweight matron attending. He waited outside in the car, chain-smoking. Same syringe of soapy water, same inner-core pain. I lay in our bed at home, swaddled with towels. Ewan was terrified, beginning to realise what I had gone through alone the first time. Sitting on the toilet and an enormous wad of blood and flesh emerged. The Cruel Mother needed to punish herself. She fished in the toilet for the lump. It was like raw liver. In the middle of the mess was a shrew-sized morsel with a pinpoint penis. No tears. No reaction. Just shock, fear and confusion. She . . . someone else did it, yes? *Oh Dio* . . . she was still trying for another baby in 1953. Betsy used to say, *Life maun aye be some way.* Yes, life must always be somehow – or life must be as it was meant to be from the first time that a single cell divided to give birth to life on this earth.

*

217

1962 saw us traversing up, down, across Great Britain, as it was known then, singing in folk clubs. We could now afford another child. Near the High Force waterfall, Forest-in-Teesdale, County Durham . . . the sky was blue, the walls and floor green. I told Betsy I was pregnant. We were in the kitchen. She was standing at the stove in one of her stand-and-tap-your-foot-on-the-floor-and-stare-into-space moods. Her aura was charcoal grey. Her response, without looking at me, was – and this is an accurate quote for it hit me like a slap in the face – *I'll tak' care o' yen child, no' twa*. When you tell your man's mother that you are expecting again after three years, she is supposed to beam, sit you down, ask when the happy day is, have a cup of tea and chat. *Dio: you would have loved the prospect of another baby in your life. You'd have waited those nine months with me, eager for the first moment of the child in your arms. I want my mother . . .* when I abort and when I'm pregnant. I'd had no plans when I was in my teens but where I was now would not have been a young girl's dream. As a spoiled middle-class girl from what was then termed the *intelligentsia*, I'd have set my rules: no married man twenty years older than I; no man with another family; no home on the top two floors of a Victorian house, a dozen concrete steps down to a garden dozens of long paces away. Certainly no bitchy, moody, live-in putative mother-in-law. Yet – when I look at the photographs of those days, I am happy. I am fit and capable and, as with all three of my pregnancies, I was *we* for nine months.

Ewan fretted when I was pregnant. He didn't take pictures, wasn't one of those fathers who continually have their hands on your belly feeling the baby moving. I'd have liked to have one of those. He was frightened of my body when it held a baby, maybe remembering the number of Salford women crippled or dead from childbirth, a process which is still the most dangerous natural event in a woman's life. One spin-off though: he drove much better when I was with child. My cravings were startling. With my first pregnancy it was pickles and salted herring. With my second, tomato soup with Smarties in it. With my third it was macaroni and cheese in the second darkness of night. With all of them I had morning sickness for six or eight weeks – then I would sail with full rigging into the open ocean of pregnancy. I didn't really like being pregnant. I loved what I called *my fineness* – the sense of control over the size, state and contours of my body. I liked being fit and active. Pregnant, I was an elephant harbouring a precious extraterrestrial. Old wives' tales told me this child was a boy, because I was carrying low. Needless to say, it seems to be common that when you've had a boy you then want a girl. I was so heartsick over Kirsty. I felt that a daughter would restore some of the purity of our love affair. Was I in competition with Jean? Or was it that Charlie loved me so much because I was a girl? The Travellers and Gypsies say that any man can father a boy, but it takes a real man to father a girl. Nonsensical. I bore Kirsty no ill will, none at all. Whatever result her birth had had on me, she was a beautiful addition to the family, to the world of music, a one-off and, like my boys, an exceptional musician and singer. In the mid-1970s, we took her to France with us on an eating holiday. The teenage trio in the back seat of the new second-hand Citroën ID provided continual entertainment. I wrote 'Nine-Month Blues' on that trip. Kirsty thought it was wordy but liked it.

Calum was born on 27 March 1963, another late-night home birth. I heard my blood thrumming, my own High Force waterfall. He was a large baby. Forget Neill's dainty birth cry, Calum gave a high-pitched howl of indignation. They laid him on my chest, his head squashed, lavish black hair on top. Neill's head had been similar, but practically bald. Like all newborns, Calum had that *where am I?* look as he tried to focus. He grabbed my finger. My body isn't big enough to hold my heart. I stop writing for a while and wallow in Memory. *Welcome, son – welcome home.* The next morning Neill came into the room in his pretty red dressing gown. He peered closely into his brother's face. *He isn't very good to look at, is he?* Calum had a pair of lungs like a longshoreman. He shouted and cried and screamed and tore the place down. High Force indeed. Neill had become a quiet, pleasant person. Bedtimes were not a problem. He'd turn on his bedside lamp and read. Lay Calum in the crib and he would begin to grizzle, then murmur. The murmur would rise to a cry, the cry would escalate into a shriek that would have passed muster in a horror film. *Is he dying?* Rush upstairs. Neill is reading quietly. *He's noisy, isn't he?* Lean over the crib. *Immediately* the noise would stop. *Immediately* the long lashes, dew-dropped with tears, would flutter. You just had to laugh. Our colt had to be broken of this. Let him cry till he falls asleep. Calum could go on for several hours. I had to stop Ewan going upstairs and he had to stop me. Calum took a week to learn. Neill read peacefully through it all.

24

The Radio Ballads

1962. Calum's not born yet. The Director General of the BBC sails through the cafe trailing obsequious dinghies behind him. The plummy voice: *And what is the Radio Ballad team doing next?* Coal mining. *Not another working-class epic!*

One of the reasons that our Radio Ballads were so successful was that the triumvirate of Charles, Ewan and Peggy went on site to directly confront the work conditions and speak to those whose lives the Ballad was to document. For *The Big Hewer*, we went below. Kitted out with gloves, a pit helmet and pads on my knees and elbows, I was directed to speak as little as possible. Miners, like fishermen, are superstitious about women in their workspace. Or maybe they want just one place in the world without women, just as many women want places without men. It was a soft-coal pit and our guide was the singer/miner Jack Elliott of Birtley, County Durham. You go down in a *cage*. It clanks and wobbles, banging against the sides of the shaft, and lands softly or with a jolt depending on the skill of the setter at the pit head. The drop down was easy but oh, the sight of that small black hole into which we are to crawl on our hands and knees. Jack's a big man. His cavil – working section – is about three feet in diameter. You enter on your hands and knees, propelling yourself forward with your elbows, a worm going back home. The Northumbrian miners call it *swimming*. Jack showed us his short-handled pick and joked about taking it in facing the wrong direction and having to *swim* feet first back to the entrance to turn the pick around.

My back and helmet graze the ceiling. My elbows touch the walls. The soles of Jack's boots are ahead of me and Ewan is crawling behind me. No spare room above, beside or behind. I have mild claustrophobia. I don't lock toilet doors – I hold my foot against them if possible. *How far do we have to go, Jack?* Matter is conquering mind. *About three hundred feet, flower.* I love that endearment. I tell him I need to rest for a moment. What I really need to do is talk to myself, head down, eyes open, on my hands and knees. It is never silent in a coal mine. The earth is creaking and groaning all around me. I'm twenty-seven, I'm a mother, and I want to live. I am in a man-made world where I am regarded as the weaker sex. I must not reinforce the stereotype of the hysterical female. I *will* live through this. By the time we emerged at the other end I believed that a miner should be paid just for going down a mine, never mind for working there.

Years later, we take teenage Neill down a Yorkshire pit as part of his political education. Here the ceilings are high and the road from pit bottom to the workings is wide. After a half-mile or so, we turn right and enter a cul-de-sac, a gallery where the shot-firers ahead of us are placing the dynamite high on the wall of a new seam. We head off to the right. Alice in Underland, a four-lane highway running away into the distance. This is hell, not a painting – but see it with me. The ceiling is about four feet high. The uncut coalface is a solid wall about ten feet to our left. The coal-cutting machine is moving along that wall, back and forth for hundreds of feet, shearing a spray of coal off onto the thick metal-studded rubber belt (McClintock's garden paths) that runs alongside, nearer to us, conveying the coal to bogies up ahead. Machine and belt comprise two lanes of the highway. To the right of this, we are crawling on hands and knees in the third lane, separated from the belt by a row of wooden pit props. To our right is the fourth lane, another row of props holding the roof up. Behind them, into the near-right 'countryside', are scattered roof-high piles of coal, rock and slack. The whole of this set-up will, as the seam is worked, keep creating new left-hand lanes and closing right-hand ones. Soon our crawling lane will be de-propped and the roof will fall in on the fourth lane. My body is vibrating with the noise as the coal-cutter comes abreast of us when suddenly there is a huge explosion. Whoooooosh! and . . . there is . . . no air . . . no . . . air. At all. Body wants to breathe in but . . . no . . . air . . . no . . . I'm dying. I lie down. A flood of cool air rushes in, drawn by the vacuum, and my lungs fill automatically. Apparently, when the shots are about to fire, a signal warns anyone within earshot. Miners know to take a deep breath and hold it. That signal, sent down our line of crawlers, never reached me; or perhaps I wasn't told about it; or the sound of the coal-cutter drowned it out; or I was just in my inner world holding my claustrophobic self together, for the miner crawling ahead of me kept on going and Ewan, behind me, bumped into me.

Most of the people we recorded for the Ballads are still in my picture gallery. We were interviewing for *On the Edge*, about teenagers. I had never been one. Big Business created teenagers as an economic category after my time. We'd been told that teenagers would not talk frankly to us oldies. Wrong – they were dying to talk. East London, a dance hall. In a side room we are interviewing girls and boys picked at random. Vera, fifteen years old, way up-to-date and dishy: *You gotta have your fun while you're young 'cos when you're twenty you've 'ad it!* At the time, I was twenty-eight, Ewan and Charles were in their late forties – all of us as out-of-date as the word *dishy*. Vera will be sixty-five now.

The first four Radio Ballads were placed squarely amongst the British industrial, male working class: *The Ballad of John Axon* (railways), *Song of a Road* (road building), *Singing the Fishing* (herring fishing) and *The Big Hewer* (coal mining). *The Body Blow* (polio) and *On the Edge* placed more emphasis on individual than community experience – attempts to mollify the Director General by getting off the subject of politics and class warfare. Our last two Radio Ballads were *The Fight Game*, about boxers – most of whom come from the working class – and *The Travelling People*, dealing with Britain's traditional nomads, who could be described as a section of the unorganised, unorganisable working class. Coming from a white middle-class family in the 1940s in racially segregated Washington DC, I had known working-class people. They came to work for us and then went home to their own world. They were menial workers – an insulting term – and they were all darker people of African descent. I had had no contact with either white workers or organised working people. My participation in the Radio Ballads brought me directly into the homes, pubs and workplaces of the *folk* of my folk songs. Ewan had a definition: the *folk* are those who do the basic ground-level work in a society, those without whose work life could not go on; the only indispensable class, the working class. They were the basis of every Radio Ballad and of my real political education. Their stories held me as the fairy tales had.

Snapshot: The Welsh miner Dick Beamish was one of the most articulate people I had ever met. He'd been our guide underground and this day, at a place where the road took a sharp bend, he motioned us to sit down and turn our head-lamps off.

In total blackness you become dizzy, losing all sense of up, down, sideways. We sat in silence while the pit creaked and cracked and groaned around us. *My mate died near here. The roof fell on him.* We moved on. Beamish stopped again. *Wait – she's moving.* A few yards ahead of us a huge section of roof crashed to the ground, closing the road that forked off to the right. Snapshot: We're sitting in the kitchen of a Welsh miner. He's in his sixties. He has advanced pneumoconiosis and his lungs fill up constantly with liquid. A cough comes up as if from below his feet, pulling off pieces of virtual flesh as it rises. It is continuous, with occasional simulations of a death rattle. His wife brings him hot tea. Charles turns pale. *Dai, shouldn't we call the doctor?* Another wrenching cough. *Doctor? No, bach. Around here we call the plumber.* Dai laughs, his wife laughs, Ewan laughs. They all have the same class background and understand that life is so perilous that you have to laugh. Charles and I look at each other. This is entirely off our middle-class Richter Scale.

The Elliotts of Birtley laughed a great deal, no subject out of bounds. Jack and Em had four grown children – Pete, Bill, Doreen and Len. We are all crowded into the tiny back room of their terrace house. Doreen is recalling her teenage courting years. She had come home late one night. *So me dad asked where we'd gone and I told him. He says, Oh, and did you cross the little stream? I says, Aye, Dad, we did. Me dad says, And did you come to that little patch of grass under the big tree? I says, Aye, Dad. And did you sit down on the grass, nice and soft, like? Aye, Dad, we did.* Doreen is already beginning to crack up. *And me dad says, I shit there.* Everyone laughs. Of course, they've heard the story before but, like the songs, it's worth hearing again and again. Ewan repeated – and my best friend Irene retells – bits of their life stories again and again and I would never stop them because

(a) the telling is different every time, and (b) it's a valuable story about a way of life still foreign to me. It's a ballad, a fairy tale, domestic kathakali. The Elliotts' kind of humour *never* existed in our Seeger family – and still doesn't to my knowledge. As I write, I'm still in touch with Doreen, an octogenarian firebrand whose political flame has never flickered.

We were visiting and staying in houses where no one had any privacy, where parents and four children shared two bedrooms while the downstairs front parlour was shut off and saved for formal occasions and where the piss pot was under the bed and you carried it downstairs in the morning for emptying. Sharing time and space with the speakers on the Radio Ballads probably did more than anything else to drive home to me the class distinctions, the real impact of the Industrial Revolution and the survival capabilities of human beings. My sheltered upbringing didn't keep me from recognising how truly protective a very small space can be for a very large family. It can be excessively constrictive under adverse circumstances, but then – as Princess Diana and Prince Charles proved – so can a royal palace. The thread of shared hardship ran through most of the people we interviewed. John Axon and his workmates comprised a railway community. The boxers in *The Fight Game* had a community at the gym. My songs came from community living but I did not. Silver Spring, Chevy Chase, my schools, my very large but very scattered family – none had given me a lifetime community. Yet here were our interviewees, whose principal pronoun was *we*, telling stories of community adhesion and dissolution, all dependent on their position as the foundation of a ruthless capitalist system. Revolution began to make sense to me.

A memoir becomes a succession of anecdotes becomes a gallery of Radio Ballad snapshots. 1959: A freezing, rainy day and

we're sloshing through the mud on the soon-to-be M1 motorway. A very young Irish boy is weeping as he runs a huge buzz-
saw down the field of set concrete, cutting expansion fissures
that will be filled later with tar. His tears are bigger than the
raindrops. 1960: We're in Winterton, Norfolk. A tiny living
room and Sam Larner recalls the sexual hunger that accompanied his returns from sea. His eighty-year-old blind wife,
Dorcas, smiles her agreement. I'm crocheting a large blanket as
we record and Charles – irritated by the uninterested BBC engineer, who records from a pantechnicon larger than Sam's cottage – snaps, *Stop clicking that needle, Peggy!* 1962: Birmingham.
I'm pregnant with Calum and we have near-to-ringside seats at
the boxing match. The Brummie fans stand and cheer local boy
Johnny Prescott on his entrance. They boo him when Henry
Cooper (a.k.a. *Our 'Enery*) drops him fifteen feet away from
us, jaw awry and eyes glazed like an ox at the slaughterhouse.
Striding in through cheering fans with both fists raised and carried out on a stretcher to the sound of booing. The following
year, the Romany Gypsy woman whose infant had drowned
in a mud hole on the Cobham site in Kent; the miner waiting
to collect his pay packet speaking of an official: *He's lower than
whale shit, and that's at the bottom of the ocean.* Dot Dobby, fifteen years old, works in a factory in Manchester, sewing pockets
onto aprons. I'm interviewing her in our living room for *On the
Edge*. A single lamp illuminates half of her face. Her eyes are
on her Salford street on a summer night and her mouth is open
listening in wonder to someone telling her story.

We come home with boxes of analogue tapes that must now
be transcribed. Ewan runs the big Ferrograph and I clatter
away on the old manual typewriter. The transcript is not word-
for-word. The folk songs have taught us that generations of

singers have edited as they went along, balancing what sings well and what best tells the story. Poetic passages of actuality emerge like passers-by approaching in a fog, only to be recognised in detail as they come close. We must sieve out the memorable. This is art, not reportage. We build up a transcript of excerpts, with rough guides as to *where* on the seven-inch reel of tape this or that piece of actuality can be found. A narrative shape is emerging, dramatic units begin to present themselves. Ewan closets himself for a few weeks, helping the tale to tell itself. He suggests points at which sound, songs and instrumental breaks could take place. We discuss continually. The script takes shape, sprouts legs, then wings. He is so good at this. He writes the songs, incorporating breathing patterns, words, whole phrases and tonality from our speakers so well that when Sam Larner first hears 'The Shoals of Herring', made out of his own recorded speech, he declares, *I known that song all my life.* In 1978, I would record Jayaben Desai, the key figure in the Grunwick dispute.* Desai's language was biblical. I put it word for word into my song 'Union Woman II'. When I play the song for her, she says, *I hear myself speaking.*

> *Born rich in the womb,*
> *As you say, with a silver spoon in the mouth.*
> *Born female, learned early to work but never had to labour.*

* The industrial action at the Grunwick Film Processing Plant, Willesden, London, from August 1976 to June 1978, was the first strike led by an ethnic minority, mostly female, and the first to involve paramilitary policing. The dispute related to pay and overtime issues, and the lack of union support was disgraceful. The strike was a tipping point, setting a precedent for Margaret Thatcher's dismantling of the power of unions in the UK. Go to the internet for the full story.

The luxury life is a knife in the heart and mind,
Every day, all day, nothing to do but waste your time.

We give the script to Charles – Charles, who later will be the one to whom journalists talk, who will give the impression that he was responsible for the whole shebang. Our joint work will become *Charles Parker's Radio Ballads*. He apologises on page 17 of the newspaper in which the original article appeared the day before on page 2. He sends us a letter apologising for having strutted for a pretty journalist. But – he's a friend, a great producer, director and editor. We're all fallible sometimes. He isolates the spoken passages and sound effects that we've designated and places them in order on a master tape. I choose musicians, then start on the musical score which will join the strands together, weaving in and out, complementing or contrasting with the speech or sound that it follows or accompanies. We take great pains to keep changing pace, content and focus so that you will not get bored and turn off. The rehearsal sessions require patience and diplomacy. Bruce Turner, superb jazz clarinettist: *I can't read music very well, Dad.* Bruce called everyone Dad. Sometimes I doubted whether he could read music at all, so I would make simple chord charts for him. We'd run through a unit and he'd be standing there with his clarinet held well away from his mouth, gazing into space. *Bruce, are you with us? Yes, Dad. Let's take it again; tell us where you're having trouble, Bruce. The whole thing, Dad.* He was hopeless at rehearsals but produced diamond-sharp improvisation on the recorded takes.

In the later Radio Ballads, we would invite one of the actuality-speakers into the studio. Norma Smith came in her wheelchair during the recording of *The Body Blow*. A boxing trainer turned up during the recording of *The Fight Game*.

Belle, Elizabeth and Jane Stewart sang in *The Travelling People*. After prolonged rehearsal with singers and musicians, we go into the studio. The floor manager has put all the microphones and screens where we'll get the best separation of sound. We can't always see each other but we all wear headphones. The ingredients that have to be mixed together are: (1) the singers, (2) the instrumentalists, (3) the actuality on the master tape, and (4) sound effects, which are on large vinyl discs up in the studio. Gillian Ford, radio engineer, is in charge of five or six huge turntables that run continually. She can drop a needle on any groove on any disc, on any cue, any time. The master tape of the actuality is situated on a TR-90 tape machine, placed in the midst of the musicians. A microsecond delay can mean that the rhythm of the actuality is out of sync with the background music – but Alan Ward can start and stop the massive machine on a farthing. I am the conductor and music director, placed where everyone can see me. Charles, the puppet master, sits up in the gods, behind a huge glass window, directing and producing. He suffers terribly with migraine headaches. Sometimes he will be lying out of sight doubled up with pain on the cubicle floor but still running the show. Occasionally, in a fury, he will interrupt a take with a deafening shriek on the intercom. Sometimes he purrs through our headphones with ill-disguised sarcasm. There is no such thing as multi-tracking or superimposing one track over another. Everything is fed simultaneously onto quarter-inch tape and the whole unit must be done in one go. If *anyone* misses their cue or messes up, the whole thing has to be done again. The long fight scene in *The Fight Game* was recorded some seventy times.

All this must seem bizarre to musicians and engineers these days, when an A-sharp sung flat can be adjusted digitally, when you can record each instrument on a different track, record the vocal, then mix the whole thing down to the final product. These new techniques can take away the community aspect of music-making but they do assure perfection – if that's what you want. A little imperfection can be just what's needed. Our team back then could energise one another almost to the point of a mystical experience: we had *all* gotten it right this time! It's *not* like a symphony orchestra or a football team. The Radio Ballad crew came together for a one-off production, rehearsed and recorded within a two-week span, after which we disbanded.

Our eight Radio Ballads are now considered seminal works. We developed new recording and editing techniques on manual equipment that is now totally out of date. The Ballads broke the radio documentary mould and challenged the political stance that had dominated the BBC ever since its inception. We used folk music disciplines to create a dramatic form that documented and validated working-class experience. Best of all, our contributors spoke for themselves – their words were not given to BBC actors to read. The Radio Ballad days were probably the best days of my creative life and our musical team were my temporary community. The BBC discontinued them because of budget considerations, even though *Singing the Fishing* won an Italia prize; even though they are now regarded as works of genius.* The subsequent Radio Ballad series have yet to get everything right – the songs are good, the subjects are really interesting. All they need is a Ewan MacColl.

* The Radio Ballads are available from Topic Records, UK. Go to *Set into Song* by Peter Cox for anything else you need to know about them.

25

Charles Parker

Charles Parker was the Proper Englishman to Ewan's Working-Class Artist. He was a seasoned BBC producer. In January 1959, when I arrived back in England, full-blown in pregnancy, he invited me to lunch in London. The two of us were magnetised by Ewan's lightning creativity and thrilled with the success of *The Ballad of John Axon*. From now on he and I were going to be working together and Charles wanted to sort us out, hanging as it were onto the tail of the MacColl comet. His meal got cold while he lectured me. I had sinned against God, against Ewan's wife and son, and, it would seem, against Charles himself. I left the restaurant unchastened.

In the summer of 1959, the three of us were on our way to Scotland, recording for *Singing the Fishing*. Our trip took us to Winterton, where we recorded Sam Larner and stayed at the Mariners' Arms. They were beautiful wind-blown days with a cloudless sky of un-British blue. One morning I woke up snuggled next to the father of my son, looking at the bright summer sky. I was deliriously happy. I fell back asleep and woke up again, feeling watched. I peered out from under the covers and Charles was standing at the foot of our bed. He would undoubtedly have knocked but we always slept very soundly. His ascetic face bore such a look of longing that I nearly invited him into the bed for comfort. He admitted once that he'd never had a real, mutual love affair.

We drove on up to Scotland. We ranged up the coast from Aberdeen to Gamrie (Gardenstown), where the Open Brethren were warring with the Exclusive Brethren. Charles was very religious. Ewan had told me that on their collecting trip for *Song of a Road* they'd occasionally had to share a room. Ewan would read in his bed and Charles would kneel like a child beside his, saying his prayers. On this trip he kept hopping out to go into churches. It almost didn't matter what denomination they were – Charles wanted to talk to any God. When he got out of the car, Ewan would say, *Put in a good word with God for me, Charlie boy*, and we'd wait for him to come back. I followed him once into one of the more interesting churches. He was down on his knees, eyes shut, his hands clasped together so tightly that the knuckles were white. Charles was very patriotic. They used to play 'God Save the Queen' at the end of the film in the cinemas. When we attended with Charles he would be instantly on his feet, saluting Her Majesty smartly.* He'd been in the Royal Navy and he really knew how to salute. Ewan was rather unkind on these occasions. He'd sit there chuckling throughout the whole of the short anthem. If Ewan was thoughtless, Charles was mixed up. Like me, he was still growing up, although he was the same age as Ewan. His mother had kept a boarding house and had definite ideas about social hierarchy. He felt insecure when he went into working-class houses. He had no social flexibility. He was almost military in his bearing and was so formal when he was interviewing that it was embarrassing.

We were in Gamrie when we heard about Lucy Stewart of the Travelling family, the Stewarts of Fetterangus, Elizabeth

---

* In New Zealand in 2017, I was at a cinema where they stand up for the anthem.

and Jane's aunt. We drove over and got a warm welcome. She gave us endless cups of scalding, sweet tea and bread and butter and cakes and biscuits. We three hadn't had dinner. Ewan and I tucked in heartily. Charles refused and asked only for a glass of water, which he didn't drink. He ate nothing, although he'd been starving before we came in. A companionable evening with songs and jokes and banter, Lucy singing old ballads and interested in my American versions. Charles . . . it was like having a party with a cigar-store Indian. On the way home, Ewan went on the attack. *Charles, you accept the hospitality even if you've just had a five-course meal! You do not etc., etc., etc.* Charles commanded me to stop the car and said he'd walk back to Gamrie, five miles away – and we were in the midst of cold, cotton-wool fog. I drove very slowly, keeping him in sight in the mirror. After a few minutes I stopped and he got into the back seat again. He burst into tears and said he just couldn't help it. He thought that Gypsies were dirty and he was afraid of using their crockery and silverware. A year or two later we visited Charlotte Higgins of Blairgowrie – an old, calm, song-full Traveller woman. She offered up a beautifully set table for tea – homemade scones, jam and butter. Her diction was courtly. Before pouring the tea she lifted each cup and showed us how clean it was. My eyes filled with tears. I glanced at Charles. He gave me an affectionate look and lifted the cup to his mouth without a moment's hesitation.

We were headed back to the Gamrie Arms after recording in Banff on the north coast of Scotland. It was late and all the food joints and pubs were closed. In northeast Scotland that means lockdown. The streets are bleak, deserted and windswept. Petrol stations didn't have food back then. We were ravenous. Ewan was driving and in the rear-view mirror he saw Charles chewing on something. I'd gotten a faint whiff of chocolate but as we'd all been hallucinating out loud about what we'd love to eat I thought it was an olfactory mirage. Ewan, casually: *What are you eating, Charlie boy?* Charles, mumbling: *Nothing.* Ewan brought the car to a quick halt, turned around and repeated, *What – are – you – eating?* Eyes down, like a naughty child, Charles brought out the remains of a bar of nut-and-raisin chocolate. He must have really worked hard to keep the wrapper from rustling as he'd secretly opened it and broken the little squares off. Ewan said in a flat, quiet voice: *Share it.*

Frozen silence all the way back. We went to bed. Charles broke out the EMI recording machine, walked down to the end of the pier and recorded the sea until the cold brought him back indoors. From that point on, he would deliberately buy things to hand out on trips. He became one of the most generous people I've ever known, leaning over backward to share himself, his time, his ideas, his skills. We all battle our upbringing and our lesser selves. More than anyone I've known in my life, Charles Parker turned himself around. He could even joke about the Queen. Like all of us, there's more than meets the eye. Oh yes, there's still that question of hijacking credit for the authorship of the Radio Ballads – but that's small stuff compared to nut-and-raisin bars bought especially for not sharing.

> *Time, tide me over a few more years,*
> *Please allow my comrade's friends to thrive;*
> *We're part of all that he held dear –*
> *We keep our friend alive.*
>
>   ('Song for Charles Parker')

26

Collector's Fever

New Year's Eve, an Alaskan snowstorm, one helluva night. You could hardly see but a yard ahead. Only fools and folk song collectors would venture out on a night like this. We were both. We'd never been to Harlow, fifty miles away. We didn't even know the people we were going to see. A Dickensian bod who came regularly to the Singers' Club had told us about them: the Stewarts of Blairgowrie. They are related to the Fetterangus Stewarts but both branches of the clan kept themselves kind of . . . *separate* is the only fair word for it. Sad remnant of some ancient feud? As time went on, we had more contact with the extended Blairgowrie Stewarts. They were a singing family of Scots Travellers whose men were helping to build Harlow New Town. Their women were taking local work, their children temporarily attending local schools where – most likely – they were being bullied. The Stewarts were holding a hooley tonight to say goodbye to 1961 and we were invited. Ewan had told me about Hogmanay, the Scots New Year: merriment, music, drinking and drinking and drinking till you were down and all the way out or hanging legless over hedges and walls as January rolled in.

We had a small-scale map and Harlow was on the A1 about an inch northeast above London. Beckenham was about a third of an inch southeast below. We were in the Light 15. The road was a vast white meadow. We were the only vehicle on the road so there were no tracks to follow. Our headlights picked out dim stalks, octagons, squares and triangles – snow-covered lampposts and road signs. We were struggling up and sliding down hills, skidding around curves no matter how slowly we went. The journey was endless, but in December 1961 so was life. In 1962, we reached the address we'd been given. The windows were dark and there were no little footsteps in the snow up to the door. We turned around and headed home. The Stewart family had moved on two days before. As one does. We got the new address and travelled to a Day-to-Remember. Belle Stewart was in full flight, a handsome, full-blown, grey-haired matron. Her daughters Sheila and Cathy were there with their families. Husband Alec played the pipes. Ewan and I sang. It was a Night-to-Remember as well – and a Dawn. We arranged to record them on a regular basis, with a view to writing a book about them.

This was very different from collecting for the Radio Ballads. We were recording in deep depth. It would be a long project. We toured incessantly. The Stewarts travelled incessantly. Put your arms down by your sides then lift them up above your head. If you can make your index fingers meet over your head, it's a sign that you're crazy. We met and recorded them whenever our crazy paths intersected. For months during the early 1970s, they came down to Beckenham. I would drive up to King's Cross train station to pick them up or, to the consternation of our neighbours, they would park their Flintstones van in front of 35 Stanley Avenue and sleep overnight in it. You never knew how many of them there would be, which could be problematical as we were paying for their train tickets and supplying supper.

We recorded everything: songs, jokes, stories, riddles, family history. Belle was happiest when she was the centre of attention. Sheila was the best singer in my opinion; she would lose herself totally in the ballads. Alec was a piper – not extraordinary, but competent. Cathy's storytelling exhibited a deep understanding of drama, an ability to create the epic out of the ordinary. They were a functional *family*. They enjoyed each other's company, and even though they'd heard and told the same stories and songs over and over again, they loved hearing them over and over again and again. Many of their riddles were in rhyme and most of them risqué.

> *Doon on his knees and he's at it*
> *Wi' a thing in his hand that'll fit it.*
> *'Is it in?' said he. 'Aye,' said she,*
> *'It's a richt ticht fit and I like it.'*

The answer is at the end of this chapter. They always stayed till the last minute. Then it was back to King's Cross to pop them onto the last train home.

You can live stories while collecting them. We were at the raspberry-picking in Blairgowrie before going home. We'd asked Belle if she knew 'The Twa Sisters'. *No, but Jacky White kens it. He's no' here the noo but I'll phone when he is.* She phoned on a Wednesday morning. Jacky was *here the noo*. We were in Beckenham. We only had the Light 15. By late afternoon on Friday we were in Blair, needing to drive back on Tuesday. *Och, he'll no' sing the noo. This is the nicht he beats his wife* – and gets too drunk to sing anything. Saturday, and Jacky had left for Aberdeen, so the four of us pile into the Citroën and head northeast. Aberdeen's large. We're nearing the centre, stopped at a traffic light. A man with grey stubble is lounging against a telephone pole. Alec barks, *He's a McFee*, opens the car door and steps out. I follow. They face each other in ritual stance. *You're a Stewart. You're a McFee.* Between them they work out which branch of McFees, which limb of Stewarts. The jungle telegraph is buzzing between them. Three more such stops and we find out that Jacky White has moved on, this time with no forwarding information. *How did you know he was a McFee, Alec? His cheekbones. How did he know you are a Stewart? My big nose.* Belle and Alec hitch a ride with a Blairgowrie-bound Traveller family, and Ewan and I return home.

That was the beginning of our love affair with collecting, most of which was done among Gypsies (those with the Romany heritage) and Travellers – the descendants of the Scots population that had been disinherited and dispersed by the Highland Clearances in the sixteenth and seventeenth centuries. I understand that these days the distinctions between them have blurred and 'Traveller' seems to apply broadly. We came at the end of an era. The powers-that-are were making it impossible for these nomads who, since Memory itself began to travel, had trekked Britain's roads, resting or stopping overnight at traditional places. Most of the Travellers we recorded were grounded, like the Stewarts, renting houses and travelling out in their caravans to whatever/wherever work was available. Some of them lived rough the year round – like Scotswoman Maggie Cameron and her family, who lived in benders, bow-tents: saplings bowed over and tied together, tarpaulins thrown over and pegged down. The Cameron family lived in a tent that was maybe twenty feet in diameter. It's nearly dark and damp-cold. We stoop to enter and encounter a scene straight out of the Middle Ages. The only light comes from a peat-brick fire in a bucket in the middle of the tent. Another bucket, upturned and holed, acts as a flue. Some of the smoke escapes through a small hole in the ceiling, the rest drifts about in a haze. No chairs, no tables, just a few mattresses. The only place you can stand up straight is right by the fire. Everyone squats or sits on the well-swept old carpets that cover the packed earth but cannot keep out the elemental ground chill. The Arctic is underground as well as at the Poles. There are three or four generations here, about twenty people. Children wander in and out of the perimeter gloom. Maggie, her face a seamed, peat-browned leather map of wrinkles crowned with a cloud of white curly hair, looks about eighty – she is probably much less. She is the matriarch and the younger members of the family give her a privileged place by the fire. She sits dignified, cross-legged, describing the winter mornings when they have to hack the children's frozen mattresses away from the ground. She weaves a story around the death of her little daughter, incorporating the flight of the phoenix from this very bucket of coals. Murmured sympathy wafts around her, providing soft accompaniment to her droning voice. No one else chips in. Maggie is speaking for everyone.

Ewan is holding the mic and I'm monitoring the tape machine. We had given up on the little battery-hungry EMI Midgets supplied by the BBC and invested in a new Nagra, the top-of-the-range Swiss recording machine. It made no noise but its dials were bright and harsh. At the very end of the Radio Ballad *The Travelling People*, a Birmingham councillor suggests that certain of the Gypsies and Travellers should be exterminated. Here, as we sit in the bow-tent, the two sources of light – dials and peat fire – seem as far apart in time and value as the councillor and Maggie Cameron herself. Among the Gypsies and Travellers from whom we collected, the older women were the main repositories of the tales and songs. When they were holding forth, the men and children were very quiet. The children had no bedtime, no babysitters. The teenagers were not out partying with troupes of their peers. During the day, they had all picked raspberries, dug potatoes, picked stones with the adults. Now they were all part of the evening's entertainment. Everyone was part of everything. Listening was every bit as important as speaking, sometimes more so. One by one the very young dropped off and were homed on warm laps or under piles of coats and blankets.

Some of the nomad people were well off indeed. At Appleby Horse Fair, we recorded a Lincolnshire scrap dealer, the Gypsy Sylvester ('Wester') Boswell. In the back window of his large, spotless Airstream caravan was a foot-high solid silver statue of a rearing stallion. Mrs Boswell served tea in a complete Spode china tea set on a silver tray. At the other end of the economic scale was the family of the Dorset Gypsy Queen Caroline Hughes, the Romany singer and storyteller. With no running water, no waste collection, no toilet facilities, the site was as tidy as could be expected. One group was sorting rags. Another was cooking over an open fire. Several men were mending a pickup truck. Horses grazed; lurcher dogs growled and lunged against the leash; children wandered dirty and barefoot; the Poole bypass thundered along, fifty yards away. Queen Caroline, paralysed in a car accident, was lifted reverently out of her traditional painted caravan and placed gently on a cushion by the fire. We asked her about the songs – the old ones. She opened with a 1920s tear-jerker and looked at us quizzically. *You didn't like that 'un, didja?* We asked her about 'Barbara Allen'. *Ohhhh*, she said. *You want our relegends. Them's our history, them songs. Without them we're nothin'*. She sang 'Barbry Ellen'. We asked her about the ballad 'Little Sir Hugh', in which a child is stolen and ritually murdered by the Jew's daughter in Lincoln. She told the story, recited the text, lilted the tune but refused to sing the whole song. She didn't like it, didn't want to sing it. John MacDonald, a Scots Traveller, sang it, then said, *I dinna care for that yen*. Many field singers have exhibited similar dislike of the ballad, changing the murderess to an aunt, a beautiful lady, a duke's daughter, a Gypsy. Regarding the last, Gilbert Boswell, Sylvester's son, had chuckled when we mentioned the ballad. *Why'd we steal children? We got enough of our own*. We crossed the bypass to the housing estate whose residents were trying to evict the Gypsy encampment. One woman had lots to say. No books, a flock of ceramic ducks flying across her living-room wall. She turned down the sound on her huge television set, but the silent shifting images dominated the room. She was vitriolic about the Gypsy site, which she could see from her kitchen window. *They just don't want to live like us*. We visited Queen Caroline several times and she gave us dozens of songs and told endless stories. When she died in 1971, she was laid in her caravan and the caravan was set alight.

*

Many of the songs we collected were incomplete, or they had confusing features. At one of our 1970s collecting sessions, the English Gypsy Nelson Ridley came out with the line: *the birds they sang in High Germany*. We asked him what it meant, as the song hadn't previously mentioned Germany. *Well now – that means harmony. They sing in harmony in Germany*. Ewan said, *Why not sing 'the birds they sang in high harmony'?* Mr Ridley hadn't learned a new song since he was twelve. It was his father's father's song and if it was good enough for his grandfather, it was good enough for him. Harmony, hermony, Garmoney, high Germany – it does have a kind of mad logic. Ridley was one of the honoured band of singers who kept the continuum going, form and content, from his grandfather's generation down into that of his own grandchildren. The American singers Aunt Molly Jackson, Clarence Ashley, the Carter Family, Almeda Riddle: the songs they sang were created in the community in which they lived, in which most of the people were illiterate or semi-literate. The music was passed down orally. Keeping the songs the way you learned them was important, although I do suspect that many field singers added their own bits and pieces – but within a style and form set and recognised by the community. When Alan Lomax was collecting from Emma Dusenbury, the Arkansas field singer, he asked her if she knew any Robin Hood songs. *Who's Robin Hood?* Alan tells her a Robin Hood tale. The next morning, he comes to record again and she has *just remembered* a Robin Hood song. She sings the tale that Alan had told. She'd made it up overnight. Alan said it was like an unhoned folk song.

We collected mostly from Gypsies and Travellers because their isolated, pariah cultures valued and preserved the old songs as part of their identity. Some of the people from whom we collected went on to perform on stage regularly, with varying consequences. I'm of the opinion that entering the folk revival is not necessarily good for some singers who are brought out from their small, cohesive communities. Once they go out on the performing circuit – however modest it may be – the field singers tend to crystallise. They're on show and, like their grounded Gorgio – non-traveller – counterparts, they often cultivate a reductive stage persona to hide behind: Paddy the Irishman, the music-hall Scot, the hick American southerner, the romantic, wandering Gypsy. We singers/performers: when we first start out, our new skin can feel too big for us. It takes time to grow into it. Once we get up on stage, the audience perceives us as larger than life and we begin to believe it. One might think that the Clancy Brothers were like that – the hail-fellow-well-met Irish singing group – but they knew exactly what they were doing. They came to the Singers' Club one night but stayed downstairs drinking. We joined them during the interval. *We've come to tell ya, Ewan, not to watch the telly tonight. We're on, slauthering one of yer songs.* Get them one at a time by a fireside and they reverted to the old style of singing.

Folk singers fresh from the field have an added pitfall. They bring a rich but limited slice of life out into the glare of performance. Keep that word *slice* in mind – the rest of the pie is left behind at home. They come away to halls full of strangers and the self-confidence and ease that they had at home is absent or at risk. I cannot imagine what it must have been like for Fred Jordan, a Suffolk farm worker who was *discovered* by a well-known English folklorist in the 1960s and sent out on the folk circuit. It was – and probably still is – common for working-class people to dress up when going out. Fred wanted to appear on stage in his going-out clothes – a suit with shirt, waistcoat and tie – but his handlers felt he would look more authentic in working shirt and worn trousers. So he went on stage in front of strangers dressed as if for work to sing his country songs. If that's not calculated to cause an identity crisis I don't know what is. When he and I talked backstage, he apologised for his denim overalls. *But at least they don't make me wear 'em dirty.*

We brought the Stewarts to the Singers' Club. Belle fretted over what to wear – to go to a folk club! She was a natural entertainer and in the first half she sang only lightweight funny songs. Alec sat like a statue, playing only well-known jigs and reels. Sheila, dignified and leisurely, told a few children's stories. Cathy went to the loo, returning dressed in a skimpy bra and a grass skirt, and performed a seductive hula dance to a strathspey on the pipes. She danced well with sinuous, graceful enjoyment, but she was in her forties and had a physique and face reminiscent of Dorothea Lange's 1930s photo 'Migrant Mother'. We bowed our heads. The Singers' folk club audience sat, mouths open in disbelief. This disjointed foursome was not the family that we'd recorded in Beckenham. During the interval we asked Belle to sing 'The Twa Brithers'. We asked Cathy to tell 'Wee Appley and Orangey'. We asked Alec to play a slow air and Sheila to sing 'Tifty's Annie'. To all of them: *Tell the jokes!* Belle and Sheila said the audience wouldn't understand the long ballads but they sang them to please us. Alec regained his dignity and pleasure. Cathy listened and put her street clothes back on again. 'Appley and Orangey' and Bawdy joined in and the second half was wonderful. The family never looked back. They learned that their lifestyle was unique, their culture fascinating, their ballads rare and that they were exotic to the Gorgios. They embarked on a career of singing and henceforth were known professionally as The Stewarts of Blairgowrie.

Reproducing the same programme, the same fixed personality, the same jokes and chat at each show can become habitual and stultifying. You begin to wonder who you really are, for Who You Are has been narrowed down to that very small slice. You're bored – and exhausted. This is what happened to the Stewarts. John Cohen, my brother-in-law and member of the New Lost City Ramblers, wanted to film them. In the late seventies, we sent him up to Blairgowrie with a letter of introduction. Belle phoned several days later. She was very direct. *Peggy, dinna send ony mair o' they film people. The Stewarts are sung oot. We're talked oot.* We sent no more collectors or media people – and whenever we visited after that there wasn't a recording machine in sight. There also wasn't the same open enjoyment at their singing gatherings. It had been difficult for the family to fit back into the community pie, whose members, like an audience, now regarded the Stewart family as larger than life and now had larger-than-life expectations of them.

*

Sometimes, when you're sitting opposite the singer, you don't know exactly what you've collected. Alan Lomax . . . he'd recorded Ewan, me, Shirley Collins, Hally Wood, Jean Ritchie, Bert Lloyd, and we all declared that he was a superb collector. He could make you think you were the best singer he'd ever heard in his life. There he was in the 1950s, recording a gaggle of Scots Highland women singing waulking songs. Waulking is the technique of soaking woven tweed in urine and water and thumping it rhythmically to shrink and soften it. The songs help the work. They sound like shanties, all in the Gaelic, with solo call and chorus response. When a Gaelic speaker back in Edinburgh heard one of these pieces, he asked Alan, *Do you want the translation?* Why ever not? The women were singing about Alan's big nose, suggesting that some other protruding part of him was also large.

Finally: the slick young New York singer who wanted to collect folk songs in the Scottish Highlands, like his hero, Alan Lomax. It was a Singers' Club evening, on the fourth floor of the ACTT building in Soho Square.* Way down there, taking two

* Association of Cinematograph, Television and Allied Technicians.

parking places, was an enormous American station wagon. We went downstairs to inspect it. Our man had filled up the back space with the very latest recording equipment. Alan, whose entire complement of similar gear had been stripped from his van in Naples while he crossed the road to ask directions from a policeman, warned Jerry that the machines were rather visible. *Pooh-pooh, this is Scotland, not Italy.* Alan tried again but Jerry wanted to do it his way. Say this for him, he came back from his Scots trip chastened but laughing at himself and in possession of a good story. It was hell itself getting the vehicle over to the remote island on the microscopic ferry. It was hell itself transporting all of the equipment halfway up a mountain by Jerry-power to the little croft where his singers lived. It wasn't heaven, setting it up for the first time ever while his singers sat watching by the peat fire. Machine, mics, tapes in place, now . . . *Where do I plug in? Och, laddie, we've nae electricity.*

*

(Answer to the riddle: a man fitting a shoe on a woman in a shoe shop.)

27

The Women Who Came to Work

I'll take care of one, I'll not take care of two. We took Betsy at her word. Two children under four, parents home and away, shops further than walking distance . . . although a workaholic, Betsy was seventy-seven and she had already given more than her willing body could stand. The house seemed full but we had one empty room left. Sandra Kerr was one of the new singers at the club, showing promise. A month before Calum was born, we invited her to come live with us. She would help in the house in exchange for a small stipend plus general music and singing lessons. She ate with us at every meal. Her laundry went in with ours. She occasionally sat and watched television with us at night. Neill was entranced and followed her everywhere. This wasn't Betsy's idea of a live-in *servant*. She fired shots over Sandra's bow, delegating jobs, elevating herself to housekeeper and demoting Sandra to skivvy. It's an old story. Ex-servants can make cruel masters. Sandra worked hard at music and diplomacy. She stayed a whole year.

From this time on, we always had a helper living in the house. They deserve to be chronicled. Mary Davenport left saying we'd only ever keep a helper who didn't mind being watched all the time. When introduced to four-foot-eleven Betsy, Aris (a tall, stately German *au pair*) announced in a matter-of-fact voice: *I do not like small people.* Betsy called her Arse. Lily, a square Norfolk woman, sat on the stairs complaining that her son should have taken care of his mother in her old age, like Mr MacColl was doing. Maggie, African American, cheerful and (as in the novels of Alexander McCall Smith) *traditionally built*, came with two steamer trunks, one laden with weight-lifting gear and the other with programmes of all the London events she'd attended. She came downstairs each day in a nurse's cap and white apron but did very little actual work. Gillian, a hard-working, intuitive woman with mild Down's syndrome, had an uncanny connection with her twin sister, who lived three hundred miles away. Sylvia had left her abusive husband and parked her five children in homes all over London. She spent her evenings doing their mending and laundry and her week-ends visiting them. Suddenly, she gathered them all up and went back to her husband. Mary Rice, easy-going and cheer-ful, Liverpool Catholic-then-born-again. We are still in touch, Tosh Mary and I. Maureen, Irish, red-haired and playful, four-teen but claiming to be seventeen, did little other than enter-tain our boys. A down-on-her-luck alcoholic, a tragic woman who styled herself Lady Dorothy Annan, bought fillet steak for her enormous snooty Persian cat, Joseph – *the only male who's ever seen me with my hair down.* Felicity Owusu, a plump, joyful Ghanaian woman who did her housework singing with a huge basket of cleaning cloths and fluids balanced on her head.

We owe this fast-moving procession to Betsy, who got rid of them as quickly as I could hire them. I didn't interview new applicants very carefully because I knew they wouldn't stay. I always felt that these women should be interviewing me as well. Needy women; women too old or too young for the job; women deserted by men and betrayed by society. I felt immense empathy with them, obliged as they were to live in someone else's house, observing a happy family that they no longer had

– or maybe had never had. I also felt for the man who called to be interviewed, confessing that he had a passion for washing women's underwear and *hope you understand, please missus, I need the job.*

Of course, Betsy was the First Helper. I tried to set ground rules but trivial battles sprang up like mushrooms in the night. She waited hand and foot on Ewan and the boys. Shoe polishing, for example. I wanted our kids to polish their own shoes. Betsy got up early to do it. I got up earlier. She got up earlier still. Then she took to polishing them the moment the boys got home from school. Tottering and swaying, she insisted on carrying ten-month-old Calum downstairs under her arm. I'd get up earlier to do it. Betsy would get up even earlier until we finally took Calum into our own bedroom. She was not evil – just monumentally frustrated, aware that she had been fashioned by an unfair life, grinding poverty, duty and overwork. My secret name for her was God Almighty, giving with one hand and taking away with the other. Looking back on it from yesterday's future, she was the anvil upon which I was forged. She was hoping to create an adversary with whom she could have a fair fight. Her real adversary was Life itself but I was within reach.

The only helper to whom Betsy took was Mattie, a whippet of a middle-aged Glasgow woman. We bonded at first sight. She had schizophrenia, which had landed her in an asylum where she was given electro-shock therapy then summarily discharged. Mattie was upfront about it and gave me the name of her doctor. He confirmed that she was indeed very unbalanced, but was up to the job, wouldn't hurt a fly and loved children. Mattie was convinced that there were spies outside her window. She could hear them plotting. We put a mic out of her window. Her 'voices' came from pigeons and from the builders who were turning the next-door estate of the shoe manufacturer Russell and Bromley into a development of ninety shoebox dwellings. Mattie was convinced that MI5 had inserted a microphone in her coat lapels. I looked. *Of course ye canna see it! It's invisible. They wadna put a visible one there!* She finally snapped. Late one evening, she fled our house into the backyard of one of the cookie-cutter houses, where the young yuppies were toasting their new pad. There they were, the beautiful people, champagne glasses in hand, when a wild-eyed Scotswoman scrambled over the fence begging to use the phone because the *musicians next door are trying to cut off ma airm!* This wasn't funny – not at all, for Mattie was probably one of the smartest, kindest, most tolerant-of-Betsy women that came through our house.

Bianca Michelux's arrival should have been announced by a blast of trumpets. Italian, middle-aged, matron-plump, a breath of fresh air; her voice could be heard at the other end of the block. The first time she laughed, Betsy nearly fell over. Bianca had never conquered English properly, although she'd been in the UK for over a decade. Kingston was Kinkie-*sto*ny, Wimbledon was Wimbling-*doe*-nee. She nicknamed everyone, family and visitors alike. Sandra was Cleopatra; Ewan was The Dear Boy; Charles Parker was Il Professore. Betsy was De Ol' Leddy. Neill was Il Dottore (the Doctor), so named – according to Calum – because he feigned illness to avoid challenging days at school. Hamish was Jerus*alem*-eh. I was Peggy. Betsy's pin-pricks, stiletto jabs and machete slashes rolled off Bianca like raindrops off a jolly duck's back. *De Ol' Leddy she not feeling good today.*

Bianca fitted in with any dinner guests we had. When the Stewarts shared our table, Betsy was dismayed. She'd been brought up with the usual Gorgio attitude towards nomads, Gypsies, tinkers, Travellers. *You dirty tink!* was one of the epithets that she used for the boys – once in front of Belle, who just laughed. The Stewarts bantered with bawdy barbs that went straight over Betsy's head, travelling to Ewan, who would translate the Scots for Bianca while adding bits from his own Voltairean vocabulary. Bianca's lusty laugh put feathers on Belle's arrow as it headed straight for Alec's funny bone. He'd reply in kind, and husband and wife would carry on lightning-quick pseudo-flyting till one of them bowed out. I translated for Calum and Neill, who listened eagerly – I'd already been objecting to their misogynistic words for sexual intercourse. I was glad the Stewarts were there, for bawdy humour had not been part of my upbringing. Bawdy is very different from pornographic. Lust in both men and women is celebrated in bawdry, where there can be a shared recognition that the sex act, viewed from the standpoint of a Martian, might seem comical.

Bianca was heavy on sexual innuendo. She flirted outrageously with any man who entered the house. A handsome but generously built boy-man member of the Critics Group was standing in the doorway of the kitchen, his beer resting on the shelf of his protruding stomach. Bianca looked him squarely in the eye and sidled seductively belly-to-belly past him, murmuring, *Big belly, little stick*. When Granada Television was filming me for *The Exiles* series, Bianca sat on the top step with her shortest skirt hiked up to belt-line, making improper suggestions to the handsome cameraman, whom she called Jesus. Be you friend, journalist, Labour MP . . . if you were male and staying overnight, Bianca was waiting for you. Her room was right next door to the guest room, which doubled as a space for the attic cistern. A BBC producer was benighted. Our Rabelaisian arachnid had been eyeing him speculatively at dinner. The house was soundproof as regarded nightly shenanigans, for which our renegade sons were grateful later on. Bianca came down the next morning declaring at top volume, *No good. He finish before he start.*

Bianca was larger than life. The house shrank. Betsy retired to her room, only stalking out to make her tea – a teaspoon of leaves in the mug, boiling water, stir around, put milk in, stalk back. Bianca's dream came true: a visiting radio journalist proposed to her after one night of acceptable stamina. He had the added attraction of a *Rang*-ee Rover (hard 'g' instead of the correct soft 'g'). She married him and moved down by the railway, happy as Larry with her new house, new sofa, new carpets, new curtains, new husband – in that order. Our house went quiet again. We missed her. Somewhere in this procession of women the current helper left after Betsy locked the boys in her bedroom and wouldn't come out. Irene Scott – my Irene – stepped into the breach and came to help till we returned from tour. Her version of her stay and my behaviour is very funny. In a sentence: I apparently played the Lady of the Manor. It was not the end of the women who came to work. The next one, Alice Dawson, our jewel, was to stay for fourteen years.

III

1960s–1989

28

The Critics Group

Jim O'Connor and I have thirty seconds to fall in love. Then
. . . *She got up behind him and away they did go.* We dismount
and enter the living room. Hand in hand, we walk to the
water's edge *where deep water flows* and sit down on the little
Persian carpet. The watchers are attentive on the far shore.
I'm with child and I'm child-happy. We're going to *get married, there'll be no disgrace.* But Jim can't meet my eyes. He's
different. Something's terribly wrong. *John Lewis, John Lewis,
tell me your mind* . . . the cliff behind me is dangerous, overfilled with books. My heart is trying to escape. I'd always been
fear'd of his way. His arms go round me with an unfamiliar,
tight urgency. *He hugged her, he kissed her* . . . Roughly, Jim
turns me around. *He throwed her in the river where he know'd
she would drown.* Jim lets me go. *I can't do it, Ewan, I can't do
it.* He has tears in his eyes. I have to sing 'Omi Wise', right
then and there. The lights go up, the watchers scribble in their
notebooks. A Critics Group meeting in full swing. The subject: Emotion Memory, a.k.a. the Stanislavski Method. John
Lewis killed Naomi Wise in North Carolina in April 1808. She
got away from him tonight. Whenever I sing 'Omi Wise' in
concert I relive my terror as I rolled away from Jim across the
carpet as fast as I could. I talk to Naomi as I sing – *Don't get on
that horse. Don't ride away with him.* Emotion memory.

*

The 1960s. Folk music was becoming respectable. Folk clubs were springing up and sinking down like mushrooms. Generally speaking, they operated below the commercial radar. We'd visit clubs where no one – sometimes including the organiser and the resident singers – had any idea what a folk song was. The club was just a splendid meeting place for anyone of any age. For a small entrance fee or a donation at the door you could enjoy a whole evening of music in which you could participate or not. You didn't have to buy a drink. You could nurse one pint for the duration of the evening. Us Singers' Club residents found ourselves in a defensive position. Rumour, misunderstanding and malice had blown the Policy up out of all proportion. Gordon McCulloch and Enoch Kent, Singers' residents, suggested that the principles of the Policy should be examined more closely. *Let's form a group of singers and discuss it.* Good idea. *Which mice are going to bell the cat?* asked Aesop.

Ewan and I began to recruit for a study group. You didn't have to be a recognised singer to join. Bert Lloyd preferred to keep away and to take under his wing those who felt that studying folk singing as an art was an oxymoron. To each his own. Everyone liked Bert. Ewan wanted to teach and didn't much care if he was liked or not. The purpose was to create a space where you worked and discussed the role of folk song in contemporary life. It felt like a political duty. Like Bert's, our home was opened, and like Bert's, our library and teaching were offered gratis – but two different camps arose. A shame, for Bert and Ewan had been such friends and they'd worked and sung so well together. Competing egos – and a woman with a banjo – came between them. Charles Parker gave the group

With Kitty, *c.*1975

Alice Dawson: my right hand, Ewan's post-prandial smoking
companion, Kitty's second mother, Neill and Calum's nemesis, *c.*1975

Calum, Ewan and Neill singing shanties at the Singers' Club (I can tell
by the wallpaper), *c.*1978

Kirsty married Steve Lillywhite in 1984. She and Ewan arrived at the church in a pink Cadillac convertible. *From left*, Ewan, Calum, Kirsty, Neill

Kitty wearing my specs, early 1990s

Recording, 1988. I look tired. Probably the weight of the glasses

Irene, *c.* 1990. She didn't always win, but I always lost

Daughters-in-law. *Clockwise from top left*, Kerry Harvey-Piper, Justine Picardie with baby Jamie, Kate St John, Kate Jones

Siblings Neill, Kitty and Calum recording, sometime in the early twenty-first century

Siblings Mike, me and Pete, 1995

The Woodlawn Witches, Asheville, NC. *Clockwise from top left*, Sharon Hynes, me, Irene, Kathleen McLoughlin, Beth Duttera, Pat Buehler, Clare Hanrahan

Maggie-the-Van with her minder, *c.*2000

About time! Civil union, 15 December 2006

Irene and the Fiery Cello in Patrick Sky's wild instrument shop, NC, 2008

Having a good time on stage in Charlotte, NC, 1999

2017: Neill, me, Calum and twelve guitars hanging on the wall. If one guitar happened to fall, there'd be . . .

Ready to turn eighty-two, March 2017

an unfortunate working title which stuck: the Critics Group. The original purpose was to educate ourselves, not to criticise others. We felt that folk song was socially different from other kinds of music and that its inborn disciplines should be studied and applied consciously. After all, that's what classical music training does – it teaches you to keep performing it the same old way, within its historic parameters. Singers dropped in and out of the Critics until we had a core of about twenty regulars. Gordon and Enoch were not among them. Wherever Ewan and I went, we would talk about this new and wonderful crusade: folk songs come from the working class and have performance styles all their own. Let's study and preserve the songs via learning to sing them as truthfully as possible. Truth: what does it really mean? Everyone has their own interpretation. Now everyone has their own definition of folk song as well.

If you're on tour singing night after night, you might want to expand your repertoire. You'll need techniques for keeping the songs fresh. Ewan was a riveting teacher. In Theatre Workshop, he had travelled and taught for twenty years, writing plays and coaching actors who needed to keep their roles fresh. Now he was going to teach singers using the same techniques: Application of the Idea of IF; Emotion Memory; use of Given Circumstances. We got whole-body relaxation routines; Wagner to help with pitch and stamina; Gilbert and Sullivan to develop pronunciation and speedy delivery; music hall to help with humour and connection with the audience. Rudolf Laban, the dance/movement theoretician, had devised the Theory of Efforts (a.k.a. the Eight Efforts), the purpose of which was to notate on two-dimensional paper the three-dimensional act of dancing. We applied his theory to voice.

Once a week, the several dozen members would fill our big

living room from 7 p.m. to 10.30. They came straight from work with chips in a bag or sandwiches in a knapsack. Calum and Neill, young as they were, occasionally sat through the first hour or so. I think they learned something useful during a particular session, the subject of which was *believing that you belong on stage*. Dennis is to be the Burglar. Rumour has it that lots of money is stashed in the living room. He must find it in the dark of night. The curtains are drawn, the lights are extinguished and the group sit huddled in the theatre. Dennis creeps in with a flashlight, searches but doesn't find the money. Jack is next, then Terry. No one finds it. Lights on. Each Burglar is challenged as to whether they *really believed* that the money was there. *If you'd believed it, you would have found it*, says Ewan, going to the most obvious place and pulling out a sheaf of bank notes.

We'd nearly always begin with relaxation and voice exercises that consisted chiefly of learning to produce clearly the non-diphthong vowels *ah, aw, ee, oo; ah-aw-ee-oo*. Regularly, one person would be singled out. *Brian, next week you'll be singing in the folk club at Winchester. Prepare a programme.* Brian would be expected to keep the Winchestrians interested for half an hour. The choice of songs had to be tailored to the audience: a convocation of students at the local technical college; a social night out for members of a union; a gaggle of secretaries (always female, even though feminism was on its feet, learning to walk). It was advisable to find out something about Winchester before you planned your half-hour. Concise, interesting introductions please, with no *ums, ers, wells* or awkward pauses. Look the audience in the eye and speak authoritatively. Don't sway or look at your feet while talking. Learn to pitch unaccompanied songs accurately, to tune instruments quickly.

Treat the stage as if you belong on it. The rest of us sat with pen and paper, sometimes scribbling while you sang. A critique session followed, in which the singer took notes. It would begin with what went right, followed by anything negative delivered in positive terms. For example, instead of saying, *I don't like the way you sang that song*, you'd say, *Frankie, that was a lovely opening. I think in the second verse you might . . .* Or *Bob, try pitching that song differently. I think it needed the resonance of your lower register.* The Critics members weren't all singers. One had a little stutter when he spoke but could hold a tune and was an excellent critic. Another had trouble holding a tune – a problem which, interestingly, was overcome after the group broke up. Some gave stunning performances but didn't have staying power – like Luke Kelly, who left to become one of the Dubliners. Later, John Faulkner and Sandra Kerr went on to plough new furrows in Ireland and northeast England. Frankie Armstrong added voice teaching to her touring. Jack Warshaw writes a variety of contemporary political songs. Others still sang but went on to do something entirely different.

The word *perform* bothers me, as does the fact that I've used it so much. It doesn't feel right when talking about folk music. The singers whom Dio transcribed were not performing as such – they were singing an inherited song to an interested collector, who recorded them in their home surroundings. *Performance* has an air of artificiality about it, suggesting the delivery of a prepared piece in which you yourself are part of the scenery. Once you hire a hall and admit a miscellaneous group, each of whom is parting with an entrance fee, it becomes one-off entertainment. The element of pay and the fact that you are singing to strangers are crucial. Take field singers or folk singers away from their community into the outer musical world and many of us feel like orphans in a commercial storm – insecure in a world which seems to need anything except what we have to offer. What do we so often do under these circumstances? We do too much. We try too hard. We jazz the music up, put glitter on it, play it too fast, smile or laugh nervously, employ histrionics, borrow features from other musics in order to – we hope – make it acceptable. In a word, we lose our trust: in the material, in ourselves, in those who listen. In seven words: we perform in order to gain praise.

You don't need to add a great deal of backing to the Anglo-American folk songs. Ted Egan, the Australian singer, accompanies himself by tapping cardboard boxes. A Pittsburgh songwriter – sorry, friend, but I've forgotten your name and I cannot find you on the internet after all these years – sang to the percussion of two spoons. British folk songs had been unaccompanied for centuries, but now many folk revival singers with guitars were keen to accompany them. The Critics Group spotlight swung onto instrumentation. I went through our considerable record collection listening to accompaniments in traditions and cultures that, like the Anglo and American, depend primarily on melody and words rather than on harmony or rhythm. I wanted to know what the instrumentalists did and didn't do, how their accompaniments differed from those in popular and classical music. I was astonished at how consistent the principles of folk accompaniment are from nation to nation. I worked up a lengthy lecture entitled 'A Theory of Folk Accompaniment', meant chiefly for British folk singers. Songs do tell you what they want, especially if you learn them unaccompanied first. Application of the Idea of *IF I were this song, what accompaniment would please me?* Sounds silly, but the answer affected what range we sang or played in, what speed, what chords, what instrument, what effort. Sometimes the song would say, *Play simple*. Or *just don't accompany me at all*. Big Bill Broonzy said it took him a lifetime to learn to play simple. Me too.

Accompaniment – a pertinent glimpse into 2001. Brother Pete is lamenting the loss of his voice. My friend Irene points out that he sings excellently in his lower range and invites him to talk about his song 'Sailing Down My Golden River'. Chris Seeger, one of my nephews and engineer for *Larry King Live*, takes us to an off-hours CNN studio in New York City. Irene interviews Pete, who then records a lovely version of 'Golden River', accompanying himself on the twelve-string guitar. I add a few twiddles on the banjo. Surprise: Irene wants symphonic background. I'd met Michael Kamen – composer of music for feature films – at the house of David Gilmour, of Pink Floyd. Michael had a framed letter from Pete on the wall of his home. We ask him to put background music to Pete's rendition. He is delighted and sends his arrangement to us on a CD. It is luscious, syrupy – it has more buds and blossoms than a hundred Chelsea Flower Shows. I phone David up. *How can we tell Michael that Pete wouldn't like this? It's more than way over the top of Everest. Could he be persuaded to edit it under supervision?* David offers to be present at an editing session and Michael agrees. He gives us three hours of his precious time in his impressive little studio. Irene knows what she wants but she doesn't read scores. I begin. *We'd really like it to be more minimal.* Michael: *Michael Kamen does not do minimal.* David sits quietly, saying nothing. Peggy the same. It's like that vital silence between two decisive verses of an unaccompanied ballad. Michael grows up instantly. *What would you like me to do?* Peggy: *I'd like to start by removing the first thirty-two bars of your score.* Very, very long silence.

David nods, Michael wipes out the pertinent bars. We work our way through the score, eventually wiping out three-quarters of what he'd written, coming out with Michael Kamen Minimal. I add a few twiddles on the banjo. Pete loves it and sends Michael another letter.*

*

The Critics Group days were just plain exciting. Ewan was secretly aiming us towards formation of a theatre group. He wrote a modern adaptation of *St George and the Dragon*, the traditional mumming play. The group bought a Bedford van and took old St George out on tyres to folk clubs within a hundred miles of London. The first half of the evening would be filled with songs and stories. The second half was devoted to the play, with its stock-in-trade folk characters, some of which were co-opted by the Marx Brothers: the hero, the lawyer, the doctor, the braggart captain, the inamorata and two simpletons (friend Dave Smith and myself) to introduce the plot. Our most memorable presentation of *St George* was at a folk club in Wolverhampton. The organisers had warned us that the club was regularly disrupted by heckling Ton-up gatecrashers.†
The first thing we saw when we came in was a line of bikers monopolising the bar, a loquacious phalanx covered in leather, spikes and chains, helmets looped on arms. Ted Culver, a.k.a. St George, chatted them up before the show. He was similarly clad, having come up from London on his Harley-Davidson.

* This stately version of 'Sailing Down My Golden River' appeared on the Appleseed album *Seeds: The Songs of Pete Seeger, Vol. 3* in 2003.
† The Ton-up Club has a website. To be a member you had to break the 100 mph barrier on a motorcycle.

When the play began, the lads in black went quiet. When George strutted about they whooped. When the captain, an American general, was about to kill George, they yelled, *Turn around, he's behind you, mate! Turn around!* and made to charge the stage. Ted held up his hand to suggest *Cool it!* or *Wait and see!* Then he dies, stabbed in the back. He's brought back to life by The Kiss and we sing the last song. The bikers went mad with cheering, lining our pints up all along the bar.

The group travelled out to clubs, giving them a choice of themed programmes – love songs, political songs, ballads, work songs, women's songs. We looked up new material in books and on records and wrote songs about current affairs. We recorded themed albums. The gossip and rumour never let up. Some of it was scurrilous and some of it bore a grudging admiration for what we were doing. Members were reproached for sounding like Ewan or Peggy when they sang. In 1965, Ewan broached the concept of the *Festival of Fools*, a full-length yearly dramatic presentation based on the old folk custom of the World Turned Upside Down. Henceforth, the first nine months of every year from 1965 to 1970 saw us collecting interesting clippings from the papers and cataloguing them by subject. In early September, issues were chosen according to importance or oddity, the main purpose being to present happenings of the past year in varied styles of music and drama. In October, Ewan would write the script and songs. November and December were filled with rehearsals. For the final *Festival*, in 1971, he was overburdened and asked me to write a women's song. Swiss women had got the vote that year and women's issues were popping up everywhere. 'I'm Gonna Be an Engineer' was one of those songs that just appear. Standing unbeknownst on the threshold of feminism and never having wanted to be an engineer, I wrote it in two hours and took it upstairs to Ewan's cubicle in the cistern room. He was brisk. *The last verse is depressing, Peg. You need some hope there.* Downstairs again, rewrote the verse, Mabel's Your Auntie and back to doing the accounts. Five not-yet-feminists sang it on stage in very short mini-skirts – *pussy-pelmets*, as they were called.*

Each *Festival* took on volunteers from the Singers' Club audience. One such temp, a dedicated alcoholic, dried out for the show and did a brilliant job working the lights. Later in life, he managed a pub in Baker Street. Americans would come in looking for Sherlock Holmes. *Oh, he's just popped out on a case. Have a drink while you wait.* Each *Festival* lasted three hours from beginning to end. We opened with a traditional wassail song and a long introductory speech about the age-old festival. Each month would then be introduced by a weather rhyme or piece of folk wisdom, followed by a major scene. Funny, tragic, frightening, satirical – quick skits, long complicated ones. Songs, jokes, dances, then the show would close with a philosophical poem and a reprise of the wassail song while we're trooping off. All this was presented in the rectangular function room of the New Merlin's Cave – now demolished, I believe. We had three stages: a tiny one in the corner by the outside door, a larger one on the long centre wall, and the third being the high plat-form at the end of the room. Every available space between the stages was taken up by 170 chairs, set without a spare half-inch between them. There were very narrow aisles along which we would run in the dark, always aware that someone's bag, pint, foot or chair leg might send us sprawling. Often you had to run

---

* A pelmet is a framework or decorative fabric above a curtain, hiding the curtain fixtures.

these aisles in the dark, between scenes. My longest such run was seventeen seconds. Step off Stage 3, take six strides down the aisle, left hand on the wall for guidance; three steps up onto Stage 2, cross it in four strides, dodging the props; three steps down off the stage; five strides along the wall to the five-step staircase to high Stage 1, two steps catty-corner and sit down at a desk with a typewriter on it before Lights Up. I practised running it with my eyes closed.

Ewan wrote for his cast. He wrote for Bob Blair, who would play Jack in the Toilet Paper Sequence; for Brian Pearson or Mike Rosen, who would speak the very long gobbledegook stories about Northern Ireland or Rhodesia. I took one over on short notice, a mammoth job of memorising. Those who were good at costumes acted *and* made costumes. Those who played instruments acted *and* played instruments. We tapped into the overhead electric wires outside the pub for the lighting and the big room-heater. On the BBC's dime and premises, Charles built up a tape of sound cues. The sound and lighting technicians were stationed behind the little bar in the back corner, following their scripts with tiny desk lamps. I made sure everyone had their parts and worked out rehearsal schedules. I arranged the music, trained the musicians and got the singers to sing together – almost impossible as some of the pieces were quite atonal. I mostly sang and played in the show. I'm not a good actor.

The boys attended the *Festival* regularly. When Calum was four, five or six he would sit on the counter of the bar, rooted to the action. During one pregnant silence between two scenes, his voice piped up out of the dark: *You don't know what's going to happen next, but I do!* He would still be awake at the end of the show, reciting whole sections of the script before falling asleep on a pile of coats in the rigged-up excuse for a dressing room. One night Betsy sat in the front row with Neill, aged nine. The lights went up on Stage 1 and there's Sandra in my luscious red tapestry dressing gown waiting for husband John to come home from the factory and tell her about his exciting day of making screws on an assembly line. It was quite a long scene, at the end of which she threw off her dressing gown and stood there totally naked. Neill looked down and Betsy's acidic Scots filled the awestruck silence: *No need to look doon, son. You'll see plenty o' that in your life!*

Exhausted at the end of each show, we would get Ewan's notes. Scripts in hand, we had to sit and take whatever he handed out – no debate, no defence. Diplomacy had no seat at his table. He laced into this one for milking a speech, that one for walking too slowly or for a wrong pace of song, the chorus singers for messy cadences. Tired? Sick? No excuse. The show got better and better. Actors from the West End were coming nightly. We got rave reviews. The *Festival* was often so good by the time the run ended that we all felt we should be moving it to a proper theatre, to a larger audience, for a longer run. Why on earth not? No – we always took it off stage and started on our next project: a recording, clubs to sing at, a new look at some vocal style or other. Ewan and I had made good albums and paid no attention to marketing them. We'd written good songs and signed them away to publishers who never did anything with them. We spent years on books that were issued in a run of hundreds and then remaindered. The Critics Group caught our contagious fatal flaw and their work was only known to the folk cognoscenti. Ah, but we all had such a good time at it . . . the Como Festival, improvising *Romeo and Juliet* for BBC Radio – and more and more.

In September 1967, members of the group were invited to a festival of progressive songwriters in Cuba – such a tiny island, such a vulnerable economy boycotted by the USA, supported by the Soviet Union and struggling to keep afloat. Snapshots: A celebration of the anniversary of the Cuban Revolution. A million people gathered on the plain outside Santiago waiting for Fidel to speak. Cuban time – hours pass and no Fidel. The English are wilting – fiery thirsty. Estelle, our translator, takes us backstage. The line is too long. *Come on, we'll join the VIP line.* A wooden picket fence divides the Cuban government and its people. At the gate stands a teenage girl with a rifle. *These are comrades from England, compañera.* She lets us through. One by one, Estelle introduces us to the entire Cuban government. Raúl, Fidel's brother, is busy talking but offers his hand kindly. We go back to our seats. At last The Man appears. *Comrades, there is something very wrong here. Too many of you have your backs to me.* That was us, looking at a sea of expectant, upturned faces. We all turn our seats around. Fidel talks for three hours. No one leaves. The next day we attend a meeting between Fidel and his ministers and the expatriates who took part in the Bay of Pigs misadventure. All get a chance to speak. When it's his turn, Fidel turns to one of the invading expats and says, *Why did you want to kill me, comrade?* Fidel looks into our eyes when he shakes our hands. A few days later we are in a bus going to a coffee plantation. It's filled with teenage boys and girls who are going to an isolated village to teach the old people how to read. Our Group put on a reasonable show but I suspect our contributions were too wordy, too tight, not entertaining enough, too English. Ewan and I didn't drink or drink in the whole picture, so we didn't stay up late and socialise. Much of this was due to Ewan's severe dehydration in the debilitating August heat – the sweat spurted from him like those little geysers in the front yards of houses in Rotorua, New Zealand. The rest of the Critics stayed awake for every possible second of this extraordinary experience and almost overnight we and the group were just . . . separate all of a sudden. We weren't ready for either bang or whimper.

29

From Overcoat to Sandstorms

It happened on the night of the last *Festival of Fools*. Half of the group made off with the heart, body, soul and most of the equipment of the whole group – a carefully planned heist. They formed a new group using the techniques Ewan had adapted from theatre to song, apparently putting them to use quite successfully until they too dissolved. Ewan took it hard even though he'd long suspected that something was wrong. He could have borne a mature, negotiated split. It was the behaviour of those who left – those with whom we had worked, studied and played for six years – that broke him. Despite the best endeavours of the remaining stalwarts, the Critics era came to an end. Ewan was a wreck. He swore off theatre, the love of his life. He vowed never to work with a group again. Flame and embers of his theatre self were snuffed out.* It was as if half of him had died. He braved the five long blocks down to our little shopping parade with Calum, the express purpose being to buy me some flowers – for the first time in our life. *He's been crying all the way back, Mum.* He withdrew, sat for hours saying nothing with a vacant look on his face. For some reason, I was no comfort but I had

---

* He tried to stamp on the ashes, as the Travellers had done to erase any trace of their presence, but a remaining spark rekindled the fire in the 1970s, when he wrote his last play, *The Shipmaster*, in which a sailing ship's captain loses not only his vessel but the use of the compass between his legs.

the usual domestic multitasking to keep me busy. Calum played simple games with him, took him walking around the block – Calum's turn to save us. Talkative and funny and strangely *sympathique* for an eight-year-old, he identified with his father's state of mind.

Ewan fervently believed that art and democracy are not compatible. He had run the Group like an autocratic father – and then the children grew up. Formal theatre has a history of top-down dynamics. There is a chain of command and the play must go on even if the director is sleeping with the producer's wife. Actors learn to put up with the behaviour of eccentric tyrants, the hierarchy of leading man, leading lady, legions of extras. In folk music, no one oversees the learning process but the singers and musicians ourselves. We are looked on with veneration if we reach certain standards or advanced age, but we don't aim for the limelight because there is no limelight in living rooms and pubs. We don't have a history of organised discipline. If we did, we'd probably have more really skilled folk singers and more of a value system as regards folk song than we have here in the UK. Right from the beginning, the grassroots network of folk clubs tolerated amateurism on the stage and – as in much popular music – had an anything-goes attitude. In the early days, this value assessment gave singers and players who could hardly sing or play access to public platforms. Tony and Jenny Dunbar, two members of the remaining Critics, reckoned that what Ewan handed out to the Group was mild compared to what they had received in their own theatre experience.

Post-Critics days lacked focus and interest. Now that we had time, we began to pay serious attention to our chronic addiction, Antiquarian Bookshop Syndrome. For centuries, collecting and anthologising folk songs, stories and lore had been a respectable British pastime for enthusiasts of all classes. There's a new perfume called Paperback that advertises itself as *sweet and lovely, with just a touch of the mustiness of aged paper*. When old paper breaks down it produces, among other volatile compounds, a polymer that is chemically related to vanillin. Like male moths, some of whom can detect a willing female moth from two miles away, Ewan and I could smell an old bookshop several cities away. Vanillin junkies. Oh, the excitement of entering that dark little book-maze in Newcastle-upon-Tyne – before the city was torn apart by traffic, developers and mega-concessions – and finding, on yon dustie shelffe, a book that we'd been seeking for years. *The Gude and Godlie Ballatis,* I presume?

We couldn't afford new books. That's where our friend Joe came in. He was a lost soul, a fatherless boy with instinctive, almost manipulative intelligence. When he was eight, his mother left him on the steps of a Christian Brothers children's home in Dublin, telling him she'd pick him up in the morning. She never came back. Joe got a downbringing, a childhood of cruelty, molestation and rape that removed a huge chunk of his survival skills.* He was a principled book thief. He only lifted books from Foyles on Charing Cross Road, a shop with an aggressive anti-union policy. He wore what he called his Foyles Overcoat on pilfering days. It had rows of large pockets sewn inside for volumes of different sizes. You commissioned him to nick this or that, but he'd only comply if he wanted to read them himself first. He went to jail several times, came out and went right back to Foyles in the Overcoat.

* For a similar story, try and get *800 Voices*, Danny Ellis's songs about his childhood.

Joe was a poet. His poems were brilliant, sad to the point of being unbearable, political to the point of insurrection. He could recite any or all of them at a moment's notice. He carried sheaves of them around from one homeless shelter to another. On the night he liberated the thirteen-volume hardback set of *The Golden Bough* for us, the Overcoat dragging on the ground, he came to stay while he read through them. He didn't know how to live, how to care for his body or mind, how to be with people. He knew it. He stayed for a week. Then, without a word, he left – and didn't come back.

Joe was just one of the teachers, writers, artists, folkies of every ilk to whom we offered the use of our library, tapes, photocopiers, dinner table or bedspace. When we heard of promising new singers, we would invite them to the house to record, for archive purposes. We occasionally held a mass teach-in over a weekend and twenty or thirty singers would turn up, cramming the front room to bursting. I liked having them in the house. I'd make enormous pots of spaghetti and hold three sittings. Occasionally a singer would stay over. Often we wouldn't know who was in the cistern room till they came down bleary-eyed to breakfast. If they stayed more than two days, they had to do gardening. I think Anne Briggs, young and a crystal-true singer, was the poor soul who got the job of watering the lawn with worm extractor chemicals, then raking them up for extermination. It's possible that worms are the chief thing she remembers from Stanley Avenue. One Scotsman stayed for over a month. When he complained that his laundry was taking rather a long time, we let Betsy deal with him.

*

Ewan was easy to be with. Night and day together for thirty years and I was never bored. His world made sense. He could correlate events in history, make connections between disparate subjects, bring related problems into one solution. He, who left school at fourteen, could coast swiftly through a book much as a whale sieves krill through its baleen comb, delivering a précis to me if I didn't have the time or patience to read it. He was untrustworthy with numbers and statistics and could be wildly inventive in recounting them. Neill and Calum would call his bluff. This would end in bluster, which in turn resulted in a tendency on the part of both boys never to believe a word their father said. Ewan was ill at ease in non-English-speaking countries or in respectable hotels and restaurants. His mannerisms would become exaggerated and faux-formal. He would put on what the kids and I called his *restaurant voice*, very proper and self-conscious. 1971, in Paris, we're a little English family out strolling – Mum, Dad and two boys, aged about eight and twelve. Ewan begins to sing very loudly in mock-Chinese, giving passers-by grotesque salutes. Neill and Calum, heads down, drop further and further back. *He's someone else's father, not ours.* Apparently, Neill did the same with his two boys. Honouring traditions runs in our family. A moment later, Ewan would be giving a detailed history of the French Revolution over cheese, bread and wine. Both boys are good at that, too. When Calum was in his cheating-at-cards stage, Ewan would cheat even worse until we were all laughing hysterically. Then he would go off to the toilet, leaving his Chase the Lady hand face down on the table. We'd change everyone's cards around, giving ourselves the best and leaving Dad with a hopeless hand.

We couldn't give up teaching. We began to include extended workshop sessions in our tour schedule. Most of these were sponsored by local folk clubs and could last for a week or more. We used Critics curricula and lectures, including songwriting. In 1968, inspired by the student unrest, I had started a little magazine of new songs, the *New City Songster*. It was a dandy little pocket-size mag, twelve inches by four, like a miniature broadsheet, illustrated by Dave Scott, the Belfast political artist and brother of my friend Irene. Throughout the seventies, I appealed far and wide in English-speaking countries for topical songs for the *Songster*. It put me in touch with songwriters all over the world and highlighted current issues, many of which are still with us. Political songs often have a limited lifespan – they need to be spread abroad quickly. It was a small venture but became an extraordinary collection. One volume per year, 376 topical songs over an eighteen-year span.*

Knowing that we could *tak' care o' twa, no' three*, I had a third illegal abortion in the mid-sixties. Two irresponsible adults whose necessary contraptions were always . . . somewhere else. This time I was in the hands of a caring nurse who took me into her apartment and made me stay for two or three days until she was sure I was safe. We were still on a financial see-saw in the late sixties and my fourth abortion was carried out in a hospital. The after-care doctor was coarse and needlessly rough. *You would not be in pain if you hadn't killed your baby*. Reluctantly, I went on the pill. That's another horror story – horrendous headaches and even more horrendous periods. I felt like the guinea-pig that I probably was. In the mid-seventies, Ewan agreed – under duress – to a vasectomy, after which he confessed to feeling less of a man. Tough titty. I feel more of a woman.

---

* You can access the *New City Songster* online in microfiche format at www. wcml.org.uk.

Now 'Gonna Be an Engineer' has taken off and I'm asked to sing at feminist meetings. Once I'd sung the 'Engineer' it was, *Now sing us another*. My 'anothers' were folk songs featuring murdered women, girls left with babies in their arms, females complaining about men and parents – victims and self-pity all over the farm. My own lot as a woman had been relatively soft and easy and I not only wasn't a feminist back then but didn't know what a feminist *was*. Par for our course: when Harold Leventhal phoned to say we'd been nominated for a Grammy for our Argo ten-disc series, *The Long Harvest*, we didn't even know what a Grammy *was*. Ostriches don't bury their heads in the sand. People do.

I began reading feminist classics and familiarising myself with feminist issues. In 1976, I made a soft and easy women's album, *Penelope Isn't Waiting Any More*. It didn't do justice to the subjects, so I embarked on writing songs for the main issues: rape, housework, domestic violence, motherhood, abortion, birth control, wage and power differentials. I was proud of *Different Therefore Equal*, with its varied songs, for some of which I had used the Radio Ballad technique of recording women and using their own words.

I volunteered at the Sydenham refuge for battered women. My job was to be a listening ear, either on the phone or in person at the big old run-down Victorian house donated by the council. Often, a Mr Wrong would hang around outside the refuge, so I'd escort Mrs Wrong to the shops, the courthouse or her lawyer. One day one of the women looked out the bay window and shrieked, *Oh God, it's Joe!* The name is not fictional. He'd come with four of his mates to get his woman. The big old front door was no match for their crowbars. We grabbed the children and ran to the top of the house, barricading ourselves in the attic. The men were demolishing the attic door when the police arrived. Nonetheless, sanctuaries were still the safest place for a besieged woman. There'd always be other women ready to help when trouble was battering the door down. Some of the women were too wounded to do anything but retreat into themselves. Emily, a diminutive Irish woman, turned up with four young children, all of them with heart problems. She fed them, bathed them and kept them in her room always at her side as the California quail hens do, squatting down over their young so that you only see little chick-feet under their spread feathers. Emily never spoke – until I asked her if I could make a song about her. She asked why. *Because you have a story.* She began, speaking poetry. Her sentences were memorable and all short as if she were too exhausted to make long ones. Fourteen verses of her speech set into song and the story is told.

> *Once we were single, once we were young,*
> *Once we were happy husband and wife.*
> *But fourteen years married, thirteen years harried,*
> *Now I don't care what comes of my life.*

When I sing 'Emily' at concerts I watch the audience. If a woman goes stone-faced, if the man at her side is inspecting his nails, leaning down to tie already-tied shoes, then *yes – I know you and I know what happens at home.* I finish the song, often to total silence. They don't know whether to applaud. That tells me the arrow has hit the mark. Once, after 'Emily', a woman slapped her husband hard in the face and strode out, chin up and (I was told by a woman in the back row) eyes ahead. Looking at a future, I hope.

Politically, the 1970s felt ... scattered. I resented that the country had adopted decimal currency. I had been so proud to learn the zany pounds-shillings-pence monetary system. Try adding and subtracting when there are four farthings (or two ha'pennies) in a penny, twelve pence in a shilling, twenty shillings in a pound or twenty-one shillings in a guinea and three columns to add up or subtract from – a nightmare if you have to divide or multiply. Troubles thick and fast – Nixon, Watergate, *Roe vs. Wade*, Three Mile Island, carnage at the Munich Olympics, the USA pulls out of Vietnam. Now here's something strange: We marched re. Vietnam. We lobbied re. Vietnam. We gave benefits re. Vietnam and belonged to Folk Singers for Vietnam – but I wrote no songs about Vietnam. It's the same now – the world seems to me to be in such dire straits that writing songs can feel fruitless. We spent whatever came in, saving little. We donated here, donated there, gave benefit concerts, took vacations in places that were just opening up to tourists, therefore affordable. Our favourite was Djerba, the Tunisian island. We had been there in 1968 with Calum and Brian Byrne, a treasured member of the Critics. He had terminal leukemia and wanted to travel abroad before he died. He answered Calum's continual questions with patience and humour. *Why does the tide go out, Brian? Because God pulls the plug. Dad, Brian says so. It IS true, Dad!* A born-Dublin-poor Catholic boy, Brian – a lovely singer. Towards the end he went into Brompton Hospital. We got a phone call from him late one night. *I'm dyin'! I'm dyin'.* Ewan went to see him. Unable to walk, Brian had managed to get out of bed, find change, crawl to the pay phone and call us. *Not possible*, said the night nurse. *He couldn't have* – but he did. Ewan sat with him till he died. *I'm dyin', Ewan, I'm dyin'!* Ewan died in that same hospital.

*

One morning we're opening the post at breakfast when Ewan goes uncharacteristically quiet. A royalty cheque for $75,000 – for 'The First Time Ever', sung by Roberta Flack. As per usual, we'd never heard of her, but the song was on the bottom step of a 1971 viral staircase. It's the end of twelve years of scraping, worrying, having to take every single paying job.

March 1972. This time Ewan and I came to Djerba alone, to the same hotel. One morning, all of the house staff gathered at the windows of the inside crescent frontage of our hotel. Ranks of formally dressed strangers lined up downstairs at the mock-palatial front door. A band of horses caparisoned with braided ribbons and coloured blankets appeared on the horizon. A huge palomino bore a small empty saddle. The manager brought his six-year-old son out and lifted him up onto the horse. The little boy, royally clad, sat straight upright, eyes forward. He took the reins and led the whole cavalcade out across the desert and out of sight. He was going to be circumcised. That night, the manager's extended family dined at a thirty-foot-long table, with belly-dancers footing it between the serving dishes, candles and a copse of wine glasses. The men, talking business, never even glanced up at them.

The five-mile walk took us to the flamingo colony, then biting sandstorms kept everyone in the hotel for days. Only one double pack of cards and one set of Scrabble to be shared amongst dozens of guests. You had to book the games days ahead and relinquish them after an hour or two. Lots of time left over and we hadn't brought many books.

A salmon-pink bedroom at Cap Gris Nez – Neill, March 1959.

A waterfall at High Force, Teesdale – Calum, March 1963.

Flamingos and sandstorms – Kitty, December 1972.

30

The Golden Years

In the spring of 1972, I was seeking, yet again, a woman who would act as housekeeper and minder of our nutty house. Our Alice – Alice Dawson, a steadfast, middle-aged, very conservative Lincolnshire widow-woman, the archetypal salt of the earth – blessed us by agreeing to the job. She had been sad and uncommunicative at the interview, humiliated by her situation. When I told her I was expecting, she was hooked. A week before my due date, Kitty was still the wrong way up in my womb. She'd have to be turned. I'd never heard of such a thing. Dr Scott's big hands pushed and shoved, moving her inch by inch, frightening and painful, neither of us liking it, shifting the head gradually from top to bottom. It was nearly my third home birth. The midwife, Miss Birtwhistle, saw me through the first stages and called in Dr Scott. *We're in trouble, little one – we have to go to the hospital.* My minders went out to consult with family and call an ambulance. When they returned, I was gone. Toothbrush, hairbrush, glasses, slippers and dressing gown in a plastic bag, I reached the brick wall at street level in time for the next contraction. Ewan followed the ambulance, sat with me and had to be resuscitated for the third time. *You were blue when you arrived, Kitty, the cord around your neck. You nearly died on your birthday.* That was just the first scare. She was soon in an oxygen tent, a precious little six-week-old scrap of female humanity gasping for breath while her atheist mother sat praying to a god she didn't believe in. Kitty's early time was filled with sudden hospital visits, physical therapy sessions, years of sleeplessness and dread that one of these bouts of asthma would take her from me. Weariness instead of marrow in my bones, fear so deep it became natural, coursing along with blood through my body.

Alice wasn't the mother I needed at thirty-seven but she was instinctively maternal. I dubbed her Kitty's Second Mother early on. Alice is dead now. I talked to her in my mind for five years as she gradually faded away in the Newton Abbot rest home, paralysed down the left side by a stroke, a huge section of her brain inoperative. She'd been the rock on which the house rested while waves of Betsy, Peggy, Ewan, Kitty, teenagers Neill and Calum and torrents of visitors washed over it. Always there, always working beyond the call of duty and, I suspect, harbouring a secret disapproval of our way of life. She learned to sit at table with Travelling People, communists, darker people. She moved left from a far-right, closet racist Conservative to a far-right Liberal. We rarely discussed our personal histories – but one day, at a Ewan-less breakfast, Alice and I ventured onto the rare subject of sex. Alice was horrified to learn that I didn't shave all my pubic hair, as she had done through her whole marital life. A one-man woman, her mouth pursed up and turned down at the corners when I told her Ewan had not been my first lover. *Didn't Ewan mind getting used goods?* Alice had to adjust daily. One morning, she opened Neill's bedroom door on her way to the paper room – where we kept old magazines, tax records, letters, documents, photos – and encountered South London Romeo and Juliet in the single bed together. She came downstairs, bristling. *What an example for Kitty!* Kitty was fascinated by the parade of girls that passed her bedroom door on the way to those of both brothers – she made friends with several of them. Nonetheless, Alice was just what our children needed. She was the only really normal member of the household. She noticed everything. The kids trusted her for she never snitched on them. She found cannabis growing in Calum's wardrobe. *But Alice, it's a biology experiment for school!* I see it now, her granite Alice-face. *I won't tell your mother. Just get rid of it.*

*

The stratospheric success of 'The First Time Ever' changed our lives. We stayed home more. I began to cook five-course meals. Ewan, born into poverty and dedicated to revolutionary politics, began immersing himself in the wine and cheese reviews. We'd take gastronomic foraging trips into London, loading up the Citroën at the kerb of the wine shops on Old Compton Street. Next, Jermyn Street, to Paxton and Whitfield, the appointed cheesemonger to Queen Victoria. Sawdust on the floor and antediluvian gnomes standing ready behind the display case. Relics from the Old Queen's reign? One of them is beaming. He gives each of us a small chunk of a corpse-grey sponge-like substance – its name escapes me. *You'll feel like spitting it out, but don't.* Dusty and crumbling in the mouth, it produces an immediate desire to retch. You struggle to banish the image of a human body in the last desiccated stage of decomposition. *Keep it in your mouth, keep it in your mouth!* The old man tries to lean over the counter as if to clamp our jaws shut. A warm glow invades the taste buds. We praise it with full vocals. The couple next to us gape. The woman, like the one in the restaurant mesmerised by Meg Ryan's vocal orgasm in *When Harry Met Sally*, tells our little provider, *I'll have what they had.* The Paxton Princes taught us how to impregnate (in alternating stages) a whole seven-pound Stilton cheese with port and Guinness. It's complicated and takes six weeks. When it is fully seasoned, gooey and revolting to look at, you scoop a tablespoonful out, pour a teaspoon of hot bacon fat over it and go to a Promised Land.

I spent decades trying to get rid of ten pounds of cellulite located on my thighs – dubbed saddlebags. Are women horses? My present digestive problems may be due to decades of serial dieting. This particular time, after three months of aromatherapy, steam baths, pummelling and rigorous self-denial, my size 16 jeans hang on me like Kipling's rhinoceros skin. Off to Carnaby Street, the *in place* for people twenty years younger than me. The sales boy, aged around sixteen, advises a size 15. I insist on size 12. I get them on but can't zip them up. The Method: lie on your back on the floor of the shop. The boy places his foot on the stomach of the lady and pulls the zip up. He helps me to my feet because I can't bend my knees. Turning in front of the mirror like a chicken on a spit, I look great. Insouciant, I toss my old jeans to the boy and swagger out. John Wayne probably owed his manly stride and immobile expression to over-tight trousers. Back to the Underground, where you need to bend your knees in order to get down the stairs. I try hopping down, then work out a way of leaning back, forth and sideways while holding onto the handrail, a grotesque routine that adjusts my self-image to the age I actually am – forty and the mother of three children. A little old lady coming up the stairs stops beside me. *May I help you, dear?*

1974. It was bound to happen. Betsy had shared control of the boys when we'd been on tour but now – at eighty-eight – she was insisting on lifting Kitty out of her playpen and carrying her, legs unsteady and trembling, to her room. Alice tried to stop her. *She's my grand-dochter. I'll lift her when I want.* Alice handed her notice in, not wanting to be present when the inevitable came to pass. I read Betsy the Riot Act: stop lifting Kitty or leave. She piled her clothes up in the middle of her room, sat staring out of the window with her feet tap-tap-tapping, demanding nothing, expecting who knows what. After a month of changing of the guard around Kitty's playpen and crib, Betsy moved out to a room in a nearby private residence. The story of housing Betsy before she finally went into a nursing home is hilarious and tragic. Corner me in a bar with a bottle of Merlot – mulled in winter – and I'll tell you about it. All she needed to do was to stop lifting Kitty. She ended up in a shared room in a nursing home – an institution that we'd never have considered otherwise.

The boys became excellent singers and musicians in their teens and we took them with us on several tours – Germany, Canada, the USA. They had immersed themselves in popular music, which their snobbish parents eschewed. They learned the jargon and began to play and record with others. Their music stretched them far beyond the folk techniques. Playing with us was adventurous for them, for I am an erratic player, too accustomed to being the only kid on the block. They still raise eyebrows at my so-called *tuning* and have to hold me rigorously to the beat. They are still the best of the best with me on stage. In 1975, Hamish, now twenty-five, wanted us to start a record company. *Then you can record what you want, when you want and have all the profits yourselves.* What profits? We'd never made a profit on a single recording. Un-musical chairs in the house. Betsy had just moved out and Alice had moved downstairs to her room, so there was an empty room upstairs for a studio. *A recording studio* – not a private space for me and all the office work. I wasn't enough of a dictator then. The three boys and Steve Hardy, an off-the-wall recording engineer, moved the walls, ceiling and floor inward, a pit-and-pendulum job. Blackthorne Records – it was a huge amount of work, a foolish undertaking. I think we recorded only one disc in our studio. Ewan and I were used to simple analogue tape. The old Ferrograph had an on/off switch, a forward-and-back switch and a volume knob. By 1975, recording had gone way beyond that – control boards of sliders and buttons and equalising and panning and . . . even to *turn the system on* we needed Steve or one of the boys. If anything went wrong, if anything needed upgrading, if, or, whether, well, hopeless. Reluctant to lose a space that only the boys used every now and then, we took it apart. It became Calum's bedroom and its fireproof double insulation probably saved the house from burning down when Someone torched the top floor playing the old Shove-the-Live-Butt-in-the-Ashtray-Under-the-Bed game. Thousands of Blackthorne records were stored in the adjacent eaves. The heat buckled them. Straighten them out a dozen at a time in the airing cupboard between sheets of plate glass. For two years.

Kitty needs an ally in this house of three doting adults. She invents Helena, who is always to blame for anything wrong. We get daily updates on Helena's opinions of things, people, food, school. We only hear Kitty's voice when they converse with each other. One day, *We haven't heard about Helena recently, Kitty. How is she?* Casually: *She's gone to America. She won't be coming back.* A very pregnant woman had been visiting us. *Kitty, would you like a baby sister or brother? NO!* Half an hour of reading, a kiss, a cuddle, a catlick, goodnight and *Mum, how does a baby get out of there?* The boys had asked how the baby got *in there*. I'd indicated what I called their Little Mousie, commenting that it had been rising visibly on and off since babyhood for a very good reason. Boys wanting to know *in* and the girl wanting to know *out*. Hmmm. Mike and I had asked Dio the same question when she was expecting Penny. The forty-three-year-old Methodist minister's daughter lay down naked on the bed, on her back with legs spread, and showed us – boy and two girls aged nine, seven and five – exactly where the baby emerged. OK. Just another moment in the life of a family that walked naked around the house on Sundays. But tonight I do my best by tapping my pussycat and then Kitty's. Wait – as you do between significant verses in ballad singing or at awkward moments involving prominent film composers. Children are like flowers in a hanging basket. Give them too much water at the top and it just flows out at the bottom. Kitty is quiet for a long time. *Can we have chips for dinner tomorrow night, Mum?* The birds and the bees and the chips, all in one basket.

*

We'd chosen 35 Stanley Avenue quickly and without thinking. We did the same in 1976 when we bought the roof and walls of an old shepherd's cottage in Sandyford, eleven miles from Lockerbie, a Scottish border town that was being torn apart by north–south road traffic, the town whose life would be changed forever when Pan Am 103 ended its doomed flight there in 1988. Our cottage, one of four houses in Sandyford, was right next to a hideous water filtration plant. Bang in the middle of a pine forest in a rain pocket, we were drinking newly chlorinated water. Hamish, Neill and Calum (ages twenty-five, sixteen and twelve) renovated and modernised the cottage. Now every holiday was taken in Scotland, where we spent all our time stripping paint, planting trees, scouring the hills for firewood, taking endless walks over the bleak Lowland Scots hills and teaching the boys to drive rally style on the forest roads. Hardly holidays – but good days with special outings. We went to the international bagpipe competitions in Jedburgh, run by the Royal Scottish Pipe Band Association. Imagine a double score of Japanese pipers all kilted out in bespoke plaid. The winner was the Glasgow Police Pipe Band. Of Course Why Not. Every last Friday in July it's pack up a picnic and go to the Langholme Common Riding, one of many traditional observances that take place in the Scottish borders. Each border town observes the ritual in its own way but the purpose is to make sure that no shared border markers have been moved. A marker moved inch by inch over a millennium will gain quite a lot of land. Age-old poetry, totems (a herring nailed to a plank, a giant thistle and more), dozens of pipe bands, hundreds of horses, thousands of people and multiple thousands of whisky shots with pints to follow make for a day you will never forget. If you remember it at all the morning after.

When you have a house in the country, the world drops in. They came, were fed and watered. If they stayed overnight, they had to saw logs or mow the deer grass, surrounded by clouds of blackflies. Hogmanay was a free-for-all. Our Sandyford neigh-bours, the Cochrans, the Richardsons, the Thompsons, the Lawsons, would *first-foot*, bringing good luck and prosperity and keeping of tradition. On the dot of midnight come three knocks on the door. The first foot over the threshold should belong to a dark-haired person. Red hair: thumbs down. Bring a lump of coal, some bread and salt. Welcome here, glasses of whisky and stay as long as you like. Willie Cochran, the gamekeeper who took rich Texans into the hills to shoot deer and who shot himself in the foot once, would come in with a huge Gladstone bag full of every possible beverage for every type of drinker. Friends would come down from the north and up from the south. Ewan's childhood was full of Hogmanay sagas of Scots visitors who stayed for weeks. Self-appointed guests turned up at Sandyford, some of whom overstayed, overdrank and under-worked. After a few days, we would want new acquaintance to be forgot and never brought to mind. Ewan refused to shift them. Tradition dictated that it was their job to leave, not yours to tell them to go. Betsy only came once to the cottage. Low flyovers by war planes from nearby RAF Carlisle and RAF Spadeadam had shaken her little body to such an extent that she never came again. In her absence, I took on the job of expelling scroungers and didn't like it. We sold the cottage in 1980. Too much work – and I'd never really approved of owning a second home. It was bought by a bachelor who stripped out most of the bohemian features we'd installed. I'd papered an entire wall with large-scale Ordnance Survey maps, Xs marking the spots where ballads or border fracas had occurred. Our new man put busy wallpaper over it – and welcomed me in warmly to view his handiwork when I visited in 2008.

*

1977. Ewan and I are going to have to get married. Tax laws have changed. I sit on Calum's bed and give him the news. Neill probably took it without comment, but Calum sits upright immediately. We talk. He flops back down with a grin on his face. *Great. When they call me a little bastard at school, I can say yes, that's what I am.* Calum was always direct. One of his mates had filled a Thermos flask with little trickles from the liquor bottles in his parents' home bar. When it was full, the neighbourhood gang met behind the deserted Clare House School to drink it. Calum is leaning on our doorbell now, twelve years old and pissed as a newt. *Mum, Andy has passed out and we can't wake him up!* I have no doubt but that Calum had milked our liquor bottles as well.

1979. Britain's tipping point came in May, when Margaret Thatcher became prime minister. Ours arrived in the summer. We were at the cottage when Ewan came into the kitchen and collapsed on a chair. The nearest hospital was in Moffat, a thirty-minute drive away. I made it in twenty, over winding, narrow moorland roads, with Ewan giving me last-minute instructions. We both thought he was dying. He was rushed onto an oxygen machine. It turned out that he'd been having small heart attacks for the past two years, never mentioning it because he didn't want to *worry me*. Scans of his brain showed several previous mini-strokes. He'd given us a hair-raising suicidal drive in the West Highlands earlier in the year, after which his face had taken on a slightly lopsided look – apparently indicating the occurrence of a stroke, which I didn't know at the time. With fully-fledged heart trouble, we were now on Ewan's front line. One day in the early eighties I'm opening the mail and here's a card from a friend sympathising with me re. Ewan's death. I take it to him. *Is there something you haven't told me?*

> *We've been through every weather, you and me,*
> *Forever twining ourselves together till death will us part,*
> *But death seems nearer than it used to be.*
> *Thoughts of time will break my heart.*

('Thoughts of Time')

Fear carved a new home for itself deep down, right next door to where hope lived. Legs in trouble, fracture of a backbone? You just live with it – but you live. When the gallant engine that's thumped away in your chest for sixty-four years indicates its true importance and vulnerability, a big hand has turned the hourglass over and plonked it hard on the table. Ewan already had a number of other ailments: hiatus hernia, slipped disc, gout, chronic bronchitis, acid reflux and diverticulitis. Now we added angina and arteriosclerosis. The medicine for one condition cancelled out the action of the other and it took a year to balance his medical programme, during which time he went from walking like a snail running to a gazelle window shopping. He made jokes about his condition, referring to himself as a whited sepulchre – but his intermittent attacks were a black cloud over our last ten years. Panic and relax, fear and calm, *Is this the one . . . am I going to lose him today?* For ten years. He was beginning to get what I call *the old man look*, a kind of lost expression on his face, mouth slightly open and eyes begging for things to make sense again. At one point our joint tension and depression were so debilitating that we went onto heavy doses of Librium. Decidedly addicted, we came off them a year later, a process as bad as the original depression. I wasn't a good nurse but I was immolating myself, like many of my women friends, on the emotional pyre of an older partner's terminal condition. Fear cemented my vertebrae together. One day I headed out of the house to take the bus to Beckenham and found that I couldn't walk. I was vertical, on the driveway, and I could not put one foot in front of the other. I signalled to Brenda, our over-the-road neighbour. She drove me to a chiropractor, who cracked my back regularly thereafter. Loosen, tighten, loosen, tighten, like a Greek chorus. Our Golden Years were over.

31

Napoleon and Me

> *Long, long gone family time,*
> *Honey on the comb,*
> *So many treasured hands in mine,*
> *All those years of home.*
> *Now all those years are past and gone.*
>
> ('Bring Me Home')

The touring life is reputed to be romantic. We'd finished our gig at a Midlands club and the organiser was paying us in cash in full view of the departing audience. Bad form, but he was new to the business. The tall, beardy fellow in the front row, who'd instigated the standing ovation, was passing by. He was astonished. *Do you get paid for this? But you enjoy it so much* . . . Classical musicians are esteemed for their years of learning. Folk singers? We're just doin' what comes natcherly, which includes practising for hours; seeking out gigs and planning a viable tour itinerary; hours of travel and traffic jams; accommodation, food, and laundry problems; late nights and early mornings; unforeseen mishaps and the worst – leaving our children. All this has led to a universal mantra among us: *I sing for free. You pay me to travel.* Finally, does it occur to an audience that we might not *feel* like singing on the night?

Alan Lomax dismissed our profession in two short sentences. He visited in the mid-1980s and, like Charlie, took three hours

to eat his breakfast, during which he talked about his innovative Cantometrics project, a theory which links gender roles to
traditional styles of singing. Alan was way ahead of his time.
His next project was Choreometrics, which linked work to traditional dance. He wasn't interested in our life at all. He'd come
specifically to recruit us. *You're going to be Cantometrics teachers.*
Ewan stopped chewing: *Alan, we're singers. We sing for a living. We like it.* Alan always wanted to be a singer. *Singers are a
dime a dozen. Cantometrics teachers are not.* The subject switches
quickly to politics. Ewan is a Maoist, Alan a Stalinist, neither
is a pacifist. Time for Alan and me to slope off to the West
Wickham baths. A whale of a man – when he jumped in a tidal
wave travelled down the length of the pool. He suggested that
we swim lengths, co-ordinating our Australian crawl, face to
face, a face I've known all my life. Mystical – turning that bison
face first down and then to me, eyes communicating, his lips
parting in a broad smile as he breathes, his prominent piano-
key teeth centre stage. Peace and some singing when we get
home. Alan's a Texan but has Scots ancestors. He's come for a
day and stays for a week.

I was efficiency plus. I made lists. My Duty Book – a spiral
notebook attached to a diary with an Extra Large Rubber Band
– was always with me. Ewan left the banking to me, so I just
signed for him on cheques, letters, semi-official documents. He
tried to take money out at the bank one day and – recognising
neither him nor his signature – the teller refused to cash it. I
was a Demon Organiser. I organised Stanley Avenue. I organised you if you visited. I organised our touring life, lock, stock,
barrel, kids, Uncle Tom Cobley and all. You don't just organise the tour – you organise the home that you're leaving. I was
Napoleon planning his march on Moscow in 1812, except he

didn't have to include an ungovernable mother-in-law in his manoeuvres. My American concept of distance had never left me. I wasn't mentally equipped for planning routes through little British villages strung like beads on a necklace of ancient roads. Motorways improved it for a while, until nature in the guise of more traffic rushed in to fill the vacuum. Glasgow to Bristol? Look at the map, easy peasy – only four hundred miles. We can get up early. Yes – and arrive five minutes before gig-time, hungry and exhausted. Scoff a packet of crisps with a shandy then *Hello, glad to see you all tonight.* Ewan never complained about my organisational mania and mishaps. It was almost as if he was just coming along for the ride.

I still calculate the time backward from the moment I am to walk on stage. Here's the backward list, each with allotted minutes: relaxation before curtain-up; put on makeup and concert clothes; small snack; sound check; set up stage/instruments/merch table; the load-in; arrive at venue; maybe get lost; two hours' rest/quiet; drive to digs; lunch; load the van up and leave; shower and breakfast; wake up. Read that list backward. Add a just-in-case hour and set the alarm for 7 a.m. Is everything in? Checklist: tour correspondence and maps; five instruments, two suitcases, record boxes; flasks of hot tea, sandwiches; anoraks, boots and tent – just in case. Whisky, butter, the Gilwell potz-n-pans and a little blue fold-up cooking stove in case we want to make steak Diane. Cross everything off the list and I'm tapping my feet impatiently at the bottom of the stairs. *We're going to be late! What the hell are you doing?* His face is an inch from the mirror and he's clipping a micrometre off an invisible hair in his beard.

I'm a gypsy at heart – I love leaving and I love arriving back. That moment of heading away for the land of Somewhere Else is unequalled even if I've been there before. We were chiefly invited by folk clubs, by the British Council and the Arts and Music Councils. Advocacy organisations chose any old place – picket lines, sports facilities, schools, churches, working men's clubs. Each venue had unique acoustic characteristics, traditional personnel relationships and long-standing routines which were already in second gear when we arrived – bar, chairs, stage in place. Ewan and I took up a lot of space. When we entered, the clutch would be pressed and the juggernaut would leap into third or fourth. Selling merchandise was necessary – it made up a large chunk of our income. At one time, we were also carrying a fourteen-by-thirty-inch book of broadsides designed by Irene's brother, Dave Scott. Upon entry, Peggy – a.k.a. control freak – might completely rearrange the room, or commandeer bar space. *Please move the record table over there, where the light shines down on it.* Sitting down for the whole show, we required a small platform. Lacking this at a show in Chester, we used a long, high table as a stage. It was barely wider than the span of our chair legs. Apparently, bets were being taken in the back of the room as to whether we would fall off. Punters still occasionally lay wagers on the possibility of my earrings getting caught in the autoharp strings.

Some premises had curtains and soft furnishings that sponged the sound up and many had no stage or platform at all. Any one or combination of these factors would result in our voices being deadened by the physical presence of audience flesh and bone. Ewan had a strong voice and I did not. My technique over the years was to sing higher and louder – almost shrill – just to be heard at the back of the room. In the early days, microphones were a rarity – they weren't *folk* – and if they were supplied they were usually inadequate. Along with a plenitude of other singers, we gave a CND concert at St George's Bristol (capacity six hundred) with one Reslo microphone, designed for speech. Mickey and Minnie Mouse sang and the instruments went unheard. When I moved back to the United States in 1994, I found that every stage was equipped with standard Shure SM58s. Now I could move my vocal range back down to its natural register and treat the venue as someone's front room – which is where the songs belong.

We toured nonstop, were tired nonstop. No St Helena for us. At one point, Ewan and I were on stay-awake pills. For about five years we would pop a Dexedrine ten minutes before the show started. We would also down the little uppers while cutting records. This probably explains why some of the songs on our Argo *Long Harvest* series are sung at breakneck speed. When the government declared its intention of making our little saviours illegal, we went off them cold turkey. Fourth to neutral gear overnight and you discover just how tired you really are. I began to take the maps at their word and brought our energy levels into line with longitude and latitude. I also began to sort the elements of this crazy way of life into categories for raking over the coals at leisure.

32

The Occupants of Hell

At its height, the British folk revival boasted hundreds of folk clubs, giving rise to a veritable army of musicians and singers continually on the move. The itinerant artist has always hoped – often in vain – to be made welcome at the fire of those who have remained in one place most of their lives. We usually prefer private accommodation – but if not, then a clean bed in the home of a local arts enthusiast who doesn't feel ignored if after-hours entertainment isn't forthcoming. Get a couple of us folkies together off stage and out come the demons we have encountered in our travels.

The Gig from Hell. (1) A Lancashire folk club, held in the bar of a bowling alley. The only way for the players to reach the bar was to cross close behind us as we sang – which they did several times during each song, occasionally mimicking Ewan's singing stance on the way. Cheering, boom of bowling balls, children running about . . . well, *we* were the intruders. (2) In Canada, sharing the show with the superb Canadian fiddler Jean Carignan. Ewan was in the middle of 'Lord Randal' when the fire curtain came down with a bang, right in front of our chairs. Union rules. Show stops at eleven. Bribes brought the curtain up again and Lord Randal *fain would lie down*, but down came the curtain before he could finally do so. Curtain up again. Five minutes later, in the middle of my – *whack!* down came the curtain again. The organiser was maybe paying the stage manager by the minute? (3) A folk club in a pub some-where near Newcastle-on-Tyne. One of our No-Nos had been ignored and we found that we were singing in a bar, orders taken and pints drawn nonstop. The bartender – not a tender bone in her body – loathed folk music. Start on an unaccompa-nied song and she would empty the drawer of the cash register into an aluminium baking tray, then drop every coin one at a time back into the drawer.

Gigs That Could Have Been Hell. (1) An outdoor festival in the USA. The mic was not on a stand but on a vertical stalk that came up through a hole in the stage floor. As I sang and tapped my foot the mic stand moved down and down right before my eyes, like a thin tree trunk being pulled back into the earth. Luckily, it was a funny song and I was fairly fit. I followed the mic down and down, finally lying on the stage until it disap-peared through the floor, too overcome by laughter to finish the song. (2) February 1974. Germany, a dark cellar with graffitied walls. Young louts lout-lounging. The routine under such cir-cumstances is to leave the instrument cases open on stage for a quick getaway. I open the show with 'Sweet Willie', fast banjo and pitch the song high up. A barrage of barracking drowns me out. I stop. Six hefty blokes are sitting at the front table, two dozen beers at the ready. One calls out in cheerful Cockney, *Carry on, Peggy.* I carry on. The louts carry on. Our chaps rise and fan outward and onward. My forsaken damsel begs Sweet Willie, *How could you leave me here?* to the tune of fist against jaw and a body dropping, another fist against another jaw, another and another. A mass rush for the door. Our Magnificent Six come back and sit down at their table. *Carry on! We've come a long way to hear you.* They were British engineers working on an electrical installation a hundred miles away. (3) Stockholm

– on tour with Calum and Neill. One song only, on a nation-
ally televised show. At the last moment, the organiser decides
on 'Ballad of Accounting' instead of 'Song of Choice'. He tells
Ewan, who tells the boys but doesn't tell me. I begin on 'Choice'.
Ewan begins on 'Accounting'. The boys are meerkats, instantly
alert. Whenever Ewan and I differed thus on stage, one of us
would override the other with no accusation or change of facial
expression. I switch to 'Accounting' and my men fall in behind.
The two songs were in related keys and their opening notes
created a bold sympathetic interval. We open in one key and I
play another on the guitar. The Stockholm newspapers hailed
it as a brilliant opening.

The Organiser from Hell is occasionally a well-meaning
but completely unorganised personage, in dubious control.
(1) Picture us headed in the Citroën DS from Manchester to
Sheffield in a blizzard. Any sane person would have phoned and
said, *Don't think we'll make it*, and holed up in a B & B to watch
the telly. But we were – and I still am – shareholders in The-
Show-Must-Go-On, Inc. The A57 – known as the Snake Road
– divides the Bleaklow and Kinder Scout moorlands. It's driver-
unfriendly even under ordinary conditions. A blacktop version of the rambunctious, hairpin-curved Whistling River that
plagued Paul Bunyan – until he hitched Babe, his big blue ox,
to it and removed the bends. Babe was ahead of us, pulling the
A57 into that long, straight, uphill stretch just before Sheffield.
On this night, we slid back down to the bottom several times
before getting up enough speed and purchase to make it to the
top. No time to clean up, change or eat, we arrive starving just
as the show is starting. We ask the organiser, *Please get us some
fish and chips.* Interval arrives. No fish, no chips, no hot tea, no
drink, not even a lousy pack of peanuts from the downstairs

bar. Now this may seem a paltry reason for projecting someone straight into fire and brimstone – but after driving through hell you need an organiser from heaven. (2) November 1991. A folk club in Northampton, Massachusetts, with Irene. Twelve people turn up, claiming they only found out via word of mouth that we were appearing – not an ad anywhere. The organisers don't want to pay us at all because not enough people came. I'd have just left with some excellently chosen insults. Irene sits there like Buddha, hands in lap, refusing to leave till they cough up.

Digs from Hell. (1) The Bradford hotel in which a double room had been partitioned off to make two 'double' rooms. Ours contained only a four-foot-six bed in a room six feet by ten, cupboards high on the walls, hooks on the door, one bare forty-watt light bulb on the ceiling, bathroom down the hall. Reader, are you saying to yourself, as Irene indeed would have, *Where is your self-respect? Why not leave a place like that?* One of the problems was that we had determined to do grassroots touring. This chiefly meant folk clubs, which often could not afford to put us up at even a fifth-rate B & B. Also, we often had very tight schedules and we'd arrive in town with just enough time to change before going to the venue. Furthermore, not all organisers vetted the digs before booking them. The truth? Not so far back in the Them Thar Good Old Days, some just assumed that a folk singer had expectations well below those of other human beings. (2) In Berkeley I arrived at a promoter's house where the sheets on the bed had obviously had considerable recent usage. I insisted that they be changed. *Oh, but L——* [an iconic singer on the circuit] *slept in it. We thought you'd be honoured to sleep in her sheets.* I stripped the bed before leaving so someone else wouldn't be similarly honoured.

We have all shared the stage with Performers from Hell.

We never minded if they couldn't sing, couldn't play, had body odour (which we have been known to have ourselves) or had eaten excessive garlic (ditto). What we *did* mind was when they overran their allotted time. Belfast, March 1967. My Irene was on the bill. She remembers it but I don't, the sight of her goddess-long copper-red hair eclipsed by my memory of the concert. It was an event for which we had been flown over from London to top the bill. In Ireland – even Northern Ireland – everything starts late, this time by forty-five minutes. We were sharing the concert with a singing family loved by us as well as by the Belfastians. Their allotted time was thirty minutes. After seventy-five minutes they had to be physically escorted off stage.* Unaware that there was a time limit on the hall, the organiser (from Limbo) allowed a very generous Irish Intermission. At 10:45 p.m., Ewan and I came on for our stint. After fifteen minutes the organiser tiptoed on stage. *I didn't read the contract properly. Sorry. We have to close down at eleven.* Ewan and I did not get a big hand. The word went round that these high-flyers sing for as little time as possible. Overrunning your time is one of the hallmarks of an amateur. It sends you straight to hell without passing GO.

The Audience from Hell. (1) The Grafton Cinema in Dublin at lunchtime, late sixties or early seventies. A strange bill: Joe Heaney, Luke Kelly and ourselves. Audience: about three hundred raucous Irish, nearly all male and all drunk. Luke sings at the very top of his lungs and cannot be heard at all. Joe Heaney, one of Ireland's most treasured traditional singers, is booed off after thirty seconds. We should have stood down in protest but, to our shame, we didn't. As before a firing squad, we walk on stage.

* One Scots folk club had a real shepherd's crook *in situ* for this job.

I'm in my prime, a female dressed sexily to stereotype. I was not a feminist back then. Hooting and hollering until a uniformed official promises hall closure if they don't shut their gobs. I open with fast banjo, then Ewan does the 'Shoals of Herring', which at that time had not yet become so popular as to be renamed 'The Shores of Erin'. I sing 'First Time Ever', which gets a bit of hush. A new bunch of drunks roll in and we finish our set to unbroken heckling, vomiting and wayward voices trying to join in on every single song. The usher-cum-bouncer congratulates us for reaching the interval. (2) December 1970, Maidstone, Kent. I am here by myself. I zoom into my song 'Uncle Sam' with tricky guitar work. Folkies have almost all been against the Vietnam War. At that time, some thirty air bases around Britain hosted our American cousins – and undoubtedly still do. In the front row are five or six burly Yankee soldiers. The interval arrives and they accost me. *How dare you sing against the country that bore you, fed you, educated you*, the litany is long and predictable. In the second half, I sing another anti-Vietnam song – not wise but irresistible. A Defender of the Free World stands up and pours his beer over me. His companions start tearing pictures off the walls, breaking windows and smashing chairs. The audience and organiser are young and frightened – they vanish. My luthier friend Peter Abnett helps me pack up the instruments and records. Another friend joins us and we get the gear downstairs. The Freedom Fighters appear behind us just as I get into the driver's seat of the Citroën. Two of them start beating Peter up and the others proceed to chase me down the M20. At last a real excuse to dispense with the reins. The DS shakes them off at a reassuring 120 mph.

The Audience from Hades can come as single spies as well as battalions. (1) I'm giving a concert at the English Folk Dance and Song Society with brother Mike and I've done my hair up in an elaborate style. Mirror-mirror-on-the-wall tells me I look lovely. I'm nervous and am just mounting the stair to go on stage when a Singers' Club regular collars me. *You look better with your hair down, Peggy.* Thank you for sharing that with me, John. You're the John who told me that you'd write songs too – if only you had the time. (2) The Arts and Music Councils had life members, many of whom came from the British middle and upper classes, whose sense of humour as regards sexual matters was more restrained than that of most of us folkies. At one such event, Ewan sang the Scots song 'The Mowdiewark'. The mowdie is a mole and *kickin' at the mowdiewark* on the wedding night cannot be misconstrued. Mid-song, the front-row man with the Lord Kitchener mustachios rose, grabbing his wife by the hand. His stentorian tones reverberated as he stalked out. *How DARE you sing that song in front of my lady wife?* Lady Wife had been enjoying it.

Audiences from Heaven for a breather here. The Daventry club which had no seats. The audience stood for the whole show. The Melbourne hundreds who braved a monsoon to come to the concert and sat soaked to the skin for three hours of protest songs. The steam rose from their dripping clothes like a bank of clouds in which an Ozzie angel choir bellowed the choruses.

Food from Hell. In the early days, before we were blessed with migrants, refugees and immigrants, the cafes opened for breakfast, lunch and dinner, each meal of two hours' duration, and closed tight as a box in between. You've slept in and want to break your fast at 11 a.m.? Breakfast is over at ten. You want to eat at 3 p.m.? Lunch is from twelve until two. Takeaway joints were still in the future. By six you are hungry again and dinner doesn't start till seven – the time at which you need to be at the venue. We were saved by the transport cafes (pro-nounced *caffs*), but you have to know where they are. The food is starchy and greasy and generous and cheap and moreish and the company interesting.

We began to cook in hotel bedrooms. The Scottish Arts Council booked us in at the very best old hotel in St Andrews, part of the legendary golf resort. That night Frank Sinatra and his entourage had commandeered the whole place – like the good old days when royalty in Great Britain traipsed up and down the country visiting each other, some with hundreds of staff. Little royalty would often be bankrupted by a Royal Progress. All meals at the Old Course were booked up. No room service, no bar service, *no food at all* if you weren't Frank & Co. We bought a haggis and boiled it up in the mahogany wardrobe. It takes an hour to cook haggis for two, especially as the little Gilwell sauce-pan doesn't hold much water. A good haggis shares its aroma generously and Frank hadn't yet laid claim to the air. Knock! knock! I open the door. An Official Haggis Hunter reels as the wave of offal and onions washes over him and out into the hall. *Are you cooking in here?* I am outraged at the suggestion. His eyes are on stalks, probing the corners. *Well, no cooking in the rooms –* but he's smiling as he closes the door gently. Maybe Frank hadn't allowed him to eat either. We also cooked in the car – wherever hunger caught us – in towns, on mountain tops, beaches. Our friend Geordie McIntyre will testify that it's possible to create a superb pepper steak for three in a lay-by in the footwell of a Citroën DS, flaming it in single malt and reducing the jus, add-ing a tablespoon of scalded cream – *and* serve it up with French bread, linen serviettes and wine in glasses.

My father came over every two or three years but refused to stay at Stanley Avenue. Our house was already overfull but, well . . . there was that matter of cooking smells. Hot food in my childhood had never included onions or garlic – and cabbage belonged only in coleslaw. If ever blind, Charlie would have found his way around via his nose. He was probably a dog in a former life. He always came out with us on tour when he visited. Gallant, as he had to tolerate our schedule, with food catch as catch can. One night we had forty-five minutes in which to eat before due at the gig. There was only one eatery open, a frightful place a stone's throw from the Manchester Town Hall, which, according to Ewan in one of his creative flights of fancy, boasted features from dozens of architectural eras. Well, certainly three, all Gothic – Early, Victorian and Neo. Each unwiped table in this awful place had a plastic cruet stand and a stained and frayed menu. A stained and frayed teenager came to take the order. Charlie ordered fish, with instructions that it was to be broiled (grilled) no more than ten seconds on each side. It came, rubbery and dry, accompanied by cold French fries and grey mushy peas. The Chinese call such fare *wrecked food*. Charlie asked to see the chef. Our waiter didn't understand the term. Ewan was deadpan, laughter in his eyes. He interpreted: *The cook.* Out came a very stained, very fat, very irritated un-aproned man. Charlie gave the ten seconds routine again. Cook listened. *Your piece of fish was the last. Got no more.* Charlie got a fried egg, also rubbery and dry, which he left on his plate.

Company from Heaven. Charlie was grand to travel with. On tour, he lived as we lived, interested in our way of life. He always lay across the back seat of the car with his feet, soft-shod in moccasins, out the back window if the weather allowed. Like Mike, he preferred my driving to Ewan's. So did I, so did carsick Neill and probably every driver we ever shared the roads with. I was at the wheel this day and Ewan was dozing in the passenger seat. We were on one of my favourite roads, nearly always deserted – the two-lane up-hill-down-dale tarmac track that goes north over the Cheviot Hills. Dips and crowns, perilous at high speed. When you take it like a motorcycle scramble, the car leaves the road and flies. Wheeeeee! then bump gently back to earth on the Citroën's designer low-pressure tyres. The road had levelled out into a straightaway and a Driver from Hell was channelling Donna Mae Mims on the home stretch at about 100 mph. Charlie's voice comes soft and measured in my ear. *Peggy. Slow down. Ninety is probably the best speed for this road.*

It should be said that there are undoubtedly organisers somewhere who remember that Singer from Hell who insisted on changing *everything* around in their clubs. All these incidents are humorous in retrospect and are completely outweighed by the upsides: the community-friendly institution of the pub and its function room; the organisers who did get our fish and chips and who paid for good digs out of their own pockets; the humble open-all-hours Indian restaurants that began to dot the country; the caring and interesting members of the audience who fed us and put us up in their own homes; and the many talented resident singers who opened the club evenings and didn't overrun their time. Good people, good times, good company.

33

Break the Other Leg

23 March 1995. I've driven for four hours to get to Nassau Community College. I feel rotten, ill prepared to face a pod of Long Island students. There are four acts tonight, each to last forty-five minutes. Oscar Brand takes the first set. His light, companionable humour sets the right tone. Then a Boadicean women's drumming circle has the audience stamping, clapping, dancing, then collapsing into their seats. The walls are still a-quiver with drumbeats. What *am* I doing here? What does this twenty-something audience want that a nearly sixty-something solo female folk singer can possibly give? Every audience has a *sell-by* date, which in my concerts usually arrives about twenty minutes into the second half. This audience is getting there, unaware of the battering their nerves have taken from the percussion. Application of the Idea of *IF I were in this audience what would I want now?* At whatever age, everyone needs a change after a while. I would want melody – and quiet, reflective words.

I open my set with the unthinkable, a nine-minute unaccompanied ballad. People love stories and Annie's is a doozy. It's somewhere in this book. Like a short children's story, I give an account of the Border Reivers – the Scots and English raiders who devastated the lands at their common border from the thirteenth to the seventeenth century. Cattle and women – in that order – were the most prized loot. At this very moment,

Americans are pillaging and raping in other countries. The students are savvy and they go very quiet. I begin. *O, the bandits stole Fair Annie away as she walked by the sea.* The proverbial pin would have clattered. Of course, they could have been dozing. But asleep or awake, they're with me for my forty-five minutes. Richie Havens follows. I've done him a favour and he owes me big time for they are now ready for a second dose of upbeat energy. He builds them up to mob frenzy but makes a key mistake – he goes on for two hours. They peel out one by one after an hour. Their *consume-by* date has arrived.

Ewan and I rarely departed from our performance format. For us, the whole point was to sing really well, to have a minimum amount of introduction and to showcase new songs, both traditional and contemporary. There were those who wrote to us afterward in glowing terms. There were those who blogged on the grapevine – Facebookers would find its speed pitiable – that our concerts smacked of lectures. We certainly weren't a bundle of laughs but we had quite a lot of variety. We sang for each other and the audience was welcome to listen and join in on choruses. We never made set lists, other than agreeing on the top and tail of each half. We sang endlessly in the car getting to and from gigs. This had secondary spinoffs in that we were in good voice by the time we arrived and in that we learned each other's songs, thus rendering us able to cue one other if necessary. For those thirty-five of my sixty stage-years I felt that it was enough to just sing the songs, to be a folk singer. Now I am a folk-orientated entertainer who sings folk and contemporary songs. I try to turn the stage into a living room. The audience and I create what happens. The ingredients of most baked goods are the same. It's how you combine them that makes the different breads and cakes. My ingredients: guitar, banjo, dulcimer, autoharp, piano, English concertina, voice and repertoire. I juggle major/minor, accompanied/unaccompanied, duple/triple metre, folk/contemporary, fast/slow, long/short, serious/humorous, loud/soft.

Ego, bravado and the desire to share or show off can get you on stage but nothing substitutes for preparation once you get there. Be prepared for anything to happen. Chelmsford folk club – a man in the front row who gives uncontrollable whoops once or twice a minute. Bernard, a super-intelligent politico with cerebral palsy, apologises at half-time, communicating at lightning speed on an alphabetised abacus. Be prepared for anything. My mobile phone rings in my onstage bag at Passim's in Boston while I'm introducing a song. I put the phone on speaker and hold it up to the mic so the caller can talk to all of us. Be prepared. On stage, I discover that my dress is wrong side out. *It's a fashion statement, folks. Do you like it?* Take lessons from Life and apply them on stage. When stuck in sand, let some of the air out of the tyres. When the dirt road turns to deep mud, don't stop. Just keep going. These days I go out front and talk to a few members of the assembled company for ten minutes or so before curtain-up. It gives me some familiar faces to which to sing, rather than a sea of unfamiliar ones. It also defuses the formality of the occasion – folk music seems to require that. Part of my preparation.

When I'm not feeling up to scratch, I open with a song with which I am absolutely comfortable – 'Peacock Street' or 'I Been a Bad, Bad Girl', sung half conversationally. Or I open with a reading from the *Fact and Fantasy Book*, my collection of trivia, statistics and jokey whatevers. We all laugh – we're on the same page. I try to keep the audience on their toes, wondering what's coming next. Sometimes I don't know what's next myself till the applause dies down. There's nothing wrong with periods of silence, especially after a very moving song. If you need to think for a moment without talking, just stay quiet. That's what you'd do in a living room. Talk before each song, but briefly. If you have a tendency to repeat *um* or *like*, try shorter sentences. Yattering on about when it was recorded from what informant or where it can be found on what page in what book is fine only if your audience is a swarm of folklore academics.

*

A percentage of a folk audience has come to produce as well as consume the show. Up on stage, the singer starts with *Join in on the chorus!* then launches into the first verse, followed by (for example):

> *Rissolty rossolty, hey bom bossolty,*
> *Nicklety nacklety, rustical quality,*
> *Willaby wallaby, now now now . . .*

The audience won't join in. They can't. They'd love to sing but need to run it through a couple of times. They appreciate being taught to sing it to their – and your – satisfaction. That done, here they are, everyone singing and one or two people sitting there, mouths pointedly clamped shut. Of course, they may have been dragged screaming to the concert by their folkie friend or by their great-grandmother who attended one of my concerts aeons ago. Or they may be tone deaf, refraining from singing for the sake of near neighbours. Or they don't like being told what to do. Give the zipped lips a bit of encouragement – *You'll feel guilty for not joining in when you get home.* Give them an excuse

– acknowledge that anyone who's a Martian or doesn't speak English can opt out. After all, I sometimes opt out myself and have the audience sing to me. That particular man in Sydney, Australia – a John Cleese lookalike – was *determined* not to sing the chorus of a song against (p)Resident Dubya Bush. Every now and then his mouth would start to move and he would force it back into a rictus of disapproval. Immovable as a boulder, the flood of chorus-voices surged against and around him:

IMPEACH! IMPEACH!
That's what we've got to do;
IMPEACH! IMPEACH!
Get Dick Cheney too.
It's pull the plug and down the drain,
Dubya, toodle-ooo!
GOODBYE TO GEORGIE!
GOODBYE TO GEORGIE!

He came up to chat in the interval. *I guess you didn't like that George Bush song?* My man is from South Carolina. *Waaall . . . I guess you can recognise a Republican from a long ways off, ma'am.* Pause. *But that's a damn good chorus!*

I nearly always know ahead of time when I'm going to forget a line. If it's the first line of a verse in an accompanied song, just play a break. If it's unaccompanied, hum the melody of the line. Or speak the story, hoping to latch onto the next remembered bit. Or maybe signal that I'm thinking and sit quiet for a moment. The audience is sympathetic. Everyone forgets at some time or another. If the interrupted song is light or funny, I've prepared pertinent punditry for the occasion: *I have photographic memory – I just don't have same-day service* (Diane

Sawyer). Or one that I think is mine: *I forget nothing. I just postpone remembering.* There are big onstage No-Nos: mumbling your intro while tuning; chatting *sotto voce* at length with other performers; cracking in-jokes; overrunning your allotted time; turning your back on the audience; wearing very short tight skirts if the stage is high, the audience is close up and you play the harp, cello or banjo. Above all, behave as if you belong there. They belong out there too – they've paid their money, they've come to share with you and to enjoy themselves. The fee you walk out with came from their pockets. You have a debt to pay off.

Be prepared. Anything may happen. Hecklers . . . My earliest experience of these sadists was at Yale University – a private, elitist institution for men. I was nineteen when I dropped in on a raucous student bash and was asked to sing. Banjo out, here comes 'The House Carpenter'. Wrong choice. But nothing I sang would have been the right choice. They were in the mood for cruelty and I was a female with a banjo. From the back comes *Sing 'Melancholy Baby'!* Everyone takes it up, clapping in rhythm together: *Melancholy Baaa-by, Melancholy Baaa-by!* I stood there, helpless. Tom Paley saved me, coming up with his guitar and starting an easy-to-sing Carter Family song. Nowadays I'd just laugh and tell them I don't know the song, invite them up to the mic to sing it themselves and leave. In my latter days, the hecklers are always men who object to feminist songs. In Princeton, I sang 'B-Side' (violence against women), then 'Gonna Be an Engineer'. A burly man got up and stormed out shouting, *Didn't think this was going to be a fucking concert about women!* A good riposte, had I been quicker off the mark, might have been, *Oh dear. The weaker sex.* It's also good to have creative ways of mentioning the CD table. *Hold your ticket over a flame and you'll see these words appear: Buy a CD before you leave.* I once saw a woman during the interval checking her ticket over her cigarette lighter.

Practise spontaneous creation. Freyda Epstein, delicious fiddler and singer, was MC on a show in Tennessee and there was a hold-up of some kind. It'd take a while to sort it. Freyda took the only working mic in her hand, gave the musicians a chord sequence and proceeded to improvise a very funny song about all the things that had happened to her on stage in her performing life. She swayed and crooned a leisurely, formless melody till the next act was ready. Freyda was peerless at being in gentle command. I took vocal tuition at a seminar she gave in Asheville and on the first day I made a joke during class. She turned to me, expressionless. *I crack the jokes here.* Right on the ball. Smart alecks can derail the train of thought. I was a newcomer to teaching at summer folk camps and tended to give a great deal of extracurricular tutoring – because people asked and because I could give them what they needed. I was exhausted by the end of the week. As we drove back to Asheville together, Freyda advised me to dole my energy out in smaller portions. I had used up all of mine by the third day. *There will always be people who want more from you than you can give.* Giving is what folk musicians do – I just didn't know where to stop. Freyda comes often into my head. She was killed in a head-on crash in Virginia in 2003 – a drunken driver snuffed her candle out.

*

Mike, Pete and I – we each had our own stage persona. Pete threw himself *out* there, arms wide, and brought everyone in. Mike sat there, alone, and the audience had to come *in* to him.

I kind of do both but neither with the exclusive skill that my brothers developed. Each way worked for its maker but the three of us together on stage had trouble and the audience had to adapt from song to song. Pete continued to give concerts till his last year. It took lion-hearted effort to keep doing what he'd always done effortlessly. In his nineties, he knew that everyone wanted him there in whatever condition. He stood proud in the spotlight, no singing voice left – and started a song off. The audience took it up and sang for him while he directed them like a conductor, mouthing the words. I'm ready to cry. We gave three yearly concerts together a couple of years before he died, each of us handing the audience over to the other with understanding and love.

I'm a singer of folk songs, one in a line of long-distance runners in a centuries-long relay race. My most recently hard-learned bit of performance ethics: know when to leave the stage. You've gotten a standing ovation. Ego tells you to stay and keep going. Common sense tells you to quit while you're ahead.

I will always be able to walk on stage as if I belong there – but the time when I can no longer travel, sing or play is fast approaching. Be ready for anything to happen – including having to leave the stage for good. Irene has already bought the shepherd's crook. She's prepared.

34

Living the Songs

Lord Thomas is obviously in his midlife crisis. Or he's on the prowl for the dowry that a new young wife will bring him. Or he's probably finding monogamy boring. Or he wants a younger model to display behind him on the saddle of his new convertible.

> *Comb down your hair, my Annie dear,*
> *And bind it up into a crown*
> *That you may look so fair a maid*
> *As when first I brought you home.*

He brings his new bride home. Annie – *Fair Annie* – the mother of his seven sons, the youngest of whom he has never seen, prepares and serves the wedding feast, smiling *sweetly upon them all*. At bedtime, she fetches her banjo and sings outside the bridal chamber:

> *O, but if my sons was seven grey rats*
> *Running on the milk-house wall,*
> *I myself to be a big tomcat,*
> *I soon would worry them all.*
>
> *O, but if my sons was seven grey wolves*
> *Running in the brushy hills,*

I myself to be a good hound dog,
I soon would chase my fill.

O, but if my sons was seven buck deer
Drinking at the old salt lick,
I myself to be a good shotsman,
I soon would make them kick.

This is high drama, a mother ready to kill her children to regain her husband. Medea, wounding Jason in the only way she knows how. Or perhaps the impossible: *Carrying and birthing my sons has made me old and unattractive. Kill them and I will be young again. He will love me again.*

The ballads are special. I approach them with anticipation similar to that of surveying the menu in a gourmet restaurant after a gruelling hill-walk. I recreate Annie and her motives for myself every time I sing her. The tune is plain enough to move into the background. But how do you sustain the drama, unaccompanied, for nine minutes? Histrionics would turn this thirty-verse ballad into a melodrama. Accompaniment would divide your attention. I turn myself towards a figurative corner and begin to tell myself the story again. Verse 15: If I were Fair Annie, meeting Lord Thomas and the new bride at the quayside, how would I sing her greeting to them? I answer the question by singing the verse with one set of thoughts for addressing Lord Thomas and another for addressing the bride:

You're welcome home, Lord Thomas, she said,
To your mansion and your farm.
Welcome, welcome, you fair young bride,
All that's here is yourn.

Then we have the following verse, in which the young bride asks her husband and her husband replies:

Who is that lady, my dear lord,
She welcomes fairly you and me?
That ain't nothing but my housekeeper,
Your friend she's going to be.

Given Circumstances and Emotion Memory. For the first two lines, let's assume that the bride is innocent, unworldly. I could have a picture in my mind of a born-yesterday child-woman asking the question of her experienced lover. Or I could picture myself at that mean little kitchen table, pregnant and naïve, talking idly to Betsy before she drops her bombshell. So think or remember innocence – and sing the lines. Or imagine this bride as not jealous but pragmatic, grasping immediately who *that lady* is and realising that she has an ally – and sing the lines. Or visualise the bride as immediately ready to make war with this *housekeeper*. Thought communicates as you sing. The bride is no longer a lay figure. The story is not just recited. The audience are smart – they may even create their own given circumstances and run with them.

Now the last two lines of that verse, in which Lord Thomas replies. These are aimed at both women with different messages. The bride receives simple information if she is naïve, reassurance if she has suspicions, diplomacy if she is aggressive. Annie receives two unspoken messages, one per line: *You've been downgraded to housekeeper* and *Her friend you're going to be*, with an implied *or else*. It's easy to call up memories from my own life when I sing that line. The chain of emotion memories helps me sustain the tension through thirty verses.

Why go through all this just to sing a ballad? I know the words well enough to reel them off – but without these techniques I'd get bored. *If Einstein's scared, I'm scared.* When the singer is bored the audience gets bored. They begin fidgeting even before Lord Thomas puts the silken towel on the silver pin, *Fair Annie, you may wipe your eyes, As you work out and in.* In Ireland, traditional singers would turn their chair to the corner, the *coineagh*, to sing the big songs. It was not a retreat – it was the kind of isolation that draws listeners in as a magnet draws iron filings. We close our eyes or gaze into the distance as we enter the age-old world of storytellers. We hope that you will follow and see it happening in your own other world. I was singing for Calum's primary-school class in Beckenham, children of five and six years old. I told them that I kept my eyes shut so I could see the story happening, that I saw the characters coming in from right to left as the song went by. I sang 'Old Bangum', in which our hero battles with the wild boar. I opened my eyes a tiny slit while I was singing and there they were, the little dumplings, sitting with their eyes shut tight. When I was leaving, a little girl rushed up to me and pulled on my skirt. *Mrs MacColl, Mrs MacColl, I saw the whole story happening! But from left to right.* Proud now: *And I didn't need to shut my eyes.* Her own other world. The *coineagh*: the word is also used in Scotland. Belle Stewart held that if a song made the hackles rise on the back of your neck, if it raised the hairs on your forearms or gave you goose pimples, it had the *coineagh*, i.e. the real deal. When I sing 'Fair Annie', I get the *coineagh*.

An emotion is not just an emotion. When I sing ballads I am carried from cause to effect to cause to effect until I am living a series of inevitable chronological events in my mind. That hourglass again. The narrator disappears and the story takes over. Telling it becomes a community endeavour and often there is total silence at the end of the ballad as the bride and Annie – with Thomas between them like the hyphen in Father Jos Vloebergh's depiction of God and Jesus – settle their case. Calum has commented that some of my renditions smack of too much thought. Charlie said he could hear me thinking when I accompanied myself – he didn't mean it as a compliment. That's why I'm a performer, an entertainer, not a field singer. I've just touched a tip of the performance iceberg, but that's all that is needed right now.

35

The Shows Go On and On Until

The 1950s: I'm on the loose in Massachusetts, Europe, Russia, China and finally settled in England. The 1960s: our two boys, the Radio Ballads, the Critics Group. The 1970s: the boys are testing their wings and Kitty has arrived. Collecting. Songwriting. Big projects and mad activity. The 1980s: the boys have left, Ewan's health is failing, the power base has shifted. They say gold doesn't tarnish but ours became pitted and scored by illness and constant fear. Right through the 1980s Ewan endured attacks both on and off stage, first weekly then daily. If minor, he carried on after a rest. If major, lying down was the only recourse. We made stabs at getting him off his favourite foods of fat red meat, cheese, wine and puddings. I took a Chinese cooking course – it helped, but Ewan missed the stodge. Now he could only walk on the level and was scornful about city walking unless there were goals in mind. Beckenham had no goals. So – it was swimming. He baulked. As a child, he had nearly drowned in the Irwell River, a body of water so clogged with industrial filth that it couldn't flow. I nagged and scolded and when he finally went he enjoyed it. He could only swim on his back. Those who frequented the West Wickham pool in the 1980s may remember the old guy who kept bumping into them.

On 1 September 1982, the matron of Thornton House called us. Betsy was dying. She'd been unable to get up that morning and had asked one of her three roommates to kiss her goodbye. Ewan and Calum and I went round. Ewan was rooted to the floor. He couldn't go near her. Calum and I stayed with him, holding him, afraid he'd fall, standing about ten feet away across the room. The matron held Betsy's hand as she died. For weeks afterward, Ewan would walk around the house, his hands clasped behind his back (Betsy's stance), peeking through cracks in doors – just as Betsy had done. And exactly what I'd done when Dio died, taking on several of her physical habits. Reverse birthing – our mothers held us safe inside. Now we'll hold them safe inside.

*

Family, touring and travelling had held us together. Now I was frequently driving out and taking gigs solo. Until now, Ewan's passion had held us together – about every five years he would fall in love with me again and we would be carried off on a wave of lust. When I had a Vidal Sassoon haircut at age thirty-six, he rediscovered the back of my neck and off he went again on the chase. The last of these sprints was about four years before he died. In his final five years, he was forbidden to drive – a mercy to everyone. Now the age difference seemed to have doubled. We lost our joy of living somewhere along the road to survival. Through the decades we'd developed a power structure: Ewan the instigator and Peggy the facilitator. Ewan would get an idea. *Let's conduct a survey of the folk clubs.* Peggy draws up the forms, sends one off to every club in the EFDSS Folk Directory, requesting *information about your club and any other clubs in your vicinity.* The forms arrive back in hundreds, with dozens of references to other nearby clubs on the back. I catalogue the new ones, circling the towns on the map, and send off a form to each of them. I spend three or four hours a day on this project while Ewan goes on to the next idea. But now, in the 1980s, there was a major shift. I began to instigate, facilitate and work on my own.

They were still golden years – but in lower case. I was home more but Alice kept the household grounded, taught Kitty house care, sewing, crochet and polishing the silverware and brasses. Kitty held us together by dint of her intelligence, her easy disposition, her patience with her asthma and her position as the last child. She and Ewan had bonded very early on but she doesn't remember her father as a healthy man. Our children were so different. Neill is a Seeger. He baffled Ewan. I probably did too. Calum is a MacColl. He kept me on my toes and kept Ewan in a boxing ring. Kitty was a mixture. She held Ewan with one hand and me with the other. She gave us a focus and companionship that lightened the burden of Ewan's illness. She came to concerts and clubs with us, often practising her gymnastics when – chairs cleared away – we were packing up. She learned songs and sang them on stage with us, disappointed when we moved on to the next issue, the next new songs.

When you sing against the System, the March of the Issues never ends. Ewan concentrated on Margaret Thatcher, whose successive terms triggered a decade-long series of political earthquakes and destroyed decades of citizen-friendly legislation. I wrote songs about Reagan, Greenham Common, El Salvador, apartheid, Nelson Mandela and various strikes. In 1983, I discovered that nuclear waste chugged daily through our local train station. I discussed it with several of the mothers who stood at Kitty's school gate. We formed BANG, the Beckenham Anti-Nuclear Group. It solidified with a few men and half a dozen older women, of whom my Irene was one.

None of us knew anything about nuclear power so we home-schooled ourselves once a week, guided by the Big Blue Book, Anna Gyorgy's *No Nukes*. I wrote five songs about nuclear power, each from a different point of view. BANG members went out to schools and women's groups to lecture. We rode suburban trains dressed in white coveralls with the radio-activity logo, talking to commuters. We dropped flyers through thousands of Beckenham doors. We petitioned and petitioned. We women are in Bromley High Street with our clipboard. Man and woman approach, a couple. Make eye contact with both. Common response: woman looks our way, interested that women are asking her opinion on something. Man surveys us, puts his arm over woman's shoulder, then around her waist and steers her away. We held local debates, which were packed. The nuclear industry sent emissaries who were no match for us. One of them even declared confidently that the Sellafield reprocessing plant could *withstand a nuclear bomb*. Nice to hear the old Beckenham Town Hall filled with laughter.

Some of the protesting was fun. One technique was to with-hold 11 per cent of your electricity bill, that being the pro-portion of electricity produced by our thirteen nuclear power stations. Then you paid the 89 per cent with imagination. You could legally write a cheque on anything. One protester wrote his check on the side of a cow and marched it into his bank – no doubt inspired by the fictitious *Board of Inland Revenue* v. *Haddock*. Bank protocol used to dictate that cheques must be stamped and physically returned with your monthly statement. I wrote my first cheque on a door; the next was on a small coffin-shaped Appalachian dulcimer case; then on an egg, accompanied by a note letting the bank staff know just how long I had had the egg. Each of these was duly stamped and returned to me, the money deposited. After a year or two the London Electricity Board threatened to cut us off. Not possible with Ewan's heart trouble and Kitty's asthma. My last payment: a cake with the cheque written on the top in blue icing – blue for the colour of radioactive water.* I wrote a note instructing the bank staff to please eat the cake instead of redirecting it to me. They did just that, whispering through the grille that it was yummy and that several of the staff had refused to eat it in case it was poisoned.

*

Nuclear bombs had appeared in my life on 7 August 1945, when I saw giant headlines on the front page of Charlie's *Washington Post*. The ensuing photographs lit a fire in my child's heart. They have never left my picture gallery. Despite the fact that the subject went to the inside pages of the papers during the dragged-out Cold War, the embers were fed continually. The Bikini tests. The Cuban Missile Crisis. Peter Watkins's *The War Game*, which we saw in Edinburgh, coming out of the cinema astounded that the world had been put back together again. I wrote 'Four-Minute Warning', referencing the UK public alert system giving us four minutes' warning between confirmation of a nuclear attack and the landing of bombs on UK soil. This warning, written in Never-Never Land, was discontinued in the 1990s, probably killed off by sick laughter.†

In September 1981, hundreds of men and women marched from Wales to nearly-London, protesting the placing of US

---

* Investigate Vavilov-Cherenkov radiation.
† The text may be found at news.bbc.co.uk/1/shared/bsp/hi/pdfs/03_10_08nuclearattack.pdf.

cruise missiles at the RAF base on Greenham Common, near Newbury. Ewan and I sang to them in Melksham, a collection of exhausted marchers who, thank goodness, fell asleep during the concert. Originally the camp was dual-gender but the men did very little work and expected to be waited upon. With neither men nor cruise missiles welcome, the camp became Women Only Territory. The press assailed us. They would turn up looking for a leader, a spokeswoman. We were all spokeswomen. *Why are you all here?* The drill was to say, *Well, I'm here because (etc.) but you might want to ask Anne/Mary/Samantha, etc., why she's here.* No head honcha, just a memorable body of memorable women. Helen John, a married woman, had just upped and left her home to come to Greenham. Rebecca Johnson sang her nightmares through the barbed wire to the soldiers. Sarah Hipperson stayed the whole nineteen years of action. Forty years on, they are still active against nuclear arms. I went to Greenham with BANG-woman Marion Watson first. The American political singer Dave Lippman was there at the time. Can't kick a good songwriter out just because he's male. No place to sleep. Slender Dave won't have forgotten sleeping squashed between two generously built compañeras in the back of an estate car. Later I came with Irene. We always found weeks' worth of filthy pots and pans awaiting newcomers who, like us – feeling guilty for not being there full-time – would set to with Scotch-Brite, Brillo, elbow grease, curses and companionship. Once, Irene and I walked the whole nine-mile perimeter, through swamps, blackberry patches, suburban backyards. Sometimes we took the night shift so that the women who were there 24/7 could sleep.

At the beginning, each of the gates had a fire and a tent. When the evictions started, you had to be ready to run, so protection became makeshift, easily packed up. Often men would approach the fire, some with gifts of food and blankets. *What does your husband think of you being here? Does your mother know you're here?* They were forbidden to sit down or stay and talk. Blankets and food were not barter material for a place at the fire. The nine gates were given the names of colours. No gate was left untended and the resident women had walkie-talkies to communicate. We'd sit with backs to the huge gate right through the day, singing, talking, laughing or just being quiet. Sleeping all night by one of the gates and waking to see six police boots, two pairs large and one pair small, right by my head. A heavy boot nudged me. The female officer: *Don't! You'll get your boot dirty.* In 1984, I was arrested at a cruise missile pro-test sit-down in front of Westminster, put into a paddy-wagon. Each one-person cubicle held two people. My cell-mate was Caroline. Face to face, back to back, chatting, battling claus-trophobia, occasionally singing – for four hours. At my trial, I tried to sing my song 'Tomorrow' and was sent down to the cells, next step contempt of court. My lasting contribution was a song – 'Carry Greenham Home' – which became one of the anthems of this extraordinary action. In 1992, the RAF returned the base to common land, and in 1997 Greenham Common was designated as public parkland again. I have a piece of the fence in my treasure chest.

Irene and I worked together in BANG and then formed Jade, a women's singing group, with three other women. Greenham, BANG, Jade: you can see the emerging pattern here – all of these campaigns and groups of comrades (mostly women) excluded Ewan. We still got considerable attention as a duo. In 1984, Mary Orr and Michael O'Rourke, media bods from Portland, USA, interviewed us, our friends and family extensively. They put together a radio documentary, a comprehensive study of our life and work.* That same year, the Miners' Strike brought us together again. Ewan wrote some superb songs for it. Calum was at his musical best and the cassette helped raise funds for the strike.

Ewan's attacks were getting worse and usually came without warning. At Liberty Hall in Dublin he had to leave the stage mid-song, coming on again in the second half in great form. At Heathrow en route to a holiday he just collapsed and we got a hospital stay instead of a Mediterranean villa. The only certainty was that it would happen again and again. One summer we went to Venice. Our room was on the fourth floor of a historic hotel. Ewan got a sudden attack in the dark of night and we called the emergency services. Two tiny old men turned up with a stretcher and manoeuvred Ewan down the medieval stone stairs and into a vaporetto. Kitty and I had just got aboard when it started off at top speed. Ewan rolled off the stretcher onto the floor, in pain but helpless with laughter. His ward at the dignified old hospital contained both men and women on beds so high that you had to abseil out of them. The nurses were nuns in full habit. Ewan was there for three baking hot days, during which they neither bathed him nor allowed me to do so. He was drowning in sweat and by the beginning of the fourth day he was frantic to get out. But look! Today the nuns come in with huge pails of water and cloths. They pass Ewan's bed and start washing the windows. Speechless with laughter, my man discharges himself. We go for a slap-up meal and head back to the hotel. Holiday, Round 2.

* *Parsley, Sage and Politics*, available in a three-CD set from Radioman@aol.com.

*

Alice had dealt with the boys' teenage years and had promised herself that she would leave when Kitty was fourteen. In 1985, at the age of sixty-six, she threw in the towel – the end of yet another era. Kitty sat weeping at the dining-room window.

I've asked each of my children to tell me what they remember from their childhood. Most of it is good. Kitty was embarrassed by my doing yoga on the floors of airports; trying too hard to engage her friends in talk. She enjoyed recording with us. Neill wrote about our camping holidays. He'd been very outgoing till Calum came along, when Betsy's obvious preference rained on his only-child parade. Neill *learned to be silent.* That broke my heart. Calum learned to be frightened – nuclear war was a common dinner topic. He confronted Ewan physically. Each of the boys moved relentlessly towards manhood, both of them now taller than Ewan.

I had little contact with my birth family during the 1970s. Charlie came over regularly. When I left him at the airport in late 1978 he gave me an especially long hug. I should have known. On 8 February 1979, brother Charles phoned to say Charlie had died. You think you're prepared but you're not. I stood stirring the stew and crying, doing the pre-supper washing up and crying, sitting at the supper table crying. As if on a political march, I had moved forward to the front line by the time the meal was served. Weeks later, on my way back from the USA, after dividing up Charlie's possessions with the family, I stood outside the airport terminal slamming my fist at the sky and screaming at Charlie that he had no right to leave me.

*

Who takes care of the carers, who are mostly women whose lives are taken over by another person's state of body or state of mind? *Caring* is an umbrella word. The lover: *I care for you, darling.* My niece Tinya spent five years *caring* for her parents, my brother Pete and his wife Toshi. For Tinya, a New York Cordelia, *care* meant regulating and administering medicines, monitoring social situations, ignoring her own needs, trying to balance subjectivity and objectivity . . . all of this adding up to five years of 24/7, 52/1 vigilance and responsibility. When you next visit an ill friend or relative, pay attention to the carer, for they need *care*. They are giving and giving and giving until their Community Chest is empty. Ten years of caring and the ever-present fear depleted my store of energy and hope. By 1988 I was on the verge of breakdown. I needed tender, loving care by the truckload. Ewan was unable to give it other than by never complaining, never betraying his fear, trying to keep up with me wherever possible. Kitty, thank goodness, was more away than home, doing what girls do at age sixteen.

A born carer, Irene could see the state I was in. Her support ranged from being a confidante to giving me hugs when I needed them, holding me when I collapsed. She occasionally sat with Ewan, alternating with Kitty so that I could get away. I loved Ewan as a comrade, as between soldiers in a war. We were not friends in the true sense. There were confidences with which I couldn't trust him, secrets that I *could* share with Irene – and, strangely, secrets that he could share not with me but with Irene when she sat with him. Desperate for outdoors, hill-walking and freedom, I asked Irene to go rambling in Derbyshire. On the way home, on 30 November 1988, in the morning, drinking Nescafé's excuse for coffee in a dreary little pub on the moors, I realised: I love her. *Dear mother of God*

– how am I going to . . . I don't know . . . As we drive back home, I pretend to work diligently in the passenger seat on the upcoming recording of *American Folk Songs for Christmas.* Mike and Penny are coming over. My mind is whirling. *Ewan . . . Irene . . . This is silly. I'll get over it. No, I won't. Way down in that heart that does have a bottom, I know I won't. I've been hit by something so big . . .* I cast a sideways glance at her as she drives. I look back in case she looks at me. I think I look different already. *Does she know?* I'm silent most of the way home in case she can tell by the tone of my voice . . .

I realised that I had never been totally *in love.* All through December I was filled from core to beyond skin with pulsing life. I was shining with inner light, obsessed with keeping it from Ewan, too ashamed and confused to tell Irene. She had a husband too – Philip, with whom she worked at their veterinary surgery. All through December, she came out with me to concerts when Ewan couldn't. On Christmas Day, she flew away for a month to Australia and I mourned as if she had died. I howled in a space I didn't know I had. I spent January preparing what I would say to her. It didn't occur to me to keep it secret from her. When she returned, we went up to London to the Sanctuary, the women's spa. On 1 February 1989, I delivered my prepared confession. We drove back home making small talk. *You don't have to say or do anything, Irene. I just wanted to tell you. Goodnight.* The next morning over a cup of tea at the local bakery . . . she loves me. Just like that. All of her daisy petals say *she loves me.* Up the ladder and walking a high wire with my eyes closed. Until 22 October.

36

1989

The memory of love will burn in my heart
Till embers and ashes are gone.
The light in your window is my Northern Star . . .

('Heading for Home')

My dear man must know. How could he not? He loves me but doesn't know me. I don't know me. I've lost weight. I feel that I have become unrecognisable in appearance and behaviour. We are on the way to the club and I'm driving. Ewan is singing 'Mill o' Tifty's Annie':

Love comes in at my bedside
And love will lie beyond me,
Love so oppressed my tender breast
And love will waste my body.

It's dark. He can't see the tears rolling down my face. Love will waste my family. I go through the motions at home. Dinner-time – try to remember what *normal* was like. Pick up your fork. Ask for the salt. Pay attention. Breathe. I'm sure they can hear my heart beating. *Pay attention.* Speak when you're spoken to.

Ewan's in hospital again. At least something's stayed the same. We visit and play games on his bed. He is cheerful, funny and communicative. He battles his fear with macabre humour. He sends a poem about hospital life to Bruce Dunnett, our zany, somewhat picaresque Scots friend.

> *Aince mair the poet's fa'en swack*
> *And noo lies flat upon his back*
> *In Bromley hospice, whaur a' day*
> *Weel-faured sonsie lasses play*
> *At piercing him wi' lang syringes,*
> *And greet each new series of twinges*
> *Wi' eldritch laughter*
> *And stroke the patient's head thereafter*
> *While thinking up new ploys and caintraips fresh*
> *To execute on his poor flesh*
> *And here comes that auld wife,*
> *Mistress Dracula, the deevil's dam,*
> *For mair o' my blood.*
> *Here, tak' aff your dram.*

For years Ewan had worked hard to keep things as they used to be. Now he yo-yos down and up and down further, in a place he has always dreaded being: the older, ill partner of a vital, younger woman. I am in a place of which I had heard and read. I'm ripe fruit. Prick me and I will give forth sweet syrup. My skin is too small. I'm bursting. I'm too complete. I explode into poetry, one a day for months. Irene smiles and holds her hand out for her poem each time we meet. They are simple offerings, liquid and flowing compulsively up from a churning caldera of passion and guilt. At last I understood how *Sweet William on his deathbed lay, for the love of Barbara Allen.*

1989

I am ill with love
But hope to live.
I am sick with need,
My body will not forgive your absence.
I have not seen you for two hours.
Flowers have died in less time.

Life holds me newborn in careless hands,
Love has washed and cleansed me
And I must learn once again
The feeling of sky on my skin.

Fire – Air – Water – Earth,
All present at the birth
Of their sister element Love,
Without which they remain
Unperceived.
I love – therefore everything is.

Life: I am fragile.
Don't drop me.

('I Am Ill with Love', 1989)

I love therefore I am. Never before have I felt so in control of a relationship, so out of control of myself. I am running the beach in Santa Barbara again, in sync with the passion and inevitability of the seasons and the flow of tides. I'm offering myself up totally for the first time in my life. I grieve for Ewan, for us. We never used the term *our love*. It's unfair that the teeth which had always been missing in our heterosexual set of gears were now fully present between me and Irene. I tried to remember when I had last told Ewan I loved him. I told Irene

333

dozens of times a day. I didn't call myself a lesbian. I didn't love women – I just loved *a woman*. I never called myself heterosexual because I loved Ewan. I just loved a man. Love is. I need to talk to someone who's gone through this. I only know one such. Back in 1956, Ewan travelled this road with me until Jean read my diary. *Ewan, help me. How do I deal with this terrible need to be with her, have my hands on her? She's so lovely . . .* I'm tired of lying. I almost want him to know. I learn 'Locks and Bolts' and sing it at the club.

> *I dreamed last night of my dear girl, all in my arms I held her,*
> *Her shining hair like links of gold came tumbling down my*
>   *pillow.*
> *When I awoke she was not there, I had to lie without her.*
> *She is in my mind both night and day, her name I cannot tell*
>   *you.*

Will he understand? He sits next to me. Irene sits in the front row, her hair glowing. Be careful – remember where you are. Don't reach out and stroke it.

I had no intention of leaving Ewan. Irene had no intention of leaving Philip. They were a unit. Ewan and I were a unit. Now Irene and I are a unit. Time took on a whole new meaning. Irene lived two miles away. Just time to drop a letter at her house. *I have to go to the post office, Ewan. It'll only take fifteen minutes.* I was always back on time. We arrange our lives so as to find ten-minute/half-hour/half-day segments in which to meet. We invent false appointments, excuses for going to town together, reasons why we are late getting home. Like two teenagers we seek dark places in which to be together. The police interrupt us in parking lots, side streets, deserted schoolyards.

I get good at lying. If you have voyaged thus, you'll know that you find a whole new duplicitous self. You despise it but you have an odd pride in its skill and planning.

*

Heterosexual kissing in movies looks dangerous. They look at each other, they come close and then, wham! a sudden violent meeting of mouths that, logically, should break two sets of front teeth while denying both participants a good supply of oxygen. With Irene, I was learning delicacy and patience. Love was being made. No one was screwing, getting laid, fucking, having sex. Not that that was ever the terminology that Ewan used, nor the technique. At seventy-four he was still very capable, very skilled, loving, familiar. But now . . .

*

Ewan and Kitty and I are in the front room and the phone rings. It's Irene. I sit on the floor, we talk and I ring off. Ewan is standing above me with the bleak look on his face that I last saw at the train station in 1956. *You haven't used that tone of voice to me for years* . . . He is watching me leave him again. I couldn't look at Kitty. Dearest Ewan, my comrade lover of thirty years, of course you know. And you know my photographic mind will never forget that look on your face. *I feel your pain* is trite, but can be razor-sharp true. And yet . . . and yet . . . we never talked about it.

In June, there's a birthday party for me at Stanley Avenue. Several dozen of us sit in the piano-cum-library room and I sing my new song, 'Garden of Flowers', set to a Sicilian folk tune that has earwormed us for several years. Irene helped to hone the text. She joins in the singing and we entwine, making vocal love. Ewan tells me later that it is the best song I have ever written. He knows what my song is about. He loved his wife and he left her.

They live in the garden of flowers,
They live in the garden of flowers
By the riverside.
They tend it every hour,
They tend it every hour
That it may never die.

He sings to her in the morning,
He sings to her in the morning
From the riverside.
The river tells the story,
The river tells the story
To the waiting sky.

She held him while he was sleeping,
She held him while he was sleeping
In the light of day.
When he awoke she was weeping,
When he awoke she was weeping
And she turned away.

Tears flow into the river,
The tears flow into the river
Through the winter garden.
She carries flowers with her,
She carries flowers with her
And lays them in his hand.

1989

She sings to him in the morning,
She sings to him in the morning
From the riverside.
When the song is over,
When the song is over
She will sing the song again.

*

In September, a giant leap into the future: our first grandchild is born, Neill and Justine's Jamie. Ewan sits quietly holding him, a peaceful expression on his face for the first time in months, respite from the turbulence that's been coming at him from every quarter. Political was personal in his books. Margaret Thatcher had launched the Poll Tax and Britain was in an uproar. The last time such a tax had been imposed was under Richard II, resulting in the Peasants' Revolt of 1381. Ewan wrote a superb five-part motet, *Bring the Summer Home*, about the earlier uprising. He fitted his text to the forms of five Sicilian folk songs whose melodic shapes he wished to mirror. He'd always made his own tunes – but now, probably trying to lure me back into the team that we'd been, he asked me to make the melodies for his texts. I used the Sicilian songs as jumping-off points and the piece sprang into life. *Bring the Summer Home* was written for two choruses, one male and one female. We already had Jade – now we trawled the Singers' Club for male singers. Four young men came forward and did their best with what really should have been sung by the Fishermen's Friends. Our lads couldn't produce the oomph. Ewan encouraged them. *Sing this with passion! Imagine you're singing a shanty and you've been without women for several months.* Two of our boy-men exchanged a look and then Peter said gently, *That would be difficult, Ewan. We're gay.* Never again did Ewan crack a joke about homosexuals.

We're finishing off the new album, *Naming of Names.* We're all crowded together in the little studio. Neill, Calum, Kitty and the chorus members are standing around at close quarters. Ewan and I are singing our swan song. He puts his arm around my shoulder. Quietly, wistfully, *Peg, this is like old times, recording and singing . . .* It was Peg when he was affectionate, Peggy when he wasn't. I love a man, am in love with a woman, and my heart cracks. It is truly broken – and its pieces belong to Irene. Ewan's heart has finally broken too, irrevocably. Angioplasty has been in the offing for several months. At Brompton Hospital in London, they'll insert a stent into his struggling coronary arteries. There are grave risks and Ewan wants to take them. Do I? No, I don't. He says if it doesn't work, he doesn't want to live . . . these past two years have been . . . this past year . . .? The operation fails and he maelstroms into delirium. He is going to die. I'm angry with the hospital staff. *Why? Could we not just take him home and carry on as we were?* Oxygen-starved, Ewan is sure the doctors and nurses are trying to kill him. *You'll remember this for the rest of your life, Peg, you'll remember this . . .* Peg. He's not angry, not loving, just matter-of-fact. I believe deep down that from the moment he knew about Irene he resolved never, not even on his deathbed, to reproach me.

He wants to leave and has to be restrained from pulling out the tubes and wires in which he's laced like an animal in a trap. Calling my name over and over, *PEGGY, PEGGY, PEGGY!* then *What a terrible death, what a terrible death!* then my name, over and over till he lapses into a coma. I ask for life support to be withdrawn. Neill standing at the head of the bed, Calum on one side and Kitty and I on the other, Hamish and Kirsty

across the room, impassive and mute, refusing to come close –
like Ewan when Betsy died. We sing him away with 'A Wee
Drappie o't', then he's gone. Jean has come. She sits alone with
him for a while. I sit alone by him with an absence of feeling
that makes me suspect that I've died too. Our children take me
out of the hospital, down the corridor under Brompton Road.
I don't want to leave him here, I don't want to leave him here . . .
Dio, Charlie, Penny, Mike – they all knew how much they were
loved. Pete knew and came to me when I stood at his open coffin in Beacon. There they are inside me for safekeeping. When
Ewan died, he didn't know how much he was loved, both of
us doubting whether I would be a haven for him. It was years
before I took him in – till I was sure I was forgiven.

> *When our time is gone and others' time begun,*
> *Our lives swept aside and others' lives about to start,*
> *Then we'll join the past as countless more have done.*
> *Thoughts of time will break my heart.*
>
> ('Thoughts of Time')

I remember little of that time other than that my central
life force was thrashing about trying to find something to hold
onto, a purpose, a meaning. Love for Irene kept me from drifting away totally. Mother love and duty to Kitty flickered on and
off for seemingly no reason. She and I confronted one another
daily, each in hormonal turmoil. She's on higher ground. She
is a teenager and her mother is a lesbian. Like the salt mill in
Why the Ocean Is Salty, the poems, letters and delirious typed
nonsense for Irene kept churning out – no magic word to stop
them. I tried to lure Ewan home again.

If I sit very still
And hold my hands in my lap
Just so –
He comes.

If I compose myself
And make a circle on the floor
Just so –
He'll come.

I am open.
Come in.
Where does he go,
My dead love,
When I close?

('Death III', 1989)

No rest in peace for any of us. I'm half mad.

37

The Little Wooden Box

tornado headache dry heaves nothing left to vomit crying when there is no energy for crying the vortex wide bowl razor wire in my throat whole body shrieks headache can't make a sound. i'm dead and alive your arms Irene an ICU unit your full bed full. Kitty's waiting I have to go home the British Queen she said she would waiting drag yourself to the car go home. home where are you my girl down Crystal Palace Hill past the crematorium where they reduced Ewan to ashes through a red light Mary Goes Round headache open the windows my wolf cry at 50-60-70 mph. no Kitty pubbing at the British Queen because I *YOU'RE NEVER HOME NEITHER ARE YOU* you're never you're nobody's home. Cleo the Cat sneaks around the vortex swirls lying outside his workroom door beating the floor hate him so sorry Ewan leaving me hate him hate him love him. headache meowing phoning the British Queen cars pass me silent in the air a foot off the ground.

Sixty-five ties? he didn't even wear ties any more. Shed's full of old tins of paint and garden tools throw everything away, give it all away. Copeland's gave him back to us in a little wooden box. Our papers fill sixty boxes Ruskin College comes to collect them don't follow the truck Charlie followed Dio down Kirke Street I can't follow Ewan any more. No point in having anything you'll lose it all I'm losing Kitty. down in that coal mine, which way is up? black hole expanding and deflating and defenceless. *What did you say, Ewan?* He's talking to me in my head. I'm terminal No-Sense NoNsense Numb with deepshard headaches. I am sick. So sick. I put the box of Ewan's ashes into his old holed knapsack and go up to London. Plenty of ghosts there, maybe he's . . . Stand head down at Bruce Dunnett's door. *May I sleep on your sofa, Bruce? Aye, a cup of tea? Sofa's yours, lass.* So sick. When he hugs me he has to hold me up. Sleep till the mid-dark hours and take a taxi home.

I need intensive care and no one is giving it but Irene. She stands on the spectators' balcony waving a white scarf as the plane draws away. I find a little room high up in a small hotel in St-Germain-des-Prés and decorate the table. Flowers, an enormous candle, photos of our children and the wooden box. The candle burns through the night. I leave it lit, put the box in the knapsack and we head out, looking for 1958. It's so cold – I am glad that he's with me, not Amontillado'd in a frozen grave. I search our courting grounds. I visit No. 5 Rue Jacob. Idoine is gone. She went to Algeria to help with reconstruction. The new Cerberus at the entrance to the courtyard doesn't even remember her. Late at night, crying at an iron railing. A stylish, middle-aged woman stands close beside me under the street lamp, tears making runnels through her makeup. Her husband has left her. Mine has too. We hold onto each other for a long time. A messenger from another world has cleaned my room, blown the candle out and left a note about fire regulations. I light it again and eat a takeaway. I stay in all next day, guarding the flame. I bring out the guitar and sing and write drivel. At the airport, I buy Kitty a scarf. £70. My taste, not hers. I never saw her wear it. I don't know who she is any more. She thinks she knows who I am and doesn't like it.

Headaches that last for days into weeks. Irene takes a

unilateral decision in the spring of 1990: we're going to France. Friends lend us their holiday house in Mastrouby, Tarn et Garonne, two days down the N1. Irene is a good driver. Her companion is a zombie with splinters in her brain, alternating silence with singing Ewan's songs, 'Alan MacLean', 'Bonny at Morn' and 'Waly Waly'. The ancient cottage has been hibernating. Irene hauls the double bed into the living room and brings logs from the woodpile. A huge fireplace, Belfast on Guy Fawkes Night, instant summer. On automatic pilot, I light the Neanderthal stove and create rough delicacies for my lover out of whatever winter ingredients the little local *épicerie* can supply. Huge spiders lurk in an ancient bathroom that's as dark and dangerous as the Silver Spring basement. They bungee down from the high living-room rafters while we're sleeping. We walk over the countryside, go for breakfast to little cafes in surrounding villages. It's good to speak French again. We're having café-au-lait and croissants at the kerbside in Roquecor when the whole Tour de France cycles right by our table.

Home again to a ruptured world. A therapist tells me to write a letter to Ewan. I was unaware that I had been living on a pot of lava; it poured out, a stream of scalding vitriol. *Dear Ewan, I hate you.* Every grievance, every regret, every difference, abortions, Kirsty, Jean, Betsy, pages and pages of rage and sorrow, the years of power differentials, of partnering a . . . was I really just a satellite of a shooting star? *A poxy little agent called me 'a leftover of a dead duo', Ewan. Did you just take me on because you loved me?* I hadn't known that I hated Ewan. I'm feeding on myself, tearing out chunks of the past to feed to the piranha letter. *How could you get sick and then die? I hate you . . .* I'm out of control, there in the little cistern room that was his office, crying

343

that terrible gut weeping that starts at the toes and moves up, speaking the terrible words aloud as I type, not knowing where it's all coming from. You know I'm not telling the whole story – but there are no scandalous secrets, no hidden violence, no real recriminations. I burn the letter. I write another, knowing exactly where it all came from – the decades of companionship, work, love, parenthood, communicating without speech. *Dear Ewan, Dear Ewan, Dear Ewan: I'm sorry. I love you, I need you, I hurt all over. Do you remember when . . .? I loved it when we . . . Dear Ewan, our boys left home a hundred years ago. Kitty hates me. We need you. Help me, Ewan, my heart is breaking. I can't do this alone. I forgive you for Kirsty. Dear Ewan, forgive me*, pages and pages. I burn the letter.

Kitty told me in 2015 that in 1989 he used to come to her bedside to talk. *Your mum hasn't always been like this, Kitty.* True – I hadn't. We'd had a wonderful life. We were middle-aged mother and teenage daughter *before* Ewan died and now, in joint grief, we are two lifeboats unable to find what we're supposed to save. No wonder. I learn decades later that she thought at that time that I'd been deceiving her father with Irene for years rather than for nine months. I didn't ask Irene to accompany us when the remnants of the family hiked up to Bleaklow Stones to scatter Ewan's ashes, Calum's Kate heavily pregnant with their son Alex. We took turns carrying the little wooden box in the knapsack.

> *Take me to some high place of heather, rock and ling.*
> *Scatter my dust and ashes, feed me to the wind,*
> *So that I will be part of all you see, the air you are breathing.*
> *I'll be part of the curlew's cry and the soaring hawk,*
> *The blue milkwort and the sundew hung with diamonds.*

I'll be riding the gentle wind that blows through your hair,
Reminding you how we shared in the joy of living.
(Ewan MacColl, 'The Joy of Living')

The wind changed as we flung the ashes – they flew back onto our hair and clothes. It was a beautiful moorland day and we lay in the sun for a long time before heading back down.

*

The headaches took over completely. I had had them for years, mostly fuelled by stress and the birth-control pill, but now, intensified by life in general and death in particular, they felt dangerous. Head earthqu-aches. I want out, to sleep – hopefully not to dream – for a long, long time. The NHS doesn't support such self-indulgence, so Irene and I visit a Harley Street doctor to enquire about sedation. Too expensive – but he'd help. He trusted Irene, who, through her work at her veterinary surgery, was used to handling and dispensing drugs. His programme will put me to sleep for six weeks, at home. Kitty is going to work with Irene. I'm tucked away in the little attic room that Kitty slept in as a baby, the one that Ewan, a DIY enthusiast with a kindergarten diploma in ability, tiled surprisingly well with pink linoleum squares. Pink feels prenatal. At a certain point we all need to go back to the womb, a time when every single mortal thing was done for us. It makes sense to me. Just put me out till I'm ready to be born again into a person that I can live with. My two Mothers keep the Good Ship Diazepam's log and regular reports are made to the doctor. In shifts, Kitty is on duty more than Irene, who has a day job. They bathe me and help me semi-somnolent downstairs to the toilet. They wake me, drug-dazed, for small feasts. Peanut butter, honey and bananas on toast. Warm milk drinks and porridge. Smooth savoury soups, before pushing my boat out again on the dreamless sea. Irene's lover is a baby. Kitty mothers her mother. I leave her on shore alone while I sail away into the night-walls of my own safe warm wooden box, never asking if *she* needed intensive care. I dream now of dreamless nights for I dream every night and wish I didn't. Usually, the dreams are not frightening but I wake exhausted with telling myself sleep-stories that have no chronology, no sense, no ending, night after night. Most of them are about being lost, or losing things. Back then, the Diazepam gave me the second of only two such undisturbed trips into the land of Lethe that I've had in my life. If death brings a third, I will welcome it for I am weary of subconscious make-believe.

The box – there will be a scrap of Ewan's ashes somewhere in it. First I filled it with stones that we had collected and polished. Then for years it housed instrument paraphernalia. Since then it has contained keys that open the locks of houses belonging to someone else. When I'm done with houses, I'll make it an odds-and-ends box. I wish it to hold my ashes. I bought a small silver amulet – probably meant to carry drugs – and filled it with tiny spoonfuls of the remains of Dio, Charlie and Ewan. I sealed it and had their full names fine-engraved on one end. I wear it whenever I need to. I wear it on all long-haul car and plane trips, on special family occasions. Dio: I'm seeing this for you. You never flew or saw these mountains of clouds beneath the wings. Charlie: I've made a song you would love to *kind of* hear. Ewan: I'm walking with one of our sons and his wife and children in Richmond Park. Come with us.

IV

1990–2016

38

No Spring Chickens

The flow of sympathy letters and cards has eased off. I settle into chronic exhaustion. My head is full of things and things and things that need doing. Irene brings me paper and a pencil. *Write it all down.* I title it What There Is to Do. Without stopping I fill up four foolscap pages in shaky cursive, ending with *amend this list.* It will take four years to clear it. Irene locks my office and engages a personal assistant, Penny Smith, to plough through the list. When I move away in 1994, Penny puts the office into her bedroom on the other side of Beckenham. News gets out and Ewan MacColl fans come and stand in front of Penny's terrace house on Cromwell Road. Penny hands me on to Jane Chapman of Shooters Hill in Greenwich, but official grief – like fame – doesn't last long and Jane's house enjoys privacy. The headaches ease up. I'm singing well and Irene and I are fulfilling the Ewan/Peggy commitments. My wellspring of new songs is gushing. I write off to clubs but no new dates materialise. Without Ewan I've become invisible. It's time to get an agent.

Throughout our working life, Ewan and I had avoided agents as much as possible, part of our determination to be non-commercial, independent, short-sighted and professionally idiotic. In 1956, Alan Lomax picked Felix de Wolfe to handle the Ramblers. Felix: an apt name for this charming, vulpine, very English Englishman. He was smooth and suave – a walking, talking representative of conservative conviction, self-assurance

and sartorial elegance. His stable was full of high-flying establishment actors and musicians. He couldn't figure out why
anyone wanted to listen to folk music but he recognised its
burgeoning potential. He had no idea where to place it, us
or our ill-matched group of skilled musicians. He booked us,
duo or group, as interval entertainment at theatres, at corporate conventions and once in a circus tent between the clowns
and the high-wire merchants. We went along for the ride and
the money, the latter sorely needed. We were advocates for the
music but were painfully aware that we – and our songs – were
misfits in the culture at large.

If David Attenborough had been interested in filming our
exotic species, he would, like Felix, have accepted an invitation
to visit our native habitat, the weekly Ballads and Blues Club
session at the ACTT building in Soho Square. Felix climbed
the three storeys of killer stairs, tricked out in bowler hat, cash-
mere overcoat, Savile Row suit with cravat, handkerchief *just so*
in waistcoat pocket and shoes polished to blinding perfection.
I admired him for coming at all. There he was, a dutiful sore
thumb among the clean unwashed, in the back row of this down-
at-heel firetrap of a room, leaning on a cane which he didn't need
but which accompanied him everywhere. It proclaimed above
all else his position in society, having obviously been bought from
James Smith and Sons' Umbrella Shop on New Oxford Street.*

At the interval, Felix made to leave. *Peggy, it's all so dreary and*

---

* This iconic establishment, founded in 1830, still has its nineteenth-century
Victorian shop frontage and signage intact. It sells not only umbrellas but a
wide variety of designer canes with inbuilt dice, pipes, flasks, corkscrews and
more. I always suspected that Felix's cane was a swordstick. I asked at James
Smith for one such a couple of years ago. *No, madam, I'm afraid that model is
no longer available.*

dismal. I saw his point. Our ballads, love laments, complaints of miners, weavers, fishermen, convicted and transported felons, deserted maidens and such were certainly no party – but neither were the lives of their makers. It was probably the only time Felix was brought face to face with working-class politics or culture. After that he confined his efforts on our behalf to negotiating radio, television, movie and random well-paid gigs – at which he was totally in his element. Folk musicians are rumoured to be grateful that people listen to us at all. The public seemed to believe that as folk songs are The People's Songs, The People shouldn't have to pay a lot to hear them. Felix took this as a challenge and charged accordingly. He nobbled an astronomical fee for a Royal Command Performance in Oslo. Two songs only. The King disliked music but there he was, on duty in his box, head down as if listening intently, reading a book. The front two rows glistened with government glitterati and Oslo aristocrap, including Madame Quisling. We hadn't counted on that. Pavlov spoke to Ewan and Ewan spoke to me: *'The Highland Muster Roll'* and *'The Ballad of Accounting'*, Peg.

> *Did you stand aside and let 'em choose while you took second*
> *best?*
> *Did you let 'em skim the cream off and then give to you the*
> *rest?*
> *Did you settle for the shoddy and did you think it right*
> *To let 'em rob you right and left and never make a fight,*
> *Never make a fight, never make a fight?*

From the third row all the way back, enthusiastic clapping and stamping. From rows one and two, a silence so loud that the King looked up from his book.

1991. Irene and I approached several agents, but they all turned me down, except for one – Rob Something-or-Other. The meeting place was a desolate, empty northern pub on a winter's night. I was rapidly losing my sense of self and this bleak deserted place was the perfect setting for a budding nobody. Someone-or-Other, a stocky middle-aged lad in braided pigtail and motorcycle gear, was late and unenthusiastic. After perfunctory chitchat, he said he would need a demo. Thirty years of singing in this country, dozens of recordings, radio, television, awards, numerous foreign tours under my belt and the man wants a *demo*? I just made it to the loo before breaking down. No matter how small, a fragment of broken pottery can be broken into even smaller pieces. When I returned, Irene was standing with her Easter Island face holding our coats. En route home, I learned that I had been deemed (a) *not commercially viable* and (b) *no spring chicken*. Looking back on it, the little autumn rooster was right about (a), but then that could be said of most mature folk musicians trying to hold onto their ethics in the commercial world. As for (b), he was right but he could have been more diplomatic about it. By the time I got a good UK agent, Henry Chesterton, I was living in the States.

During those years in which I disappeared, Irene held me steady, leading me back from Ewan's death to Peggy's life. Regardless of its advantage to herself, she always pointed me in good directions and shoved. This night on the way home she says, *We'll make a CD and entitle it 'Almost Commercially Viable'. We'll go on tour as No Spring Chickens*. Perfect. Peggy fifty-six, Irene forty-four = one hundred years. She'd never recorded, directed or produced but she – then we – undertook all three and *ACV* turned out to be a splendid piece of work, my favourite of my albums up till then. It has only one very small cringe-point, a note sung slightly flat. I have told the story of its title many times. Gossip gets around. Whatsisname came up to me after a concert recently and introduced himself politely with a quarter-hearted excuse for his 1991 self. I kind of owe him thanks – he pushed me over a cliff. After bouncing down like a gannet chick, I had to fly.

It isn't hard to remember my childhood, and age nineteen to thirty was too jam-packed to forget. I can access age thirty to fifty-four by referencing the age of one of my children or, trivially, by which hairstyle I had at the time. But when I try to cast myself back into the early 1990s I hit a wall. The days, weeks and months deal themselves out like playing cards in speed poker, their only consistent feature my deepening love for Irene. Events in my nineties life are being moved around by memory much as products in superstores are shifted by market-driven managers and manic supervisors. It's all still there but no one can find anything. Part of my parental identity went astray when Ewan died. I had two beautiful little grandsons but did I spend quality time with them? Kitty and I lived in the same house but I couldn't find my way back home to her. She decided to leave school six months before the final exams and I was too lost in myself to stop her. I had waited years for her and now I was losing her. I can't write about that.

*

The 1990s. I meet one of my favourite comedian commentators, Billy Connolly, who apparently thinks the world of my banjo playing. I'm as tongue-tied as I would be if I met Paul Simon, to whose early work I turn over and over. Love, unions, ecology, Poll Tax, abortion, Thatcher, Iraq, you name it and I made a song for it. Bra burning is old hat. Now we can say *penis* out loud, largely due to the ground-breaking in-your-face HIV campaign (*Don't Die of Ignorance*). Soon Monica Lewinsky will let the world know that Bill's tackle has a kink in it. *Vagina* will be kind of OK after *The Vagina Monologues* hits the bookshops. In 1992, Calum came back home to live, bringing Alex, two years old, for days at a time, cooking gourmet meals for him. Alex is sitting in the bath playing with what little boys play with. Calum is teaching him the names. *What does Daddy have?* Alex, at top treble volume: *A penis!* And what does Peggy have? (I'd insisted on the grandkids calling me by my name.) *A vagina!* Menstruation and its permanent cessation, sexual harassment, orgasms, rape, mid-life crisis, erectile dysfunction – no privates left un-public. Flies were unzipped, condoms recommended. In the noughties, actual sexual intercourse could be seen on London streets, videoed for television audiences. Ruby Wax is interviewed with a copulating couple going at it in the background. On the positive side, sexual identity came centre stage. In the 2000s, a teacher at my grandson's school is dealing with same-sex relationships. *What do you know about it, children?* My grandchick holds his hand up and says, *My grandma is a lesbian.* That must have earned him Brownie points with his mates.

The 1990s. Thatcher exits for the last time from Number 10, waving and smiling. Not a glimmer of shame for taking the country back a hundred years. That's what Donald Trump will do when he leaves – if there's still anyone around to wave at. The Iron Lady is succeeded by John Major, who is decidedly minor. You feel a tad ashamed to go on the offensive. I only write squibs for him, one of which refers to him as *A slow, slow, slow, slow velociraptor.* Ewan would have felt out of place in this decade. He would have used crossbows against Major, bringing up a tumbril to execute a mouse. His Movement targets were disappearing

– big industry closing down or transported abroad, workers job-
less, the Boss now called a Manager, a CEO, or concealed name-
less within the Corporation. Ewan's 1980s stabs at ecology had
produced splendid eco-songs – 'Nightmare', 'The Vandals' – but
the fate of humanity was his concern, not the fate of the earth.
Would he have adapted? Or did he die just in time . . .

The 1990s. The Poll Tax is still with us. I had great fun with
that in 'Can't Pay, Won't Pay' and 'Fifteen Ways to Beat the Poll
Tax'. Plus I refused to pay it. I should mention that through all
these decades – 1960–90 – gritty pop songwriters were shouting *PROTEST* at the top of their lungs. Ewan and I paid little
attention to this procession of outraged, mostly male, black popular singers. Overheard in Brixton, spoken by a very old black
American in a cafe: *These spades are really calling a spade a spade.*
They were on another musical planet, one which, tunnel-visioned
as we were in folk music, we never visited. Multicoloured –
James Brown, Country Joe and the Fish, Gil Scott Heron – they
appeared on our sons' horizons but never on ours. Shame on us,
for their work was giving millions a new voice.

Voices: the hills echo with *lesbian, lesbian!* The media drones
home in for the kill. One of the tabloids puts us on Page 3,
double spread, big header to the effect of 'The face of First
Time Ever I Saw Your Face takes lesbian lover'. Three dreadful photos. Irene and I get the Camilla-and-Charles treatment
and Ewan is Diana, downcast and devastated even though he's
dead by now. Jenni Murray has me twice on *Woman's Hour* and
Sue Lawley invites me onto *Desert Island Discs*. The BBC's Jim
Lloyd devotes seven half-hours of his *Folk on Four* radio programme to me. We win the 1995 Sony Silver Radio Award in
the Specialist Music Sections. Gosh – maybe Ewan and I should
have thought of this earlier as a 'What If' theatre exercise . . .

Irene takes it all in her stride. She's spur-of-the-moment incarnate. She takes us to Belize, to a tropical jungle resort. We paddle up the crocodile-infested Macal River in a dangerously overloaded canoe and sleep out in hammocks. Clouds of mosquitos attack after the hasty cookout and we are bundled into mosquito-netted hammocks. Battalions of tiny hedgehogs are poking their quills in at me. Damn, I forgot to pee. Out of hammock, escorted into the bush, where I squat on a plant that gives me a mountainous rash, race back to hammock, where mozzies have been waiting at the door. Howler monkeys approach, trumpet overhead and pass on. Our guides stay awake for prowling wildlife. We stay awake because we don't want to miss a thing in this marvellous place. Next stop, Ambergris Caye, which at that time was modest and so-called *undiscovered*. We stay at the less populated end of the island in the Green Parrot, run by a couple firmly attached to the bottle. We find a huge dead tarantula floating in a neighbouring swimming pool. Irene fishes it out with a net and taps its carapace. Audible. She tells me to tap it. I am so frightened of spiders that I can't. She holds my finger and makes me touch it. I go cold all over on this boiling hot day. I search our little cabin very carefully when we get back to the Parrot. Back to Beckenham and life in black and white, while Ambergris Caye begins its descent into discovery.

It was a huge step for Irene to join a *leftover from a dead duo*. No Spring Chickens toured the USA, Australia, New Zealand but never cracked the UK. Nor did we ever develop a style. I wanted to stick to the programme no matter what. I didn't know how to share the stage with anyone but Ewan. I was tied to our thirty-year-long performance style: static continuity with the emphasis on singing every song as well as possible and getting the audience to sing on choruses. Irene was very funny on stage, ready to detour at any point. She's a natural story-teller with a good sense of timing but no sense of time passing. I was not what she needed on stage and neither of us knew how to adapt. She didn't like touring, sleeping in a different bed every night, battling with half-deaf sound engineers and airline Nazis. Example, from 2012, but typical: Here we are in Kingsford Smith Airport in Sydney, toting Irene's 1906 Martin guitar in a soft case as hand luggage. *Oh no*, said Ticket Man, *not allowed.* We stood our ground. *Air New Zealand allowed us to bring it IN as hand luggage. Why can't we take it out the same?* He called his supervisor, a woman who relished her position of power. *Oh no*, says she, *it's a dangerous weapon.* We, in unison: *Whaaaat?* Straight-faced: *You could garrotte someone with the strings.* Of course. Passengers look passively on while we bring the case down, unzip it, get the peg winder out (little wire-cutting pliers having been confiscated) and unwind a string to garrotte the pilot, who's behind a locked door. It was a rigged match on home turf. I was flying off to England an hour after Irene. Ozzie compañera Margaret Fagan went way beyond the duty of a friend and picked it up, packaged it and sent it to Irene's home out in the New Zealand sticks. Three months later, this $6000 guitar was left lying in its soft case on a rainy day in full view of passing traffic, next to an NZ boondocks mailbox. Irene still comes along on some of my tours, but back then we couldn't pull a show style together. (Mike and I hadn't been able to do so either, but we occasionally gave duo concerts.) No Spring Chickens hopped off the perch permanently. What I took away from its demise was Irene's legacy: be funny and entertaining, *then* sing as well as possible. She picked me up, dusted me off, instigated the *Fact and Fantasy Book* and shoved me out of yet another nest. I seem to always need saving.

39

Alone Again, Naturally

In my hour of need
I truly am indeed
Alone again, naturally.

('Alone Again', Gilbert O'Sullivan)

I found it impossible to work in Beckenham. Ewan was still wandering from room to room. In December 1993, I upped sticks and rented a small renovated stable in Breighton, a tiny village just south of York, a city in which I'd live if it wasn't so friggin' cold. The Arctic wind whips across the North Sea from Scandinavia with the express purpose of making the lives of everyone on the east side of Britain miserable. It was a seminal move. It was a decision I took *by* myselfish, *for* myselfish and *with* myselfish, with no regard as to its consequences for Irene or Kitty. It was a necessary move. It placed me alone out in the country. I would live away from family, friends, partner – by myself for the first time in my life. It galvanised me. I'd begun work on two mammoth songbooks, one of my songs and one of Ewan's, and I needed to be away from everything familiar.

Despite the fact that you can now produce music scores entirely on the computer, I chose to type each song text on staff paper and hand-draw the music, following Dio's precept of laying out the song on the page as one would lay out poetry. I slogged all morning on the books, rested and took a long walk in the afternoon, played and sang in the evening. I found that recording and supporting women who had suffered domestic violence had given me more than information. For the first time in my life I was afraid of men in general. Out in the countryside walking, if a woman came towards me I was ready for the acknowledgement that usually happens when two female loners pass each other. If it was a man, my heart would speed up and my fight-or-flight finger would get ready to hit the switch. If I went to York for the day, I'd try to get back before dark – that more-than-deep country darkness, with no person near me should I need help. A perfect catalyst for fear. I began to carry a walking stick and tried to put my key in the lock without turning my back to the night, casting my eyes 180 degrees around me till I was indoors. I would carry this apprehension and unlocking posture into every home in which I lived alone.

*

Early 1994, USA. My six-foot little sister Penny is dying. Cancer stalks women in our family. She is wasted and very pale, opening her bony arms wide and wider to pull me towards her in the bed, hugging me gently. She'd waited till I arrived and then she drifted off into a coma – no crying or calling, just gracious and quiet. Her hand is in mine, limp. She lies there and I talk to her. *The water's warm, Penny. You can walk in. Look at the little fishes swimming with you, Penny. You can float and look up at the sky. We're all ready for you to go now.* Her fingers clasp mine. She's back in her bunk bed in Boston, listening. Family and friends, we were standing and singing to her when all of a sudden she sat upright and said, *What ARE you all doing here?*

359

Then my six-foot-tall little baby sister lay down and died. She hovered above me for several days, then came inside with my other beloveds.

Thus began my real reconnection with my birth family. Back home in Beckenham again, I felt incapable of anything except being with Irene and slogging on the songbooks. All of a sudden, loud and clear, the United States was calling me – after nearly forty years' absence. Would Kitty come? No, emphatically. Would Irene come? *I'm going somewhere warm. You'll like it.* No. I decided to go by myself. I know now that I needed to find out who I had been. I had left before I had grown up. Witness my mother's desire a year before her death to *find out if Ruth Porter Crawford still existed*. She had answered the question with a remarkable spurt of composing, then died. I had been Charlie's daughter, Pete's sister, Ewan's lover, Neill/Calum/Kitty's mother, Irene's lover and whaddaya know, I don't know who I am.

The United States government knew who I was, along with hundreds of people like me – Americans who had lost or given up their citizenship. Here comes an amnesty for political exiles and I go to the American embassy in Grosvenor Square to apply for a passport. No more Georgian house, no more talking to the consul, nicey-nicey all gone. This place is a fortress with a simulated moat, armed Marines at the door, security checks and Mrs Andrews (not her real name). She hands me a form. It wants to know how I lost my citizenship. I comply and take it back to the counter. Mrs Andrews is English. *You know*, she confides, leaning over the counter, *these people think that American citizenship is the most valuable possession you have. You gave yours up as if you didn't care at all.* She waves the form. *This won't do. Go back and beat your breast and wring your hands, tell us how you suffered when you lost your citizenship. And print. They don't like longhand here.* I tackle the form again, figurative tears blotching the page. Mrs Andrews surveys it. *These people don't like long sentences. We're closing in five minutes. Here's my phone number. Go home, rewrite it, phone me up and we'll make sure it's right. And type it. They don't like handwriting here.* I phoned, we talked and I took it in the next day. As I left, she leaned over the counter. *I love your music.* Folk music may not get you to the very top but it helps in securing passports.

I needed to tour North America. Three American agents turned me down. No surprise there. Josh Dunson threw me a lifeline. He was invaluable as I figured out a solo approach to the US folk scene. More than an agent, he did the work of a manager as well, he and his wife Jean becoming my friends, their home my Chicago haven. He contributed ideas to songs, published a brochure for me, arranged photo shoots. The photographers Irene Young and Dave Gahr captured the best of me at that time – or at least how I wanted to look all the time. Dave's technique was to tell dirty jokes then snap my reaction. After one of our sessions in the early nineties, Dave – upon learning that I was going alone with suitcase and instruments from Washington DC to New York City – insisted on accompanying me. We get off the train in NYC carrying our luggage, which he doubly secures with a rope through the handles and around our waists. *They'll run up behind you and grab the guitar out of your hand, Peggy.* That happened to me on Oxford Street in England, a Martin guitar lost. We're outside Grand Central Station now, looking for a taxi. Setting my baggage down on the sidewalk, Dave now secures his end of the rope around a lamppost. If one passer-by tested the accessibility of my banjo or guitar, a dozen did. Alone, I would have lost them all.

Through all the early 1990s, Irene and I were absorbed in each other, finding out who we were together. Our star didn't wane – but we made no plans to live together, no plans for a joint future. We just existed in our own universe. Now – inexplicably – I'm determined to go back 'home' to the States and my plans are cruelly unilateral. I had grown up at 35 Stanley Avenue, from the age of twenty-five to fifty-four. Now I moved the library, mementos, everything valuable into our old bedroom and locked it. Kitty was twenty-one – she'd already moved out. I hired a useless rental agency, closed the front door and walked out. Just like that. Unbeknown to me, Irene and Philip came in shortly afterward with their consummate perfectionism and cleaned it up, redecorated it and made it safe and fit for tenants. Love is. Philip and Irene were work soulmates, as Ewan and I had been. They separated a few years later – I hold myself responsible, for Irene misses their joint work. Repeat: I closed the front door and left, just like that. I left lover, sons, daughter and grandchicks behind. My house was on fire and on 1 September 1994, Ladybird, Ladybird flew away.

40

Personal Political Progression

The human race has a fatal knack
Of going full speed down a cul-de-sac.
After running so fast, working hard,
There's a helluva mess in the backyard . . .

('Progress Train')

The other day I passed a hedge, immaculately groomed by a manic perfectionist who probably pruned it hourly with nail scissors. One two-inch sprig had escaped and was hitch-hiking skyward on shafts of sunlight. Even while tucking it back out of sight, I was tempted to doorbell its minder regarding the hedge needing one more snip. When you flaunt a set of principles, even if only via your topiary, 100 per cent adherence to it will now be expected of you. A target appears on your forehead the minute you express an opinion and you must defend yourself constantly. As the saying goes, the world is divided into people who think they are right. It took me a long time to learn not to wear myself out trying to 'convert' dug-in political opponents.

When I met Ewan, I had good political instincts but no political experience or party allegiance. I espoused immediately his 360-degree definition of politics as the *science of human organisation*. That will make it easier to fight social inequality and injustice on every front when we finally have a 360-degree

One Big Union of the human race.* Ewan was two years old in 1917, when the Russian Revolution finally overturned a brutal feudal system and set up a new Marxist-based working-class social system. He cut his teeth on communist texts and believed that the left wing will always fragment into smaller factions, while the right wing will remain stolid and solid. He espoused what are loosely called Movement Politics. For decades, I was Ewan's echo chamber. I read the books faithfully and mouthed the slogans, many of them deep and true – but not a continual, not a complete story, as I realised when 'I'm Gonna Be an Engineer' hurtled me into the women's movement. Ewan and I argued about the role of feminism in the working-class struggle. I was for tackling women's issues immediately. He felt that it was more important to have the working-class revolution before liberating women. *Liberating* . . . Hey – we're more than half of the human race. So why fight side by side as unequals, with men Making the System Work Better while women Made Better Tea and Coffee? Kind of like black men in the US armed forces, defending their country in World War II and being lynched at home. I'm not the only one who has difficulty correlating one issue with another. Stokely Carmichael – black and radical – was national chairman of the Student Non-Violent Coordinating Committee (1960–6). When asked where women

* Traditionally, workers organised according to their trade or craft and fought each battle for themselves. The OBU (One Big Union) was a concept, and the IWW (International Workers of the World) proposed a radical, revolutionary method for making that concept a reality. Both offered a vision of just ONE union to which all workers would belong. Efforts to bring the ideas of either organisation to pass were subverted not only by the government but by many of the existing trade unions. Their history and fate are well worth studying.

belonged in his organisation, he replied, *The only position for women in SNCC is prone.* No – the revolution is only truly possible when men learn how to make the hot drinks.*

Right through the eighties, I had been interviewing women for new songs. My most memorable session was the one with Ana María Navarrete Mulsow, whose daughter Murielita had been *disappeared* in 1974 by the Pinochet government in Chile. *Disappear* is a very exact term. The authorities remove every official trace of a person's existence: hospital records, school reports, exams, degrees, driver's licence, birth certificates and so on. Pinochet told Ana María in person that she was deluded – that she had given birth to one daughter, Berenice, not two. For seven years, mother and daughter lived the life of those seeking vanished people. They went every Sunday to demonstrate at La Moneda, the presidential seat of Chile. They carried photographs of their *desaparecidos*, asking on buses, trains, in shopping queues: *Have you seen this woman, this man, this person?* They followed leads that took them to outlying hospitals, prisons and detention centres. Murielita was never found. Berenice spoke little English, Ana María none. The terrible story unfolded in halting translation. We were all in tears by the time the tale reached the point where the two women abandoned the search and emigrated to the UK. It took me six weeks to recover enough emotional energy to make 'Missing' out of Ana María's words. Muriel Dockendorff Navarrete's story can be found on the internet, along with a beautiful photo of her. I'm very proud of our song.

I suggested to Ewan that we write a Radio Ballad on women. I would choose and record the contributors, then we'd proceed

---

* PS: and equal wages for equal work. PPS: and child care and no sexual harassment and . . . and . . .

as usual. He seemed all for it. I began with survivors of domestic violence, chiefly at the refuge in Sydenham. I recorded several of the inmates – they referred to themselves as such. The perpetrators are free to circulate and the victims have to lock themselves up. Kind of like North Americans who have put ourselves into a cage for fear of people whose countries we've encroached upon. My recordings bore fruit. I wrote 'Emily', 'Winnie and Sam', 'My Friend Pat' and 'Reclaim the Night'. I branched out into south London and recorded thirty hours of varied female experience. I found the older women intriguing – and still do. Children love, ignore or make fun of us old dears. Many people use *dear* to address women but there's an added tone of voice when kind men of all ages offer, without our request, to escort the old girl across the street. I tell them, *Thank you, dear*, and make grown-up conversation as we link and cross. We older women have tremendous untapped energy but we are marginalised when we can no longer produce children. Redundant when the baby factory closes down. Men of or near my age are attracted to Beaujolais Nouveau or at least a middling vintage. Fashion ignores us, and to judge from our presence in printed media we exist chiefly as proof of what happens if you don't use anti-ageing creams. We are invisible. But we watch you – and you won't see us coming.

The feminist dictum *personal is political* is now in common usage. Sex, being very personal, is very political. I recorded a number of older women on this subject, sessions of cackling and storytelling. We explored the subject to its inner- and outermost limits. Unlike men, women aren't reputed to think of sex every seven or so seconds. How do you manage, gentlemen, carrying between your legs an organ with a mind of its own – a second brain, a third eye, an alternative beating heart below the belt line, an Achilles heel continually kickstarting you without your permission? Penis envy? Not a chance, Sigmund. How frustrating it must be to know that half the world's population has what you want and that you can't have it whenever you wish. You have to work or pay for it, sometimes even marry for it, occasionally resort to violence or pretend to be what you're not in order to get it.

Every women's issue became political, e.g. will we ever be able to dress completely *as we wish*? Doing what you wish is not always sensible. A soldier in the trenches *wants* to stick his head above the ramparts to get a breath of fresh air. Bam! A woman *wants* to walk city streets ultra-scantily dressed. Bam! Forehead-targets all over the place, sourced from the lofty heights of Opinion and Instinct. Close to home, possible Bam material: Can a man be a feminist? Not having had the gut experience of growing up female in a patriarchy – an experience unique to women – could it be patronising for him to declare himself a feminist, especially when he doesn't participate actively in *any* feminist organisation; doesn't object to wage differentials based on gender at work; doesn't rally other men to battle sexual harassment or domestic violence, et necessary cetera? Marching on feminist demonstrations and washing the dishes are appreciated but they don't make a man a feminist. Closer to home: did Ewan (who called himself a feminist) ever go to the kitchen to make coffee and bring it in while the visiting journalist talked to me first? Would the terms *feminist empathiser* or *feminist supporter* be more exact? Home in: Do those of us with hereditary wealth or penises or whitish skin (or or or or) realise how deeply entrenched are the privileges that they/we received at birth? I, along with anyone else earning more than a four-figure number of pounds a year, am not part of the famed 99 per cent of the world's people, the majority of whom live at a subsistence level unimaginable to us in the 1 per cent. How much of what I have would I be willing to share or give up to be a true Egalitarian? Does all this belong in a memoir? Some of these are not questions. *Politically correct* is tiptoe territory. Labels are important – they shouldn't be lightly assumed. They tell us and others who we are, how we have processed our experiences. Aching for community strength, we employ labels as both sword and shield as we go into battle.

I began declaiming feminism from mountain tops, hoping for an echo from Ewan, who neither read the books nor mouthed the slogans. He had trouble with *personal is political* and was horrified by most of the interviews. There were so many women who were frightened of men; so many deceiving, macho, violent men; so many jokes about young and old men and their sexual abilities; so many women who loved women; so many vibrant older women; so many women who discussed their men and their *pride* as if they were children. Oh yes, and so many of those distraught wives whose middle-aged husbands had left them for girls in their twenties . . . His lack of enthusiasm discouraged me and we moved on to I forget what. But the interviews had moved me into the wider arena of patriarchy, men in general – and violence.

Three women in a kitchen make war. Men make war everywhere. *Young people with guns* are committing mass shootings in schools, streets, crowded markets? No, they are all young whitish men. The 'terrorists' are almost all young darker men. Asheville, 1994. My rental house has a TV and tonight's programme features a half-circle of eminent US army generals, navy admirals and White House staff, almost all pale men in late middle age. They are discussing what war is going to be like in 2050. Don't forget: war is natural and will always be with us. I had sung it since I could sing: *If it is a girl, she can wear a gold ring. If it is a boy, he can fight for the king.* Ah, the soldiers, the young men sent off to war by old men. The *war game*, our beautiful boys are pawns. *Theatre of war*, enticing the youths into drama, lights, camera, action! The boys are walk-ons, limp-offs, carried-offs, buried. When the curtain comes down on the current show, Business As Usual is ready with helplines, health programmes, rehab centres and secluded establishments where ex-warriors completely beyond repair spend what's left of their shattered lives hidden from those who might learn something unforgettable about war by just *seeing them*. Destroy and repair. Enantiodromia – everything contains or suggests its opposite. Victims of domestic abuse can be sent home in presentable condition thanks to makeup kits in Moroccan police stations; packs of clean clothes for rape victims are standard kit in hospitals in Lincoln, Nebraska. The same company makes swords that pierce any shield and shields that repel any sword. The global war industry flattens a country and the global construction industry rebuilds it. The male dynamic is in control: road rage, pederasty, kerb-crawlers, pussy-grabbers, competition, even if it's rivalry to see whose penis is *smallest*.* There you have the basic cause: the fascinating, demanding, urgent penis, the elephant in humanity's room. Herds of elephants, a multitude of rooms, one of them Oval. In *Flawed Giant*, the first volume of his biography of Lyndon Johnson, Robert Dallek wrote: 'During a private conversation with some reporters who pressed him to explain why we were in Vietnam, Johnson lost his patience. According to Arthur Goldburg, LBJ unzipped his

---

* Google the Smallest Penis Contest in Brooklyn.

fly, drew out his substantial organ and declared, "This is why!'"
Oh, do let's discuss war in 2050, gentlemen.

What female would not be a feminist in the face of all this?
On a lighter note: as feminism progressed, us women were
beginning to study our bodies. We started to take certain
aspects of our health into our own hands. For instance, to learn
how to inspect the insides of Down There. I did this and found
a small polyp on my cervix. I told the doctor. His face was a
picture of abrogated authority. *How do you know?* I told him I'd
used a mirror and a speculum. *Did you sterilise it first? Anything
that goes in there has to be sterilised.* Welcome, lover. Swab your
wick in Dettol or dip it in boiling water before we go to bed.
Feminism: it's pistols at dawn every day.

Feminism pointed directly to Mother Earth. Stage 1:
Conservation. That good old household practice of reusing
everything possible. I soaked and compressed old newspapers
into brick-size blocks, dried them and used them for firewood.
Turn out unnecessary lights, put on another sweater and turn
the central heating down. After the Great Storm of 1987, I took
a chainsaw around Beckenham, cutting fallen trees into firewood. We began to buy in bulk with neighbours. Repair, Reuse,
Recycle, Rejoice, small acts committed by Edmund Burke's
little platoons of society. Stage 2: Environmentalism. Work with
nature to improve the environment. We planted a vegetable
garden and installed solar panels on the house. Britain's intermittent excuse for sunlight could actually bring cold water up
to warm.* I wrote one of my best humorous songs, 'It's a Free
World', in which I fence with a quarrelsome restaurant smoker

---

* Improved technology makes it possible for Calum and Kerry to run their
house on solar energy *and* sell extra sun-watts to the National Grid.

via farting. Small acts. But environmentalism was concerned almost entirely with the *human* environment, reminiscent of the north-country toast: *Here's to me and my wife, our Bill and his wife. Us four and no more.*

A hail-and-farewell peek at this point into Humanism. Arrogant and anthropocentric. Stage 3: Ecology – the chain of life. There are other living organisms on earth besides humans – but pick and choose, for only the ones that humans love or need are worth bothering with. The chain can operate with a few links missing, eh wot? But which links . . .? In our coliseum world, little pollen-collectors can put wings up or wings down on whether mankind lives or dies. Maybe bees are God. In 1992, I turn our whole Beckenham back garden into a wildlife refuge. The plants and animals take it over completely. 'Weed' wars: bindweed battles with nettles that battle with dock that battles with clover, all unhindered. Bird droppings bring the endangered cowslip and oxlip. Two types of buddleia inter-marry. Grandchick and I sleep overnight in the garden shed and see the fox cubs playing at dawn. Stage 4: Deep Ecology. The philosophy that all living beings, regardless of their use-fulness to humans, are important links in nature's chain. Zika? Ebola? HIV? Maybe Earth is trying to rid herself of an excess of humans. Recently, I wrote 'Baby Welcome', 'Nero's Children', 'Progress Train' – small acts, pathetically small compared to the enormity of the Mother's plight. Whatever happens, She will continue to make her run around the sun, adapting to the new little wobble on her axis brought on by the melting of the ice caps, retaining or evolving species that can manage the pro-jected four-degree Celsius temperature rise that will reduce humans to cinders or at least to manageable proportions until She falls into the sun billions of years from now.

Stage 5: Eco-feminism, the belief that nurturing, sharing and reciprocity are the clue to human survival. These values are present in both women and nature, and both nature and women have suffered at the hands of patriarchal societies. Only with immediate, major input from human females can we turn our dire situation around. This is hard for men as a gender, for *conquering nature* has long been a dominant male occupation – in the interests of women and children, of course. Cheek is full of tongue. Christian Dior declared that his purpose was to *save women from Nature*. Ladies, only we can save ourselves from Christian Dior. Small act: via Women for Women International, I pay monthly to educate a woman in a developing country, enabling her to support herself and her children, to free herself if she is in a violent relationship, to learn to read and write. I confess my own Achilles heel: I employ fossil-fuelled vehicles to get to concerts where I sing songs about deep ecology.

I get angrier by the day. I grew up in a home in which anger was suppressed. *Now, Ruthie dear, don't get peppy.* I remember no deep rage, no resentment, no lasting discord. My early political songs set forth event and repercussion, all reasonable and measured. My Radio Ballad songs turn someone else's aggregate of experience into a highly charged emotional song. After 9/11, America's petulant cry was *Why do they hate us?* Seismic fury – I let rip with 'The Cavemen', one of my best songs. In May 2009, George Tiller, a surgeon who ran a late-term abortion clinic in Kansas, was murdered by pro-lifers as he ushered in church. 'Right to Life' flew out like a cannonball. Yesterday in 2017 I saw Ken Loach's film *I, Daniel Blake*. The crowd came out from the cinema heads down, many of us ashamed to go home to our comfortable lives. My mind ran off its rails and I didn't even know how to *think*. My brain was dark. I took a pill and slept for twelve hours, aching to be away from the cruelty of the human race. Today I have been incapable, unable to function. My picture gallery won't go away, its persistent replaying of drowning migrants, dead elephants, Hiroshima, Buchenwald now joined by the image of starving young single mother Katie, opening a can in the food bank to scoop the baked beans out with her hand and stuff them into her mouth. I am outraged, wondering what I can do. My political life has intertwined with song-making. Something wrong? Make a song. Something unfair? Sing about it. Sounds neat and tidy, doesn't it? It doesn't seem enough any more. What use is a songwriter whose songs are not in the current popular idiom and may never reach mainstream media? What use is a protest singer who gives concerts, the ticket price of which would buy a full day's food for Katie and her two children? Richard – my walking partner – phones and I unload. *There's too much misery, too much injustice, too much just plain horror. It's all too big – a song can't cure it.* He's my Richard: *From each according to their abilities . . . small acts . . .* measured talk, considerate but neat and tidy. He's right, of course – but I go for a walk by myself.

You either have to be part of the solution, or you're going to be part of the problem, said Eldridge Cleaver. Small acts in any political arena are the only possible starting point for most of us. Here are some of my Small Act role models. The Solidarity Sing Along in Madison, Wisconsin; Nigel Gibson and Jane Alexander, indomitable in the battle to save my local Temple Cowley Leisure Centre and swimming pool; Si Kahn and the campaign to stop the proposed Pebble Mine in Alaska's Bristol Bay; Amina Marix Evans and her Borderline Books project; Ted Power, not letting the council get away with anything detrimental to Brighton without a battle; my granddaughter

Morgan going on her own to Lesbos to help migrants living in crisis conditions; my grandson Alex, recycling used Mac computers and undertaking a bizarre variety of sponsored activities to raise money for motor neurone disease; the community organisations confronting local issues, the activist groups that rise overnight to fight fracking, the Friends of Iffley Village where I live, all instigated and run by locals for the betterment of the community. Each of my own benefit concerts is one of these small acts which add up to what Paul Hawken discusses in his book *Blessed Unrest*: an upwelling of positivity.

Justine Picardie, the British writer, was married to my son Neill back in 1992 when she did a wonderful small thing. Her local north London park had so much dog shit on the green sward that the children couldn't step off the pavements. She approached the other mothers with a plan. They purchased hundreds of small white flags on metal sticks and put a flag by each dog-stool, then contacted the local press. By the weekend both article and photo were in the local rag – you could hardly see the grass for the little white triangles. The council cleaned up the park and installed collection stations with bag, gloves and disposal facility.

Speaking of faeces – it's 9 November 2016. The Old Order of barely controlled disorder has come to an end. First Brexit and now the world wakes up to an American Nightmare. Two Wrongs are making a Big Right turn. I lie in bed listening to the new POTUS accepting his crown. He's Donned a thin cloak of humility and moderation for the occasion. His voice is oily, his delivery steady. His pace is stealthy. He seems to taste it as he speaks. A leopard crawling through high grass, belly to the ground, just a leap away from its prey. Most likely reading from an autocue, a hypocritical solo in the a-dodgio section of a political shamphony. I wish I could get drunk. I'll learn to disseminate my songs on the web. I write and Vimeo a little one immediately, 'Donald's in the White House'. If more women had been feminists, maybe . . . I want to phone Irene quick before Hocus-POTUS declares war via Twitter, giving the world only 140 seconds to say goodbye. Her number's busy. She was phoning me. We always make contact. Always. End of.

I am a pessimist. *Homo sapiens* is an incredibly intelligent and monumentally stupid species. Having learned little or nothing from previous failed civilisations, we continue to make the same mistakes over and over.* I am an optimist. At last we have one survival issue that will, hopefully, unite us: climate change. We will *have* to work together now. I am a realist. I believe that we won't work together in time. We'll decimate our species but enough of us will survive and evolve to maybe do a better job next time around. I am an atheist but I wish I did have a Guide somewhere. Deep in the earth's core? Enough power and mystery down there to birth more than a religion. Up there, maybe? The sky is too big. God would get lost. The Greek gods were delightfully imperfect. So are the gods of every human religion – they are all probably up there laughing at our gullibility. The first god I didn't believe in is almighty – presumed perfect. If he created humanity in his own image, then humans must be perfect. We know we aren't, so he can't be either. But take a political stance and you're expected to be 101 per cent perfect and there will always be Someone who will point out the sprig in your hedge. Or they'll hit the contact button on your website and ask why an eco-feminist is driving a diesel van. I'm on it . . . I'm shifting to hybrid or electric as soon as possible.

* *Collapse* by Jared Diamond. A necessary read on this subject.

41

Asheville, North Carolina: Part One

She saw me coming. Seasoned shopkeepers spot easy prey long
before we walk in the door. It was ostensibly a shoe shop, but it
had a variety of other wares shoved onto ceiling-high shelves,
multi-draped on hangers, strewn in glass cases, lying in heaps
on the floor. Forty years before, I had attended square dances,
kitted out in white ankle socks, sneakers and flaring knee-
length skirts. In England, I didn't dance because Ewan didn't
dance – a stupid reason, but I wasn't a feminist back then. In
later years, I'd venture out to the Cecil Sharp House dance evenings. The good dancers – skilled amateurs – came in unlock-
able couples, so I sat out playing the concertina or scouring the
room to pounce on an unwary lone male. Every now and then
a professional troupe of folk dancers from the American South
would turn up in oh-me-oh-my dance costumes – matching
shoes, skirts, trousers and smiles. Is that the way they dress for
square dancing now?

Asheville, North Carolina, headed for Warren Wilson
College and I'm about to find out. The music and dancing
are a large part of what I came for. I'm wanting desperately
not to look fifty-four and foreign. In the South, anyone from
north of Virginia is a furriner, a Yankee. I'm from three thousand miles away northeast. But now, When-in-Rome wants
local dress-code information and this shop looks to be full of
it. *What do people wear at square dances here?* The generously

built Ashe-villain assured me that white Mary Janes worn with nylon tights and a neon triple-striped, deep-gored, knee-length flared skirt *will do just fine, honey*. I turned up at the college gym looking like a biped candy cane. Half the women were clad in jeans and trainers, the other half in a multicolour array of comfortable peasant skirts, dresses, shorts, any old shoes. Most of the men were similarly informal – plus hats, or the ubiquitous baseball cap about which I will not comment here. The MJs killed my feet but during the ensuing twelve years I still patronised the shoe shop, for Milady nearly always had just what I wanted somewhere in the Higgledy Piggledy. She'd give me a friendly grin. I'll grin back, honey. We are enablers, giving each other's stereotypes a helping hand.

Asheville was first deposited in my memory bank when I was about six years old. Charlie was taking Mike along on a trip down south, stopping at Galax on the way to Asheville. Ashes were something in our big log fire and *What's vill, Dio, what's vill? Why can't I go too, Dio? I want to go!* Galax was a magical word, *GAY-lax, GAY-lax*, around the house, chanting for days. By 1994, Mike had become an integral part of the southeastern folk music community. *Mike, I want a small, southern, relatively civilised mountain town that survived Sherman's March, a town where I'll find the folk music we grew up with.* No hesitation: *Asheville.* I flew over to have a look. Asheville is nestled in a bowl surrounded by mountains – a position now to its disadvantage as air pollution is trapped after rolling in over the hills from the paper mills and coal mines of neighbouring Virginia, West Virginia, Tennessee and Kentucky. Every entrance was a malled highway – but in the centre, many of its historic buildings had survived the assault of the 1960s developers. It had a memorable skyline, complete with a pink city hall. Asheville was a little pearl of a relic back then. It has now been discovered, hotelled, trafficked, touristed and mauled – but is still known for its traditional musicians and storytellers. I hired a car and for two days I quartered the little town as a hawk quarters a field, marking in colours where I wanted and didn't want to rent. I put an ad in the paper and flew home. Gay Fox Agency sniffed out a fine house. I took on a year's lease over the phone without realising that the house I'd rented was not in Asheville.

Gemini from head to toe, my heart has two homes. I have two families in two countries. I have had two life partners. I want to be both home and away, both bound and free. A homemaker for thirty-five years, I wanted, in 1994, to rediscover the foolhardy free spirit that I had been. I was escaping from a self that I didn't like any more. It was the second time in my life that I settled in as a stranger from overseas. I was looking for a warm, interesting place for Irene and me. I found out later that, other than Spain, the USA was Irene's least favourite place to live. Neill phoned in 1995. *You're not coming back, are you, Mum?* He remembers it as a statement, not a question. I felt that he was sad, a child's sadness. I was stunned. He was thirty-seven, with two sons. It hadn't occurred to me that my grown-up children would miss me. Having had no grandmother myself, it hadn't occurred to me that my grandchildren might want or need me in that capacity. I thought I was returning to a familiar place, America of thirty-five years ago. Later I would decamp to Boston expecting to find the town of my college days. Even later, returning to Britain, I expected to find the country that my heart had nested in for three decades. I never learn. People kept telling me how brave I was to take off and relocate to a little mountain town in another country. It turned out to be an adventure but my English self went before me the moment I opened my mouth. *Are you Canadian? Irish?* Early on, Betsy had filed the edges off my American accent with caustic comments and pretence of misunderstanding. I have a mid-Atlantic accent. In the USA, my British sense of humour often brought me trouble or blank looks.

My rental was the top floor of a two-storey modern house in Montreat. The warlike evangelist Billy Graham stabled his Trojan Horse in that strange place. Sixteen miles east of Asheville centre, two miles up the hill from Black Mountain, it's on the edge of a huge National Park. My work desk faced a mountain through the uncurtainable cathedral windows. Anyone on that hill behind had me in their sights, especially at night when those black windows reflected back at me the target that a sniper would have no trouble hitting. I was very aware of my isolation as a lone woman. In my first North Carolina year, a young female hiker disappeared. She was found dead weeks later, tied to a tree. Hunters roam these forests, ersatz militia men preparing for the apocalypse, the Rapture or just their own personal war. Escapees from prison or wanted criminals have no trouble vanishing into the greenery here. Gun ownership is normal. The yearly North Carolina Gun Show fills the huge Asheville Civic Centre regularly. Irene and I attended out of curiosity. The clientele covers every class, colour, age and gender in the human rainbow. Fathers bring their five-year-old sons, both dressed in camouflage. Husbands and wives choose pistols together. Dainty women with dainty handguns in their handbags. Pistol-packin' Mamas you wouldn't want to meet in a lighted alley much less a dark one. Men you wouldn't want to meet anywhere. On the roads, pickup trucks tote an array of rifles on the cab wall, visible through the windscreen. The fear of men that was a seedling in Breighton springs full-blown in Montreat. The Interstate 40

(I-40) takes me back and forth to Asheville. If I'm returning at
night, I'll put on a tacky baseball hat, slip a lit cigarette in my
mouth and slouch in the driver's seat like some of the men down
here. The under-deck car space is dark. There are steps up to the
wraparound porch. As a child, I was never afraid of the dark.
Now I'm regressing, in a place where almost everyone I meet is a
retired Presbyterian minister, every one of them probably handy
with a gun. I'm frightened of a gender that I've borne, nurtured
and lived peaceably with till now.

Montreat has no real centre, just a little convenience store
with a post office. It has a huge convention centre, bedrooms for
the multitudes and an artificial lake should Billy's Man decide
to walk on water. Swannanoa Terrace is a cul-de-sac. Mail is
not delivered to the houses, so every morning I take a fifteen-
minute walk along the creek path to post my letter to Irene
and unlock my post-office box. Even if it's just bills or junk
mail, it's like opening a present every day. Irene comes to visit
and likes Asheville. She edits my songbook, making sure that
I'm not saying stupid things or opening myself to libel. She's
already visited Jackie Fleming, the prima feminist UK car-
toonist and illustrator, and chosen or commissioned the visuals
that will give my book its distinctive character. We choose the
photos and Irene corrects the odd layout that's been provided
in-house by Music Sales, who don't really want to publish the
books. Peter Pickow, one of Jean Ritchie's sons, fought the good
fight and *The Peggy Seeger Songbook, Warts and All* (weighing
3½ lb) comes out via Oak Publications in 1998. *The Essential
Ewan MacColl Songbook* (weighing 4 lb) appears a few years
later. I'm bringing the *dead duo* alive again.

1997. Hara Sitnick is my American personal assistant at
this point. Cheerful, off-the-wall and funny, she corrects my

slapdash trash routines, pointedly picking little pieces of paper out of the garbage can and putting them into the recycle bin. Her mother is running for mayor in Asheville, where she's everything the stereotypical southern establishment seems to dislike. In her early fifties, Leni is five foot five, has long wavy curls and wears trousers. Worse than that, she's northern, Jewish, female and feisty. Her only redeeming feature is that she's not brown or black. I enter the fray with a sixty-second piece for the radio, 'Leni in a Minute', frisky and tight. Then a longer song, 'Vote for Leni Sitnick'. Rhymes for Sitnick? Easy.

You're fighting for a better deal, you're not about to quit-nick,
She's right there in the ring with you. VOTE FOR LENI
> *SITNICK!*
She sticks to all her promises right through thin and thick-nick,
For politicians that's a record. VOTE FOR LENI SITNICK!

She won and was the best mayor Asheville ever had, even up to now, 2017.

Touring took on a whole new meaning. In Britain, the only long journeys were those pre-motorway nightmares when my estimations of travel time rarely coincided with reality. Now I'm touring a gigantic country. At Irene's behest, I've exchanged my car for a small, second-hand motorhome – twenty-one feet long by seven feet wide by nine feet high – the perfect vehicle for a travelling singer. All mod cons, including double bed, shower, toilet, fridge, sink, hob and oven, plus space for instruments and CDs. Turn the front seats around when you wish to dine. I christened her Maggie, after those sturdy, square, older working-class Scots and Irish women with names like Bessie and Fanny. She was my refuge at festivals – perfect when you need to get away from the throng or entertain a friend with cinnamon toast or a glass of bubbly. Speedy snail, carrying all I need on my back. Perfect for a Gemini. You don't leave home when you have a Maggie – you hop from a stationary residence to one on wheels. A treasured period of my life.

Maggie also made it possible for me to invite my grandchildren over for a fortnight of travelling to wherever we wished to go. One by one, from age six to ten, each of them arrived, was tucked into the passenger seat and off we went. Calum's wife, Kerry, put a self-sticking plastic EJECT button on the dashboard when she brought one of theirs. *Just press it when he gets too much for you.* They all got homesick after the first four or five days, *sittin' in the corner with your mouth poked out.* Dio: *I can sit on your bottom lip, Peggy.* Want to go home? Too bad. You're stuck with me for the next ten days. We'll stop at the next RV – Recreational Vehicle – camp and phone home. We'll have a look at the other motorhomes. Some of them are motor-palaces, forty-five-foot vehicles that arrive jammed tight with upholstered furniture, a huge television, kingsize bed, sets of matching crockery and ceramic knickknackery. The residents welcome the English in for inspection, proud of their rig. Grandchild and I watch as pop-out sections are popped out, the stuffed sofa and armchairs moving sideways and *voilà*, just like the home they left behind. Smaller, but enough space in the middle to do six twirls of a polka with my little Limeys. Outdoor scenarios are set up – miniature picket fences, fake flowers in fake pots, strings of fairy lights, composite wishing wells, *Bev and Buddy's Homestead*, Snow White and the dwarves, Bambi and smiling pussycats, the ubiquitous Star-Spangled Banner and (usually) Republican Party accessories. Democrats didn't seem to shout so much – until Obama.

1995. My first RV camp. It's nearly midnight. You enter the camp, get your papers and head for your designated spot. Not always easy to find. I hop out with a flashlight to find the location of the electrics and water. *Damn, I'll have to back in.* Maggie's reverse bleeper went on, loud and steady. The door of the adjacent motor-mansion burst open and a very large man emerged shouting every possible form of the F-word. His very large wife hovered behind him, their indoor light casting shadows that reached my feet. Abject, apologising, *This is my first time at a camp, very very sorry.* He comes over. I back away. He's come to help. Your RV is like a dog. Dog owners make friends with each other. I get Maggie's bleeper fitted with an on–off switch. I buy a pepper spray and a stun gun – a hundred thousand volts at the touch of a finger – and keep them right by the cargo door. I tell the grandchildren when they come, *If you even look at that shelf, your life won't be worth living.*

The huge highway and roadside signs provide entertainment for us. A church with on-off-on-off lighting proclaiming *Sinners Welcome. Jesus Saves* right next to a sign for the Fifth Third Bank. *What Really Happened in Eden* right next to *Adult Fantasy Store Next Exit.* My chickadees give me such pleasure. Alex communicated by CB – Citizens Band radio – with passing truckers and had a prolonged fit of laughter when we passed a truck carrying Portaloo cabinets, toilet-paper streamers waving out of them like comet tails. Tom cooked pasta carbonara for us both on Maggie's tiny stove and left his wallet with all his holiday money on the counter at the camp store. Gone. He took it like . . . Tom. *Let's play ping pong.* The money was found and returned. He puts it in his pocket and *Let's play ping pong.* Morgan, at the instigation of our Okefenokee official guide, hopped out of the boat with me into an alligator-infested

Florida swamp, water up to her waist. In the evening she sat on my lap singing 'Rattlesnake Mountain' for our hosts by their fire in the camping ground. Ella, smile watermelon-wide, whizzing down the enormous slide at the James Island water park, forgiving me (I hope) for letting her get sunburned. Jamie interrogating me about my life late into the night and getting tearful trying to use chopsticks. Harry's mouth dropping open when he heard and saw the guides at Williamsburg, Virginia; when he noticed before I did that brother Pete's name was one of those inscribed on the wall of the stairway of one of the towers of the World Trade Center in New York City. Fraser moping, sitting homesick on the kerb as we wait for the hot-air balloon to inflate, then leaning out of the basket to pick a leaf from the very top of a tree. Tanith and Esther never got the Maggie trip – but at least, unlike the visitors in 'She'll Be Coming around the Mountain', they didn't have to sleep with Grandma in the narrow double bed at the back.

I toured and toured, parking up at RV camps, on residential streets, on concrete Walmart prairies or filling-station forecourts. The Interstates are scary at night. Once, at dusk, Maggie broke down and I drew up on the shoulder. I put up my big sign: HELP CALL THE POLICE in huge capitals. I wait. It's getting dark except for head and tail lights thundering past. I wait, hoping that someone has reported at the next gas station that there's a white motorhome stranded somewhere back a ways. I wait into the dark, vowing to buy a cell phone. A pickup truck screeches to a stop. My heart is in my mouth and it's not tasty. A man gets out and stands hands up in full view in his own headlights so I can see him. That's thoughtful. I put my hand in my pocket as if I have a gun and tell him to keep his distance. He has a nice face. *Are you broken down, lady?* I ask, *Can I trust you?* Stupid – Jack the Ripper would have replied politely, *Of course you can, madam.* My man scratches his head and replies, soft-spoken: *Waaall . . . I work for the telephone company, ma'am.* We both laugh. He has a new fan belt in his truck, a Colossal Whopping Extra Large Rubber Band. I give him a CD. He has a new fan. At the next pit stop, I'm told that three tractor-trailer drivers have reported a broken-down motorhome back a ways on the road. The police were nowhere in this story.

Ah, officialdom. I was steaming up California State Route 1, the fabled coastal highway that runs up the west coast of the Eldorado State. Post-*that-woman*-Monica Lewinsky, I heard someone call it the Kinky Prick State. Florida has long been called the Penis of America. Pointing down. Aimed at Cuba, waiting for stimulus? Busy songwriting in my head, I didn't watch the speedometer. Blue lights blue lights blue lights! I steer Maggie onto the shoulder. A handsome young policeman sticks his head in the window and asks if I know how fast I was going. My Maggie could indeed gallop at full tilt. I admit that I only glanced at the speedometer when I saw the blue lights. 95 mph on a 65 mph road. *No, officer, I'm a musician and I'm very sorry and I was writing a song in my head and I wasn't paying attention* and his face lights up. *I write songs too! What's your song about?* Off we went, commiserating on the difficulties of putting thoughts and emotions into verse and melody. *You play folk music? Do you know Bobby Dylan and Joanie Baez?* He was impressed that before they were Bobby and Joanie they'd both asked for my autograph, but he zipped back to our songs. He just wanted some tips. He let me off with a warning. Ah, officialdom. That Customs officer at Heathrow who, every time I turned up carrying my guitar case, would ask me in hushed tones if it was *the 1907 Martin.* I tour with no other and he knows it. We swing into our routine. I open the case and he takes it out reverently and plays it. The other officials are busy stopping anyone with a brown or black skin.

Maggie-the-Van was very white, practically invisible that night, en route from Charlottesville to Lexington, fifty miles west, on the I-64 over the mountains in a Virginia blizzard. I'd been advised not to make the trip but whoever listens to the Romans? The wind was whipping the snow into tornado-cones and I was following icy wheel tracks. The truckers know the road and they whiz by in the fast lane. I switch on the CB. *I'm a small white motorhome going west slowly in the right lane. I have my hazards on. Please watch out for me. I think I'm between exits such and such . . . over . . .* An immediate answer: *I just passed exit whatever and I'll pass you real slow and move over in front of you. You just stay behind me, darlin' . . . over . . .* A huge tractor-trailer passes, indicates and pulls in ahead of me. He puts his hazards on and I draw up behind him. Another voice chimes in: *I'm coming up to exit so-and-so now, honey. I'll come up behind you. Over.* A cliff with two blazing eyes is right behind me. A Maggie sandwich with bread sliced thick. Three of us in communication, they shepherded me over the mountain at my pace, talking to me all the time. *English girlie. Honey. Darlin'.* The one behind said nothing about my anti-establishment or eco bumper stickers but loved the funny ones. They deposited me safely on the I-81 and went on their way, talking to each other until they were out of CB reach. Two southbound guardian angels – undoubtedly with guns on board.

In the States, if you're parked up beside the road and need help, you hang a white cloth in the driver's window. On this sunny southern day, there's a station wagon on the shoulder with the fluttering flag out. As I pass I see the driver slumped over the wheel. It could be a trap. I am a thoughtless do-gooder. I'm not boasting – I'm still alive. I pull to the side and walk back, Stone Age cell phone hung on my shoulder, pointing index finger in pocket. A hunter – and he's shot himself in the foot. A dead deer, its head hanging over the back seat. 911 is, like the batteries, Ever Ready. I get in the passenger seat and we engineer his leg up onto my lap. We talk while we wait. He's from Texas, sounding *exactly* like Alan Lomax, *honey* this and *honey* that. The police and ambulance arrive and I make to leave. Texas motions me over. *Look, honey, I'm real grateful you stopped. But don't make a habit of it. You know what men are like, honey.*

Is there some vibration between people that tells us, *Yes, pick up this person; no, don't stop for that one*? It's midday, roasting hot. I pass a young couple hitch-hiking – illegal on the Interstates. The girl doesn't look so good. She's stumbling and he's holding her up. Are they acting out a little hook-play? Do I want to read in the papers that a young woman dropped dead on the highway in the summer sun because no one would stop? Or that an old lady driver was . . . No, don't think that way. No one stopped for me except the telephone technician. Pass it on. I move onto the shoulder and reverse for half a mile. The woman is dangerously dehydrated. We manhandle (peoplehandle?!) her into Maggie and onto the bed in the back. We sponge her with water and give her small cups of sugary tea. If it had been two men, I would have reported it and driven on. As a gender, men have shot themselves and each other in the foot.

42

Asheville, North Carolina: Part Two

The two main women in my life live in England now. Kitty –
she'd excelled in school but in the chaos following Ewan's death
she'd left before matriculating and we'd drifted apart. I felt that
I'd committed a crime by falling in love with a woman. Guilty.
Same-sex relationships wore that coat of shame back then and
Kitty and I . . . well . . . Long phone calls from Asheville didn't
constitute mothering. Strangely but not really strange, I trusted
her to find her way – and I was right. She went back to school,
attained a brilliant A level in English and then started on a
career of – as far as I am concerned – knowing how to do anything on a computer. She has a lovely singing voice, knows most
of my songs, but chooses to be the visual artist of the family, a
graphic designer. On and off she has appeared on stage with me
and has supplied backing vocals on my *Home Trilogy*.* I'm three
thousand miles away and I know little or nothing about her
life. In 1997, she came to visit me in Asheville. She was a breath
of English air and it hit me hard: I am English, not American.
That was the beginning of my knowledge that England was
really home.

Irene – back and forth we went, visiting each other in our
respective countries. Each year, when warm weather came,
Irene would arrive from England. I'd terminate my rental and

* Three albums of traditional songs issued by Appleseed Recordings, 2003–8.

put into Maggie what we'd need for the summer. Dump the rest into storage and we'd take to the road and the summer festivals. One summer we took a three-month trip over to the west coast and back. In September, Irene would fly back home and I'd look for another temporary Asheville home. In 2001, Irene decided to come on over to live, so I bought No. 3 Woodlawn Avenue, a plain, square, four-bedroom wooden galleon of a house, five minutes' uphill walk to get to the town centre, ground zero for the worst mosquitos ever – pre-Zika. They were tiny, with zebra legs, and they didn't play fair – no *zzzzzz* before they landed. Their bites raised mountains. No. 3 was a couple of blocks from the growling I-40 that literally cut Asheville in half. The real-estate lady said, *Just imagine that it's the ocean*. I did – because I loved the house. I painted it a vibrant yellow. Down on the backstreet, very old Mr Young – he'd refused to put mosquito-dunks in his water butts, *it'll pizon my termaters* – sat on his porch chewing and spitting tobacco, cursing and slapping mosquitos and watching the paint go on. *That's the darndest, yallerest house I've ever seen*. He gave us some perfect tomatoes.

It was my first unfurnished home in the States. We haunted the auction houses, the second-hand recycled household shops. We bought a gigantic antique Welsh dresser which fitted into the nine-foot-three-inch-high kitchen with half an inch to spare. Six-foot-long chopping-board tables from a defunct Chinese restaurant made food preparation and big parties possible. We paid $25 for a 1950s cook-stove that was thrown out into the yard of a house that was being butchered – a.k.a. modernised. It was one of those totally civilised appliances, the four gas burners of which have different functions. Baking and broiling instructions are on the enamelled inside surfaces of the oven doors.

Herewith an instructive backstory, the purpose of which will be clear by the end of the next paragraph. October 1990 and No Spring Chickens are on tour in the States. We visit Pete and Toshi on their hill. I do the laundry and carry it out to the line in a large, heavy enamel bowl. I stumble and the dish falls on my hand. Hand swells up to twice its size so it's off to the local hospital in Cold Spring. I've broken a metacarpal bone and the surgeon books me in for a next-day operation. Irene: *Excuse me, but you make your living with your hands. If you broke your hand, where would you go to have it mended?* Without hesitation, he gives the name of the top hand specialist at the Roosevelt Hospital in New York City. *Please don't be offended. My friend, like you, makes her living with her hands. We will be going to the Roosevelt.* On her second day in the USA, never having driven on the right, Irene drives us into the chaos of New York City. I want to go home. Irene insists that we finish the tour, mostly unaccompanied singing except for my attempts at left-hand-only on the piano.

Back to our old stove. One of the burners doesn't work. We contact the gas board and Rumpelstiltskin comes to the door with a toolbox that he could have slept in. His face lights up when he sees our vintage cooker. *My grandmother had one just like that . . .* he tails off wistfully. Then decisively, *But you'll never get the clock or that burner fixed.* OK, three burners it is, but the little man operates on some of the stove's entrails, mends the thermostat and leaves. A few days later, Irene spots a truck emblazoned with MR FIXIT CAN FIX ANYONE'S OLD STOVE. Frankenstein comes to the door with a tool-box that he could have put in his pocket. His face lights up when he sees our vintage cooker. *My grandmother had one just like that . . .* he tails off wistfully. Then, decisively, *But you'll never get that burner or the clock fixed.* Irene: *What would you do if this stove was yours?* Without hesitation he says, *I'd go on the internet.* There it is on my computer: The Old Appliance Club. The parts arrive and we send the clock off to be repaired. Frankenstein is delighted when he comes to fit everything in. The Application of the Idea of IF. It moves problem solving onto a different level.

Woodlawn Avenue was one block long, a street of older women. We formed a coven, Beth, Clare, Irene, Kathleen, Pat, Peggy and Sharon – the Woodlawn Witches. We met once a month for potluck gossip sessions and occasionally slugged it out in heated political discussion: local council elections; whether or not the State House in the capital of South Carolina should fly the Confederate flag; what to do about the blocked-up alley next to Kathleen's, a dumping ground for litter; teasing Beth, a pastor, about the frequent, drawn-out visits of Brownie, the activist councillor. We had a big front porch with a swing that accommodated four and front steps that accommodated twelve. It was a good life, perhaps the most normal I'd had since Ewan died. We'd sit out front greeting passers-by. Neighbours and friends dropped in unannounced. The weather was made for it, summers hot and humid and slow as a river of molasses, winters cold and sharp with bright blue skies. One year there was a small tornado. Another year there was a blizzard followed by an ice storm. Every bit of flora was sheathed by the Ice Queen. The circus was in town that week and elephants picked their way gingerly along snowblown streets.

Irene entered the Green Card Lottery several times, but no go. The conditions of her stay were now laid down by the USA. The options: (a) pay an enormous amount for a Green Card allowing permanent residence; (b) take regular paid employment;

(c) start a business that employs Americans; (d) go home after ninety days; (e) marry an American – man, not woman. She'd already joined with four other women to renovate the huge old Castanea building (Haywood Street, Asheville) into shops and flats. The project won the prestigious Griffin Award but that wasn't enough. She chose (c) and converted an old laundromat in the historic suburb of Montford into a small, homey cafe-cum-restaurant. She christened it Pyper's Place, after her mother, Bessie Pyper. A nine-foot leopard-design couch sat in front of a classic 1960s orange woodstove. Zena, a full-size woollen zebra, stood in a straw-filled corner. The atmosphere was cosy, the piped music soft and easy and the food vegetarian, although not advertised as such. One man came in every day for Pyper's special Quorn Kiev. He didn't ask what Quorn was. After two weeks, he came up to the till with a horrified expression on his face. *This place is . . . vegetarian!* He'd thought his lunch was chicken. He continued to come.

I had breakfast at Pyper's every Sunday morning when we had classical musicians in. Billy Jackson on the harp accompanying Irene's potato bread with Pyper's chutneys and a poached egg on top. An atheist's church. We had live music three or four nights a week: singers, songwriters, storytellers, instrumentalists. John Hermann, Meredith McIntosh, Vollie McKenzie, Rayna Gellert, Laura Boosinger, Beanie Odell and Vince Fogarty, Connie Regan-Blake. Bruce Green – esoteric fiddler always bringing out tunes no one else ever played – and ballad fiend Loy McWhirter, who learned the fifty or so verses of 'Tam Lin' so she could sing it for me at a fireside get-together. I name them for myself as well as you. I loved those evenings. Some of the acts were wonderfully crazy – Billy Jonas, the Mad Tea Party. Foot artists . . . Rodney Sutton with

his subtle soft-shoe shuffle and Ira Bernstein, spaghetti-leg
magic, leaving his dancing platter behind the Kawai concert
keyboard for his next visit. Professional out-of-town musicians
made lightning appearances if we were on their flight path. Pay
was a free supper and a divvy of the donations. I'd take the big
lidless teapot around, standing by each table, refusing to move
till *something* was dropped in, preferably silent money. Irene
had never done anything like this before but she ran it like a
professional. She worked 20/7, opening at 7 a.m. and closing
at 11 p.m. That meant getting up at 5.30 and going to bed long
after midnight. I helped when I could, arranging the music ros-
ter, washing dishes, clearing up, sometimes sitting down at the
piano to play – but then I would just take off on a tour and be
away for weeks on end. That's not *living together.* An Asheville
friend asked Irene about my long absences: *Are you afraid someone will steal her away?* Irene didn't miss a beat: *They'll soon
bring her back.* To say that Pyper's Place wore Irene out is the
understatement of the decade. In 2005, we had a grand closing.
That cancelled her permission to stay. Now she'd have to leave
when the immigration militia discovered her status.

So in 2006, when Judith Tick, our friend and my mother's biographer, offered me a teaching post at Northeastern
University in Boston, I said yes. Just like that. *Yes.* No conference with Irene. Peggy just says, *Yes, I will move to Boston.* Irene
will go . . . where? She has stuck by me thin and thick. Her style
is to plant herself and put roots down – that's what she's done
here in Asheville. She's adjusted to my wanderlust for years.
How could I? The phrase haunts me, drives me to weekly sessions with a therapist. When I wake at the not-so-proverbial
3 a.m. my mind begins beating up on me. The depressing
thing is that I will probably do it again. And again. We'd been

together in England and boom! I fled solo to the USA. We're in full bloom in Asheville and boom! I feel the need to be a seed again. Teaching songwriting in Boston? Of Course Why Not? The Woodlawn home was sold, at a good price thanks to Irene's passion for real estate. Goodbye yet again, leaving casually without a backward glance a house where we'd been settled, a town of which we had been part for twelve years, leaving friends, acquaintances, Witches. We packed Maggie full to the gills and drove north, with Babou-the-Cat prowling unhappily around the boxes. I'd already scoped Boston out and chosen a small two-bedroom flat. Another bitter lesson for Irene, who undoubtedly noticed immediately upon entry that it was really meant for one person – one bedroom for bed and the other for office. When Irene visits, she has but a corner in the living room for herself and her computer.

Love is frightening. It can make you go where you shouldn't go, stay where you shouldn't stay. You stay or go because you love someone, because someone loves you. We flew to England and held our long-awaited civil union in Woolwich Town Hall on 15 December 2006. We both know there will be no one else. Nonetheless, after decades of encouraging me to fly solo she decided to put the Wind of my Neglect under her own wings – and moved to New Zealand. Sunny weather; low population; trees and water; and life somewhat as it used to be. Once, upon my arrival in Auckland, the flight attendant announced, *Welcome to 1950*. No one laughed.

In 1958, I made a good decision – good for Ewan and myself and for the children to come. From the early 1990s onward, my choices were for myself alone. I have to live with that.

43

Boston, Songwriting

My father's people come from this neck of the woods. This is where Grandmother Seeger tormented her enemies with her three-legged teacups. I settle on the other side of the tracks, Paul Gore Street, in the Jamaica Plain district of Boston. I liked the name. The Gore family first appears in neighbouring Roxbury in 1635, and Paul purchased his section in 1743. There was a farm right here on my street. Sold and broken up into parcels in 1876, it is now covered in block after residential block of family homes. An enormous multi-storey project on the other side of Centre Street houses Latinos, Filipinos, blacks, browns, light browns, down-and-out darkish whites – an interesting series of communities. My apartment was No. 1, the ground floor of a triple-decker, those quintessential community-friendly New England houses. Each storey consists of an entire apartment with two full-width porches, one in the front and one in the back. Front and back doors give access to the two staircases that join the whole structure from top to bottom, one leading down onto the street and the other to the back garden. The back staircase winds further down to the cellar, which contains shared storage and laundry facilities. The upper floors of No. 91 are still home to my good neighbours, two friendly German families with interesting children. We visited up and down, helping each other when needed. Dunja – just above me in No. 2, mother, opera singer and my special friend – saved me when I had a shoulder operation and had to drag around the flat for three days attached to a cumbersome ice-machine, christened Trifidette. Our next-door neighbour, Jenny Jones, became the catalyst that turned our street into a neighbourhood, instigating regular meetings, street parties, yard sales and a watch committee. Every couple of weeks she and I walked the street from top to bottom collecting rubbish in huge black bags. Fewer people seem to drop trash on a clean street.

It's hard to make a neighbourhood out of a narrow, one-way, downhill three-lane thoroughfare: two lanes for parked cars and one lane for buses, trucks, rat-runners and litter-dropping, speed-happy customers on the getaway from the excellent Mexican takeaway at the top of our five-block street. Maggie fits into a normal American parking space but my rental didn't come with parking. Sometimes, coming home late at night, I'd have to leave her five or six blocks away. There was a dedicated collector of hubcaps on Paul Gore. I replaced at least a dozen during my four years there from a shop that specialised in hubcaps. Probably owned by our dusk-to-dawn collector. We also had a serial vandal who skateboarded down the street in the dark of night, caught once on video. Beautiful economy of movement as he passed each car, arm up, baseball bat shattering the windscreen of this car, the next car and the next but – strangely – never my Maggie. The sturdy, square, older working-class women of Belfast and Glasgow command the same respect.

It was in Boston that I saw my first silent rave. The empty parking lot in Lexington was filled with several hundred people, identical music in their earbuds. The dominant sound was hundreds of feet moving, synchronised, each participant hermetically sealed into their own world by their determination to do everything their own way. No couples dancing together, no squares, lines, organisation or attempts to make physical contact with anyone else. Hundreds of human globules of oil and water mixing at a near distance. Headphones are dangerous. Mike's beautiful Woodstock girlfriend Mary Lou, a mother of two, was hit by a truck while jogging, her head filled with music. My mother developed mould in her ears from hours-long sessions of listening through earphones to recordings at the Library of Congress.

My exercise was walking, especially around Jamaica Pond, a link in Boston's Emerald Necklace of parks, designed in 1837 by Frederick Law Olmsted – sixty-eight water-filled acres, lovely at any time of year, a forty-five-minute brisk-pace delight. The trees are aflame in autumn, a-flower in summer. Around Halloween, the Lantern Parade draws participants from near and far, from toddlers to the very old – a 1.5-mile ring of candle fireflies, reflected in the pond waters. The apartment seemed capacious before I arrived. Furniture brought up from the 2400-square-foot Woodlawn house was now squeezed into 1200 square feet, leaving little space in the centre of every room. Like wearing a warm coat several sizes too big. I slipped into a hermit lifestyle that was not conducive to making or keeping a circle of friends. Visitors had to sleep in the living room on a two-foot-high blow-up mattress. Rosalie Sorrels, *sine qua non* Utah singer/songwriter, comes to visit, record and entertain me with the story of her Rosalie life. She is spare, a scaffold of bones, skin filled with spirit. Her stories keep us up very late and I sleep in. I creep to the bathroom around noon the next day. A squeaky mouse-voice is calling *Peggy . . . Peggy.* We hadn't secured the valve. All I can see is Rosalie's head. The rest of her is totally captured by the collapsed mattress. She is a larva peeking out of its cocoon, laughing and begging to be released. It is 12 June 2017, and I'm proofreading this book. Rosalie died yesterday.

*

I begin teaching in September 2007. Here come the young students to look me over. I'm looking *them* over. Twenty – far too many and all of them with guitars. I know how to weed out the ones who won't work at it: rules.

No baseball caps in class, forward or backward.
You sit not in the middle of your spine but on your coccyx.
What's a coccyx? I spell it for them. Two students leave.
You will be on time or it will affect your grade.
No instruments at all – you'll sing unaccompanied for
twenty weeks. More deserters.
You will create a song a week.
You will work with a thesaurus and a rhyming dictionary.
What's a thesaurus?
You will read *A Is for Ox: The Collapse of Literacy and the
Rise of Violence in an Electronic Age* by Barry Sanders and
be ready to write short commentaries when required.
You will read *The Necessity of Art* by Ernst Fischer and be
ready to write (etc.). The warmth of prolonged commit-
ment melts a few more snowflakes.
You will be encouraged to find alternatives for the words
awesome and *cool* when describing anything from an ice-
cream cone to the upcoming presidential election.
You will attempt to remove the word *like* from endless
usage in your speech.

I am now Professor Seeger, terrified. I have never taught anything solo, formally or at length. I am facing a dozen de-capped, de-guitared, ill-assorted eighteen-to-twenty-three-year-olds who are allowed to desert the course if the first sessions aren't to their liking. Roughly half of them are involved in music and the music industry. It occurs to me that the non-musicians might be here just to get an easy credit. I sing a few of my own songs for them in the first session. My pupils are flummoxed. Not their idea of songs at all. My songs are powerful – they make students disappear. We're down to eleven now, mostly male. First assignment: bring me tracks of your favourite music. Most of it consists of a melange of deafening instrumentation and percussion whose main purpose seems to be to hide the vocal. Is it a song? Are there words? When asked to sing one of these pieces unaccompanied . . . well, hopeless. No guitar, gotta sing unaccompanied? Us oldies, we have ESP, extra-sensitive powers. I hear them exchanging glances. *What is Professor Seeger going to teach?* Melody and words are my bread and butter. Another duckling flies off and my dutiful ten sit there, capless with straight backs, ready to take notes.

We write a song because we feel we should; because we're being paid or commissioned; because our communal life gives birth to it. We write songs to help heal a disaster or a personal tragedy. I wrote 'Love, Call Me Home' for my Asheville friend Christine Lassiter, who had terminal cancer, courage, grace and no medical plan. She sang her song continually during her last weeks. We write songs because we just can't help it; because the song is begging to be written. Would Ewan have written 'The First Time Ever' if I hadn't left him? I had asked Alan, a dedicated lover of women, why the Anglo-American folk songs didn't celebrate happy love. *Honey, when things are*

going right you haven't got time to write songs. We write songs
because we've signed up to a songwriting class. My course was
described as *Some Perspectives on the Art of Song Writing.* The
only tunes they'll use will be of my choosing – the words will
be theirs. I have 5500 items on my iTunes and each week I give
them twenty-five songs to download off the Northeastern website. Probably illegal. By the end of the course they'll have over
five hundred songs of all sorts, chosen for their melodies and
the way the words fit – a variety of styles and artists from unaccompanied Irish singer Paddy Tunney to Tracy Chapman via
Paul Simon, on to Dolly Parton, Clarence Ashley. Then I give
them a general subject: dreadful accidents; something you're
afraid to write about; something funny; something from the
newspaper. They don't read newspapers. Occasionally they can
choose a personal subject but the melody must come from my
list of songs.

The reading is difficult for them. They hadn't expected
theory, philosophy, cultural politics. Nor had I expected to
have to suffer their essays and give them grades. The fun stuff
was the songwriting. Day One. *We'll start today with simple off-
the-cuff rhyming couplets.* Confusion. *What's a rhyming couplet?*
Dear God. 1 + 1 = 2. *Well, like Muhammad Ali's war cry to Sonny
Liston:*

> *Float like a butterfly, sting like a bee –*
> *His hands can't hit what his eyes can't see.*

Who's Muhammad Ali? Ali was a black boxer who . . . *Oh,
him! The old guy who's punch-drunk sick?* Yes, that one, a superb
fighter, punch-drunk maybe, Parkinson's definitely, a man
capable of creating delightful runs of words and rhymes on

the spot. *It'll be a killa and a thrilla and a chilla when I get that gorilla in Manila.* I think the youngsters are bored. Never mind, I'm the boss here and we're going to create spontaneous poetry today. The purpose is to break down the fear of seeming foolish and to improvise text on the hoof. I sing:

> *There was a man and he was mad*
> *And he jumped into a pudding bag.*
> *The pudding bag it was so fine*
> *That he jumped into a bottle of wine.*
> *The bottle of wine it was so . . .*

You only need to put in a new adjective, kids, then a rhyming noun and pass the need for a new adjective on to your neighbour. *Why does it need to rhyme?* Good question. Only in this song. Rhyme or No Rhyme: that's when we get to 2 + 2, quatrains and narrative.

I'm standing outside the classroom and here comes Dan down the corridor, designer headphones and volume high enough for me to hear thirty yards away, the heavy bass martial and barbaric. When he was standing next to me the din from his headphones felt physically dangerous. Dan was a photography student. He couldn't carry a tune and I don't believe he played the guitar. His voice disappeared when he tried to sing, but he wanted desperately to write a song. I thought that was wonderful. Dan was the first one to turn up with a singable song, a direct and charming piece, delivered in Dan-croak. He basked in my delight. Astounding, that he could listen to that cacophony of percussion and yet write that simple song. Many of my students indulged in insanely loud music. Sam invited me to hear his band play. Pre-showtime he walked around the whole audience of a few oldies and many ex-teenagers giving everyone a set of businesslike earplugs and a warning: *It's going to be loud.* By God, it was. I think he was singing – his lips were moving but nothing resembling a song came to the fore. Fearing for my eardrums, I left. I waved, he smiled, put thumbs up and saluted. He knew from the get-go that I would leave. Then he turned up in class and wrote good songs.

Music: I have widespread preferences and they are reflected in my output. I can write childishly simple songs – 'One Plus One', 'Chunk of Cheddar Cheese'. My songs 'RSI', 'Different Tunes', 'The Plutonium Factor' are complicated, almost classical, pieces whose format differs radically from the verse-by-verse approach of my more traditionally based compositions. The distance between their disciplines may be considerable but they all regard melody and text as more important than rhythm and harmony. In class, it turned out that the choice of tune had an enormous influence on the type of text, the placement of words, the aptness of the subject. My selected tunes were what made it possible for the students to work together – that and the tutorials, when six of us would sit around a table for two hours with rhyming dictionary and thesaurus, to work on one person's song. Consider moving the second line to fourth position. Choose a synonym for a word that doesn't fit in or doesn't rhyme. That verse – it's good but does the song need it? You don't have to spell out every little detail. It doesn't always have to rhyme – I sing them 'Dirty Old Town'. They love it. It has to fit in the mouth and the mind has to be involved. You're telling a story here even if it is not in chronological or narrative form. It was hard for me. I would see the word, line, verse or rearrangement that was needed and had to refrain from saying it outright. I learned to lead the maker of the song via questions towards what I thought was suitable. The *folk process*: the gradual alteration of songs and stories as they pass orally from person to person. Traditionally, the changes usually occur vertically, *down* through generations. Our tutorials generated a horizontal folk process, singers in the same generation and the same time zone helping to hone a song across a table.

An end-of-semester concert was required by the head of the music faculty. The guitars came out in the last three classes and rehearsals began. Up till now, most of my students had been consumers of music. Now they had to be producers. The a cappella singing had revealed vocal problems that normally would have been concealed behind instrumentation. When I was at home attached to Trifidette, I gave over a whole class to Northeastern's vocal teacher, Martha Peabody. The improvement was more than noticeable. By the time the concert came along, Dan's croak had a melodic edge but his pitch and attack were shaky, his nerves unreliable. Nevertheless, he wanted to sing his songs himself. On the big day, it became obvious that he was struggling. His class-friends understood what his songs meant to him. As he sang, they joined in, humming quietly in unison. *We're here, Dan. Here's a bed of accuracy for you to lie back on.* He responded by singing better than he ever had. There were tears in my eyes. I have the *coineagh* on my fore-arms as I sit here typing. In those twenty-two weeks, ten singu-lars became a plural.

I learned along with them, not only by watching the bond-ing of tune and text, content and form, politics and art, but by observing them networking with one another to help everyone create something of value. Even though they have most likely gone back to their chosen musical genre, we wrote a lot of very good songs. The Time-Tested Tunes and Tutorials for Texts saw to That. All t's crossed. Twenty-two i's dotted in two years. They did complain. *Professor Seeger, these tunes! I can't get them out of my head. I hear them when I go to sleep and when I wake up. I walk around humming them all the time.* Yes. That's the whole point.

*

What kind of new songs can a singer of folk material make to deal with the issues of these treacherous days? So many of the formats, the loyalties, the performance styles have been based on traditions that sprang from working-class culture, however tightly or loosely organised. That culture is a thing of the past, seen off by television, globalisation, migration to cities, advent of mobile phones, Facebook, Twitter, social fission and community disintegration. The potential audience for new songs, to judge from the mass rallies and demonstrations, covers exceedingly wide age, gender, political, heritage and religious ranges. We need to explore, steal, invent new formats. We need to capture the public imagination, sing to the fence-sitters, bring factions together. Righteous outrage and complaint are common features of folk-orientated protest songs. Let's stop complaining and write – with as few complacent clichés as possible – about hope, compassion, gratitude, cohesion and, above all, action. Sounds simple. It is.

44

Are Lawnmowers and Folk Music Political?

1960s. The phone rang during dinner. An American, with that no-nonsense, self-confident voice that wants to sell you something. The Music Industry was meeting in Geneva. *We're going to take over the British Folk Revival and we want you on board, Mr MacColl.* Ewan: *Which other singers are being approached?* Not many, it would seem. *Well – if you're not needing a lot of singers then what is it that you're taking over?* The reply was brazen: *We don't need singers, Mr MacColl. We have engineers.* Geneva wanted neither our input nor our output, only your support in pushing a corporate lawnmower over your grass-roots movement, Mr MacColl. It felt like an invitation to sail on the *Titanic*. Of course, we were already part of the Music Industry – the collection agencies that make sure that we get royalties; the legal processes that investigate copyrights and permissions; our precious Musicians' Union. The company that he and I formed, Ewan MacColl, Ltd (I wasn't a feminist then), is now safely in the hands of our children because I was hopeless at running it. They keep me in their loop, hoping that I will remain at a distance. I am at last being professionally managed, publicised and distributed by various arms of the Music Behemoth that was born in the latter part of the twentieth century when it became plain that music could earn big bucks – mostly for the network of publishers, producers, studios, labels, shops, venues, media . . . oh yes, and for the songwriters, if they didn't make the mistake of signing a contract without a lawyer present. Which Ewan did in the early 1950s. He signed away into perpetuity at a 50–50 rate – incontestable – the royalties for one of his best songs, 'Dirty Old Town'. T's dotted and eyes-crossed, dory hunky, dear man, grateful for the pitiful advance. These days he'd have gotten 85–15 or even 90–10.

*

> *The man that hath no music in himself,*
> *Nor is not moved with concord of sweet sounds,*
> *Is fit for treasons, stratagems and spoils . . .*
> *Let no such man be trusted.*
>
> (William Shakespeare, *The Merchant of Venice*)

How is it possible to dislike music when there are so many different musics, including the controversial, totally 'silent' *4' 33"* by John Cage? Music – it lights up the whole of the brain. Singing vibrates every part of the body. Listening can also jostle things. You can now have that energising, booming boom-box strategically installed in car seats. Music – it's more than meets the ear. It is proof of our existence. Our musical productions are as birdsong, trumpeting, *This is my territory. I am here. Because of my song I will always be here.* Touching, really, each of us our own Ozymandias. Without art we are truly alone, incompletely connected to our inner selves, disconnected from each other. Like every form of art, music has political status according to the class in which it originated, why and for whom it was made, taking on all the hereditary baggage of that class. The production, appropriation and commercialisation of music in an exploitative system is a political act.

Other musical disciplines tend to dismiss folk song and folk singers as simple and unlettered. Folk songs are generally not created for patronage and if they make a profit it's either amazing or because someone has changed them into something marketable. Folk songs originally expressed the experience and values of those at the bottom of the social heap; those who take home a weekly wage, not a salary; those who can be dismissed with little or no notice; in short, those who walk an economic tightrope insecurely fastened at both ends. Who 'the folk' really *are* and what folk music really *is* have become arguing points too sticky to deal with. New definitions abound. *Folk* can mean amateur. *Folk* can mean new songs that sound like old songs. *Folk* can mean a folk song given a classical or pop-music treatment. *Folk* in the UK can mean acoustic music of any sort. Enough, already. Folk songs were originally hewn in memory. Their pared-down-to-the-bone texts are unpretentious, close to spoken language. Their melodies are so reminiscent of the rise and fall of colloquial speech that they are often regarded as an elemental ingredient – embryonic, therefore belonging to nobody, therefore the property of everybody, therefore a resource which creators in other disciplines can borrow when they need flour, butter, eggs, salt, fat or sugar for their new musical recipe. The temptation to plunder folk music, to change it into something else seems universal. It's a process that can totally alter the meaning and the social – i.e. political – purpose of folk song.

One of the political strengths of folk music is that it is immediate. Write the song today, sing it tonight. We are unplugged, portable, can sing and play anywhere. Recognising the escalation of interest in *listening without seeing*, the BBC is increasing its volume of radio programmes. I read the final draft of this memoir out loud – what a difference from silent reading! *You can't cheat the ear in the way you can cheat the eye*, as Jeanette Winterson says. Another political strength of folk music is that it originates in orality and aurality rather than via literacy. Too much of the latter and too little of the former alter the functioning of the brain. Back in the sixties at a concert in Cambridge, Massachusetts, I was teaching the audience to sing the five times table in a children's multiplication song. Father Time was sitting in the front row scratching his head, befuddled. He finally took out a pencil and a little notebook, wrote the numbers down and read them off the page, singing happily. I spoke to him in the interval. He was Niels Bohr, the Danish physicist – atomic structure, quantum mechanics and all that.

*

I have chiefly been part of the UK folk revival. I know diddly-squat about any folk tradition other than the Anglo-American, whose songs are full of social comment – mostly descriptive with minimum-to-nil interest in redressing injustice with violence. The procession of the powerless vs. the powerful marches on: haves vs. have-nots; children vs. parents; workers vs. the boss; women vs. men; Scots vs. English; love vs. everything. Folk music employs a multitude of confrontational methods, from thumbing of noses to trickery to force to murder. Class and family strife boil up in folk songs down the millennia, the ever-changing System kept eternally simmering by money, which always trickles up. Clever nature, yearly dropping your colourful coinage to rot, to compost, to feed your whole body next year. Would that our human coinage were thus. Physical work has a prominent place in the folk song repertoire. Your trade, your social position or lack of it, determine who you are and what happens to you. Massive stereotyping and romanticising in the folk songs:

I would not marry a doctor, he's always away from home;
I'd rather marry the gambling man, he'd never leave me alone.

Massive misogyny in the folk songs:

I had a wife and got no good of her.
Here is how I easy got rid of her,
Took her out and chopped the head off her,
Early in the morning.

And if lovers in the songs keep dying it is because love, like politics, is worth dying for. In these days of ruthless capitalism, such sentiments are definitely political.

*

Brother Pete took folk music onto a wider political stage, believing that if people sang together they would work together more effectively when group action was needed. He encouraged generations of young and old to produce music and pass it on rather than simply consume it. This was un-American, apparently, bringing him to the notice of HUAC, but normally folk music in its *ur* forms doesn't sell or attract mass attention. Talent scouts from big media still turn up at folk gigs like the dealers who cruise the charity shops and car-boot sales looking for bargains. When singers are enticed out of the grassroots, polished up and sold to the public they can lose what they had.

Long songs, wordy songs, unaccompanied songs, unorthodox styles of singing can be so easily commercialised into musical Esperanto. In 1966, an audience member came up to us during the interval at Keele University. *We've lost X. She's got her own show on television now*, said as if it was a betrayal. *Thank you for not selling out.* We didn't tell him that no one had offered *us* our own show, our own opportunity to sell out – but what if they had? Needing money so desperately, would we have danced to the tune of the company, the investors, the media critics, the hired lawyers like those who, for fear of libel, insisted on one radio show that we cut the final verse from Ewan's 'Ballad of Tim Evans'?

> *They sent Tim Evans to the drop*
> *For a crime he didn't do.*
> *It was Christie was the murderer*
> *And the judge and jury too,*
> *Saying, Go down, you murderers, go down.*

We cut the whole song out instead.

Senator McCarthy & Co. were right to suspect folk musicians. He and his buccaneers panicked if we gathered in groups. We create and pass on our art without a dollar sign or patron in sight. We help to slow down the pace of change. We are handing down the family jewels in as good a condition as possible. We bring the past forward, even as the El Salvadorean guerrillas, always on the move, took the bones and ashes of their ancestors with them. We spread the songs like a benign contagion. The bottom line: once released like a dove into the air, a song cannot be controlled. The singing of it can be forbidden or discouraged – in the British army it was believed that to sing

'McKaffery' was a chargeable offence – but, unlike a dove, it cannot be shot down. In hard times, we will be able to pick up and go, making up new songs, singing them into the ear of a comrade and fading into the crowd. Folk singers and musicians are the young ones sitting at the bedside of old, old, very old Memory. In the future, memory may be the one and only reliable 'device' to carry with us. Music passed on via memory is a political and cultural weapon. Guarding a wondrous body of traditional music is a radical act – a political duty. A most pleasurable one.

45

From There to Here

Mike phones. *Peggy, I have two weeks to . . .* He hung up mid-sentence. July 2009. The chronic lymphocytic leukaemia with which he'd been dealing for eight or nine years had metastasised. Multiple myeloma swept in just short of his seventy-fourth birthday. We're coming. He's bent way over, my special brother. Like Charlie, he has always worn scarves wrapped around his neck, but the scarf can't disguise the huge tumour that swells like a discoloured melon. *Will it hurt if I hug you?* His bones stick out, living skin draped over them like fabric. No self-pity, Mike hushes conversation on the porch in the evening so we can hear the Cooper's hawk. He sits for the last time on the side of the bed, looking up at me. *Peggy, you're a good mature woman. You can do this.* He lies down to die. Ewan died in terror and rage. Dio wanted me to sing to her. Penny responded to a flow of quiet assurance. Charlie died alone on a little wooden staircase. Mike wanted no music, not even our favourites. He needed to see where he was going, not where he had been.

> *Look up and down that long lonesome road*
> *Where all our friends have gone, my love,*
> *And you and I must go, where you and I must go.*

Alexia and Mike had met at Penny's deathbed. It had been companionship at first, *to see each other out*, as Mike put it – but they fell passionately in love and married in August 1995. Irene and I wrote 'Autumn Wedding' for their ceremony. Mike would cry whenever he heard it. Alexia and Kim, Mike's doctor son, are managing the home hospice. Irene washes dishes, cooks, shops, keeps the place clean and welcomes the visitors who come to say goodbye. 5 August – he hasn't spoken for several days. He's in a semi-coma as the nurse washes his hair. He smiles and says *hmmmm*. Alexia asks him how he's doing. Clear as day, he replies: *Fair to middling.* Grief, keep your distance. Sit quiet as he fades and shrinks, beloved brother, my childhood playmate and protector, teenage compañero, my music companion, who only once told me that he loved me, but that was enough. Death as a concept makes sense but *Goodbye, Mike* doesn't. It's too soon. He joins me now in 2017 when I sing 'Lord Thomas and Fair Ellender', 'East Virginia' . . . but sometimes I miss him so much that I can't sing our songs.

Back in Boston, I was beginning to drift, capable of touring but out of kilter with myself. I had tried for fifteen years to feel at home in the USA. After my 2008 autumn semester, I had stopped teaching even though I was good at it. It tied me down. I loved giving concerts, going to the summer teaching camps, enjoying the way American audiences react to folk music – joining in on the choruses, harmonising everything even when unison would be preferable. I made friends and acquaintances all over the country. Touring reconnected me with far-flung family members. Travelling finished me. I was bucketing endlessly up the I-81, down the I-95, across the I-90, the Midwestern networks and Canada, arranging for CDs to be sent ahead and sent back, trudging up and down the concourse of this or that airport. I still walked into 91 Paul Gore Street to silence. Ever since coming back to the States I had referred to

England as home. In our travels, Ewan and I had met many Brits – chiefly Scots – who in their youth had emigrated to *the colonies*, the countries that made up the Empire Upon Which the Sun Never Set and upon which the British never stopped shitting. Most of these countries have gained independence and the rest, some fifty or so, make up the Commonwealth. All of them have settlements of expats who enjoy better prospects, more space and stable weather patterns. Like me, many of these escapees were fleeing from some aspect of their lives in the old country, even if just for a while – but when they said *home* they meant Britain. Irene has not lived in her birth-town, Belfast, for fifty-five years but she still refers to it as home.

*

It's 2010 and I'm restless, unsettled. England is calling me back. I want to live in a country whose English-speaking history is more than several centuries old. I want to live in a country where a Nottinghamshire man can be sent to jail for failing to keep a tidy home; where one can attend the Boring Conference and listen to ten-minute talks on 'Paper Bags from Independent Bookshops' or 'The Serial Numbers on Toilet Roll Tubes'. I'm going to apply to speak on 'The Personality of Extra-Large Rubber Bands', a subject dear to my heart. I crave the sight of ancient buildings; narrow, crooked lanes in small villages; and, above all, the variety of nationalities that exists all over Britain, not just in the big cities. Many of them dress in vibrant colours, rivers of rainbow textiles. By their food ye shall know them. I delight in Indian restaurants that do not, as in the USA, shovel hot spices in by the cupful at the last minute. Most important, I have missed so much of my children's adult lives, my grandchildren's growing-up years. It is one thing returning after thirty-five years to the country in which you lived from age zero to twenty. It will be quite another returning at age seventy-five after sixteen years of absence. Going Back Home – I think about it for a long time. In our Asheville days, Irene had wanted to come back. Would she come back now? Doubtful, even though I am her only family. She's well settled in New Zealand now.

When we hold the No. 91 house-cooling party on 31 May 2010, I find out how many friends I really do have in Boston: friends to whom I have not paid enough attention; friends with whose busy schedules I never seem to mesh; friends with whom I still keep in touch. I give away furniture, books and appliances and receive an evening of music, friendship, gifts and hugs. Jay Ball turns up with his wife Ricky, who forgave me early on for continually calling her Myra, the name of Jay's penultimate squeeze. Jay and I sing Memory Lane songs, everyone joining in, top-and-tailing my life in our old stamping grounds.

Maggie is sold, but to be collected after we make one more pilgrimage in her. Irene and I are not in good shape. We should have holed up by the seaside or driven into a mountain camp and just stayed there sorting ourselves out. The trip is not what we thought it would be. Too many interstates with overnights in RV camps that are packed cheek by jowl with people determined to enjoy themselves or else. Maggie is now given to periodic stalling. One day, she chooses the worst possible time – rush hour – to stop dead at the worst possible place: suburbia's edge, in the middle of a one-lane entry to one of those main arteries that keep the petrol-driven heart of America beating. No room for cars to pass, so they pile up behind us into an impatient tailback. We seasoned motorists apparently spend six months of our lives waiting at lights, accidents, suburban stop signs and highway feed roads. CB communications increase at such times, humorous, racist, misogynist, grisly. I was held up for three hours once on a major artery outside Chicago – a terrible accident. A CB sadist was chuckling. *They're shovelling her up off the road now. All her insides are falling out.* Now, at the scene of Maggie's disgrace, I turn the CB off in disgust.

I have put bumper-stickers all over Maggie's rump to entertain those who sit behind us at lights and in traffic jams. Obama features heavily on these.* Now horns are blasting. A Humvee is right behind us. Road Rage Roger storms out of it, brandishing meaty fists at my window and yelling, *Well, what do you think of Obama now?!* Pretty good, a president who can stall a van in Connecticut all the way from the Oval Office. Irene and I cooled our heels in the bleak yard of a forsaken garage for five days until the little stent arrived to get Maggie's circulatory system going again.

Bank account $5000 lighter. Two destinations 1500 miles apart: St Augustine, Florida, and Quebec, Canada. The former, the oldest European town in the USA and home of the Present Moment Café, the best raw food restaurant ever. The latter, location of the 1759 defeat of French forces by the invading British on the Plains of Abraham. The battle lasted fifteen minutes. The song 'Brave Wolfe' takes four minutes. *They stole my love away, while I was sleeping . . .* Our route through Quebec Province takes us through Thetford. You round a bend and as

---

* Rosie the Van, my little red UK post-office van lookalike, also carries stickers: WHAT WOULD PETE SEEGER DO? SUPPORT THE ARTS: KISS A MUSICIAN. CAUTION, DRIVER SINGING. WE ALL LIVE DOWNSTREAM.

far as the eye can see in all directions are hundreds of pyramids, enormous heaps of a shining, white substance. The road winds through the town. Sick men of all ages sitting hunched over on wooden benches; an enormous hospital; numerous residential nursing homes. Tourist Information has racks of leaflets, booklets, maps, photos, mementos for the thousands of visitors who come to see how asbestos is mined, who go to the mines, who walk the streets on windy days breathing in the deadly little particles. Tourists like to wander around nuclear power stations too.

Our trip was a final chance to get together – and we split. Irene flew far away south. I flew far away northeast. New Zealand is just too isolated for me and England is too cold, too crowded for her, too perilous for someone with a compromised immune system. Two lovers flying off to live as far apart as seems possible, black and white Scottie dog magnets placed together the wrong way. Sounds pretty stark, doesn't it? It was. Irene bought the house in the Marlborough Sounds, on the South Island. I'd have to rent, for 35 Stanley Avenue had been sold after attempts to tenant it proved unmanageable. There's a blue plaque on the house now. It was put there while a gaggle of policemen were renting, holding riotous parties and trashing the place. *Ewan MacColl 1915–1989, political songwriter and playwright, lived here*. No feminist comment.

*

I came back to the UK to remind myself, yet again, of who I had been – all the activism right down to little happenings. In the 1970s, I drove a Rolls-Royce in Berkeley Square, where the nightingales sang during World War II. Its owner had probably congratulated himself as he parked it perfectly about an inch from the kerb. Well done for a man. But now he wanted to unpark. He was standing by the driver's door, weeping. His treasured symbol of British engineering excellence was boxed in by a Bentley in the front and a Ford Cortina in the back with about an inch of wiggle-room. He didn't even want to *try* to get the Rolls out. I offered to manoeuvre it out for him. Still buried in his immense, immaculate handkerchief, he handed me the keys. Men gathered to watch, as they often do when women are handling machines made by men with men in mind. It took a lot of trimming and tacking, but I got it out without damage. Cheers all round. If anyone said *Well done (for a woman)*, I didn't hear it. Willie the Weeper didn't offer me a tip. Now that's class.

I came back to the UK for the fierce little red-breasted robin. I like it that Banksy, the King of Street Artists, lives here. I know the London Underground system. I look to the right when I step from pavement to roadway. When I'm in London, I sit in the top front seat of a red double-decker bus. I love having pub lunches. I like Jenni Murray's motherly voice on *Woman's Hour*. I like the layout of the *Guardian* newspaper. I know roughly the way the political system works and doesn't work. I like the English sense of humour. Accent and vocabulary change subtly every ten or fifteen miles as you go north, east or west – much as do the geological ages, visible in the type of stone used in the older buildings. Golden Cotswold in Oxfordshire and Gloucestershire; red sandstone in Glasgow, grey granite in northeastern Scotland – the story of the earth and of human habitation in tandem. Many of the limestone walls that crisscross Derbyshire are impacted with quartz, mica and sea-bottom fossils from the periods when these islands were under the sea. They gleam like jewels when/if the sun shines. I like the fact that villages and towns are now bypassed. No longer will giant trailer-trucks monopolise ancient high streets or shear off bits of Elizabethan cornerstones. I like it that small villages still have the commons where the commonalty used to graze their sheep. London has many such protected green parks. Some tiny townships still engage in well-dressing at Easter, decorating their defunct community wells with lavish traditional floral displays. I like it that Morris dancers can suddenly appear on market days. I like it that they *have* market days. Oddly, I appreciate that many *incestral* families, as Irene calls them, have by their historic greed and thievery kept enormous tracts of the countryside safe from creeping urbanisation and the litter-happy public. All in all, I came back for the dottiness of this country. I certainly didn't come back for the weather. HOME, sWEeT HOME.

My children are now in their forties and fifties. My grandchildren range from late teens to late twenties. My American and English families are functional. As far as I know, we have no drug addicts or criminals. Everyone did well at school and they come together en masse for birthdays, graduations, anniversaries, Christmas, reunions. What I didn't foresee, after sixteen years' absence, was feeling like a visitor when I returned. My family in the UK numbers several dozen members who have shared years of which I was only a transient part. Even after seven years of living here I still occasionally feel like a half-stranger at the family table. Much of it is due to just being old. Also, my family keep in touch with each other regularly via the social media that I don't use, largely for fear of addiction. I've brought this up with many crone friends and we agree that we needn't keep up with every scrap of subject matter or matters that are supposed to matter. Our starting gun went off long before the young ones' parents were born and our finishing line is much nearer than theirs. We already have one foot somewhere else. We need peace to think and get ready, practising our *retreat in good order*, as Victor Hugo would have it. Mind you, it's probably good at any age to just sit back and listen to everyone else talking.

46

The First Time Ever

How does it feel to sing 'The First Time Ever I Saw Your Face'?
The voice asks while the eyes look straight at my face. I know
what he's thinking and he knows I know and wishes he had
looked anywhere else. Like your first day in a nudist camp.
That song – those three simple verses that move from first sight
to first kiss to the final act – can be sung anywhere any time
and still sound good. How does it feel to sing it? Depends on
whether I am crooning to myself or singing to an audience. In
1957, when I sang it every night at the Gate of Horn, it was just
a simple love song. I had fled the complicated affair with Ewan
and was enjoying my singularity enough to scooter back from
Chicago to New York with a new lover riding pillion. In the
early days with Ewan on stage next to me, I felt embarrassed
and exposed. I felt a fraud, for the first time I saw Ewan the sun
still rose only in the sky. Our first kiss was the best I had had up
until that point – and I didn't put my hand anywhere near the
thing that definitely moved. The first time we lay together was
disconcerting for me and humiliating for him, so it was difficult
to sing verse 3 with any conviction. As the decades rolled by,
I experimented with the song as a performance piece, mostly
in terms of range and enjoyment of the accompaniment – and
to celebrate our wonderful life. But – a Big But – Ewan and I
were now settled parents of children. Our union went quickly
from passion to comradely contentment to enjoyment of mutual

creativity and once more the song became just a piece of lovely music. After he died, I couldn't sing it at all without breaking down. Loss and grief . . . but also because that my thoughts would stray to Irene while singing it – a double betrayal. When my emotional core returned, I sang verse 1 as if I were Ewan reliving his 27 March back in 1956. Then in verse 2, I sing to both of my lovers. Verse 3 to Irene, for our first night was what a First Time Ever night should be. These days I sing the song very high. There are swirls of colour, I'm a bird, creating wide-wing flight, celebrating Love with a capital L. My body fills with the joy of living, the joy of loving, the joy of singing, the joy of remembering. That L can embrace the whole of our blue earth and the universe in which She swims. It can conjure up the faces of each of my children, lying newborn in my arms.

In 2012, Kitty corralled me for a whole day to sing, unaccom-panied, any song in my repertoire for the innovative Broadcaster, who had an idea for his second album, *Folksploitation*. Spurred on by wine and a smashing Broadcaster meal, we recorded about fifty songs, many of which I would normally accompany. It was intriguing to sing them without an instrument – but I could do it, with pleasure. Calum wanted me to sing 'First Time Ever' for the record, unaccompanied and as low as possible, so low that you speak-sing the bottom notes. I used the tune that everyone sings, not Ewan's tune, of which only the second line remains in the popular versions of the song. Listen to any of my recordings of it if you're curious about the original. If we regard an unaccompanied six-minute traditional ballad as one param-eter, then we would regard any track on *Folksploitation* as the other: completely opposite and something I have never done before. My voice is hardly recognisable and the songs, both tradi-tional and topical, are cut, twisted, turned and interwoven with synthesised musical input of Broadcaster's genius. Folk purists were horrified but I was delighted. *Folksploitation* releases the inhibitions of my inner child, hidden teenager, closet dancer and living-room raver. I daren't put it on when I'm driving.

*

I've played instruments since I was six years old. When I first went on stage, I had my supports: the prickly banjo and the comforting guitar. As my repertoire grew, I needed variety. I took up the Appalachian (lap) dulcimer for slippy-slidy, the autoharp for rich harmony, the English concertina for its ability to extend notes and chords, the piano for its infinite possibilities. The songs began to recline in luxury on beds of strings and reeds. My voice became lazy. I began to depend more and more upon the accompaniments, which, as they became more and more complicated, started to stand almost by themselves like my barn clothes at Putney School. They also sped up the singing and corseted the melodies into set harmonies. Following Ewan's example, I began to sing unaccompanied, which expanded my repertoire mightily. I also discovered the extent to which my attention had been divided between voice and instrument. I produce a better voice when I am not accompanying myself. I taste the words fully. Best of all, I understand, in every cell of my body, what singing actually *is*. It does for the soul what blood does for the body, flowing like electricity through the grid of thought-wires, turning the spotlights onto dark corners and directing the actors in the Play of Life. Seamus Heaney's *voltage of the language* is perfect. Voice, words and melody – friends that I can take anywhere at any time.

*

2014, my seventy-ninth birthday. My children ask how I want to mark my eightieth. Whoa, wait a minute. I'm only getting used to seventy-nine, but I answer anyway. *Neill and Calum, will you tour with me for a week? You are my two most favourite musicians.* My boys say *Yes.* 2015 appears and the tour expands to sixteen dates. Calum's wife, Kerry, will be our tour manager, with Kitty occasionally sidekicking. I don't tell anyone that I no longer have the 2012 voice with which I recorded what I consider to be one of my two best albums, *Everything Changes.** I don't tell anyone that I'm losing the desire to sing. Nor can I play properly any more. They see the swollen arthritic joint on my right-hand ring finger and don't ask about the wedding rings that had to be cut off. For the first time ever, I am having trouble with the middle notes of my range. I've had an easy ride as a singer. I have a mixed singing voice with no vocal break in the middle of my two-octave range. Now those bridge notes have become difficult. Eliza Carthy – daughter of Master Martin Carthy and Regal Norma Waterson and a law unto herself, no holds barred on stage – recommends her voice coach, Dr Denise Borland, who lives in Edinburgh and teaches via Skype. Where Eliza Skypes, there Skype I. I sit at the computer and try to sing for Denise. I have to fight the tears. I have sung since forever and now I can't. Denise, with her red lipstick, pink headphones and cheerful, mobile face, guides me as I warble across the river and over the bridge to grandmother's house, where she's humming, burbling, singing with and

---

* Interesting, I think: this album contains a song with a tune that I made when I was ten and a text that I wrote when I was seventy-six.

without words, searching for the Ease of Singing that she had always taken for granted. It's hard – very hard.

Through winter and early spring, the tour begins to feel life-threatening. It will take us from the Channel up to Aberdeen. I can't sing. I'm going to be up on stage making a fool of myself. I feel the panic that some of my Boston cherubs must have felt as their concert approached. I'm practising two hours a day. On every car journey, I put on the CD of voice exercises issued by Kerry's mother, Penni Harvey-Piper, who coaches the big theatre and opera singers. Maybe God has started believing in me, for in the middle of April, with no waving of wands, no *ta-DA!* of trumpets, my voice returns.

*

Back in what my dyslexic Irene calls the *annuals of time,** Ewan and I were on tour and recovering from a rare but drawn-out difference of opinion. Somewhere near Hartlepool, we're in a cafe, coasting in neutral and ready for a lot of silence. Since we sat down, the old couple at the adjacent table haven't spoken a word to each other either, just the sounds of fork, knife, chewing. Eyes-only-on-the-plate can be noisy. Marital ease? Marital boredom? Marital war? After a few minutes, the old man, his mouth full, says, *Nice chips.* Silence. *Don't like mushrooms, though.* He likes the word *mushroom* and says it with his mouth full. He mooshes the first syllable almost as if he is *mash*ticating it. The old woman nods. Little mouth-clicks. False teeth that don't fit? A loud sip of tea. She relents. *Yes. Nice chips.* The

---

* One of my friends was worried about her son, who had maths dyslexia. *Poor Alistair*, said she. *I'm afraid he'll have to be an artist.*

warring factions in the Middle East could learn something from this. *Nice chips*, says the husband, encouraged. *Don't like mooshrooms, though.* He's hitting his stride. *Never trust a mooshroom.* Ewan leers at me and eats a mushroom, his lips poking out fish-like. *Uh-huh. Nice chips*, says the wife. I pick up a chip and mouth, *Nice chips.* That does it. Lunch half-eaten, we pay the bill and sit in the old Citroën losing it till the tears pour down. *Nice chips* and *never trust a mooshroom* became part of our repair kit when negotiations were in progress or laughter was required.

Nice chips wouldn't have smoothed over the misstep I made at the first rehearsal for the eightieth tour. On this day, a few minutes into our first song, Mother emerged, a general with an army of two privates. I forget my actual words but the meaning was *No, Calum, do it this way*, i.e. my way. Calum didn't say anything. He just started again and the rehearsal day progressed. The next morning at breakfast, *Mum, if this had been any other gig but your eightieth I'd have pulled out of the whole tour.* I had treated him like a learner. We were not mother and sons on this or any tour. We were three working musicians – one of us contrite. Off we went on the road. With a tour bus, manager and our own sound engineer, I had nothing to do but travel and sing. I was deposited at my hotel for the octogenarian snooze, during which time Neill and Calum set up the stage, my chair in place, instruments tuned. Kerry collected me when it was time for sound-check, making sure food was available and sliced ginger and honey ready for the hot water. I didn't know I was born. This was a Great Big Birthday Present. It would be hard to describe properly how different this was from my solo travelling, in which I did every living thing for myself, from planning the tour at the beginning to lugging everything back home at the end. It was like winning the lottery – all I had to do was have a good time. The boys sang songs solo and fell in seamlessly with the way I normally give a concert, patient with my inability to remember the location of instrumental breaks, accepting my dropping of beats as a normal feature. For the first time ever, Neill, who always calls me Mum, called me Peggy several times on stage. The banter was not rehearsed, often marrow-close to the bone. I reminded my beautiful big man-sons that they actually emerged from my body. Neill learned, on stage, the colour of the walls – not the ceiling – of the room in which he was conceived. Several nights later, Calum demurred when offered a similar piece of information. He got it anyway. Family in-jokes that were suitable to share, out-jokes from any-where, love and affection on stage like a fourth entity. I didn't learn until later that some of the things I said on stage were somewhat over the top or under the arm. I didn't learn until later that the family had all felt apprehension about the tour – dread, worry, fear might be better nouns. No problem. Calum had nipped in the bud any out-of-order Mother Behaviour. The tour was a One-Off Special. I want to be eighty again and tour with my sons.

47

Life with Sydney and Big Charlie

I had croup and scarlet fever when I was two. When I was six, a smartass boy bashed my head into the drinking fountain, chipping one of my new front teeth. When I was fifteen, I was on crutches with mild rheumatoid arthritis in my big toe. When I was nineteen, I was stricken with mononucleosis. At forty, ulcerative stomatitis floored me on holiday on the island of Mull. When I was sixty, I endured a colonoscopy during which the anaesthesia wore off, in excruciating pain and unable to communicate with the surgeons. All that put together is nothing compared to life with Sydney.

Ewan took reading matter to the loo and sat and waited for gravity to do its job. I, regarding elimination as just another unit of multitasking, postponed and postponed until I had chronic constipation. I've had surgery for carpal tunnel. I stumbled on uneven paving stones in 2010 and fractured my left wrist a day before my Farewell-to-Asheville concert. I played at the concert anyway, thus damaging my wrist permanently. I ate a plate of mussels in Boston and my right knee swelled up to the size of a grapefruit – inflammatory Arthur Ritis, who came to stay. Showing off on a fifteen-foot diving board at age seventy-six resulted in a second vertebra compressed and another fractured. Five breast lumps in fifty years – three benign and two malignant, the second resulting in a mastectomy in 2012. All of this pales into insignificance compared to life with Sydney.

I have fallen downstairs and upstairs, both backward and forward. I have fallen going uphill, downhill and on level ground. I routinely catch a toe in flared trousers and am flat on my face. I have fallen off swings, bicycles and motor scooters, been dragged by a moving train. I have Reynaud's, osteoporosis, cancer, bladder problems, acid reflux, parastomal hernia, chronic back pain, some form of necrosis in my right shoulder, weak knees, a bunion, fallen arches, ever-painful feet, chronic mild heart failure, night cramp, incipient glaucoma, claustrophobia, arachnophobia, dry skin, problems with recent memory and I forget what else. I will never forget Sydney, my stoma.

In April 2014, significantly near to the USA's Tax Day, I developed stabbing belly pain. This wasn't my first abortion, nor the Warsaw pleurisy. This time I knew I was going to die. I took a taxi to the A & E department of the John Radcliffe Hospital in Oxford. Immediate intestinal surgery and Sydney emerges, an end in himself. He is a clean, wrinkled little specimen, a cheeky cerise cherub, about two and a half inches long with a one-eyed opening at the end. He loves the shower. He moves as if searching for something, reminiscent of a worm coming up into the sunlight, or the end of a tiny rosy elephant's trunk. It's the way he hangs off me that gives me just a teensy idea of what it must be like to have a penis. Sydney always answers to his name. Several men have told me that their penis answers to its name. The internet lists some of these monikers – mind-blowing. The *Vagina Monologues* gave a wonderful selection of pet names for Our Lady Downstairs. A companion volume for men would need to be the *Penis Dialogues*.

In 2014, I am man-woman-cow. I've lost thirty pounds since Sydney's birth and my face depicts my misfortune. My body is a war zone, chronicling my jousts with mortality. Here I am at the mirror – Gemini Me. I close my eyes and stroke my chest where my left breast used to be. It is semi-numb, smooth and flat and quite pleasant to the touch. My ribs stick out. This must be what a man's chest feels like. Before I get carried away, I survey my remaining breast. Nothing to boast about. My belly is criss-crossed with surgery scars like railway lines, its muscles traumatised. Sydney and I – our interests intertwine. I shelter him and he serves me. His outer layer is not skin-like. It is fearfully delicate, reminiscent of entrance areas of Down Below. Like the male member, he is always on his host's mind. His demands cannot be denied. Every hour and a half, I have to pay close attention to him. Every night I set my timer to ninety minutes, waking myself up and dragging my REM-drugged body yet again to the bathroom to attend to him. He rules my life like a baby. Mother stuff – I'm used to it. Sydney as a baby, Sydney as a man . . . well, what can I say? My little Sydney – I'll miss you when we are parted on that eighteenth day of September 2014, when Scots go to the polls, many of them hoping to complete the work of Robert the Bruce and William Wallace. Some people have to keep their stomas all their lives. Hundreds of thousands the world over have to manage without an NHS to provide (free) the equipment necessary for dealing efficiently with Sydneys. Nor will they have the opportunity to reverse the ileostomy. Sydney: next week my own Mr (Robert the) Bruce George the Surgeon is going to take his little scalpel and carve an entrance next to where he carved your exit. You are going to be tucked back among your fellow toilers. Soilers. You will be reunited with Big Charlie, for whom I have had no use for five months. I hope I never see you again but I will never forget you. I will call your name and wait for the twitch of your little red reattached nose in there among the crowded organs. I will send you plenty of water, mushy food and modicums of caffeine and alcohol. Having seen you so vulnerable – and let's face it, so drop-dead *cute* – I have new respect for my innards. *Sydney: over to Big Charlie and out.* In.

*

Backstory. In 1956, I was scootering home at night from Chelsea to Alan Lomax's Highgate retreat. A London Fog had rolled in – murky and semi-solid. You breathed in black, spat out black, tried to blink black out of your eyes. The Lambretta's headlights were pitiful, reaching about two or three feet ahead. A man passed me in the middle of the street muttering, *Bus coming.* It was a conductor with two torches, one picking out the kerb ahead and the other facing back for the double-decker bus to follow, two or three feet behind him. I dropped in behind the bus. Torch-bus-scooter inching along together up Archway. The conductor grunts to tell me it's my turn-off, Cholmeley Park, then I'm alone in the pea-soup. I walk the scooter along the pavement counting the gates, knocking several times on the wrong door before I find the right one.

In the autumn of 2014, Big Charlie and I began creating London fogs of our own. After five months of separation, retraining him was not easy. He is male, subject to forces beyond his control. His gaseous emanations are frequent, lengthy, audible, malodorous and dense beyond belief. They permeate the seams of clothing and lurk for days in the corners of rooms. Ever heard of the 1919 Boston Molasses Disaster? A gigantic molasses tank exploded, killing fifty people. It flowed like sticky lava through the North End. I thought of that as my productions flowed under closed doors and seeped into carpets. Outdoors,

431

they could be seen from Betelgeuse. I kept incense sticks and perfumed candles in every room. Irene, blessed angel, said – but only when asked – that I had definitely stamped my personality on the house. WMD, Woman of Mass Destruction. I'm sure I was the reason the smoke alarm went off that day. By reading the faces of visitors I could tell whether the air in the house had reached danger level. It might have been considerate to put an early warning sign by the gate. FYI: it's safe to visit me now.

In general, I dislike hearing lists of other people's ailments and medications. Two minutes and then let's talk about something more uplifting, such as England's Fifty Shades of Grey Weather. Like Ewan, many of my older men friends talk about *the heart, the arteries*, as if their insides belong to someone else – like me talking about my second abortion. Makes pain easier to contemplate. You've read this chapter. You can ask me, *How are you?* I'll always reply, *Fine. Good. I'm vertical and breathing. And how are you?* You get only two minutes to complain. It's life. Beginning to end, the whole period of intestinal redistribution took eight months. Irene stayed from April till November, during which time she rigged up a pulley system for anything I needed to take up or downstairs. She bought me some superb binoculars and installed birdfeeders outside any window at which I had to sleep or sit, turning me into a compulsive bird-watcher. A serial lifesaver, she throws me the ring and rope every time but leaves me to put it on myself, to push the reset button – and swim.

48

The Beginning of the End

As Time's my old friend, and death's my new kin
I'm not taking the journey alone,
I am old, I am young, I am all that I've been
And I'm thinking of heading for home . . .

('Heading for Home')

I was in New Zealand when the phone call came. Pete was dying. I arrived in New York City four hours after he died, no chance to say goodbye, kiss him or hold his hand as he went. His death made world news. Barbara took it philosophically. *Well, kiddo, it's you and me now.* I felt lopsided, top-heavy. That happens when Death moves into your attic. Pete held me in his arms when I was a baby. Pete was Life. Pete was Music. He'd brought banjo and new songs to Mike and me. When I decamped to Europe he'd send me little notes with clippings, names of books, ideas . . . *This will interest you, Peggy. Have you read this, Peggy?* Most recently, they were signed 'old Pete' but always with his scrawled banjo signature. Pete was Always, he was one of the elements. Pete couldn't die – but he did, in January 2014. Up until then I couldn't get old – but then I did. Previously, I'd been observing my gradual physical dissolution with detached amusement, wondering which of my faculties, which organ or joint was going to give up or plague me next. Even worse, anaesthesia decimates my vocabulary. Every time I

433

have an operation, more words join the socks in Life's washing machine.

Post-Sydney, the humour of the situation vanished. The loss of so much weight aged my face by ten years even though it did enable me now to wear clothes that I'd drooled over for a half-century. Objective mirth changed to resignation to *O God, what next?* My inner child is still full of wonder and smart enough to avoid mirrors – but the thought of her in teenager Pete's arms tells me exactly how old I am. We Seegers have family reunions every two years at the Killooleet camp, now run by brother John's daughter, Kate. I'm next to oldest at these heart-warming get-togethers. Brother Charles's widow Naomi and I commiserate, wondering how the hell we got so old. I hold the new little ones in my arms and talk to their grand-parents, whom I'd held in my arms as babies. I've instigated yearly MacColl family parties here in England. I won't leave my young ones behind when I die. They will leave me behind. Diana Jones, in her song 'The Day I Die', captures it beautifully. Progress, Development and Growth will leave us all behind. They can run faster than we can.

In 2005, Irene gave me a splendid Seventieth Birth Day, tak-ing me to new secret haunts all over London and up on the London Eye – something I'd never have done by myself. I have a fear of heights, first realised as a teenager when I went up the Empire State Building in New York. *Hold me, Charlie, I want to jump off* – which you could easily do back then. *Life* magazine had shown us the crumpled body of a woman who did jump, enfolded in the metal embrace of the car she landed on. In 2009 – to challenge and hopefully cure my acrophobia – I skydive from fifteen thousand feet above Queenstown in New Zealand, attached to a guide who comes from Springhill, Nova

Scotia. He sang my 'Ballad of Springhill' in school. Looking back resembles looking down from high up. This memoir is beginning to feel like someone else's story. I walk with care, convinced that my gravitational field is weakening. I feel insubstantial, as if floating several inches above the ground. I want to come down to a safe level place. Death is level. In 2014, I stop pretending it isn't happening. Soon I'll leave myself behind. The Extra-Large Rubber Band that's holding me together will snap, releasing Peggy-fragments like mushroom spores. Bits of my life may appear in someone else's brain in the future, like those sudden clear flashes of someone else's experience that flick through my mind. Being old is being connected big-time, soon to join Nature's shape-shifting game. *I'll be riding the gentle wind that blows through your hair* . . . I won't deny that I have entered a new, all-embracing desire for oneness with our planet. I identify with my birds, hungry to grab the food before the squirrel gets it – hungry to grab life before death gets it. I identify with the seasons for they have all happened to me. The past and the future are just time's tug of war. I am pulled in both directions, while trying to balance living at the same time as myself with trying not to fall into the self-indulgent chasm of the fleeting present. I grind to a start every morning asking the same old question: *Why?*

I sign on with Lesley Hayes, Oxford psychotherapist and author, knowing that she won't answer with *why not*. Yesterday on Lesley's sofa, wearing the warm slippers she puts out for me, I used the word *old* to describe myself. When baby hedgehogs are in the womb, their spines lie flat under a thin membrane of skin, making their birth bearable for Mrs Tiggywinkle. This layer dissolves after birth and the little spines emerge. Lesley's professional skin softens and her felt-tipped quills appear.

What about using the word elder? No, that's a bush. *Ancient?* No, that's several hundred years older than eighty-one. *Vintage?* Some zillionaire recently bought a bottle of vintage Napoleonic brandy for a trillion-plus-one pounds, and invited a clan of zillionaire-minus-one friends around for the kill. It tasted like vinegar. I can be brandy and/or vinegar. Both are comestible and delicious – so *vintage* has possibilities, especially where connections with salad and alcohol are concerned.

*

Neill and his Kate (St John) got married several summers ago. Kate and I are on the same three pages: Neill and Music and Our Own Page. We create two new songs together, woman songs that either of us would have had trouble producing alone. Calum and I collect a BBC Radio 2 Folk Award for the best new song of 2015 – our co-written 'Swim to the Star'. In 2017, more duo songs. I will write with Neill next. Co-writing gives me company as I walk around Writer's Block. 2016 is something else altogether. Poison everywhere and trite antidotes. A drone bought on the internet is a danger to an airliner. *Teach responsible usage*, say the authorities. Mass killings in Western nations by Isis jihadists are to be expected now. *Be vigilant*, say the authorities. Someone else is clearing up the mess for now but soon it will be the Vigilant You and I who'll be tossing the legs, arms, heads and charred remains into overflowing carts after Aleppo, Paris, Berlin, Manchester Arena, Westminster Bridge. The Grenfell Tower tragedy tells us exactly who we are and where we are going. A surprise backlash: back in the eighties the authorities tried blowtorching the chain-link fences of the Greenham Common air base to get rid of the woven woollen doves, scraps of children's clothing, photos and poems put there by thirty thousand women. It melted the plastic covering. So they employed children from the schools to unpick it all, creating, I hope, some truly *vigilant* young activists.

My Gemini duo are not twins. They are Janusian, their intentions miles apart. One keeps asking *Why?* and *Are we there yet?* The other answers, *Because.* And *We're already there. Yet* ... Both join with the mirror to tell me I'm just plain *old.* That's that. Now I can laugh again and welcome the tears that water my reckless optimism. It's spring 2016. My outer child shovels in the pills, dons prosthetic breast, hernia truss, toe spacer, glasses, orthotics, hearing aid and charcoal hand-warmer and heads out with a smile to supervise the world. Think *sexy* – a word that's also used to sell cars and bank accounts – and do something new. Tour in the autumn with a young man, twenty-three-year-old Sam Gleaves, Virginia-born and country-bred. We bring out new songs every night for each other and for Kerry, our surrogate mother-minder-manager. A lot of older people come to my concerts. Sam is the son they'd always wanted. We take our bows, the little old lady and the amiable, six-foot-six package of male beauty and apple pie, down-home manners. One of my New Year's resolutions is never to tour again without Kerry.

I buy a tiny potted tree – only fairy lights and a teddy bear for decoration. I go Christmas shopping in the covered market in Oxford. You can buy all of Christmas now. If you don't like it, you can turn it in for a refund if you've saved the receipt. Kirsty's gutsy 'Fairytale of New York' Muse-axes out on the market speakers. It's 18 December, sixteen years to the day since she was mown down while scuba diving in Cozumel, Mexico. Ewan would not have survived her death. Our family . . . you don't *recover* from such a thing. We set remembrance places

437

at our tables, remembrance spaces deep down inside. Time swirls around me. Polio struck Washington so nix on shopping. *Hammer hammer* behind a closed door as Charlie and eight-year-old Mike make cradles for our dolls. Dio and I crochet dresses for Barbara's doll. Barbara's tongue is motor-overflowing as she and the blunted needle make popcorn chains for the tree. Time flings out December memories like a whirling dervish undressing. A nudist beach in Australia and here comes Santa with nothing on but a red hat, swinging a hand-bell and ho-hoing while male sunbathers move the clapper of the hotel bell from side to side to facilitate uniform crotch-tanning. We have a *Ewan is dead* 1989 Christmas, then our amputated family stands on the back porch, egg nog in hand, listening to Washington's church bells ringing 1954 in. Kate and Neill make a lick-your-plate-clean simple Christmas Eve vegetarian dinner. Family . . . soon it will be Ewan's hundred-and-second birthday, time to visit the flourishing oak tree that was planted in his memory in Russell Square.

For the first time in my life, I choose to spend New Year's Eve alone among strangers. A film, a dinner at the Old Bank Hotel, then head home in time to call Irene. The door bell. Time scrooches his time-worn boots on the coir mat and steps in. Cerberus fawns. I glance behind them. *Is He . . . have you come alone? Yes.* He hasn't come to talk. He's come to sing. A small voice calls from the kitchen: *5-4-3-2-1 ROLLING! It's getting late.* Time knows when it's time. *Are you ready? Yes.* Hot-water bottle and slippers, we climb the stairs. Lifelong companions.

49

Slow Express to Eternity

We talk every night on the phone, UK to NZ. Every conversation begins with the agreement that nothing ever changes and that things will always change. Tragedy and trivia, disconnected events and random thoughts, most of them not the kind of thing to fall asleep on but worth sharing. Have you noticed that more and more social gatherings are spent talking about our holidays – about where we've been or where we are going to go rather than where we are? Kitty came for a couple of hours today – just quiet, talking and sitting by the fire. She makes me happy. Did you get your copy of *The Positive News*, Irene? The new format is splendid. Oh, and a bunch of old duffers in County Durham have started up a free newspaper, *Hartlepool Life*. Only features good news. I'll send a donation in our name. Let's hang up tonight on a hopeful note.

*

The earth is a noisy place. From how far away can the sounds of earth be heard? The cries of newly consummating lovers, the screams of the tortured, the scrunch of tectonic plates, the call of the last remaining member of a now extinct species, the last word spoken by the last person who speaks a vanished language. The scurry of insects, the rustle of kudzu as it gobbles up the American South at a foot per day. Astronomers listen to far outer space. I have a star named after me, a birthday gift from Calum and Kerry. Near Castor and Pollux, Star Number Gemini RA 6h 27m 48s 24° 25' is called Peggy. An act of love: a micro-speck of life on a planet that's lost amongst billions of nebulae bestows the name of his female progenitor on a lump of rock so far away that it would take thought – which we know travels much quicker than the speed of light – many lifetimes to reach it.

*

What is *99-clop, 99-clop*? A centipede with a wooden leg. What is *pluck, pluck, pluck, oops*? My right hand with the swollen, half-frozen arthritic knuckle on the ring finger trying in vain to play my signature banjo roll. Life is just simple math. You grow up, adding skills. Experiences multiply and become memories. Then you grow down, subtracting skills and losing vocabulary, dividing the mind into what we've retained and what's hidden out of reach. We discover the very essence of life during this process of dissolution. It is best conducted with the same curiosity and concentration that characterise childhood – but with dignity, objectivity and patience. Life in whatever shape or form is thrilling. It begins and ends with Once Upon Any Time. I've had my wedding rings repaired, Irene. I wear them on a chain around my neck.

*

Time slowed when I was at the head of a twenty-car pile-up on the M62 in 1988. The car spun around in slow motion while Ewan intoned, *Don't worry Peg it'll stop Don't worry Peg it'll stop Don't worry Peg* it stopped. I got out of our crushed car and directed traffic while vehicles were still piling up behind us. Crash, slam, crunch, each impact a bullet shot. We went on to our gig in a rented car. Fear stopped Time when teenage Neill tumbled out of sight over the wall of the back porch to the cement path one floor down. Ewan had taken the electric saw back into the garage that day to work. Otherwise . . . Slow motion again when a van knocked Ewan and several others clear across an intersection of Regent Street. He sailed forever through the air till he landed twenty feet away, right next to a woman who had been killed. I was eight months pregnant with Calum. Ewan saved our lives. He pushed us out of the way and took the blow chest-on. He had killer bronchitis every winter after that.

*

Sweet earth, please pull on my puppet strings more gently. My body is out of joint. I am malleable, pummelled, pockmarked by love, rage, joy, grief, guilt and operations. My height has plummeted from five foot nine to five foot five, my weight from 148 pounds to a forever 117 with fat and muscle gone and ribs like xylophone keys. Mesomorph to ectomorph in one *fell swoop*. In northern Britain, *fell* means cruel, wicked. Raptors swoop. Time is looking for me again. I hide out in hospitals. The large, mocking mirrors in public bathrooms are unavoidable. I'm a skeletal tree on a wild seashore. A lammergeyer could perch comfortably on my protruding clavicles. *The old grey mare she got so thin, bones poking up right through her skin. Tra la la.*

I went to get a new bathing suit today. Two beautiful young teenage girls with the lizard figure I had always longed for went into the next cubicle. *I hate my thighs*, said one. *I hate my boobs*, said the other. *I think I'll get a boob job.* Female General Mutilation. I surveyed my ruined body in the full-length mirror. I knocked on the dividing wall and invited the girls to open their curtain. I stood there and said, *Look at this and think again how imperfect your bodies are.* No, I didn't really do that, Irene. I stared at my reflection and apologised to my courageous body for using the word *ruined*.

*

Like the universe, 85 per cent of our brains seems to be dark matter. Other fauna are smart. Their males may battle, sometimes to the death, but they don't kill or torture each other on a massive scale. They don't invent things the logical outcome of which could spell their doom. *Dumb animals.* Survival is Nature's reward for those who are good at securing territory for food, shelter and the right conditions for reproduction. Nature deals certain death to those who're not good at it. Humans have invented the science of uncertainty. Useful, for we're uncertain of 85 per cent of what is happening around us and we're not dead certain of the other 15 per cent. Animals use 100 per cent of their brains. *Dumb animals.*

*

The fat squirrel sits on the window ledge of my office room, its face set in reproach. I have cut off the tree branch that allowed it to leap onto the bird table. Down at the canal, *quack* and *honk* mean the same thing: *What-have-you-got-for-me?* The cold, damp English air is selfish, uncaring. The wind piccolos,

442

flutes, tubas to the splatter of raindrop feet – weather music. Trees dance – stoic, radiant, teenage. Geriatric, their gnarled fingers deep in the ground, innocent teenage saplings springing up where the grown-ups have let sunlight through. Sometimes they lean away if another tree has encroached on their space. *Dumb trees.* The English spring is coming, birthing warmth and hope. Bluebells, crocus, daffodils, colours reappear, like the samples shelved on the wall in Marie Marcella's quilting room. My down-the-road neighbour comes to the door. She's new to the black hole that I sank into in 1989, but it took her husband twenty years to die instead of Ewan's ten. *Come for coffee?* She knows I'm on a deadline. She also knows I'll come. We have ESP but we're not going to tell each other how good we are at it. We don't have to.

*

I snap awake at three in the morning with Saharan thirst. I leap out of bed with screaming leg cramps. By the time I've walked the muscles loose, I'm half awake but too tired to get up. I sleep late, hitting the snooze button over and over. Unless I have a gig or a memoir to write I fill an open day with loose ends, of which I am one and yet am never at one. Loose, lose, lost, looking for something to hang onto. Parents, siblings, my children, friends, my dear lovers, all have saved me in the past. Who will save me now? I wear an alarm pendant around my neck when I'm alone in the house in case I fall down or up the stairs or wander off into the past. If I press it, the Box on the mantelpiece comes alive. *Hello, Dr Seeger, is everything all right?* In April 2014, I'd have died if I hadn't had the Box. Yesterday I was practising and the banjo head pressed the capsule. *Hello,*

Dr Seeger, are you all right? Accustomed to being interviewed, I looked with interest at the Box and replied, *Good question.* I interviewed myself. *Am I all right? Where am I?* No answer. Boxes of clutter have gone off to the Helen and Douglas House charity shop. Was I in one of them? I go along to check. I see myself displayed in their window with a price tag on my toe. £2. Apparently I've been there for a long time, accumulating dust. I'm a Gemini – I've told you over and over – and a sucker for a bargain. I go in and pay the asking price for my other half, delighted that after eighty years I am managing to get myself together.

*

I've told you this before, Irene, but it's on my mind right now. On one of our charbroiling holidays in Greece (Hawaiian Suntan Oil Factor 2), Ewan and I took a little boat to a small, deserted island and set our blanket out at the bottom of a cliff. I got up to go and swim. A moment later a head-size boulder fell from the clifftop and landed exactly where I'd been sitting. I'm obsessed with the thought that something might happen to you, Kitty, Calum, Neill, one of the grandkids . . . take the phone with you when you walk down to the shore.

*

I forgot to tell you – I've ordered dozens of the film *Gasland* to send to the little villages who are fighting against fracking. What do you think about a song paralleling fracking with rape? Tumescent skyscrapers harassing the sky? They're bulldozing the Jungle in Calais today, bussing the migrants to . . . no, let's hang up on a hopeful note. Had a photoshoot yesterday with Vicki Sharp – she looks like a joyful pirate there behind her SLR. You remember her – Kerry's sister. She took that lovely sideways laughing photo of me. Oh – and there's a herb farm called Growing Underground beneath Clapham Common tube station now, in the tunnels of the former World War II air-raid shelter. It uses hydroponics. We'll visit it when you come. Goodnight, Irene. Goodnight, my treasures, my beloveds dead or alive. See you all in the morning.

50

The Last Time Ever

It wasn't a race. I was just running, creating the wind beneath my wings, a force of nature hurtling forward from one reality to another, absorbed in the glory of being . . .

*

We've come to Rome, Kitty and Ewan and I. We park the car and walk down through residential streets to the centre, a huge coliseum surrounded by ancient municipal buildings which disappear one by one till only two are left, one damaged – then both are gone. A huge empty space. I look up behind me at the identical houses – Daly City, California, in crescent rows. Lots of people live there. Immigrants, refugees? Ewan goes back to the car and doesn't return. I take my suitcase, wheelie, guitar and bag out of the little room and leave them in the big hall in the pile of luggage. When I come back, Kitty is gone. Back to the hall. It's empty – everyone's gear gone. No bag, no money, no phone. The cleaners come in. *Is there anyone I can see about my . . .* The cleaners vanish. I traverse little staircases, up, up, up. *Is there anyone I can . . .* There is no one to ask. The walls honeycomb in. Two man-size boys wander the network of capillaries with me, helpful. A little old man takes us through room after room of lost property. He disappears. *Boys, let's go!* They've disappeared. *Boys, boys . . . !* I am alone in a shrinking, deserted, grey stone labyrinth.

446

Dreams are quicksand. My time here is a bowl of water in the desert of eternity. Enantiodromia. Lost when I sleep and found when I wake. Each first time ever is the last time that *that* first time ever will happen. The first time I die will be the last time I live. I was born joyful and will probably die troubled. This is the first and last time I will write my life. Thank you for sitting in the front row. You and I have shared our lives with billions of fellow travellers. I wish you well, truly well.

*

Life offers a chance
For friends to carry us over,
Time can stop or dance forever,
Love, call me home.
Time, ferry me down the river,
Friends, carry me safely over,
Life, tend me on my journey,
Love, call me home.

('Love Call Me Home')

Acknowledgements

'Thank you' has become somewhat devalued by overuse. Hallmark cards: *Thanks to my spouse, my children, my therapist, my car mechanic, my dentist. Thank you for the thank-you card you sent thanking me for my thank-you card.* Herewith my deepest, heartfelt *gratitude and indebtedness* not only to those who made this book possible but to those whose lives I am privileged to have been part of:

First and foremost to my partner, Irene Pyper Scott, who, after the death of Ewan MacColl, urged me (as therapy) to write my life in instalments; who has put up with my single-mindedness for six years while I tunnel-sprint towards publication; who is waiting patiently for me to grow up.

Always to Ewan MacColl, who not only encouraged and took pleasure in my abilities but who taught me and learned from me in our three-decade productive partnership.

To Brian Reese, who took the plethora of life-instalments and put them together into a workable starter manuscript.

To Jean Freedman, who in writing the biography *Peggy Seeger: A Life of Music, Love, and Politics* made it easier for me to write this companion book and who was one of my two invaluable early reader/editors.

To Sheelagh Neuling, experienced reader/editor/friend – her UK perspective balanced Freedman's US viewpoint.

To Judith Tick and Ruth Perry, my two Boston (USA)

sister-friends, for constant encouragement, editing and kicks in the butt to just get on with it.

To friends who gave me information when needed: Jake Rosen, Joe Hickerson, Ken Hunt, Paul Wilson, Marilyn Tucker, Totsie Marine, Peter Cox, Justine Picardie, Ted Power, Doc Rowe.

To Peter van de Putte, who gave me vital suggestions re. writing style.

To Cathy Fink and Marcy Marxer, who, in insisting on me recording my love poetry, gave me a new idea of myself as a bona fide writer.

To Josh Dunson and Andy Patterson, who have kept me abreast of my presence on the internet, thus jogging my memory buttons.

To Victoria Johansen, my personal assistant, who took over more than her usual share of our business work while I wrote.

To Dave Watkins, my patient, long-suffering Faber editor.

To the many writers, pundits, eavesdropped people whose words, phrases, ideas I have absorbed for decades and presented without credit herein.

To David Attenborough, who had nothing to do with the book but everything to do with fanning the embers of optimism and eco-feminism. He keeps my spirits up.

Last but never least, to my children, Neill, Calum and Kitty MacColl, for their support. Like Irene, they are also waiting patiently for me to grow up.